# THE COLD WAR AND THE COLOR LINE

# THE
# COLD WAR
## AND THE
# COLOR LINE

## American Race Relations in the Global Arena

## THOMAS BORSTELMANN

HARVARD UNIVERSITY PRESS
Cambridge, Massachusetts, and London, England

First Harvard University Press paperback edition, 2003

*Library of Congress Cataloging-in-Publication Data*
Borstelmann, Thomas.
The Cold War and the color line : American race relations in the global arena /
Thomas Borstelmann.
p. cm.
Includes bibliographical references (p. ) and index.
ISBN 0-674-00597-X (cloth)
ISBN 0-674-01238-0 (pbk.)
1. United States—Race relations—Political aspects. 2. United States—Foreign relations—
1945–1989. 3. United States—Foreign relations—1945–1989—Social aspects. 4. Cold War—
Social aspects—United States. 5. Southern States—Race relations—Political aspects.
6. African Americans—Civil rights—History—20th century. 7. Civil rights movements—
United States—History—20th century. 8. South Africa—Race relations—Political aspects.
9. Blacks—Civil rights—South Africa—History—20th century. 10. Civil rights movements—
South Africa—History—20th century. I. Title.

E185.61 .B728 2001
305.8′00973—dc21                    2001024861

*For Lynn, John, and Daniel*

# CONTENTS

# PREFACE

IN 1972, WHEN I WAS fourteen years old, the ultraconservative Jesse Helms was first elected to the United States Senate from my home state of North Carolina. That a figure so closely associated with racial segregation could become our senator in the 1970s astonished me, even at that young age. By this time, however, Helms had mostly dropped the rhetoric of white supremacy and spoke primarily in the idiom of anti-Communism. With my friends and especially my older brother Michael, I made much countercultural fun of the senator's concern about "subversives," both red and black. Little did I know that the seeds of a lifelong fascination with race relations and the Cold War were being sown.

Three years later, as juniors at Phillips Exeter Academy in New Hampshire, my classmates and I were required to choose between two courses for fulfilling the second semester of the year-long U.S. history sequence. One course focused on the domestic side of American history since 1865, while the other paid greater attention to U.S. foreign relations in the same period. There was, it was thought, simply too much material to cover both stories adequately between January and June. A similar division shadows the entire field of American history, as I later found out, from the training of graduate students to the journals that reflect the research of professional historians. In 1975, I opted for the international track but was never happy—then or since—with having to make that choice. This book intends to contribute to a growing movement to reunite the internal and external sides of the American past.

The story told here ranges widely across U.S. and international landscapes in putting the history of white supremacy on the same page with the history of the Cold War. Particular attention is paid to Africa and to African Americans, both of which figured prominently in the era of the Southern civil rights movement and Third World decolonization. Recent scholarship has revealed the ways in which black Americans linked their struggle against discrimination at home to the quest for national independence in Asia and Africa. This book focuses on how the white men in Washington who wielded enormous global power after 1945 wrestled with the simultaneous demands of people of color at home and abroad for full equality, and with the parallel responses of Southern segregationists and white authorities in Africa. It was during the Cold War that one of the central tensions of American history was largely resolved, at least in the public sphere: the conflict between an older vision of an America founded on hierarchies such as race and gender, and a newer ideal of a society free of legalized discrimination and enforced inequality.

A WRITER ACQUIRES many debts on the road to publication. I am grateful to several people who took time from their own important work to read parts of early drafts of the manuscript and provide generous and critical comments, as well as much needed encouragement. They will recognize their suggestions in the stronger parts of the book. For its faults, they bear no responsibility; they truly tried to tell me. They include David Cecelski, Bill Chafe, Mary Dudziak, Cary Fraser, George Herring, Lisa Hoffman, Michael Hogan, Michael Hunt, Walt LaFeber, Mel Leffler, Gary Okihiro, David Painter, Dick Polenberg, Andy Rotter, Keith Taylor, Peter Wood, and Jonathan Zimmerman.

The Cornell History Department has provided a wonderfully supportive as well as challenging environment for carrying out this project; I am particularly indebted to two wise and helpful department chairs, Itsie Hull and Sherm Cochran, department manager Judy Burkhard, and the entire Americanist phalanx. Financial assistance from several sources at Cornell eased the book's completion: the Return Jonathan Meigs Fund of the History Department, the Robert and Helen Appel Fellowship for Humanists and Social Scientists, and university sabbatical and study leaves. Audiences at various forums provided helpful feedback on earlier versions of several chapters: the Ohio State University Graduate History Workshop, the Southern New England Foreign Policy Seminar at the University of Connecticut, the Porter L. Fortune, Jr., History Symposium at the University of Mississippi, and the Cornell Comparative History Colloquium. The editors of two journals kindly allowed the reuse of materials first published with them: "Jim Crow's Coming Out: Race Relations and American Foreign Policy in the Truman Years," *Presidential Studies Quarterly,* 29 (September 1999): 549–569; and "'Hedging Our Bets and Buying Time': John Kennedy and Racial Revolutions in the American South and Southern Africa," *Diplomatic History,* 24 (Summer 2000): 435–463.

Two literary professionals eased the publication process with consummate grace and skill: my agent, Lisa Adams of the Garamond Agency, who placed the manuscript; and my editor, Joyce Seltzer of Harvard University Press, who improved it immeasurably. Manuscript editor Elizabeth Hurwit provided superb polishing in the final stages. Long-term sustainers of the author include John "JB" Borstelmann, Tim and Barb Beaton, Dub and Libby Gulley, John Platt, Suzanne Mettler, and Wayne Grove, all of whom helped preserve my perspective on the larger journey. My deepest gratitude goes to those to whom this book is dedicated, my wife and our sons. Patient with me, they are my best teachers.

T. B.
Manlius, New York

The past is the present. It's the future, too.

—EUGENE O'NEILL, *Long Day's Journey into Night*

# PROLOGUE

"WHEN I ASKED for coffee, the good woman said she could not serve me." Malick Sow, the ambassador to the United States of the newly independent African nation of Chad, was explaining to a reporter in 1961 about his reception in a Maryland restaurant. "She said, 'That's the way it is here.' I cannot say how I felt. I was astonished. I was so angry. President Kennedy himself has made deep apologies, but these humiliations are bad." When asked for her side of the story, Mrs. Leroy Merritt of the Bonnie Brae Diner replied with what she considered evident common sense. "He looked like just an ordinary run of the mill nigger to me. I couldn't tell he was an ambassador."[1]

An "ordinary run of the mill nigger" or an ambassador? Malick Sow and fellow African diplomats created a dilemma for white Americans long accustomed to discriminating against people of color. Americans determined to preserve their leadership of the non-Communist "free world" could no longer ignore the world's nonwhite majority, whose representatives now flowed into the United States as their peoples gained independence from European colonial rule. "How can we persuade these Africans and these Asians, whose skins range from dark to black," State Department official Pedro Sanjuan asked Maryland legislators, "that we believe in human dignity when we deny our own citizens the right to this basic dignity on the basis of skin color?"[2] American foreign relations could not be insulated from the nation's race relations in an era of maximum U.S. involvement abroad.

In the twentieth century the global movement toward racial equality and self-determination gathered speed and finally broke upon the bulwarks of white supremacy with irresistible force. This happened around the world and within the United States at the same time, and the purpose of this book is to trace the ways in which the U.S. government responded to demands for an end to racial discrimination both at home and abroad.[3] Colonialism— mainly European but also Japanese and American—retreated from Asia, Africa, the Caribbean, and the Middle East in the decades following World War II; legal racial segregation in the United States was exorcised in the same years. The two world wars gravely weakened the European empires, and from the ashes of each global conflagration arose a new revolutionary state to inspire and encourage colonial independence: the Soviet Union in 1917 and the People's Republic of China in 1949. Decolonization became, in a sense, the twentieth-century equivalent of emancipation for slavery, doing for nations what had been done a century earlier for individuals. The unfolding of national self-determination across Asia and Africa, in turn, nourished the struggle for equality in America.

The twin efforts of the anticolonial and civil rights movements, and the resistance they encountered from Europeans, white settlers in Africa, and white Southerners, presented the U.S. government with a dilemma. How could it defend equality and the rule of law while not alienating its allies across the Atlantic and local authorities south of the Mason-Dixon line? This conundrum was immensely complicated by the onset of the Cold War. The American practice of the Cold War was grounded in the central belief that the liberal, democratic, capitalist order of the United States represented a more open and humane society than that of Communist states. With the Soviets and the Chinese competing for the friendship of the new nonwhite nations, American policymakers had to thread their way through a minefield of potential disasters in dealing with race and its international implications after 1945.

The essential strategy of American Cold Warriors was to try to manage and control the efforts of racial reformers at home and abroad, thereby minimizing provocation to the forces of white supremacy and colonialism while encouraging gradual change. They hoped effectively to contain racial polarization and build the largest possible multiracial, anti-Communist coalition under American leadership. This effort proved generally more successful at home than abroad. The relatively small percentage of nonwhite Americans could be reasonably accommodated within the flexible structure of American democracy. But the more revolutionary situations in much of the Third World proved harder to control, as even deeper racial divisions of wealth and power alienated nonwhite majorities from their colonial and white settler overlords.[4] The potential for racial conflicts that might derail the American pursuit of a First World–Third World alliance was most evident in southern Africa, where white settlers dug their heels in for a last-stand defense of white privilege. White violence against civil rights organizers in the American South also threatened to limit Third World sympathies with the West in the Cold War.

The story of domestic race relations and American foreign relations over the past half-century has had a particular geography. The narrative encompasses most of the globe, as does the reach of U.S. power, but the states of the old South loom especially large. It was there, south of the Mason-Dixon line and east of the hundredth meridian, that human relations along the color line conflicted most sharply with the nation's pursuit of a "free world" abroad. Much changed in Dixie during the decades after 1945, and the region was always more complicated and diverse in its social patterns than its harshest critics understood. But the states of the former Confederacy did emerge from World War II as a region of abiding racial hierarchy, coercion, and violence, whose white authorities remained firmly entrenched. This set it at odds with most of a broader world that had long endured the inequalities of predominant white power but was now moving rapidly up the road to at least formal racial equality.

The racial discrimination required by Southern state legal codes represented one pole in a growing debate between two visions of sovereignty and human rights. Traditionalists adhered to a doctrine of local authority in managing social relations and maintaining order. This doctrine took the form of defending states' rights to manage their own internal affairs. It also bolstered national sovereignty against inquiries or incursions from international organizations. The second vision embodied the opposite view: that in the wake of the Holocaust, the international community could no longer fully trust any local sovereignty to protect its own citizens. Innocent people should no longer be allowed to suffer and die owing to the sheer misfortune of which government they happened to live under. Instead, standards for human rights needed to be made globally applicable. The United Nations embodied elements of each of these visions, with clauses in its charter declaring both the common rights of all people against discrimination and the sovereignty of nations over life within their borders. In the early postwar years, the U.S. government cited the latter clause in rejecting requests for an international investigation of American racial discrimination—a position shared by European colonial powers and South Africa. A few years later, white Southerners used precisely the same arguments in making their own case against federal investigations of Southern racial practices.[5]

The South's centrality in struggles over American race relations engendered a debate in the early postwar decades about the region's precise relationship to the rest of the country. At issue was the very definition of Americans' core values and the essential identity of the United States. Non-Southern liberals tended to view Dixie as a foreign culture and almost a different country. Less troubled by social hierarchy, less committed to racial equality, and more impressed by the South's religiosity and general conservatism, moderates and especially conservatives saw the region instead as somewhat distinctive but ultimately in line with the rest of the nation. From the opposite end of the political spectrum, radicals agreed; they rejected the idea that non-Southerners should feel superior to the South. Attuned to the reality of de facto segregation and discrimination in the North and West, they tended to agree with Malcolm X's assertion that "Mississippi is anywhere south of the Canadian border."[6]

Critics of Southern race relations, including black Southerners, had abundant ammunition in a culture so marked by rivalry with the USSR. The Cold War developed after World War II as a new bipolar U.S.-Russian competition that encompassed the globe, and strident American anti-Communism presented critics with the image of a totalitarian Soviet Union that bore some resemblance to white-controlled Dixie. A short list of common features of Russia and the American South included the language of justice and the reality of inequality before the law; involuntary labor (peonage and prison labor in the South); kangaroo courts and summary executions; arbitrary imprisonment; the denial of human rights through the use of inhumane prison conditions and even torture; and the state's use of spies and terror to intimidate potential dissidents, including occasional "disappearances." Above all, the role of the government—whether in Moscow and Soviet provincial capitals or in Jackson and Philadelphia, Mississippi—was that of a crucial supporter and perpetrator of such practices.

The American South and the Soviet Union had different histories, of course, and different forms of inequality and injustice. But the parallels between political totalitarianism and racial totalitarianism could occasionally be striking. Each seemed to serve an ideological "higher truth" in its legal system rather than pursuing questions of actual innocence or guilt. Harvey McGehee, the chief justice of the Mississippi Supreme Court, unintentionally illustrated this point soon after that state executed Willie McGee, an African American, in 1951 for the supposed rape of a white woman in Laurel. McGehee's court had upheld the conviction, and he responded revealingly to a journalist's suggestion that evidence of the woman coercing McGee into a sexual relationship might have been suppressed in the case: "If you believe, or are implying, that any white woman in the South, who was not completely down and out, degenerate, degraded and corrupted, could have anything to do with a Negro man, you not only do not know what you are talking about, but you are insulting us, the whole South. You do not know the South, and do not realize that we could not entertain such a proposition; *that we could not even consider it in court.*" Truth, as in the Soviet Union, was often established long before anyone walked into the courtroom. Like many others, Willie McGee paid for that higher truth with his life.[7]

The other primary site for official U.S. anxieties about color and subversion during the Cold War, besides the American South, was Africa. The swift retreat of European colonialism from the Middle East and most of Asia after 1945 left Africa as the center of colonial contention. In contrast to the confusing "browns" and "yellows" Americans saw in the rest of the Third World, the "black and white" racial demographics south of the Sahara fit with their assumptions about their own society, though in reversed proportions. The continent even offered its own Deep South, its own centers of white supremacist resistance that would outlast less determined white colonial authorities farther north: the apartheid regime in South Africa, the white settler government in Rhodesia/Zimbabwe, and the dogged Portuguese rule in Angola and Mozambique. While the rest of sub-Saharan Africa emerged from white control between 1957 and 1964, the region below the Zambezi River remained frozen under white totalitarianism until late in the Cold War.[8]

The African and African American freedom movements encouraged and reinforced each other in ways remarked on at the time and since. The appearance in Washington and New York of dignified nonwhite leaders from the Third World, combined with their respectful treatment by white American officials, made a profound impression on segregated black Americans.[9] Conversely, the model of successful, nonviolent organizing in the American South spread powerfully outward from American shores, its influence washing ashore in freedom struggles in places as disparate as China, Poland, northern Ireland, Palestine/Israel, South Korea, and South Africa.[10] In a world increasingly linked by televised imagery and intercontinental jet travel, American policymakers could not preserve a clear distinction—much as they sometimes wished to—between the social upheaval they faced along the color line at home and in certain parts of the world abroad. The movements for racial equality and self-government that arose among the world's non-white majority during the Cold War were destined to succeed or fail, for the most part, together.[11]

DISCERNING THE ROLE of race relations and racial attitudes in American foreign policy after World War II is not a simple diagnostic exercise. The construction of U.S. relations with the outside world does not work like a mathematical equation, in which a single factor can be removed and the resulting difference in outcomes then calculated precisely. Indeed, racial thinking itself is merely one of several ways to divide the world in hierarchical and pejorative categories; others like ethnicity, class, religion, and gender frequently overlap with race in the minds of responsible officials, making it difficult to isolate completely any one variable.[12] Yet there is abundant evidence that racial considerations were regularly present in the minds of U.S. officials throughout the Cold War, as should hardly be surprising in light of the turmoil surrounding race relations in the United States and the world in those decades. In a nation increasingly absorbed by racial problems while also engaged abroad with a mostly nonwhite world, it seems only reasonable to ask how these two themes were related. The focus here on race should not, of course, suggest a downgrading of the salience of other well-known factors in American foreign policy, like economics or geostrategy, but rather encourage the inclusion of an aspect not previously well understood.

The high stakes of the nuclear-tipped contest between the Soviet Union and the United States promoted institutional and intellectual rigidity while discouraging creative thinking about the period's international history. In retrospect, the conflicts between the great powers of the Northern Hemisphere after 1945 distracted attention from the period's perhaps more significant long-term development: the emergence of the world's nonwhite majority from white colonial rule into national independence. With the democratic elections of 1994 in South Africa, the long era of legalized white rule over people of color—much, much longer than the period of competition between Communism and capitalism—came finally to an end. Continuing differences in the racial distribution of power and wealth confirm the ongoing relevance of this theme to contemporary international history.

Thomas McCormick has observed, "People do not think one way about their national society and a different way about the world society. Instead, they tend to project and internationalize conceptual frameworks first articulated at home."[13] Historians are nearly unanimous in their placing of the civil rights movement "at the center of their history of the postwar United States," according to a review of recent major U.S. history textbooks.[14] Yet scholars of that movement have paid scant attention to its international context and significance.[15] Conversely, even eminent observers of U.S. foreign policy sometimes display a notable lack of concern for domestic realities.[16] Harold Isaacs, by contrast, called attention nearly four decades ago to "the peculiar consonance that has existed between the rise and fall of Western white power and the rise and fall of white racism in America."[17] The issue of race is one of several that can illuminate the ways in which American history in the second half of the twentieth century was also international history.

Some clarity about the use of the word "race" is required. The absence of quotation marks around this term throughout the book reflects an effort at literary felicity, not an acceptance of the still common belief that race refers to a biologically significant characteristic of human beings useful for classifying them in distinct populations. In a society as suffused with anxiety about racial identity and race relations as the contemporary United States, it is worth emphasizing how much race is a social construction. Americans throughout the Cold War and after, like their predecessors, have conflated several distinct physical features—skin color, hair type, various facial features—to create a system of absolute racial identities: white, black, yellow, red, and sometimes brown. Race has become so accepted a part of "common sense" in this culture that it bears repeating here that race is a historicized construction, which other societies in other eras have built differently.[18] The tendency of North Americans and Europeans to wield racial thinking with considerable force and impact in modern history should not be understood as a permanent condition. There was, after all, a time when "civilized" peoples of the Mediterranean region viewed northern Europeans as "deficient in skill and intelligence," in Plato's words, and Britons as "utterly stupid and incapable of learning," according to Cicero.[19]

In the course of the twentieth century, American racial classifications tended to become more rigid, although Americans remained uncertain sometimes about how to apply them. Ironically, the scientific community moved in the opposite direction by refuting previous assumptions of significant biological differences.[20] The status of Jews suggested continuing malleability about race, from the 1940s—when they were viewed primarily as a separate

— 7 —

race, having an interfaith marriage rate of 3 percent and suffering intense discrimination—to the end of the century, when they had been thoroughly assimilated into the category "white" with an interfaith marriage rate of over 50 percent.[21] The legal status of immigrants from India remained unclear until the Supreme Court ruled in 1923 that they were Caucasians but still not "white persons," and thus not eligible for naturalization.[22] So few blacks lived in Hawaii in the early twentieth century that the census classified them as "Puerto Ricans," while Puerto Ricans were in turn defined as "Caucasians" and thus—unlike Indians—as whites. In other words, along Waikiki Beach, blacks were white.[23] Russians troubled American racial categorizers throughout the Cold War, appearing to some as Europeans and to others as Asians or half-Asians.[24] The anxiety produced by such uncertain identities perhaps helps explain the sign over one east Texas town: "The Blackest Land—The Whitest People."[25] And it is crucial for understanding the American institution of the "one-drop rule," whereby having any African heritage at all came to define a person as black.[26]

The absurdities of the one-drop rule were legion. Walter White, long-time president of the National Association for the Advancement of Colored People (NAACP), had fair skin, fair hair, and blue eyes. Like his parents, he appeared white, but like them, he chose to identify with the tiny percentage of his genetic ancestry that was not European. When he traveled abroad with his second wife, a white brunette, and they were introduced as an interracial couple, puzzled foreigners often asked him how he happened to marry a "colored" woman.[27] African American diplomat Ralph Bunche headed the 1960 United Nations mission in the Congo, where Americans assumed his color would be an asset. But he was so light-skinned that the distinction was lost on the Congolese, who tended to consider him just another European. Black in America, he was white in central Africa.[28] Even Malcolm X, the exemplar of black pride and, for most of his career, black separatism, embodied such ironies. His relatively light skin tone resulted in the nickname Red in his early years. During a visit to Kenya in 1964, Malcolm accompanied President Jomo Kenyatta to the Nairobi racetrack, where he was noticed from afar by U.S. ambassador William Attwood as "a white man" in the official entourage. Only as Attwood approached the presidential box could he see who the guest was—and thus what color he "really" was.[29]

Race, then, means "race." But the artificiality of the term and the often invidious meanings imputed to it do nothing to reduce the importance of those meanings to Americans in the postwar era. Most Americans, including policymakers in Washington, viewed the world in explicitly race-conscious terms, and U.S. officials made decisions that affected the lives of hundreds of millions of people partly on the basis of racial assumptions. This is the story of how those racial lenses helped shape U.S. relations with the outside world in the era of American dominance in the international sphere.

# 1

# RACE AND FOREIGN RELATIONS BEFORE 1945

ALONG A RIVERBANK in Panama in 1577, Spanish soldiers hunting for their piratical English rivals finally caught up with Sir Francis Drake's lieutenant John Oxenham and his fifty comrades. The English had allied themselves with the considerable local force of Cimarones, enslaved Africans who had escaped from their Spanish masters. Together they raided the gold and silver shipments bound for Spain from the mines of Peru. These Protestant Englishmen were intensely hostile to the Catholic Spanish, who returned the sentiment by hauling them off to be executed, but they evidently enjoyed the company of the Cimarones. What the Spanish interrupted that day along the river was an African-English encampment and barbecue, replete with large quantities of roasting pork and abundant good humor and fellowship. The Spanish described the black and white allies as "amusing themselves together"—in contemporary terms, they were partying.[1]

The foreign relations of the United States, the country that emerged two hundred years later from the colonies established by Drake's countrymen, have always involved relations between peoples of different skin colors. Natives of three continents—Europe, Africa, and North America—gathered in the land that became the United States, later to be joined by immigrants from Asia. White appropriation of black labor and red land formed two of the fundamental contours of the new nation's development and its primary sources of wealth. Like the enslavement of African workers for two and a half centuries, wars of Indian removal helped define American society and American foreign relations from the early seventeenth century to the late nineteenth. The savagery inherent in the institution of human bondage and in the frequently exterminationist campaigns on the frontier assured that their poisonous legacy would continue to afflict American life throughout the twentieth century. Slavery and westward expansion wove together issues of race relations and foreign relations from the very beginning of American history.[2]

The subjugation and destruction of people of color rests at the center of the early American experience, in great tension with the egalitarian, democratic tradition of the American Revolution. The dominant power of white Americans in most of their interactions with people of color has meant that, for most of American history, white political and military superiority has been an imposing and aggressive force in the shaping of these relations. Francis Drake himself, after all, was involved in the African slave trade. But scenes like those of the multiracial barbecue in Panama suggest that from the earliest days of its colonial past, the United States has harbored competing inclinations among its white majority: toward racial hierarchy and domination, on the one hand, and toward equality and color blindness on the other. The oscillation between those two poles has helped define the manner in which racial perceptions and attitudes have always been a factor in the American experience.

### The Color-Coded Expansionism of the 1800s

During the first half of the nineteenth century, American expansionism acquired an increasingly explicit sense of racial destiny. White Americans in these decades shared the growing European scientific fascination with the meanings of human difference and racial classification. Popular American conceptions of the nation's future in the decades immediately after the Revolution focused on the ideological power of republican liberty. Although assumptions about "Anglo-Saxon" superiority and the inevitable disappearance of "inferior" peoples were present in 1800, they did not become dominant in the language of expansion until the middle of the century. Only gradually did a specifically racial view of human destiny overcome a more egalitarian political perspective in post–Civil War America. As North and South reconciled, black and white became increasingly segregated. As renewed racial hierarchy set in at home, it weakened the perception of the United States as a model of liberty for the rest of the world to follow.

A racial perspective pervaded the debates about annexing Texas and going to war with Mexico in the 1840s. Most white Americans saw Mexicans as a people degenerated by a racially mixed heritage of Spaniards and Native

Americans, who could neither manage nor improve the vast territories they held. They stood in the way of U.S. settlers eager to occupy new lands to the west. The annexation of Texas and the rapid conquest of the land that became the American Southwest came to be seen by most white Americans as the "manifest destiny" of a racially superior people.[3]

Profound disagreements over whether to carry slavery into new territories and states in the West helped bring on the Civil War in 1861, as domestic race relations and national expansion remained intertwined. After the brief egalitarian hope of Reconstruction, white Americans put their regional divisions largely behind them in rebuilding racial hierarchies in the form of Jim Crow segregation and renewed campaigns against Western Indians. This other reconstruction—of unified white authority over nonwhite peoples—placed the United States squarely within a broader global pattern of the expansion of white power. The final decades of the nineteenth century and the first decade of the twentieth marked the zenith of European and North American imperial might, at the end of which only a fifth of the world's land remained outside the control of Europeans or the descendants of European settlers. Racial theorist Lothrop Stoddard in 1920 referred back to the turn of the century as "the high-water mark of the white tide which had been flooding for four hundred years." The reestablishment of white dominion in the American South and its final assertion in the American West came in precisely the same years that Europeans at last brought the interior of Africa under their subjugation. American immigration policies in these years reflected the broader trend of white settler states, including Canada, New Zealand, Australia, and South Africa, to define citizenship in racial terms, with non-Europeans ineligible for naturalization. Racial homogeneity seemed a defining characteristic of great nations like England and France.[4]

The growth and consolidation of white power at home and abroad did not seem accidental or unfortunate to most Americans. The legitimacy that white Americans accorded to notions of white supremacy was reflected in the rise of Social Darwinist thought, which proclaimed Europeans and their descendants as fittest to survive among the races, and Anglo-Saxonist thinking, which posited the preeminence of an even narrower British race. The common tendency was to rank racial groups by their supposed relative merit, with northwestern Europeans and their descendants at the top and others trailing off through darkening skin shades to Africans and their descendants at the bottom. Such a view of racial categorization around the world precisely reflected domestic attitudes.[5] The trend toward dividing up the human population went so far as to threaten the concept of a single white race, as Anglo-Saxonist proponents conceived of several white races: Anglo-Saxons, Teutons, Latins, Celts, and so on, down to Slavs, who were seen as partly Asian. This racialized vision of humanity emerged in the rising nativist sentiment by the turn of the century against immigrants from southern and eastern Europe. "They are beaten men from beaten races," announced the president of the Immigration Restriction League in 1894.[6]

With many Europeans not even qualifying as fully white, native Americans and African Americans fell much further down the scale. Indians west of the Mississippi River faced an onslaught of white settlers backed by the military power of a reunified federal government. The alternative to the U.S. Indian Bureau's reservation system, with its emphasis on the eradication of Indian culture, was warfare.[7] Regardless of the extent of antislavery motivation among Union troops in the Civil War, soldiers in blue were shipped west immediately thereafter to vanquish native Americans. "The more we can kill this year, the less will have to be killed [in] the next war," declared General William T. Sherman, conqueror of much of the South and the first postwar commander in the West in 1868, "for the more I see of these Indians the more convinced I am that all have to be killed or be maintained as a species of pauper."[8] Theodore Roosevelt summarized the common assumption that underlay the often exterminationist thrust of anti-Indian warfare: "The most vicious cowboy has more moral principle than the average Indian."[9] The subjugation of native Americans and their treatment as dependent wards of the state laid the groundwork for parallel U.S. actions in the Philippines a few years later. Each represented a form of colonialism: conquering and controlling culturally different peoples, and ruling them as subjects rather than incorporating them as citizens.[10] Domestic and foreign policies regarding people of color developed as two sides of the same coin.

The African American experience of segregation after Reconstruction reflected the importance of black labor in the Southern agricultural economy, in contrast to the resentment of Indian presence on valuable Western lands. But the goal was control of both nonwhite workers and nonwhite lands, just as it was in European overseas colonies in the same years.[11] While most white residents of the Confederate states accepted their defeat and reincorporation into the Union, some plantation owners refused and left. Of these, many settled in Brazil, where slavery still existed and expatriates could reconstruct racial hierarchy and the plantation economic system in their fullest form.[12] White supremacists thus indicated an international consciousness, just as they would a hundred years later in looking to Rhodesia and South Africa for support. Those white Southerners who did not leave after the Civil War succeeded in establishing a rigid system of racial segregation confirmed by the Supreme Court in the *Plessy v. Ferguson* case of 1896. In conjunction with the expropriation of Indian lands, this decision laid the groundwork for the treatment of nonwhite inhabitants of the overseas territories that the United States seized two years later in the war against Spain. Only Hawaii and Alaska among those territories with dense populations of people of color would become states, as the U.S. government sought to preserve the whiteness of its citizenry.[13]

Two prominent figures of the late nineteenth century represented to the American public the meanings and importance of white authority. Henry Morton Stanley and Theodore Roosevelt each understood race relations in international terms, tying the story of black and native Americans to that of Africans. Through the lives of these two men, Americans could link the exploration and conquest of two of the last great mysterious wilderness frontiers: the interior American West and central Africa. The fame of Stanley, the lesser known of the two, derived from his successful effort to track down missing British missionary David Livingstone in 1871 near Lake Tanganyika, and his epic three-year transcontinental exploration of the headwaters of the Congo River, which brought him, exhausted, to the Atlantic Ocean in 1877. He was subsequently involved in the creation of the Congo Free State, a colony infamous for its brutality toward the indigenous inhabitants. A Welshman by origin, as a young man Stanley came to Louisiana, where he observed plantation slavery at close range. He fought in the Confederate army and was taken prisoner at Shiloh. After the war he became a star reporter for the *New York Herald,* covering first the Indian wars in Colorado in 1866–67 and then the British punitive campaign into Abyssinia later in 1867. Stanley's subsequent reputation for ferocity among Africans—his nickname in the Congo was Breaker of Rocks, and he left his bloody mark across the continent—built upon earlier experiences with American slavery and frontier wars. There he had first learned the place of people of color in an era of white dominion, and he applied that lesson in explicit fashion, even quoting to Africans from speeches that General Sherman had made to Native Americans. Stanley represented the truly international sweep of white authority in the decades after the Civil War.[14]

Like Stanley, Roosevelt built on experiences with Jim Crow and frontier warfare in the American West in understanding Africans as an amalgam of black and red Americans. Roosevelt's life span of 1858–1919 coincided with the era of global white supremacy, and his fascination with race and racial differences reflected the Victorian world in which he lived. Though a New Yorker by origin, he learned sympathy for white Southerners and even for slavery from his Southern-born mother, as well as hatred for Indians from his years in the Dakota Territory in the early 1880s. He opposed lynching but shared common white assumptions about the subversive possibilities of African Americans and the importance of restricting non-European immigration. By the time he landed in Africa in 1909 at the head of a Smithsonian-sponsored safari, the former president embodied white American views of "natives"—whether red or black—as both dangerous and less interesting than exotic animals. Roosevelt, like Stanley, helped teach Americans about the international character of white rule over people of color.[15] In a popularized version, the Tarzan novels of Edgar Rice Burroughs that began to appear in 1912 did the same. These stories of white heroism in the jungle paralleled tales of white courage on the American frontier. Tarzan's identity as a British lord did not diminish the sense of a Davy Crockett adventure transported to central Africa in these quintessentially American stories.[16]

Issues of race pervaded the American acquisition of an overseas empire after the defeat of Spain in 1898. Most imperialists and anti-imperialists shared a common view of the world as divided between civilization and barbarism, with those possessing lighter skin in the former camp and those with darker skin in the latter.[17] Where they differed was over how, precisely, the United States should engage with the lands it had seized in the course of the fighting—the Philippines, Cuba, Puerto Rico, and the Virgin Islands, as well as Hawaii. In winning the argument regarding the Philippines, annexationists succeeded in convincing enough white Americans that the domestic racial status quo would not be upset. Anxieties about increasing the nation's non-European population had contributed to the initial refusal to annex Hawaii to the United States after the white planters' rebellion in 1893. The final decision five years later to make Hawaii an American territory reflected a growing determination to control Asian immigration to the islands to put them on a path toward someday forming a predominantly white state.

One major issue of the congressional debates of 1897–98 demonstrated the unstable and malleable definition of race, even as U.S. policymakers used this idea in powerful ways: were Hawaiian residents of Portuguese origin or descent white? According to the 1896 census, Americans made up 3 percent of the islands' population, non-Portuguese Europeans 7 percent, and Portuguese 15 percent; the rest were Japanese, Chinese, or native Hawaiian. Annexationists said yes, of course the Portuguese were European and thus white, boosting the whiteness of the territory. Anti-imperialists said no, they were not really white, lowering the whiteness quotient and the attractiveness of annexation to most white Americans. Americans spoke forcefully to one another about race, even if they were not always referring to the same category of distinction.[18]

U.S. policy toward its new colonies abroad after 1899 derived directly from its prior policies toward Native Americans. The administration of racially and culturally different peoples as dependent wards of the state without political representation marked an extension across water of long-standing governmental practices in the American West. The unanimity of white American opinion about the rightness of subjugating Indians made this precedent a powerful argument for annexationists in Congress in 1899. If those opposing the acquisition of the Philippines were right, Senator Henry Cabot Lodge declared, "then our whole past record of expansion is a crime." Roosevelt wrote to a friend that if whites were "morally bound to abandon the Philippines, we were also morally bound to abandon Arizona to the Apaches." Apaches had few white defenders at the turn of the century, and the American frontier with indigenous peoples pushed westward again, into the far reaches of the Pacific Ocean.[19]

Filipino resistance to American annexation confronted U.S. policymakers with a repetition of the problems they had just finished facing in Indian lands at home, and their response was the same. Both officers and soldiers of the American army had considerable personal experience in Indian fighting, and their racially charged language and behavior in the Philippines reflected the belief that they were engaged in a similar struggle.[20] President William McKinley spoke of Filipinos needing to be disciplined "with firmness if need be, but without severity so far as may be possible."[21] The ordeal of insurgent and counterinsurgent warfare soon eliminated most restraints, however, and produced considerable severity. From the ready use of torture and the killing of prisoners, some American soldiers descended into sheer racial slaughter. They did so at the command of their superiors, such as General Jacob Smith, who ordered his men to kill all hostile Filipinos over the age of nine: "The interior of [the island of] Samar must be made a howling wilderness."[22] A. A. Barnes, an American infantryman, expressed a racially focused rage in a letter home to his brother: "I am probably growing hard-hearted, for I am in my glory when I can sight my gun on some dark skin and pull the trigger."[23]

Some white Americans were troubled by the course of the war in the Philippines, but many openly accepted it as one of the unfortunate burdens of civilization. Charles Francis Adams, Jr., the former president of the Union Pacific Railroad and president of the Massachusetts Historical Society, explained this point of view in a public address in Lexington in December 1898. Reviewing the violent history of white interactions with people of color on the North American continent over the previous three centuries, Adams called it "a process of extermination." But, he concluded, that process was also "the salvation of the race. It has saved the Anglo-Saxon stock from being a nation of half-breeds."[24] U.S. actions in the Philippines fit into a broader global pattern of imperial severity as European powers pressed further into Africa and Asia and encountered resistance. The massive slaughter of Congolese by the Belgians, the attempted extermination of the Hereros in Namibia by the Germans, and the destruction of the Boxers in China by an international force all unfolded in these same years. Like other American elites of the time, Roosevelt understood American behavior in this global context: "The rude, fierce settler who drives the savage from the land lays all civilized mankind under a debt to him. American and Indian, Boer and Zulu, Cossack and Tartar, New Zealander and Maori—in each case the victor, horrible though many of his deeds are, has laid deep the foundations for the future greatness of a mighty people."[25]

Unlike Germans and Belgians who engaged in large-scale racial violence beyond their homogenous homelands out on the fringes of their empires, Americans constructed their campaigns against the Filipinos out of a set of experiences at home in a multiracial, hierarchical society. Indian wars provided only part of that domestic framework; the ongoing campaign of subjugation of African Americans provided most of the rest. "We do not have to go to Luzon for American barbarities," one Brooklyn minister noted in 1899, pointing to the chartering of an excursion train to carry aficionados from Atlanta to the well-advertised lynching of Sam Hose in the town of Newnan, Georgia, from which some returned with souvenirs of his charred and mutilated body.[26] The years of U.S. warfare in the Philippines, 1899 to 1902, encompassed a wave of mob violence against African Americans at home. In addition to lynchings in the rural South, the terror included race riots in New Orleans, New York City, Akron, Ohio, and Wilmington, North Carolina. Black soldiers stationed at bases in the South drew the particular ire of white soldiers and civilians who, just thirty-three years away from slavery, were enraged by the authority implied in the uniforms and weapons. The racial coding of deadly conflict on the periphery bore similarity to that in the center of the American empire.[27]

African American soldiers fighting in the Philippines found themselves caught between powerful, conflicting currents of identity. Despite their cultural and linguistic differences with Filipinos, many of them felt some admiration for the islanders' nationalist resistance to American power. Some also acknowledged a sense of racial commonality as people of color, an inclination that grew as they listened to their white colleagues refer to Filipinos as "niggers" and as the insurgents appealed to them to stop fighting in a "white man's war." A small number even deserted and went over to the other side, finding the elements of racial conflict in the war ultimately more significant than their common ground with white Americans' economic and military expansion. The vast majority of black soldiers stood strong in their American identity, however, even as they evinced little enthusiasm for the idea of the "white man's burden" and the more gruesome forms of racially tinged counterinsurgent warfare. Hoping their courage and patriotism on the field of battle would translate into better treatment of African Americans at home, they swallowed their anger at the spread of segregated facilities in the American-controlled areas of the Philippines and the other territories taken from Spain.[28]

In this process, black soldiers took encouragement from small signs of progress among their paler countrymen. Captain W. B. Roberts wrote home from Santiago, Cuba, in the fall of 1898 to report an incident where the American proprietor of a hotel restaurant had tried to eject him on racial grounds. "The dining room was full of officers and others, and you could have heard a pin fall" when Roberts loudly declared that he and other black soldiers had spilled their blood on San Juan Hill to protect American businessmen like him and would accept no such discrimination. Before the restaurateur could respond, a white general got up from his table, walked over, and shook Roberts's hand, saying, "Come, Captain, take my seat; and you, Mr. Hotel Proprietor, get it quick; and I don't want to hear any more of this damn foolishness with these officers of mine!"[29] Such outcomes were unusual in a period when the outward expansion of the American empire usually served to encourage more intense discrimination against Americans of color. But the logic of color-blind equality—that is, the logic of democracy—persistently shadowed the reality of Jim Crow, articulated by darker Americans determined to make real the promises of the Declaration of Independence. The growing American engagement with a mostly nonwhite world pointed toward an era when many more white Americans would be forced to confront and resolve the contradiction between liberty and racial hierarchy.

### White Dominion and Its Challengers in the Early 1900s

The U.S. war against the Philippines overlapped precisely with the British war of 1899–1902 against the South African Boers, the farmers of Dutch descent seeking to preserve their independence from the expanding British empire. Americans' response to events in southern Africa revealed their ambivalence about race and its meanings. Most Americans sympathized with the Boers, seeing parallels to their own revolutionary past as white settlers on a new continent far from Europe. Some even volunteered to fight alongside the Boers, especially Irish Americans resentful of continued British control of their own homeland. The U.S. government, however, strongly supported the British. The administrations of both William McKinley and Theodore Roosevelt viewed the British empire as a civilizing and modernizing force, bringing law, liberty, and commerce in its wake, in contrast to the white South Africans, whom they saw as traditional, hidebound rural folk—figures from the past rather than the future. Both presidents spoke of the conflict as a racial one between more advanced Anglo-Saxons and more retrograde descendants of the Dutch. A European or even a northwestern European identity was not sufficient to put one in the front ranks of whites. The Dutch and Irish origins of men with the names "Roosevelt" and "McKinley" added a particular irony to the presidents' emphasis on the supposed biological superiority of the British; Roosevelt did at least argue that the Dutch "down at the bottom have the great basic virtues of the Teutonic races." Sure that race was a critical method of distinguishing among peoples, Americans nevertheless demonstrated ongoing uncertainty about precisely who fell into which category.[30]

Arguments about the relative genetic merits of Europeans paled, of course, beside confident assertions of non-European inferiority. Almost completely ignored in American discussions of the Boer War were the vast majority of South Africans, who were black. Social Darwinism offered a vision of weaker peoples of all shades inevitably disappearing before the relentless march of stronger peoples. A supposedly unavoidable course of history offered a clear case of ends justifying means, when it came to matters of tactics in pacification campaigns on the fringes of empire. Professor Washburn Hopkins of Yale asked in the pages of *Forum* in 1900, "Is there not here a counterpart in the moral world to the inflexible severity of physical laws, whereby the maintenance of the race is upheld at the sacrifice of individuals?" However excruciating the forms of that sacrifice might be, it accorded with "the higher law of racial superiority" that Hopkins and so many other white Americans saw at work in the Philippines and in southern Africa—and in the American South—at the dawn of the twentieth century.[31]

In the same years that the United States and the European powers were extending the reach of white authority around the globe, signs of antiracist and anticolonial organizing began to twinkle through the imperial gloom, pointing the way to the coming decline rather than triumph of worldwide white supremacy. The first dramatic breakthrough came on a battlefield at Adowa in Ethiopia in March 1896. There, in the same year that the U.S. Supreme Court put its stamp of approval on the South's system of segregation in the *Plessy v. Ferguson* decision, soldiers of King Menelik II's Ethiopian army destroyed an invading Italian army. This first modern military defeat of Europeans by non-Europeans preserved Ethiopia as the one great exception in Africa in the early twentieth century: an independent nation. Out of one part of Africa came hope for people of color everywhere, and fear for white supremacists.[32]

The second sign of trouble for white dominion appeared in northeast Asia. The Japanese destruction of the Russian fleet at the Battle of the Japan Sea in 1905 ended the Russo-Japanese War and represented the entry of the first nonwhite nation into the elite ranks of industrialized great powers. Some Europeans had reassured themselves after Adowa that Italy had had only a second-rate army, but the Russian empire was an entirely different matter. Observers around the world interpreted Japan's success in racial terms, as a victory of Asia over Europe. On a boat crossing the Suez Canal soon after this news arrived, Chinese revolutionary Sun Yat-sen found himself besieged by enthusiastic Egyptians eager to celebrate their anti-European solidarity, even after they realized he was not Japanese.[33] Politically attentive African Americans took vicarious pleasure in the defeat of the overconfident white Russian troops in Manchuria.[34] Most Europeans, however, heard the news from the Sea of Japan with foreboding. A French reporter in Japan described the arrival of captured Russian soldiers: "Whites, vanquished and captives, defiling before those free and triumphant yellows—this was not Russia beaten by Japan, not the defeat of one nation by another; it was something new, enormous, prodigious . . . it was the awakening hope of the Oriental peoples, it was the first blow given to the other race, to that accursed race of the West."[35]

Even the British, formally allied with Japan since 1902, were uneasy about an Asian nation defeating a fellow European power. Roosevelt helped mediate peace terms between Japan and Russia in part to preserve the balance of power in northeast Asia and thereby prevent what he called "the creation of either a yellow peril or a Slav peril."[36]

The military defeats of Europeans in Africa and Asia fit into a broader pattern of rising resistance to the spread of white power in the first years of the twentieth century. Those ruled by colonialism or otherwise discriminated against increasingly sought national, ethnic, or racial self-determination. In the intellectual realm, the publication in 1911 of *The Mind of Primitive Man,* by American anthropologist Franz Boas, signaled the coming retreat of scientific racism, with its rejection of biological theories of white racial superiority. In the political realm, anticolonial agitation in India and elsewhere accelerated, and the first of a string of Pan-African Congresses was convened in 1900. Eastern European Jews, stigmatized as racially distinctive, responded to continuing anti-Jewish violence by organizing the Zionist movement for liberation. African Americans and their white supporters formed the National Association for the Advancement of Colored People in 1909 in reaction to intensifying racial discrimination in the United States. And Africans surveying the grim realities of the new dispensation of joint British-Afrikaner control in South Africa created the African National Congress in 1912. The outlines of a global struggle for racial equality were visible by the time World War I exploded across the European landscape.[37]

The carnage on the fields of Europe between 1914 and 1918 struck a mortal blow against the certainty of Europeans that theirs was the highest civilization to which all others should aspire. World War I appeared to many as a civil war among whites, especially in light of centuries of assertions about Europe as a unified culture superior to the non-European world it had colonized. Not only were Germans, French, and British slaughtering one another in unprecedented numbers, but they were even using colonial troops from Asia and Africa against each other. The "white race" seemed to be engaged in a kind of suicide, many observers noted, some with sadness and some with hope. Nation clearly ranked above race, revealing huge cracks in the edifice of white authority. Soldiers of color paid close attention, whether they came from India, Senegal, or Mississippi. People who had lived all their lives under the power of white supremacy could not avoid being impressed by the deaths of millions of white people. Most nonwhite troops who survived the horrors of modern warfare returned home less willing to be intimidated by white civilians. Young African American veterans, the *Chicago Defender* observed, "are not content to move along the line of least resistance as did their sires."[38]

Waves of new immigrants over the previous generation had combined with the processes of industrialization to create a more diverse and more contentious American society. Ethnic tensions in the United States swelled as Europe descended into war. People with ties to Ireland, Germany, Eastern Europe, and Russian Jewry observed the conflict with different emotions than did those with links to England, France, Italy, and gentile Russia. The administration of Woodrow Wilson kept the United States out of the war for the first three years, in part because of such conflicting public sentiments. Wilson's sympathy for the British side of the conflict was no mystery, however, and the start of U.S. belligerency in 1917 led to an outbreak of intense repression of domestic dissent. Wilson's ambassador to England, Walter Hines Page, responded with rage to the hopes of many Irish Americans that a defeat of England would lead to Irish independence: "We Americans have got to hang our Irish agitators and shoot our hyphenates and bring up our children with reverence for English history and in the awe of English literature."[39] Wilson's Southern roots and strong segregationist commitments also did not incline him to sympathy for the major revolutionary movements of the World War I decade, in Mexico, China, and Russia. He tended to view Mexicans as somewhat childlike and in need of American tutoring to learn how to govern themselves responsibly. His Yankee secretary of state, Robert Lansing, wrote to a friend about the loathsomeness of having to "swallow one's pride and to keep ladling out soothing syrup to those Greasers [Mexicans] while they smiled sarcastically and kept on with their insults."[40] Lansing blamed much of the Bolshevism that took power in Russia on the supposed Asian influences in that vast, bicontinental nation, equating Lenin's rule with "the Asiatic despotism of the early Tsars."[41]

American entry into World War I led to an extraordinary outbreak of violence against African Americans. The delicate balance of domestic race relations was upended by the war hysteria of thousands of white Americans, who were troubled by black migration to Northern cities for defense industry work. From the summer of 1917 through 1919, white mobs across the nation beat, shot, burned, and mutilated black Americans with impunity. The incidents ranged from rural lynchings across the South to full-scale riots in cities around the country, including the ferocious slaughters in East St. Louis and Chicago.[42] The contrast of these actions with Wilson's proclaimed cause of expanding democracy abroad was stark. Howard University professor Kelly

Miller asked in an open letter to the president: "Why democratize the nations of the earth if it leads them to delight in the burning of human beings after the manner of Springfield, Waco, Memphis, and East St. Louis, while the nation looks helplessly on?" Eight thousand African Americans marched down New York's Fifth Avenue in protest.[43] America's closest allies in the war, England and France, experienced smaller-scale versions of the same pattern. Whites assaulted blacks in Liverpool and Cardiff, while nonwhite workers imported from the colonies to help in France's war industries were carefully segregated and frequently abused. White male anxieties about social contacts of men of color with white women figured prominently in the patterns of discrimination in all three countries.[44] The French government, however, readily used African colonial troops against Germany, including a large number in the occupation of the Rhineland in 1923. Germans, whose imperial army had engaged in the near extermination of an entire African people in Namibia just nineteen years earlier, apparently did not appreciate this small bit of historical justice. They bitterly resented black authority and called for the removal of African soldiers not just for Germany's sake but also "for civilization and the white race."[45] By dividing the white nations and drawing in so many non-European combatants, the war threatened the survival of global white rule.

The extensive participation of African Americans in their nation's cause in World War I created novel problems for U.S. commanders. The army conscripted a slightly higher percentage of blacks than whites, and then sent many of them off to France, a country that U.S. commanders feared would breach American racial boundaries. As a result, U.S. Army authorities campaigned strenuously to convince French soldiers and commanders not to treat darker-skinned U.S. soldiers as equals—especially not to eat, shake hands, or socialize with them and not to praise them too highly in front of lighter-skinned U.S. soldiers. American authorities exuded particular anxiety about the likely liaisons between black GIs and French women, given the relationships that commonly develop between male soldiers and some female civilians during wars. Such links, it was feared, could lead to the breakdown of army morale abroad and segregation at home after the war. Wilson himself worried in 1919 that decent French treatment of African American soldiers "has gone to their heads." The American campaign to extend Jim Crow across the Atlantic met with only limited success, as most French were delighted to have Americans of any color fighting to defend them against Germany. And the problem turned out to be French men more than women:

French commanders generally treated African American soldiers as equal to other soldiers, as they did their own colonial troops. This was a novel experience of equal treatment for black Americans, precisely what their white commanders and colleagues had feared.[46]

Black veterans returned home from Europe with guarded hopes that their patriotic service and sacrifices would help initiate a new era of diminishing discrimination. The white hostility they encountered back home suggested the opposite. Walter Jones recalled many years later, "They told us to 'go catch the Kaiser and everything'll be all right.' We went over there and fought and the first thing I heard when I got back to Waco, Texas, was a white man telling me to move out of the train station. He said, 'Nigger, you ain't in France no more, you're in America.' He didn't even give me time to take off the uniform."[47] During the war years the urban black working class had grown considerably, as African Americans left the rural South for better opportunities in booming war industries. This brought them into volatile situations as a wave of labor conflict and political radicalism swept through the country from 1918 to 1920. Conservative whites viewed blacks as especially inclined to subversion or to manipulation by revolutionaries because of their secondary status. Army intelligence officers kept a close eye after 1917 on "Negro unrest," and Southern leaders warned African Americans against seeking equality. "This is a white man's country," warned South Carolina Congressman and future Secretary of State James F. Byrnes, "and will always remain a white man's country."[48]

Wilson's determination to create a League of Nations at the postwar settlement at Versailles revealed the close ties between domestic American race relations and U.S. foreign policy. Japan responded in the spirit of Wilson's Fourteen Points by proposing a clause in the league's charter that would establish the equality of all people regardless of race. Despite having the approval of a majority of delegates at the peace conference, the proposal died when the president, supported by Australia and Britain, declared that there were "too serious objections on the part of some of us" to include it in the league covenant. Racial equality was still a radical concept for most Americans in 1919, especially Southern segregationists and Westerners opposed to Asian immigration, who lobbied Wilson against the proposal.[49] Philip Kerr, the secretary to Prime Minister David Lloyd George, reminded U.S. diplomats of American vulnerability on matters of race when he directed them to ignore Irish American lobbying efforts regarding Irish independence; the United States had no more right to ask that Ireland speak at Versailles, Kerr declared, than a "delegation of Negroes from America" could demand from England the right to appear there and argue for relief because "they had been disenfranchised in the South."[50]

Japanese leaders resented the rejection of their proposed clause, just as they did the ongoing discrimination against Japanese immigrants in the United States. Former prime minister Shigenobu Okuma warned that "the problems of population and race will in the future form the hardest and most important issues between nations." Echoing W. E. B. Du Bois's famous dictum about the color line being the central problem of the twentieth century, Okuma concluded: "The satisfactory solution of these baffling problems is the responsibility of twentieth[-]century diplomacy."[51] People of color everywhere shared Japan's disappointment in the U.S. government's commitment to racial discrimination and the support the United States received from Britain and the white-ruled Dominions. Organizers of the Pan-African Congress in Paris in 1919 ran into opposition from the State Department, which denied passports to many Americans trying to participate in what was seen to be a radical, international, antiracist movement.[52]

For many opponents of the League of Nations, however, Wilson's restraint did not adequately protect white supremacy from international pressure. Senator James Reed of Missouri ridiculed the idea of international sovereignty: "Think of submitting questions involving the very life of the United States to a tribunal on which a nigger from Liberia, a nigger from Honduras, a nigger from India . . . each have votes equal to that of the great United States."[53] America's emergence from World War I as a global power had brought the country's internal conflicts into the full daylight of the international arena.

In the two decades between the end of one world war and the beginning of another whites attempted to reassert traditional racial hierarchies while there began a movement toward racial equality that would flower after 1945. The domestic violence of World War I slid over into the 1920s, with lynchings and race riots continuing long after the guns had fallen silent in Europe and workers had retreated from the barricades of 1919. As African American calls for greater civil liberties escalated, segregationist forces increasingly resorted to violence. Entire black communities reeled from the onslaught of armed whites, often instigated by the newly revived Ku Klux Klan: more than a hundred and fifty black residents of Tulsa were murdered by marauding mobs on 1 June 1921, and the all-black town of Rosewood, Florida, burned to the ground. The deaths of some fifty whites in the Tulsa riot illustrated the determination of African Americans to defend themselves—"I ain't looking for trouble, but if it comes my way I ain't dodging," one war veteran said— but they also suggested the risks whites were willing to run to assert their racial dominance.[54] Three thousand whites, including many undergraduates at the University of Georgia, savored the torture and slow burning of an African American in Athens in February 1921, going so far as to hunt for souvenirs among the charred remains—one of more than fifty lynchings in Georgia during the previous four years.[55] Yet the antilynching legislation introduced in the U.S. Congress in 1937 never overcame the opposition of powerful conservatives and Southern lawmakers, who viewed it as an opening wedge of federal intervention in the "Southern way of life."[56] Federal law-enforcement officials such as those in the Federal Bureau of Investigation (FBI) showed little interest in the South's peculiar forms of justice.[57]

New restrictions on immigration after World War I reflected broad white anxieties about controlling people of color and culturally distinct European newcomers. Sentiment against blacks in the South, Asians and Mexicans in the West, and immigrants from southern and eastern Europe in the Northeast flowed together in a new nativist spirit in the 1920s. The Immigration Act of 1924 created a system of "national origins" to reduce radically the number of new Americans and to ensure that none would be Asians and few would be Europeans from south of the Alps or east of Berlin. U.S. policy fit into a global pattern in the 1920s of white settler states erecting walls against nonwhite immigrants, as was done in South Africa, Australia, Canada, Southern Rhodesia, and New Zealand. The victory of fascism in Italy and the growth of the Nazi Party in Germany further illustrated the enthusiasm and vitality of white racism beyond American shores in the wake of the Great War.[58]

Nowhere in America's relationship with the outside world did racial attitudes loom so large as with Africa. American films in the interwar years revealed a fascination with African wildlife and topography and a disdain for the continent's peoples. Movies of the 1930s like *Trader Horn* and *King Solomon's Mines* bolstered white views of supposed African savagery. The first of a wildly popular series of films, *Tarzan the Apeman,* appeared in 1932, confirming casual American assumptions of white superiority and cultivation. In the minds of almost all white Americans, there could not have been a wider gap between the virtues and refinement of European civilization and the primitive and savage lands of Africa. Such a vision of ancestral continents was closely tied to the assumptions of white cultural and technological progress in the United States; Americans of African descent, it seemed, could hardly rank intellectually or morally with Americans of European descent. The most popular film of the interwar era, *Gone with the Wind* (1939), marked the end of this period with the same stereotypes of black venality and foolishness as *The Birth of a Nation* (1915) had done a quarter of a century earlier.[59]

While reprising certain familiar American attitudes, however, the 1920s and 1930s gave rise to an ultimately more important change in thinking about race. These were the years in which American and British anthropologists and biologists began to repudiate the scientific basis of racial hierarchies. Anthropologist Franz Boas helped lead this rejection of race as a biological category meaningful for understanding differences within the human population. Not coincidentally, Boas worked with U.S. Congressman Emanuel Celler of New York in unsuccessfully opposing the national origins system of immigration restriction. The decline of the view of race as a scientific designation and the progressive recognition of race as primarily a social grouping found perhaps its foremost statement in the publication in 1942 of Ashley Montagu's *Man's Most Dangerous Myth: The Fallacy of Race,* which described the biological limitations of racial categorization. The political sphere offered its own parallel to this scientific shift, as Eleanor Roosevelt and other mainstream liberals began openly to oppose racial discrimination and segregation. Her husband was not yet willing to take that position in the Oval Office, but his successor, Harry Truman, would do so a few years later. As the Depression dealt a broad blow to European mastery and self-confidence, the European Left turned to the Soviet Union as a model, and Western radicals showed increasing interest in non-European cultures. The intellectual groundwork for a broad international movement for racial egalitarianism was being laid just before the racial claims and savagery of the Nazis brought "Aryanism" to the forefront of international relations and politics.[60]

### Race and War in the 1940s

As the ruler of the powerful German state from 1933 to 1945, Adolf Hitler put race at the center of his worldview and forced the rest of the world to confront the consequences. For him German foreign policy had a racial mission: to expand the nation's sovereignty to the east, destroying or enslaving the inferior Polish and Russian peoples in the way. He wrote in *Mein Kampf* (1923) that in this pursuit he would not repeat the mistake of the Spanish conquerors of Latin America, whose intermarriage with Indians and Africans had led to what he considered racial degradation. Rather, he would follow the North American model of annihilating indigenous peoples to ensure "Aryan" or northern European racial purity and domination. After taking power in 1933, he responded to international criticism of Nazi racial legislation by having his ministers remind diplomats and the foreign press that Germany was hardly unique in this regard, pointing to the segregation and immigration laws of other predominantly white nations. He explained Nazi views of Slavic inferiority by using an analogy he thought Westerners would understand: "Russia is our Africa and the Russians are our Negroes."[61]

Italian actions leading up to World War II revealed a similar readiness to destroy people categorized as inferior. The senior statesman of fascism, Benito Mussolini, sent his forces into Ethiopia in October 1935 in a campaign of conquest, replete with the use of outlawed mustard gas, the bombing of clearly marked hospitals, and the indiscriminate slaughter of women and children. In revenge for the Italian defeat at Adowa four decades earlier and in quest of recreating the glory of the ancient Roman empire, Mussolini snuffed out the last truly independent African government. The European conquest of Africa was, briefly, complete, as the League of Nations refused to take meaningful action against Italy.[62] The brutal Italian campaign did have the effect, however, of electrifying a wide array of African Americans who had long treasured, from a distance, Ethiopia's peculiar prestige. "Almost overnight," historian John Hope Franklin has written, "even the most provincial among Negro Americans became international-minded."[63] W. E. B. Du Bois wrote in the *Pittsburgh Courier* that the status of Africans and African Americans was closely linked: "I do not believe that it is possible to settle the Negro problem in America until the color problems of the world are well on the way toward settlement." Many recalled the argument of Marcus Garvey at the end of World War I that black safety in America depended on African independence: "The Japanese in this country are not lynched because of fear of retaliation. Behind these men are standing armies and navies to protect them."[64]

When those Japanese armies and navies attacked U.S. forces in the Pacific in December 1941, American race relations and the racial dimension of U.S. foreign policy became prominent issues that would now be struggled over and forged anew in the crucible of war. Franklin Roosevelt had already laid out the basis of U.S. war aims in two forums earlier that year. In his January state of the union address he had enumerated the "four essential human freedoms" that the United States must promote, including the "freedom from fear" and the "freedom from want." In his joint statement of war aims with the British prime minister Winston Churchill in August, known as the Atlantic Charter, the president had emphasized the "right of all peoples to choose the form of government under which they live" and the need to "see sovereign rights and self-government restored to those who have been forcibly deprived of them."[65] Roosevelt and Churchill had Europeans in mind—French, Poles, Dutch—but most of the rest of the world seemed to qualify as well. Who more than colonized peoples had been "forcibly deprived" of their "sovereign rights and self-government"? Did black Southerners and Africans deserve "freedom from fear"? Filipino General Carlos Romulo recalled in 1945 how residents throughout the European colonies in Asia had been thrilled to read the brave words of the president and the prime minister, wondering only, "Is the Atlantic Charter also for the Pacific?"[66] Even in Latin America leftist political unrest was sometimes blamed on the subversive influence of the much-publicized four freedoms.[67] By framing their war propaganda as a struggle for democracy and against the Third Reich's racist tyranny, the Western Allies opened themselves to intensive critiques of their own colonial and segregationist practices.[68]

Roosevelt confronted European and American colonialism in World War II, as he had the domestic problem of racial discrimination during the 1930s. Both colonialism and racism represented distractions from his primary goals of ending the Depression at home and defeating the Axis powers abroad. The president worked closely with the British and therefore with their colonies in the war, just as he had constructed the New Deal in the United States through intimate cooperation with white Southern legislators who administered the rule of Jim Crow. Personally inclined against colonialism and racial discrimination, Roosevelt was foremost a pragmatist who accepted the necessity of working with reactionary allies for common ends. He was not about to weaken a common front in a dire global crisis, whether economic or military, to pursue what he saw as a more narrow issue of social justice. Such problems, from his perspective, could be dealt with only after the larger crisis was successfully resolved.[69]

Few places more fully embodied the racial contradictions and uncertainties of American culture than the islands from which the U.S. war in the Pacific was launched. The territory of Hawaii in 1941 was still in many ways a colonial plantation society, where a tiny white elite controlled vast estates of sugar cane, pineapples, and coffee on which a quarter of the mostly nonwhite population lived. But Hawaiian social customs, at least on the surface, did not include the pervasive segregation common elsewhere in the United States. When the war brought enormous numbers of American troops into the islands as a staging ground for operations against the Japanese, significant transracial friendships developed. Conflicts were inevitable. White Southerners urged islanders to practice more intensive discrimination, while African American soldiers defended themselves against white assaults in street confrontations with greater support from their commanders than they had received back on the mainland. Blacks' experiences in Hawaii during the war left them pleased with a degree of color-blind camaraderie but also bitter at the spread of some Southern-style discrimination to a place where it had not previously taken root. By contrast, many whites from Dixie were alienated by the absence of a racialized social order as they understood it. One wrote home to complain of African Americans that "the government is sending a lot of them out here and giving them all the privileges of a white man" and to warn that "we are going to have a war with the Negro[e]s when this one is over right in the states."[70]

The war in the Pacific following the surprise attack on Pearl Harbor seemed to draw all the racial bitterness of white Americans out into the open. World War II was not racial in its origins, but in the Pacific it became for most American soldiers a racially coded conflict. In contrast to most U.S. residents of German and Italian heritage, those of Japanese descent were stripped of their property and incarcerated because of what they looked like—not because of their actions or even beliefs. Anti-Japanese vitriol pervaded American life between 1941 and 1945, along with the assumption that "Japanese-ness" was an innate, racially determined quality that required guarding against by quarantining all its genetic carriers. This racial coding of the Pacific war troubled African Americans. The arbitrary nature of white racial thinking disgusted one Harlem resident: "All these radio announcers talking about yellow this, yellow that. Don't hear them calling the Nazis white this, pink that. What the hell color do they think the Chinese are anyway! And those Filipinos on Bataan! And the British Imperial Army, I suppose they think they're all blondes?" Fighting a war with nonwhite enemies and allies forced American authorities to try to educate the public about distinguishing "good Asians" (Filipinos, Chinese, Indians) from "bad Asians"

(Japanese). The problem of needing to supersede simple stereotyping would arise again in subsequent wars in Korea and Vietnam.[71]

The European theater seemed quite different to Americans. Lacking the exterminationist sentiment evident in the war against the Japanese, U.S. forces fought another white nation that was engaged in the organized process of actual genocide. While effectively seizing the moral high ground against the Nazi regime, the U.S. government downplayed the intensity of anti-Semitism in the United States, which reached a new peak during the war years. Jews were still categorized legally as members of "the Hebrew race" rather than "the Caucasian race." This system enabled the U.S. government to admit few Jewish refugees from Europe after the Nazis came to power in 1933. American officials hoped they would emigrate elsewhere; some even suggested various parts of Africa, an option that would have restarted the process of European colonization of that continent. This potential linking of blacks and Jews also appeared in U.S. opinion polls, which showed Jews ranked second only to African Americans as the most disliked group. Although few Americans approved of German racial practices, it was not clear that knowledge of the Holocaust would necessarily motivate U.S. soldiers in Europe to fight harder. The army magazine *Yank* decided in the fall of 1944, for example, not to use a detailed U.S. government report on the Holocaust for an article because of fears that a focus on Jews might stir up latent anti-Semitism in the army. Anti-Jewish sentiment pervaded Congress and the State Department, further hemming in Roosevelt's own limited interest in helping European Jews even after the initial reports of the Holocaust had been confirmed.[72]

Despite enduring prejudice, going to war with the most murderous racists in modern history certainly left its mark on American society. Most Americans were horrified by the pictures and stories of the concentration camps liberated by the Allies. Hitler forced the world to see where racist thinking ultimately could lead, thereby sharply reducing its legitimacy for the postwar era. This encouraged popular opinion in Western nations like the United States to begin to support the antiracist consensus that had been building in the scientific community since the 1920s. Fighting against the Nazis eased this transition for many white Americans. In part by downplaying America's own racial history, or even projecting it onto the enemy, they found it possible to protest racism—and became increasingly tolerant of the idea of integration in the process. The fierce prejudice on display in the Pacific theater suggested how complicated and incomplete this shift away from explicit racism would be. But the struggle between the contending forces of racism and antiracism continued after 1945 on a new terrain won by the sacrifices of those who conquered the Third Reich.[73]

The United States entered the war in 1941 with a thoroughly segregated military, representative of broader American society. Soldiers trained disproportionately in the South, where eight of the nine largest army training camps were built. Most black units were commanded by white Southern officers, who were widely believed to understand African Americans better than did other white Americans. White Southerners expressed deep anxiety about having large numbers of armed and uniformed black troops—and any black officers—in their region. To some whites the very idea of a black soldier with authority was literally fantastic. Edgar Huff was one of the first fifty African Americans accepted into the Marine Corps in 1942, for service in a segregated unit in North Carolina. On leave in late December to visit his ailing mother and still in uniform, Huff got off a bus in Atlanta and was immediately accosted by two Marine military police (MPs). The MPs tore up his furlough papers, arrested him, and threw him in jail for impersonating a marine. There he spent five days, including his first Christmas in the Marine Corps, before his commanding officer was able to bail him out. The MPs simply refused to believe there could be such a thing as a black Marine.[74]

The decision in January 1942 to segregate "white" and "black" blood plasma for transfusions illustrated the routine fashion in which military authorities preserved traditional racial practices. The secretary of war and the secretary of the navy, along with their respective surgeon generals and the head of the American Red Cross, approved this policy, despite agreeing that there was no scientific reason to do so. The purpose was solely to placate anxious segregationists, especially in Congress. African Americans noted how this policy gave credence to long-standing beliefs about the mystical qualities of blood as racially distinctive—as in such terms as "pure-blooded" or "Aryan blood"—and thus matched up perfectly with official Nazi doctrine. The critical role in blood plasma research played by an African American physician, Charles Drew, deepened the irony of U.S. policy.[75]

Even more controversial were the efforts of U.S. military authorities to expand segregation into areas where it had not previously existed in rigid, legal form: the North, the West, and overseas. The problem arose most sharply in determining racial policies for new army facilities being built in these areas. Military commanders needed uniform policies, which inevitably required imposing new practices on some parts of the country, as racial traditions varied across different regions. Black soldiers particularly resented what they saw as the infusion of Jim Crow rules into regions and places previously free of them. Puerto Rican recruits experienced an acute version of an expanded, bureaucratized system of racial classification, as an army officer walked through their ranks cursorily deciding who would be assigned to "white" units and who to "black" units.[76]

Efforts to extend the reach of Jim Crow overseas during the war provided one of the most visible intersections of race and U.S. foreign policy. Nowhere did this issue arise as dramatically as in England, which served as a staging ground for the vast American force that attacked the German-controlled beaches of Normandy on D-day, 6 June 1944. Of those U.S. soldiers 130,000 were African Americans, whereas England itself had only 8,000 black residents. Military authorities and white soldiers focused great attention on the relationships of male soldiers with civilian women in nearby communities. American commanders feared that Englishwomen might develop intimate relationships with darker-skinned GIs. Many white American males were determined to export their definition of racially appropriate socializing, seeing themselves as protectors of white womanhood in England just as at home, where most states in the South and West banned interracial marriages. When many British female civilians insisted on treating black and white Americans equally—allowing themselves to get emotionally and sexually involved—the results among American troops were often explosive.[77]

Both the United States and Britain tried to defuse such situations by working to isolate black soldiers as much as possible, but war had deprived British women of male companionship, and military perks and antiracist Allied propaganda limited these efforts. The British government found itself caught between its own civilians' desires and its sensitivity to two critical supporters: white Southerners in the U.S. Congress, who were enthusiastic defenders of England, and the large majority of U.S. troops on English soil, who were white. Its overriding goal was the defeat of Germany and the preservation of unity among the forces engaged in that task, regardless of discriminatory attitudes within the Churchill government or inclusive behavior among some civilians. General Dwight Eisenhower, the commanding officer of American troops stationed in England, laid down a policy of informally preserving racial segregation to minimize possible tensions. But he refused to order an explicit color bar, as he recognized the impossibility of preventing social contacts with civilians or trying to control the behavior of civilians of another sovereign country. Instead, he tried unsuccessfully to convince the Women's Army Corps to station more black American women in England.[78]

Eisenhower explained the situation in a letter to his superiors in Washington in September 1942. "Here we have a very thickly populated country that is devoid of racial consciousness," he argued, exaggerating British color blindness but revealing white American anxieties about other white people who did not adhere to strict segregation. "To most English people, including the village girls—even those of perfectly fine character—the negro soldier is just another man, rather fascinating because he is unique in their experience, a jolly good fellow and with money to spend." The problem, Eisenhower noted, arose with "our own white soldiers [who], seeing a girl walk down the street with a negro, frequently see themselves as protectors of the weaker sex and believe it necessary to intervene even to the extent of using force, to let her know what she's doing." Both those men and their supreme commander seemed to share the conviction that such an Englishwoman did not "know what she's doing."[79]

British civilians generally responded to African American soldiers much as they did to white American soldiers. When distinctions were made, in fact, they often ran in favor of blacks. Many English found black GIs more polite and less arrogant than white GIs, and less likely to complain about the relative lack of American-style comforts like refrigeration and abundant home heating. "I don't mind the Yanks," said one, "but I don't care much for the white fellows they've brought with them." Civilians leaned to the underdog's side, especially when confronted with unprovoked cruelties by white soldiers against black troops. White American insults and discrimination against nonwhite British colonial troops from the West Indies serving in England further offended civilians. The British government downplayed such incidents, seeking to avoid conflicts with U.S. forces. Indeed, one proposal by the Colonial Office—not actually enacted—would have made black Britons wear a badge to distinguish them from black Americans, presumably to enable white Americans to know immediately who was a "nigger" and who was not. Both British officials and civilians had long been annoyed by American criticisms of British rule in India, and they were swift to note how the American racial discrimination that had now washed up on their shores undercut American moral posturing. Many African Americans who had long criticized Britain for its colonial practices abroad found themselves divided between that view and a newfound appreciation for the wartime humanity of English civilians at home.[80]

When race-baiting and discrimination among U.S. forces occasionally exploded into large-scale violence, British civilians were as likely to side with blacks as whites. Racial violence among Americans abroad was rarely separable from race relations at home. The largest incident in England during the war unfolded just four days after the massive race riot in Detroit on 20 June 1943, which killed thirty-four people. A typical scenario spun out of control on 24 June, as white MPs from the nearby U.S. air force base came to a pub in Bamber Bridge, Lancaster, to arrest supposedly disorderly African American soldiers. White MPs were well known for their eagerness to punish black troops for socializing with local women. In this case, local white Englishmen sided with the soldiers, urging them to resist the MPs and helping unleash what evolved into several hours of uncontrolled violence between white and black troops. "The more I see of the English, the more disgusted I become with Americans," a black lieutenant named Joseph O. Curtis wrote to a friend in 1944. "After the war, with the eager and enthusiastic support of every negro who will have served in Europe, I shall start a movement to send white Americans back to England and bring the English to America."[81]

The unrest at Bamber Bridge, like the Detroit riot, was part of a broader pattern of intense racial conflict in American life during World War II stemming from major shifts and dislocations of people and places. Incidents of racial violence unfolded among civilians and soldiers in all areas of the country as well as at overseas bases. They reached a peak in 1943, as over two hundred racial battles flared in more than forty-five cities. The ferocity of the killings in Detroit forced Roosevelt to send in six thousand federal troops to reestablish order, an extraordinary diversion of military force in the midst of a war for national survival. Military installations in the South, where most African American soldiers were trained, served as the most common flash points. Military spending brought both economic growth and social dislocation to Dixie, as cities swelled with war workers, and army camps were carved from pine forests to hold hundreds of thousands of new troops. White civilians and white MPs and soldiers shared a determination to preserve the color line, even at the cost of beatings, shootings, disappearances, and riots on bases and in cities. Their dismay at the presence of black officers and armed black soldiers paralleled the fear and anger of black Northerners, unaccustomed to the deference expected under Jim Crow, who were sent south for training.[82]

The Roosevelt administration sought to dampen such conflicts. Presiding over a political party encompassing vast differences in regard to race relations, the president and his advisers focused on the overriding task at hand: winning the war. This produced an ambivalent approach to racial discrimination. When greater racial justice dovetailed with the needs of the war, it was pursued; when it did not, it was allowed to slide. Many officials privately and publicly rejected the idea of racial equality or integration. Attorney General Francis Biddle, for example, responded to the Detroit riot by calling for more rigidly enforced segregation. Roosevelt himself entrusted racial matters in the armed forces to two Southern aides, one of them the avowedly racist James Byrnes. Segregationist Southern Democrats dominated both houses of Congress, far out of proportion to their region's share of the nation's population. Nevertheless, the manpower needs of the military eventually breached the wall of segregation within the armed forces during the war. The sheer inefficiency of duplicating facilities resulted in an abundance of cases of greater, if unintended, equality of treatment and opportunity, including the first use of racially mixed infantry companies during the Battle of the Bulge. In the process, many whites experienced limited doses of desegregation that served to inoculate them against too easy a return to traditional assumptions about people of color after the war.[83]

While the United States tried to muffle the sound of racial conflict within American ranks, Germany and Japan strove to amplify it. German and Japanese propagandists eagerly brandished every report of racial discrimination in the United States as evidence of American hypocrisy and the hollowness of Allied rhetoric about democracy and freedom. Their lurid but often accurate stories of lynchings and race riots targeted the nonwhite peoples of the European colonies, especially those in Asia. The Nazis themselves were hardly good candidates for promoting the cause of racial equality, but their propagandists did not need to enter the realm of fiction to weaken American claims to moral superiority.[84]

As a nation of color in a region dominated by European colonialists, Japan had greater success in raising doubts in Asia about the true intentions of the Allies. Despite their own ethnocentrism and brutal treatment of conquered Asian peoples, the Japanese portrayed themselves accurately as leaders of the effort to sweep white power out of Asia. They buttressed their call to "join us in our fight for the liberation of Asia" in part by focusing attention on the anti-Asian character of U.S. immigration laws.[85] Nationalist leaders from India to Korea varied widely in their attitudes toward Japan, but they were all inspired by the possibilities created by early Japanese victories over the British and Americans, whose colonialist and segregationist practices were well known. Japan's success in highlighting American racial discrimination and violence—encapsulated in the persistent question, "Will white Americans give you equality?"—dismayed many liberal Americans. Popular writer Pearl Buck saw American racism as now too politically expensive a luxury, bemoaning "the persistent refusal of Americans to see the connection between the colored American and the colored peoples abroad, the continued, and it seems even willful, ignorance which will not investigate the connection."[86]

The Tokyo government used racial themes in making a particular effort to influence African American opinion about the war. Many black Americans had long appreciated Japan as the nation that disproved the idea that people of color were unable to compete equally with whites. Black communities around the country shared an element of vicarious pleasure in the victories of a nonwhite military over white troops in 1942. "I don't want them to quite win," went a typical response, "but to dish out to these white people all they can dish out to them." Elijah Muhammad, the founder of the Nation of Islam, and a small number of other black sympathizers with Japan were imprisoned for encouraging African Americans to abandon their national loyalty to the United States for a racial identity with an international colored community under Tokyo's leadership. But the vast majority of black Americans remained intensely loyal, sharing the national revulsion at the attack on Pearl Harbor. Few believed that any advantage could arise from an Axis victory. African Americans instead swallowed a full measure of harassment and discrimination in order to serve in the U.S. armed forces, with hopes that their sacrifices would lead to greater equality for all Americans after the war.[87]

### The Pacific War at Home

The racial lenses through which the United States government viewed much of the world during World War II were most evident in the incarceration of some 110,000 American citizens and residents of Japanese descent in the West. Japanese Americans were not interned in Hawaii, where they were too important to the territory's economy. Despite the attack on Pearl Harbor, which supposedly justified the mass incarceration, neither military intelligence nor the FBI found any military reason for the policy. By contrast, few Americans of German or Italian heritage were imprisoned. European immigrants, in other words, could become Americans, but Americans born in the United States who had Japanese ancestors remained ultimately Japanese. It was hard to imagine a more racially exclusive definition of "American." Japanese Americans were not only rounded up like livestock but were also forced to live for months in buildings designed for animals, such as stockyards and fairground cattle stalls. Several of the internment camps constructed for them in the interior of the country were located on Indian reservations, as a way of avoiding provocation of local white residents who resented the presence of the internees. Confining Japanese Americans to reservations served to obscure a new concentration of people of color within an older one.[88]

Federal and local officials did not hide the racial logic of their policy. General John Dewitt, head of the Western Defense Command, explained that in this war "racial affinities are not severed by migration. The Japanese race is an enemy race." Dewitt believed his point to be obvious, as his hypothetical construction of the reverse situation revealed: "To conclude otherwise is to expect that children born of white parents on Japanese soil sever all racial affinity and become loyal Japanese subjects, ready to fight and, if necessary to die for Japan in a war against the nation of their parents."[89] Governor Culbert Olson of California did not shy from this kind of racialized thinking with any audience. "You know," he told a group of Japanese American editors in February 1942, "when I look out at a group of Americans of German or Italian descent, I can tell whether they're loyal or not. I can tell how they think and even perhaps what they are thinking. But it is impossible for me to do this with the inscrutable Orientals, particularly the Japanese."[90] The *Los Angeles Times* summarized white views more bluntly in an editorial that same month: "A viper is nonetheless a viper wherever the egg is hatched—so a Japanese-American, born of Japanese parents—grows up to be a Japanese, not an American."[91] The internment camps represented racial segregation with a vengeance. Dixie had no corner on the market of discrimination.

Even Japanese American war heroes could not immediately overcome this racial construction of American identity. In response to heavy Japanese propaganda in Asia about the United States fighting a racist war, the Office of War Information finally convinced Roosevelt in 1943 to allow military recruitment from the internment camps. American citizens of Japanese heritage, having lost their constitutional rights and freedom, were now expected to shoulder the citizen's duty to fight for his country. Reaction in the camps was deeply divided. Many Nisei (those born in the United States of Japanese immigrants) who did serve when drafted hoped that their sacrifices—which were considerable, especially in the Italian campaign—would help grant full citizenship to Japanese Americans after the war. They did, though it turned out to be a long process. Captain Daniel Inouye, the future U.S. senator from Hawaii, lost an arm in combat in Italy. Stopping in San Francisco on the way home, he tried to get a haircut. The barber looked at him, with his empty sleeve pinned to a U.S Army uniform covered with ribbons and medals, and said simply, "We don't serve Japs here."[92]

The attitude toward Americans of Japanese descent provided the domestic backdrop for the treatment of actual Japanese soldiers and civilians during the war. Historian John Dower has demonstrated how the surprise attack on Pearl Harbor triggered "a rage bordering on the genocidal among Americans." This response went beyond the wartime requirement of demeaning and killing the enemy to create a pattern of language and behavior permeated by racial thinking. The determination to slaughter as many enemy soldiers and civilians as possible did not characterize U.S. actions against Germans and Italians in the European theater of the war.[93] Even Hollywood movies reflected the acceptability of racially coded killing when it came to the Japanese: while cries of "hell" and "damn 'em" by American gunners shooting down Japanese planes were censored as obscene, "stinkin' Nips" and "fried Jap going down!" were not.[94] Racial considerations were not the primary factor in official policy and individual actions in the Pacific, but they did help determine the peculiarly ferocious manner in which the war there was fought. Japanese audacity in attacking U.S. territory had challenged the very structure of white supremacy that suffused American life in 1941. "The thesis of white supremacy," Undersecretary of State Sumner Welles pointed out in 1944, "could only exist so long as the white race actually proved to be supreme."[95] The Japanese challenge to white power threatened not just the political order of the western Pacific, but also the social order of the United States and the European colonies.

The fact that the United States had Asian allies as well as an Asian enemy in World War II complicated the picture considerably. Since the ubiquitous epithet "little yellow . . ." appeared to cover people on both sides of the Sea of Japan, including America's Chinese allies, who were keeping millions of Japanese soldiers occupied, U.S. officials and other prominent Americans encouraged their countrymen to narrow their typically broad anti-Asian sentiments. *Life* magazine published an article soon after the attack on Pearl Harbor that sought to help readers distinguish Chinese from Japanese, including pictures that made Chinese appear more like Europeans. One Chicago newspaper took this logic a step further, declaring China to be "our 'white hope' in the East." Despite strong opposition, Congress in 1943 amended U.S. immigration laws to allow a tiny but symbolic number of Chinese into the country each year, in an effort to undercut Axis propaganda. Indians received a similar allotment three years later. These breaches in the wall of immigration restriction pointed toward the racial egalitarianism that slowly overtook the U.S. legal code after 1945. The war in the Pacific, in sum, illuminated both the deadly consequences of American racial discrimination and the beginnings of a rethinking of U.S. relations with nonwhite nations.[96]

### Africans, African Americans, and the Prospect of Equality

Like Asians who saw in Japan's initial victories an opportunity to reconstruct their national futures, many Africans experienced World War II as a loosening of their historic colonial ties to Europe. Major battles were fought on the northern littoral of the continent, and Africans served in Allied armies both there and abroad. British, Nigerian, and South African troops liberated Ethiopia from the Italian army in 1942, establishing a precedent for the process of decolonization that would sweep through all but the southernmost end of the continent over the next twenty years. From south of the Mediterranean, World War II appeared in large part as a vast European civil war. White people slaughtered white people by the millions, casting into further doubt the supposed superiority of European civilization to African "barbarism" that underpinned the system of colonial rule. Above all, Africans listened carefully as the major colonial powers on their continent—Britain, France, and Belgium—condemned Germany for its efforts to rule over other peoples. African nationalists were dismayed at the apparent surprise of Europeans at the success of fascism, which seemed not so different from colonialism. Aimé Césaire noted that before Europeans "were its victims, they were its accomplices": before it was inflicted on them, they had "absolved it, shut their eyes to it, legitimized it, because, until then, it had been applied only to non-European peoples."[97]

Africans by 1945 were unsure how to view the United States. Americans had no direct colonial connection to the continent, and they had helped defeat the racist Nazi regime by fighting under an officially antifascist creed. While still mostly segregated, U.S. forces did include large numbers of black soldiers. And American officials seemed eager to open up new avenues of trade with territories previously controlled by colonial offices in London, Paris, Brussels, and Lisbon. But behind their wealth, power, and fine rhetoric stood the shadow of Jim Crow. How the U.S. government and the white majority of Americans treated African Americans at home seemed the likeliest indicator of how they would deal with dark-skinned people abroad. Reports of American racial discrimination trickled into African colonies from a variety of sources: British and French radio broadcasts; German propaganda during the war and Communist Party propaganda afterward; African soldiers coming home from foreign battlefields; and African students returning from sojourns at American colleges. The close working relations of U.S. officials with colonial and white settler authorities in Africa also suggested something less than a firm commitment to equality. Few white Americans imagined African self-government as a viable option in the foreseeable future. Among whites racial attitudes combined with economic and strategic considerations to consolidate the primacy of European over African priorities.[98]

Black Americans, by contrast, strongly supported the independence of colonies in Africa and everywhere else. They understood during the war that the status of people of color in the United States could not be separated from that in other parts of the world. Independence in Africa would weaken the logic of continued white supremacy in the United States, as black people demonstrated their ability to govern themselves. Three major figures in African American political and intellectual circles—W. E. B. Du Bois, Walter White, and Rayford Logan—published books in 1944–45 that focused on the international character of racial inequality and the need for its demise.[99] Politically engaged Americans of color hoped in particular that the new international organization under construction in San Francisco in the spring of 1945—the United Nations (UN)—would promote both decolonization and full human equality. The problem for the UN was the inherent tension between respecting national sovereignty and defending racial nondiscrimination; the second had to be pursued without overriding the first, or else the United States and the European colonial powers would not be supportive. The UN charter thus compromised by including language supporting both principles. A divided U.S. delegation did agree to the principle of nondiscrimination—a significant symbolic step—but refused to take a strong stand against colonialism. Delegates like John Foster Dulles opposed the human rights clause in the charter out of fears that it could lead to an international investigation of "the Negro question in this country." What Dulles feared, others welcomed.[100]

Like African nationalists, black Americans emerged from the traumas of World War II with a new determination to liberate themselves from the burdens of inequality. Membership in the NAACP grew ninefold between 1940 and 1946. African American protests against discrimination escalated sharply before the United States entered the war, as the threat of a massive march on Washington organized by labor leader A. Philip Randolph led to the creation of a federal Fair Employment Practices Commission in the summer of 1941. While American troops were engaged on foreign battlefields, such activism was muted by a respect for the cause of defeating the Nazis and a determination to strengthen the war effort. But their experiences of fighting abroad for democracy rendered black soldiers less willing to return home and quietly accept their prewar status as second-class citizens. For many, the scale of wartime violence and destruction that they had survived made white supremacists at home seem less intimidating. For others, experiences of better treatment by whites abroad altered their expectations when they returned. Black Mississippian Wilson Evans remembered how quickly racial discrimination had disappeared under fire in the Battle of the Bulge: "For those what six, maybe eight, ten days there was no black or white soldiers. We was all soldiers. White was afraid of dying as blacks. And there was no color. During the [German] breakthrough I did see that Americans could become Americans for about eight or nine days."[101]

Whether Americans could remain Americans, in these terms, remained an open question as World War II wound down. On the one hand, many white Americans, particularly soldiers, emerged from the war with a more acute sense of the injustice of racial discrimination. Having faced down the weapons of Japan and Germany, some were quick to confront perpetrators of petty harassment at home. Some had seen firsthand the horrors of where Nazism led; most others had at least glimpsed the pictures of liberated concentration camps. Many soldiers had experienced intimacy and comradeship with darker-skinned colleagues, which challenged their society's traditional segregationism. Georgian Dean Rusk of the War Department, for example, invited his counterpart from the Office of Strategic Services, Ralph Bunche—an extremely rare high-level black official—to dinner at the previously segregated officers' mess. When Bunche tried to decline, Rusk insisted, "Come on, we'll change that rule right now"—and they did.[102]

On the other hand, white anxieties about returning black soldiers were high, especially in the South. Black Mississippian Henry Murphy came home to Hattiesburg with a Purple Heart earned on the battlefield. White police in the area, however, were randomly assaulting and searching uniformed African Americans; if they found pictures of white women, the assaults could turn deadly. Murphy's father therefore met him at nearby Camp Shelby with a pair of overalls for him to change into in the car, so the returning war hero could survive by posing as a simple field hand. Dabney Hammer's reception was no less menacing. He arrived home in Clarksdale, Mississippi, with a chest covered with ribbons and deeply proud of his performance in five battles in Europe. One of the first whites he met stopped to admire his medals: "Ow-w-w look at the spangles on your chest. Glad you back. Let me tell you one thing though, don't you forget." Forget what? Dabney asked. "That you're still a nigger."[103] "Niggers" or "Americans": the essential question remained.

No issue more clearly revealed white Americans' ambivalence about race and foreign relations in the 1940s than the contrasting treatment of African American soldiers and German prisoners of war, particularly in the South. Axis prisoners in transit often enjoyed access to hospitality in restaurants where black Americans—even those sometimes guarding the prisoners— were not welcome. This pattern reflected, in part, a belief in decent treatment of prisoners of war, especially with hopes that American prisoners in Germany would be treated with similar respect. But it also starkly illuminated the racial contours of many white Americans' understandings of their own identity. Dark-skinned U.S. troops, risking their lives to defend all Americans, could not sit at the same table in fellowship with white Americans, while white soldiers of the German Wehrmacht, which was engaged in killing as many Americans as it could, were invited to the table. African Americans during the war were often enraged by this confusion over who the enemy really was.[104] Nor was this pattern of discrimination limited to blacks or to the South. In Wyoming, where both German prisoners and American citizens of Japanese descent were incarcerated in separate camps, neighboring white residents frequently built relationships with the Germans that outlasted the war, while making no contact whatsoever with their fellow Americans imprisoned for the color of their skin and the shape of their eyes.[105] For many Americans of all regions, whiteness continued to transcend national borders and even enemy lines in conferring the ultimate form of status.

Nonetheless, as World War II came to a close, the long-standing tendency of white Americans and their government to see African Americans and other antiracists as potential subversives was beginning to ebb. The fears of the FBI and the military intelligence services that significant numbers of black Americans might support Japan on racial grounds proved unwarranted, as did their concerns about Communist Party inroads into black political allegiances. African Americans instead demonstrated their patriotism precisely as their white countrymen did—arguably more so, at least in terms of how they treated their fellow citizens of different hues. Governor Eugene Talmadge of Georgia did win reelection in 1944 in part by campaigning against "Moscow-Harlem zoot suiters trying to take over Georgia," and Senator Theodore Bilbo of Mississippi did ask Congress to pass a bill providing for the deportation of African Americans to Africa. But the tide was against them, as the Supreme Court's outlawing of the white primary in 1944 demonstrated. In his widely acclaimed study of U.S. race relations, *An American Dilemma* (1944), sociologist Gunnar Myrdal pointed toward an eventual eradication of discrimination. Even many Southern segregationists—like Afrikaners in South Africa—recognized that fighting a war against the Nazis was bad news for Jim Crow. "The Huns have wrecked the theory of the master race," complained Frank Dixon, former governor of Alabama. The U.S. government acknowledged this turn in quiet ways, such as the shift in policy by the Civil Service Commission's loyalty board in 1943 directing its investigators to cease asking applicants whether they attended racially integrated meetings. Patriotism no longer required segregationism. As Americans sailed forth into the uncharted waters of the Cold War, they carried with them a greater openness than ever before to reconstructing race relations along more egalitarian lines both at home and around the world.[106]

# 2

## JIM CROW'S COMING OUT

"THE RACIAL PROBLEM has . . . become not merely a moral and social problem in American life," political commentator Harold Isaacs concluded in the summer of 1950, as American troops poured into South Korea. "It has become a political problem of the first magnitude in the making of American world policy."[1] The course of World War II had drawn the United States out of its relative isolation, and the early postwar years thrust the nation into a conspicuous position of world leadership and even dominance. Like a deep-sea diver surfacing too quickly, American society hurtled upward into the unprecedented attention of the open air. Without adequate time for decompression, Americans seemed almost to have a case of the cultural bends in the late 1940s, debilitated by certain vestiges of intolerance they carried with them. Systematic racial discrimination and violence were foremost among those vestiges and caused uncertainty among other peoples who admired much else about the new North American superpower.[2]

The ethnic and racial diversity of the American population made the United States a potentially positive model for the international community as it rebuilt from the ashes of World War II's racially charged destruction. Not only was the United States enormously wealthy, militarily supreme, and democratic in its creed, but it had also marched to victory in World War II with armed forces made up of the descendants of every continent on earth. If any nation looked like the world in all its human diversity, it was the United States. As international leaders pieced together a new multiracial organization to promote peace and "respect for human rights and for fundamental freedoms for all without distinction as to race," all eyes looked to the country that would host that United Nations.[3] "The possibilities for good or evil within the continental United States are precisely the possibilities for good or evil in the vexed postwar world," American writer Wallace Stegner declared in the early months of President Harry S Truman's administration. "The problem of making one nation from the many races and creeds and kinds, one culture from all the European, Indian, African, and Asiatic cultures that the promise of freedom has drawn to our shores, comes to a head in our time."[4]

Stegner and many others recognized that the reconstruction of race relations along more progressive lines would be a crucial task on both the national and international levels after World War II. Colonialism, in particular, would not remain the same. The most important colonial powers of Western Europe had been either defeated and occupied by Germany during the war, like France, Belgium and Holland, or at best militarily victorious but financially devastated, like Great Britain. By contrast, nationalist movements in Asia, the Middle East, and Africa—like racial egalitarianism in the United States—had been strengthened by the course of the war, and in the two decades after 1945 independent states emerged in almost every former colony. Harold Isaacs urged Americans quickly to grasp this sea change in international and interracial relations: "We are going to have to learn to see Europe not as the center of the world we know, but as a peninsula dangling on the western end of Eurasia."[5]

The struggles for national and racial equality in the world system and in the United States, which came to characterize the entire Cold War era, intensified in the Truman years of 1945–1952. The domestic civil rights movement and what might be called the international civil rights movement of anticolonialism moved on parallel tracks. African Americans sought to vote in the American South, while Africans and Asians strove for self-government. Black Americans struggled to overcome the use of states' rights to justify white supremacy, promoting instead the higher mandate of human rights and the U.S. Bill of Rights, while nonwhites abroad struggled to overcome the UN's reliance on domestic jurisdiction, wielded by racially discriminatory white authorities in places like South Africa. The tradition of white supremacy in the United States was embedded in a broader global pattern of white control of people of color, and both systems of racial inequality appeared to some to be directly related. They predicted that the two systems would survive or fall together.[6]

The Cold War developed after 1945 as a state of heightened tensions between the two great powers that emerged from World War II, the United States and the USSR. The ideological origins of the conflict dated from the

Communist revolution in Russia in 1917, which most Americans abhorred for its rejection of private property, religious worship, and multiple-party political liberty. Such differences in values took on greater political and military significance at the end of World War II, as the two victorious nations found themselves face-to-face in Central Europe, East Asia, and the Middle East. Their visions of the world order that should be reconstructed after the war were largely incompatible: command economies run by Communist parties versus global capitalism free from most state interference. U.S. policymakers were deeply concerned about Communist influences in the anticolonial nationalist movements in Asia and Africa. In Western Europe, home to America's most important allies, the Truman administration feared that growing Communist parties in Italy, France, and Belgium might use public dismay at grim postwar economic conditions to win popular elections and seize control of those governments.[7]

The major American Cold War initiatives of the late 1940s and early 1950s—the Truman Doctrine, the European Recovery Plan (Marshall Plan), the North Atlantic Treaty Organization (NATO), and National Security Council document 68 (NSC 68)—emerged against a background of mounting demands for racial equality and national autonomy. People of color at home and abroad were particularly sensitive to these policies' racial meanings. Winston Churchill's Iron Curtain speech of February 1946 represented a declaration of Cold War, but it also called for Anglo-American racial and cultural unity. The Truman Doctrine of March 1947 opposed potential "armed minorities" of the left but not those of the right, who actually ruled much of the world: European colonialists. The Marshall Plan (1948) and NATO (1949) bolstered anti-Communist governments west of the Elbe River, but they also indirectly funded those governments' efforts to preserve white rule against indigenous independence movements in Asia and Africa. NSC 68 (1950) laid out an offensive strategy for diminishing Soviet influence abroad, but it also revealed American anxieties about a broader "absence of order among nations" that was "becoming less and less tolerable," when the largest change in the international system was coming not from Communist revolutions but from the decolonization of nonwhite peoples.[8] This concern about disorder abroad paralleled the Truman administration's unhappiness with the volatility of race relations at home after World War II.

In designing his big house of anti-Communist democracy, Harry Truman faced the same fundamental challenge at home and abroad. He had to build it large enough to include people of all colors, while preserving his relationships with the British and French colonialists who ruled so much of the world beyond Europe, and with the Southern segregationists who through their seniority dominated much of the U.S. Congress. In an era of decolonization and rapid change toward greater racial equality, the president and his advisers needed to demonstrate that traditional white racism would not be a central element in the domestic and international anti-Communist coalitions they were constructing. In its quest for nonwhite loyalties, the Truman administration was confronted by a more racially inclusive vision deriving from the radical Left. The Soviet Union played on Third World experiences of European colonialism and Western racism, while Henry Wallace and the Progressive Party appealed to African Americans against the intransigence of white Southern authorities.[9] Both were external sources of pressure that encouraged the administration to take a more racially liberal stance within the limits imposed by its higher priority of containing the expansion of Soviet power. Racial issues and the management of racial change were central to the American experience of the early Cold War, and the nation's borders proved quite porous in this regard.

### Harry Truman and People of Color

The relationship between race and U.S. foreign policy in the Truman years was grounded in the segregated culture in which the most influential members of the administration had lived before 1945. The president's family connections to the South are well known: his upbringing in the former slave-owning state of Missouri, at a time of fierce Jim Crow discrimination and violence; his slave-owning grandparents; and his mother's traumatic experiences as a child with Union Army raiders and subsequent lifelong hatred of blue uniforms and Abraham Lincoln. Historian David McCullough has pointed out how Truman's hometown of Independence was "really more southern than midwestern," especially in its racial practices. The attitudes about people of color that the future president imbibed from these sources were not surprising. His conversation and letters were littered with racial and ethnic epithets for Asians, Jews, southern Europeans, and African Americans, among others.[10]

People do not choose the circumstances into which they are born, but what they make of those in later life provides a measure of their character. In contrast to his siblings, Harry Truman chose to move away from the explicit rac-

ism of his childhood as his political career developed and his contacts in the
world widened. He successfully courted black voters by treating them as a legitimate political interest group and following a fairly progressive path on
civil rights issues. As a U.S. senator from Missouri from 1935 to 1944, he consistently supported antilynching legislation and the abolition of poll taxes. By
the standards of later generations and of more liberated contemporaries, Truman remained a racist in his personal attitudes: he opposed what he called social equality of the races and continued privately to disparage nonwhite peoples on occasion, as he would to the end of his life. But for a man of his place
and time, the Missourian made impressive strides on matters of race.[11]

Truman's ascension to the White House resulted to a significant degree
from his record on racial issues. His selection as vice president in Franklin
Roosevelt's last campaign of 1944 represented a compromise at the Democratic Party convention. The real struggle was between supporters of the incumbent vice president, Henry Wallace of Iowa, and of the former Supreme
Court justice and close wartime associate of Roosevelt, James Byrnes of
South Carolina. Wallace headed the reform forces of the New Deal and was
strongly supported by African American voters and unions; Byrnes, a devoted segregationist and union opponent, was the candidate of the party's
powerful white Southern wing. Truman proved acceptable to both sides, a
border-state figure strong enough on labor and civil rights without being a
complete racial egalitarian. The vice presidential contest thus previewed the
struggle that would unfold four years later in the 1948 presidential campaign,
with Truman's bona fides on civil rights again being tested by Wallace's stronger opposition to racial discrimination.[12]

In contrast to Wallace, Truman's primary foreign policy advisers all stood
to his right on racial issues. There was no equivalent on the international side
of the administration to political aide Clark Clifford's encouragement to promote civil rights more forcefully.[13] The elite white men who ran the State and
Defense Departments and the intelligence agencies were comfortable with
the world they had grown up and succeeded in, a world marked by European
power, Third World weakness, and nearly ubiquitous racial segregation. To
varying extents, assumptions of white racial superiority underlay their inter-
pretations of the postwar situation facing Washington. Even George Kennan,
the author of the containment doctrine underpinning the administration's
entire foreign policy and an intellectual widely admired for sophisticated
strategic thought, made no secret of his distrust of people of racial and ethnic
descents different from his own. He saw African Americans and Jews in the

United States as potentially subversive "maladjusted" groups.[14] As late as 1938, Kennan had written privately that the U.S. government should be transformed into a "benevolent despotism" of elite white males, with women, immigrants, and blacks excluded from the franchise.[15]

Kennan, like his colleagues in the Truman administration, was a man of the north. A Soviet specialist with a Scandinavian spouse, he later observed that his "entire diplomatic experience took place in rather high northern latitudes."[16] His occasional contact with the world beyond Europe gave him the opportunity to indicate personal dislike and even loathing for peoples of Africa, Asia, the Middle East, and Latin America. He tended to lump them together as impulsive, fanatical, ignorant, lazy, unhappy, and prone to mental disorders and other biological deficiencies.[17] In the case of Latin America, Kennan specifically singled out generations of racial intermingling as a primary source of that region's supposed neuroses and delusions.[18] Third World neutralism angered him. Nonwhite leaders needed to be seized "by the scruff of the neck" and made to defend their newly independent nations from potential Soviet incursions, he told American officers at the National War College in 1952.[19]

Perhaps most revealing in Kennan's thought about race and international relations was the unself-conscious fashion in which he, like many of his colleagues in the U.S. government, attributed ideological and diplomatic failings to racial identity. He located a major—if not the major—root of Soviet despotism and tyranny in the Soviet Union's partly Asian identity. He considered the suspiciousness and inscrutability of Soviet diplomats and leaders "the results of century-long contact with Asiatic hordes."[20] The "Long Telegram" that he sent to the State Department from the U.S. embassy in Moscow in February 1946, which first put him on the upward path from obscure diplomat to major policymaker, attributed much of the Soviet government's behavior to its "attitude of Oriental secretiveness and conspiracy."[21] The Bolshevik Revolution of 1917 had stripped away "the westernized upper crust" of the old czarist elite, revealing Russians in their true form as "a 17th-century semi-Asiatic people."[22] It was Asia and "Asian-ness" that had done so much to corrupt the healthier, "European" elements of Russian life and character, according to Kennan, and that now made it imperative to contain the USSR within its own boundaries.

What is important about Kennan's perspective on race is not its singularity but its commonness within American policymaking circles. He was no fool and could be, in many ways, a strategist of great subtlety and even humility;

he was quite critical, for example, of what he saw as the material corruptions of modern American and European life.[23] But if the most reflective of Truman's diplomatic elite—the one specifically assigned the task of long-range thinking, as the head of the State Department's new Policy Planning Staff, and a non-Southerner to boot—could be so traditional in his assumptions of white superiority, his colleagues were unlikely to do much better. In fact, they did not. State Department adviser John Foster Dulles plumbed the depths of official racial insensitivity by making his famous 1951 comment that "the Oriental mind, particularly that of the Japanese, was always more devious than the Occidental mind" to Ambassador Wellington Koo of Taiwan.[24]

Truman demonstrated just how little the opinions of African Americans counted in American public life in 1945, and how much influence white Southerners had, by making James Byrnes his first appointed secretary of state. The South Carolinian's "cool formality of a sophisticated diplomat" masked the heart and mind of a typically reactionary racist of his time and place: "a chronic, absolute, unquestioning believer in the natural inferiority of the African stock."[25] Many Americans were appalled. W. E. B. Du Bois, the director of special research for the NAACP, traveled to the capital of Byrnes's home state in October 1946 to urge the Southern Negro Youth Congress to make the American South "the firing line" for the emancipation of people of color everywhere. Du Bois situated Byrnes in a long line of other prominent white supremacists from the Palmetto state, including slavery proponent John C. Calhoun and rabid segregationist "Pitchfork" Benjamin Tillman, all "men who fought against freedom." The secretary of state instead "must begin to establish in his own South Carolina something of that democracy which he has been so loudly preaching to Russia."[26] Byrnes's successor in the State Department, General George Marshall, was no less comfortable with traditional racial hierarchies. A white Virginian whose career in a segregated army inclined him to discount the abilities of African Americans, Marshall in his brief tour as secretary of state touched on the subject of race only to reject accusations of American hypocrisy about democracy.[27]

Truman's final and most influential secretary of state, Dean Acheson, came out of the elite, all-white world of the Groton School, Yale University, Harvard Law School, and corporate Washington. A sophisticated and worldly man of strong convictions, Acheson was a fierce Cold Warrior and a close and loyal adviser to the president. His oft-cited 1946 letter to the Fair Employment Practices Commission emphasizing the damage done to U.S. diplomacy by domestic American racial discrimination seemed to indicate a sensitivity to racial issues.[28] In fact, it showed his immensely practical mind. He retained deeply prejudiced attitudes typical of his generation and class. "If you truly had a democracy and did what the people wanted," he argued privately, "you'd go wrong every time."[29] Acheson was a passionate Europhile who disliked and disparaged Asians, Latin Americans, and other people of color. Despite his partial awareness of explicit racism's cost to American diplomacy, he presided over a segregated State Department.[30] The son of a British-born clergyman who emigrated to the United States, Acheson did not share the anticolonialism common among many Americans. He supported white minority rule in southern Africa, even sharing anti-Asian sentiments by letter into the 1970s with former Central African Federation leader Roy Welensky.[31] One of the most striking aspects of his thinking about race was how it grew less egalitarian through the 1950s and 1960s, when much of the rest of white America was moving in the opposite direction. In his 1969 autobiography, Acheson rued the failure of the United Nations to be housed in a serene European city like Geneva or Copenhagen, regretting that it wound up instead in New York, "a crowded city of conflicting races and nationalities." The most influential American policymaker "present at the creation" of the Cold War offered little enthusiasm for racial equality or national independence in the colonial world, as he pursued his primary objective of containing Soviet expansionism.[32]

If Truman's leading foreign policy advisers were ill prepared for a postwar world of growing racial equality, they appeared positively prescient when compared with the predominantly Southern leadership of the Congress, especially the Senate. The judicial branch of the federal government provided crucial support for desegregation after 1945, but much of the nearly all-white legislature set off into the new era of the United Nations ridden with racial attitudes from an earlier time. The late 1940s and early 1950s marked the apex of Southern influence in the Senate, as seniority rules and the one-party character of Southern politics had elevated Dixie Democrats into the chairs of a majority of that chamber's most powerful committees—the pattern in the House of Representatives as well.[33] Mississippi's Theodore Bilbo used his position in the Senate to promote violence against African Americans, calling on fellow whites of the Sunflower state in 1946 to "remember the best way to keep the niggers from voting. You do it the night before the election."[34] Bilbo represented an extreme position on Capitol Hill regarding methods, but his goal of preserving white supremacy was in no way unusual or disreputable. The majority of his most influential colleagues agreed. Their leader, Richard

Russell of Georgia, was the "most powerful man in the Senate," according to the *Christian Science Monitor* in 1951. Southern segregationists stymied the efforts of Northern liberals to pass an antilynching bill or any other piece of what Russell called civil wrongs legislation.[35] A few years later William S. White's book on the chamber summarized its character: "So marked and so constant is this high degree of Southern dominion . . . that the Senate might be described as the South's unending revenge upon the North for Gettysburg."[36] It is worth remembering how at the onset of the Cold War "democracy" and "freedom" for the majority of human beings were alien concepts to the bulk of the leadership of the United States Congress.

### Changing American Race Relations in an International Context

Wars, by their very nature, create social dislocations and tensions, and World War II was no exception. The unprecedented scale of its destructiveness ensured that it would be followed by a contentious period of reconstructing damaged political orders. In many places, like China, Greece, and Korea, this process emerged as civil strife and even civil war. In others, like Eastern Europe, it appeared as an army of liberation transforming itself into an army of occupation. But in much of the world the conflict over postwar reconstruction took the form of anticolonial struggle and metropolitan resistance, with a veneer of racial distinction. Indonesian nationalists fought against Dutch troops; Vietnamese guerillas went to war with a French army; Indians prevailed relatively peacefully over retreating British authorities; and French colonial forces slaughtered tens of thousands of Malagasy insurgents and civilians in Madagascar.[37] Strikes and protests in the Gold Coast and Nigeria put British authorities on notice that Africa would be next, and by 1952 Kenyans were at war with white settlers and colonial soldiers. In each of these cases, the experiences of non-Europeans in World War II, especially those who fought in colonial armies, had helped embolden them to challenge white supremacy after 1945.[38]

So it was in the United States. The swelling tide of racial tension and violence that rolled through the American South in 1946 and 1947 was part of a global phenomenon of race relations being reconfigured in the aftermath of the defeat of history's most murderous racists, the Nazis. "Bringing the boys home" for most white Americans meant returning to the peacetime life of 1941. In the South most dramatically, but also above and beyond the Mason-

Dixon line, that meant a life grounded in segregation and white domination of people of color. African Americans, however, emerged from the war with very different hopes and expectations. Those on the home front were bolstered by better wages and job opportunities, and by egalitarian war rhetoric extending from Roosevelt's four freedoms and the Atlantic Charter of 1941 to the founding of the United Nations in 1945. Those returning in uniform from abroad, having risked their lives for their country and having survived the often unspeakable brutalities of the modern battlefield, were even less inclined to accept the harassments and indignities of traditional segregation. They had in mind the Double V campaign announced by the *Pittsburgh Courier,* for victory against fascism abroad and against racism at home, not a quiet return to a Jim Crow society of poverty, discrimination, disenfranchisement, intimidation, and violence. Close to a million of these dark-skinned veterans percolated back into American society in late 1945 and 1946, providing many of the shock troops for the racial confrontations that roiled American life in the early years of the Truman administration.[39]

For most white Southerners, the reestablishment of Jim Crow far surpassed other Cold War priorities like promoting democracy. Local officials in Jackson and Hattiesburg made this clear in their decisions to ban appearances of the Freedom Train in 1947, a "rolling showcase of democracy" sponsored by the U.S. government, to prevent unsegregated viewing of potentially subversive documents like the Declaration of Independence.[40] The efforts of blacks to vote and to be treated with respect enraged many of their white neighbors.[41] Following the lead of public authorities like Senator Bilbo, white Southerners unleashed a wave of intimidation, terror, and death upon African Americans that lasted for much of 1946 and 1947.[42]

The violence came from many sources and in a variety of forms. It ranged in scale from full-blown white riots with random shooting into black homes and businesses, as in Columbia, Tennessee, in February 1946, to the gruesome intimacy of the blowtorch and cleaver used to dismember veteran John Jones near Minden, Louisiana, six months later.[43] It varied in agency from unidentified civilians in the lynchings of two black couples near Monroe, Georgia, to police chief Lynwood Shull of Batesburg, South Carolina, gouging out the eyes of uniformed Army Sergeant Isaac Woodward (and then refusing him medical attention for a day)—and to the hundreds of state patrol officers and National Guardsmen arbitrarily destroying black-owned property in Columbia. It included the execution of eight African American prisoners at a state prison camp outside Brunswick, Georgia, by an inebriated chief warden and other guards in July 1947. And it incorporated untold numbers of "disappearances," near lynchings, and police beatings.[44] The best accountings suggest at least sixty known violent deaths of black Southerners at the hands of whites between the end of the summer of 1945 and the end of 1946, with abundant police collusion.[45] Most revealing, no perpetrators were punished, despite mounting international protests.[46] What Truman's assistant attorney general called "the tide of lawlessness" was evidently acceptable to much of the white South.[47] Few could miss the unhappy implications for America's reputation. Even the conservative California Republican senator William Knowland ("the senator from Taiwan") took time out from his Cold War priorities in East Asia to demand on the Senate floor—much to his colleague Richard Russell's annoyance—that "such things must not continue in the United States."[48]

This wave of "white death" in postwar America crested in the South in 1946, but it neither ended quickly nor was limited to the lands below the Mason-Dixon line. International attention returned repeatedly to events in Dixie during Truman's two terms in the White House, particularly the 1951 executions of Willie McGee in Mississippi and the Martinsville Seven in Virginia on charges of rape.[49] Racial segregation and discrimination had the force of law in the South but were almost as common in public life in the North and the West.[50] The veneer of greater liberalism outside the old Confederacy frequently proved to be quite thin, as the race riot at the military prison in Leavenworth, Kansas, demonstrated in the spring of 1947.[51] More dramatic was the crowd of three thousand whites, abetted by the police, who gathered in Cicero, Illinois, on 12 July 1951 to defend their community from invasion—by the family of an African American veteran, Harvey E. Clark, who had rented a unit in a previously all-white apartment building.[52] With the nation at war on the Korean peninsula, liberals and many others were dismayed. Francis Russell of the State Department called the ensuing Cicero riot, which was quelled only by the intervention of the National Guard, the equivalent at home of the early U.S. defeats on the Korean battlefield.[53] A letter to the *New York Times* reminded readers that the events in Illinois would bolster the conviction of many Asians that white Americans regularly abused black Americans and thus undermine the nation's security: "Every rioting participant in the Cicero incident has won for himself the Order of Stalin."[54] Many Northern whites in the early postwar years demanded more rather than less segregation, and specifically cited the Jim Crow South as a model of successful race relations.[55]

If the Mason-Dixon line failed to wall off injustice from the rest of the country, there was still no doubt of the brighter prospects on its other side that had drawn black Southerners northward in large numbers since World War I. What those migrants left behind was a society where in many states, as the President's Committee on Civil Rights reported in 1947, "the white population can threaten and do violence to the minority member with little or no fear of legal reprisal."[56] For millions of Americans, the police were not a source of safety, and courts did not provide a refuge from injustice. U.S. society was far from life under Soviet rule, but the two did have certain similarities. Even FBI Director J. Edgar Hoover, a fierce anti-Communist and a segregationist of well-known racial prejudice, recognized the resemblance. When his agents tried to investigate lynching cases in the South, they received almost no cooperation from local authorities or the white community. Instead, he admitted, "we are faced, usually, in these investigations, with what I would call an iron curtain." Hoover found the arrogance of many Southern whites "unbelievable."[57] Poverty and the absence of protection from arbitrary and cruel authority—that is, the absence of the rule of law—characterized the lives of millions of Southerners, just as it did the lives of so many Russians and Eastern Europeans. Likewise, dissent against that authority in either place was dealt with swiftly and brutally. African Americans in Dixie were not likely, then, to be deeply impressed by Truman's Cold War distinction between "freedom" and "slavery." The New York–based League for Freedom of the Darker Peoples of the World agreed with Hoover's analysis of Southern isolation and offered a novel solution in a 1947 telegram to the president: send General Douglas MacArthur and his forces, having successfully reconstructed Japan and taught its peoples "the fundamental principles of Americanism," to Georgia and South Carolina to do the same there.[58]

Despite totalitarian tendencies along the color line, the American South was not the Eastern bloc. With the 1860s now well behind it, Dixie was part of a much larger constitutional republic, just as the United States was part of a still bigger world moving fast away from officially sanctioned racial inequality. One of the most striking aspects of the late 1940s was the instability of traditional political and social structures, including racial hierarchies. The defeat of Nazism, the sharp decline in "scientific racism" since the 1930s, and the creation of the United Nations and its Human Rights Convention all encouraged the forces of egalitarianism around the globe. Within the United States, African Americans took the lead in organizing for a less discriminatory society. Their unwillingness to accept prewar white threats and practices helped lead to the white race riot in Columbia, Tennessee, in 1946. Black Columbians knew every detail of the lynching of a youth in their town thirteen years earlier and of the other eight lynchings in the state since, and news of a white lynch mob assembling downtown moved them to arm themselves and then open fire on white officers entering their neighborhood in the dark. "Most people here remember that [last lynching]," one black resident told a reporter, "and they didn't want another."[59] Even the destruction that followed could not diminish the greater confidence of Columbia's black community that grew from its demonstration of a will to defend itself.[60] Jackie Robinson's breaking of the color barrier in major league baseball in 1947 highlighted the vulnerability of Jim Crow across the country, encouraging black Americans as well as millions of white Americans who found themselves cheering for a person of enormous talent and grace under pressure.[61]

No institution in American life loomed larger in the changing race relations of the 1940s than the federal judiciary. In decisions that paralleled racism's declining international legitimacy, the U.S. Supreme Court outlawed the white primary in 1944, ruled against segregated public interstate transportation in 1946, and banned racially restrictive property covenants in 1948. Also in 1948, the California Supreme Court declared the state's antimiscegenation law unconstitutional. No judges were immune from the Cold War atmosphere that heightened international attention to American race relations, and the Truman administration made good use of these judicial breakthroughs in its diplomacy abroad. The U.S. embassy in Manila, for example, reported great public sensitivity among Filipinos to issues of color and considerable enthusiasm for the California decision.[62] Truman's Justice Department consistently intervened in civil rights cases in an effort to convince the country's highest court of the negative impact of officially sanctioned racial discrimination on American foreign relations. The Justice Department's amicus curiae briefs in the various school desegregation cases that would eventually be collated into the 1954 *Brown v. Board of Education* decision were especially revealing of the international significance of race in America in the early Cold War. The State Department's leading argument in dealing with foreign critics had been that segregation was a regional and declining phenomenon, which would soon be eliminated through the established American legal system. If instead the Court should rule against the plaintiffs in the school cases, finding that segregation was fully compatible with democracy and individual rights, the American position in a mostly nonwhite world would be devastated—and the United States revealed for the hypocrite its critics accused it of being. The ultimate decision in *Brown* followed the antidiscriminatory logic of the Court's previous civil rights decisions, and American diplomats were relieved that Jim Crow's legal sanction had disappeared.[63]

Like both the escalating racial conflicts and the rising tide of antidiscriminatory reform in the immediate aftermath of World War II, the Truman administration's civil rights policies were embedded in a larger international context. Truman's support for civil rights legislation and his 1948 executive orders to desegregate the armed forces and the federal civil service had their closest parallel in the challenges facing Britain's colonial administrators. Like Truman's Democratic Party, the vast British empire incorporated conflicting constituencies ranging from left-liberal egalitarians of all colors to staunch white supremacists. Like Truman's efforts to hold as much of his party together as possible, especially for the 1948 election, the Labor government of Prime Minister Clement Attlee sought to preserve as much unity as it could across three continents. Generally eschewing the French route of counterinsurgent warfare in Indochina, Madagascar, and eventually Algeria, Britain responded to the unyielding demands of nationalist organizers by granting independence to India, Pakistan, and Sri Lanka and setting the Gold Coast—and soon the rest of British West Africa—on the road to self-government.[64] Truman responded to similar pressures at home, stemming from the general decline in black deference that brought a violent white backlash and serious unrest across the South, and from A. Philip Randolph's campaign to desegregate the U.S. military. In both Washington and London, policymakers' relatively liberal inclinations regarding race relations were powerfully encouraged by deteriorating social stability brought on by nonwhite democratic organizing. At the same time, both governments sought to accommodate rather than alienate white supremacist forces that retained considerable influence: for Truman, the Dixiecrats, and for Attlee, arch-conservatives in England and white settlers in Africa, especially the apartheid government that took power in South Africa in 1948.[65]

Much like the next Democratic president sixteen years later, Harry Truman entered the White House in a period of rising political activism by African Americans and corresponding repression by white Southerners. Like John Kennedy, Truman had previously tried not to anger either side in civil rights disputes and did not wish to see racial issues rise to the top of the national agenda. And, like Kennedy, Truman was forced to choose more plainly between segregationists and egalitarians, stepping clearly into the latter camp.

Both men believed that they governed in times of global crisis caused by Soviet actions, and both were deeply concerned about the damage that racial discrimination at home was doing to their international priorities. Truman's earliest response to this problem—assembling a President's Committee on Civil Rights in late 1946—fended off criticism while establishing a baseline of information about racial discrimination in the country. The committee's final report in October 1947 placed great emphasis on the international reasons for ending Jim Crow, concluding that "our domestic civil rights shortcomings are a serious obstacle" to American leadership in the world.[66] That June Truman also became the first president ever to address the NAACP, telling the crowd of ten thousand and an international radio audience that "our case for democracy . . . should rest on practical evidence that we have been able to put our own house in order."[67]

The political crisis that Truman faced in his uphill battle for reelection in 1948 mirrored the simultaneous international crisis. At home he confronted competitors—Republican Thomas Dewey and Progressive Henry Wallace— with stronger civil rights stands as he fought for his own political survival, while abroad he faced the Soviet Union in what he saw as the nation's struggle for political survival in a world tilting leftward. Burdened with racist allies at home in his own party, he was weighed down with colonialist allies abroad; Dixiecrats were most obviously like Afrikaner nationalists in South Africa, but their political parallel to European colonialists on matters of race relations was also evident. That Truman would share a party affiliation with Senator Richard Russell of Georgia seemed no odder than his alliance through NATO with such white overlords of Africa as Portugal's Antonio Salazar. His domestic political advisers thus encouraged his own growing commitment to standing against racial discrimination. Clark Clifford's well-known memorandum of advice about the campaign emphasized that "the northern Negro voter today holds the balance of power in Presidential elections." Unlike the white South, which he wrongly believed "can be safely considered Democratic," Clifford argued that African Americans might well return to the party of Lincoln—much like Third World peoples possibly turning to the party of Lenin—if the president did not woo them more explicitly.[68] These were, of course, similar rather than identical situations: African American votes were clearly more immediately important to Truman than the friendship of impoverished nations in the long arc of new states stretching from Morocco to Indonesia. But the political dilemma for the president of racially charged conflict continued on both domestic and international levels.

The obviously political timing of Truman's initiatives on race in 1948, combined with his continuing effort to keep white Southerners on board his campaign, seem less significant in retrospect than the unprecedented fashion in which he placed the authority of the White House and the Democratic Party behind the goal of racial equality.[69] The Democrats, it must be remembered, had long been the party of the white South, of slavery and the lynching rope. It was Truman's rejection of racial discrimination that began to shatter that historic identification and started the seismic shift of a majority of white voters in Dixie to the Republican Party by the 1990s. His civil rights message to Congress on 2 February 1948 made explicit the international context of American race relations: "If we wish to inspire the peoples of the world whose freedom is in jeopardy, if we wish to restore hope to those who have already lost their civil liberties . . . we must correct the remaining imperfections in our practice of democracy."[70] Prominent among the pieces of legislation he called for was a federal antilynching law, as lynching—"the law of the jungle," as the NAACP so accurately and pointedly called it—probably did more to undercut American legitimacy as a leader of the "free world" than anything else.[71] Truman's executive orders for the integration of the armed forces and the civil service marked other milestones, as did the Democrats' strong civil rights plank and the president's campaign speech in Harlem to a crowd of 65,000 three days before the election. All helped him win a large majority of black votes and a narrow overall victory, to the delight of racial liberals both in the United States and abroad.[72]

One of the fruits of victory in 1948, ironically, helped limit Truman's pursuit of racial reform in his second administration. The Democrats regained control of Congress, assuring its Southern members of renewed political power through their committee chairmanships. The situation paralleled the problem of Truman's successful creation of a Western European alliance with the Marshall Plan and especially NATO, which bolstered the economic and military might of the colonial powers in Africa and Asia. The president's civil rights package ran into the buzz saw of segregationist opposition on Capitol Hill, where a liberal effort in early 1949 to weaken the filibustering option in the Senate was trumped by a successful conservative effort to strengthen it instead.[73] So Truman looked to the courts and the military for movement toward desegregation, where success was gradual but more forthcoming. But the twin crises of 1950—the onset of the Korean War and the meteoric rise of Senator Joseph McCarthy—brought a swift end to major efforts at social reform of any kind. Awash in the maelstrom of a military emergency in East Asia and a political emergency at home, the president sought above all to unite his party and the country behind his leadership. Potentially divisive issues would have to wait for calmer days.[74]

### Diplomacy and Shifting Racial Identities

The most salient fact about both race and American diplomacy between 1945 and 1953 was how contested and in flux each of them was. African Americans battled for equality at home; people of color fought for independence from white rule across the colonial world; for the first time in world history, the great powers united in the UN Charter in opposing racial discrimination; and the very idea of race as a biologically meaningful way to distinguish between peoples was fast losing its scientific authority.[75] Over all of these shifts loomed the chilling rivalry between the United States and the Soviet Union, dividing the world into competing blocs, threatening it with nuclear destruction, and absorbing most of the attention of the Truman administration. One aspect of race in the United States that was not succeeding fast enough, however, was the struggle of African Americans to achieve full civil rights. Consequently, Americans remained in peril of forfeiting their claim to leadership of a mostly nonwhite world.[76]

Yet the crumbling of many long-standing hierarchies of color helped create some hope that racial equality could be achieved. New uncertainties about the racial identities of individuals arose as blacks and whites alike tested the color line. "Passing" as a member of a different "race" had long been an option for many persons, owing to the artificiality of race as a category of absolute distinction for people of diverse genetic inheritances.[77] After 1945, the phenomenon of passing moved in many directions. Traditional efforts by some light-skinned people of color to be treated as whites—that is, to be treated without humiliation—continued, as journalist Carl Rowan observed at a whites-only restaurant outside Atlanta where he was refused service. Rowan struck up a conversation outside with a man of dark hue, who explained that he was waiting for his lighter-skinned cousin inside: "Yeah, he's passing. And he ain't much lighter'n you 'n' me. When we get hungry in these country places he walks right in and orders some sandwiches. If they tell him they don't serve colored, he says, 'I don't blame you; I wouldn't serve no damn niggers, neither.' Them crackers get so flabbergasted they don't know what he is, and they serve him. They figure that anybody who don't like niggers is on their side."[78]

With visitors from the Third World arriving at the United Nations and touring the United States in growing numbers, some African Americans occasionally enjoyed passing as foreigners. Putting on a foreign accent and donning exotic attire like turbans, they could share temporarily in the status of nonwhite visitors as "honorary whites" in Washington's segregated restaurants and hotels.[79] Such adventures could be perilous, however, as white Americans commonly made the reverse identification of dark-skinned foreigners with black Americans, offering them instead the back of Jim Crow's hand. When four black students from the British West Indies sat down for a meal at a lunch counter in Washington, D.C., for example, they were refused service until they produced their British diplomatic passes. Then the embarrassed waitress apologized, explaining that she had not realized they were "not niggers." Being a "nigger" in America's capital in 1948 was evidently a function not simply of skin color but also of nationality.[80]

It was no surprise that some white Southerners were angered by this new wrinkle in policing the color line, but many did their best to accommodate it. After a sharp debate among the waiters at a restaurant in Montgomery in the summer of 1951, visiting Indian politician Rammanohar Lohia was finally allowed to have lunch. Afterward the waitress explained confidentially to Lohia's white escort, future U.S. senator Harris Wofford, "I knew he wasn't no colored man. We're getting good at spotting foreigners. Besides, no colored man would come in here."[81] Lohia's dark skin did not quite make him a "colored man." Even for segregationists, racial identities did not always fit neatly into boxes.

As racial hierarchies and distinctions came increasingly into question in the years after World War II, a few white Americans occasionally tried to pass as African Americans to see what life was like under Jim Crow. The best known case was John Howard Griffin, a white Northerner who had his skin chemically altered to appear black and then went south to investigate the other side of the color line.[82] Less dramatic was the example of Dick Sanders, a white Southerner and classmate of Carl Rowan at Oberlin College. Boarding a segregated bus together in McMinnville, Tennessee, in 1947, they sat down together in the black section at the back. Eventually alerted by a white woman passenger who kept turning around to stare at them, the driver pulled off the road and came back to tell Sanders that he could not sit in a "colored seat."

Without a pause, the young man responded in an embarrassed whisper, "My father was white." Embarrassed in turn, the driver returned to the wheel, explaining the situation to the woman en route. When they got off in Knoxville and the driver handed him his bag, Sanders smiled and said, "Say, I forgot to tell you back there that my mother was white, too." The driver responded first with an embarrassed look, then with a smile, and finally a loud laugh, which Sanders and Rowan joined in. Not all white Southerners failed to appreciate the absurdities of Jim Crow's racial classifications.[83]

Another kind of passing in the swiftly changing times of postwar America came with a crucial change in U.S. immigration law in 1952. For the most part, the McCarran-Walter Act was a conservative bill that reconfirmed the racially discriminatory system from 1924 for using national origins to limit entrance almost exclusively to European immigrants. Truman unsuccessfully vetoed the legislation because it preserved that system, which he called "a slur on the patriotism, the capacity, and the decency of a large part of our citizenry" and "a constant hardship in the conduct of our foreign relations."[84] But the State Department had actually urged the president to sign the measure because it also included a historic section ending the ban on the naturalization of Asians.[85] For the first time in American history, residents of the United States who had come from Asia could become American citizens. A crucial step had been taken along the road toward a nonracial definition of U.S. citizenship. Asians could now pass as—in fact, become—Americans.[86]

The indeterminacy of racial identities in the immediate aftermath of World War II also helped shape shifting American attitudes toward the state of Israel, created in 1948 in the midst of Truman's campaign for reelection. Traditional American anti-Semitism and the scientific orientation toward racial categorization had combined in the 1924 immigration legislation to define Jews as members of a distinctive "Hebrew race." Anti-Semitic sentiment among gentile Americans continued to build, reaching a peak during World War II, simultaneous with the Holocaust. Then came a sharp change. For several weeks after the German surrender in May 1945, U.S. newspapers were filled with stories of the Nazi gas chambers and horrifying pictures of the victims of anti-Semitic evil. These were Harry Truman's first two months as president, and he shared the shock, revulsion, and perhaps even guilt of most Americans about what had happened. When Zionist settlers just three years later won a stunning military victory in their war of independence, gentile American attitudes toward Jews continued to shift, leading to a steady decline in anti-Semitism and a turn away from defining Jews in racial terms. No longer impotent victims of Nazis, Israelis—and, by extension, Jews else-where—were increasingly seen by gentile Americans as tough, independent pioneers who had conquered hostile indigenous peoples and opened up pre-viously marginal lands to fruitful agricultural production, much like Ameri-cans' own ancestors. With Israel on its way to becoming a crucial American ally in the Middle East, and with anti-Semitic quotas disappearing in the United States, Jews could increasingly pass as fully privileged American citi-zens and Israelis as members of a modern, Western nation.[87]

The relative nature of racial designations also characterized American per-spectives on East Asia after the war ended in the Pacific. Long-standing white American prejudice against Asians and people of Asian descent had often been complicated by an opposing tendency to appreciate those who seemed to admire American ways. Unlike the old racist adage about Native Ameri-cans, there apparently was such a thing as a live "good Asian." This bifurcated view showed up vividly in World War II, when most white Americans viewed the Japanese enemy in explicitly racial terms—as inherently fanatical, savage, treacherous, and inhuman—but regarded their Chinese allies as courageous, democratic, and business-oriented. Between 1945 and 1949, however, the ra-cial traits attributed to the Japanese and Chinese were almost entirely re-versed. Occupied and friendly to Americans, Japanese became democratic, reasonable, and pro-business, while the newly Communist Chinese took on the role of fanatics and savages, especially after they entered the war in Korea in late 1950 and began killing American soldiers in large numbers.[88]

A similar shift occurred regarding Korea in the same period, as the postwar political chaos on the peninsula encouraged American observers to reverse their prior views of Koreans and Japanese. Brave former Korean nationalist allies became suddenly uncooperative, difficult, and even subversive, while brutal Japanese forces were now seen as cooperative and orderly—and were thus used by U.S. commanders for preserving order long after their surren-der.[89] The early Cold War revealed that white American racial thinking was quite malleable in the face of changing political and strategic realities. De-spite anti-Chinese sentiment that swelled after the People's Liberation Army crossed the Yalu River, there was no internment or even sustained harassment of Chinese Americans as there had been of Japanese Americans eight years earlier.[90]

The same flexibility, in light of changing political circumstances, about meanings assigned to racial categories could be seen in the federal govern-ment's relationship to African Americans. The federal employee loyalty boards set up by the Truman administration in 1947 assessed the loyalties of black and radical workers partly by the degree of their support for biracial friendships. It remained a suspicious activity to socialize across racial lines and carried the taint of radical political associations. FBI Director J. Edgar Hoover was particularly eager to link civil rights activity and mobilization to subversive organizations, and he flooded Truman's office with reports linking the Communist Party to civil rights organizing efforts. But the president's own growing support for an end to racial discrimination kept him at odds with Hoover on this issue. Truman and his advisers might have had no use for black radicals like Paul Robeson and W. E. B. Du Bois, but support from anti-Communist African American leaders like Walter White encouraged the president to avoid simplistic conflations of racial egalitarianism with political radicalism.[91]

White Southern political elites in the president's own party worked much of the same ground as Hoover in these years. Particularly from 1948 on, they responded to the new stance of the national Democratic Party in favor of civil rights by elevating the rhetoric of anti-Communism as a more widely acceptable cover for segregationism. If Communists and other radicals supported racial equality, they asked, what clearer evidence could there be of its subversiveness? They played on rising fears of domestic subversion in an effort to fend off Truman's liberal racial legislative goals. After the establishment of the Truman Doctrine and the federal employee loyalty programs in 1947, the president and other administration officials increasingly explained demands for social change within the international system—especially immediate decolonization—as influenced by a monolithic Communist conspiracy headquartered in Moscow. Dixiecrats and other white Southern leaders brought that argument home to their own region, attributing efforts at racial reform there to Communist agents.[92]

The smearing of liberal reform with Communist associations reached its apogee in the early days of McCarthyite political anxiety, as segregationists in North Carolina sought to defeat the most renowned Southern liberal of the era, U.S. senator Frank Porter Graham, in his reelection effort in the 1950 Democratic primary. A young Raleigh journalist named Jesse Helms played a critical role as campaign publicity director for segregationist Willis Smith, whose supporters catered to voters' anti-black and anti-red inclinations by labeling the incumbent as a dupe of Communists and a proponent of the "mingling of the races." The latter was the trump card, based vaguely on Graham's support for school desegregation but played out on fliers with pictures of black U.S. soldiers dancing with white Englishwomen in London during the war, under the captions "Remember these . . . could be your sisters or daughters" and "WAKE UP WHITE PEOPLE." On the very day North Korean troops poured across the thirty-eighth parallel into South Korea, white North Carolinians took the advice of Helms and his comrades and voted to defeat Graham.[93]

While white Southerners challenged Truman from the right by conflating anti-Communism and racial discrimination, Henry Wallace and his Progressive Party pressed the president from the left by declaring both to be bankrupt policies. The former vice president became the most prominent white supporter of full racial equality in the late 1940s, reflecting the growing openness of many white Americans after the experiences of the Depression and World War II to move beyond the simple boxes of racial identification.[94] Wallace threatened Truman, in part, by linking this more liberal domestic stand with a fierce critique of the president's anti-Soviet actions abroad since 1945. Harking back to the wartime Grand Alliance, Wallace sought to defuse the Cold War by recreating a reasonable relationship with Moscow in place of the containment doctrine advocated by George Kennan. His opposition to colonialism, and to the imminent NATO alliance that would partly support it, suggested a sensitivity to international racial hierarchies that matched his actions at home.[95] He and his running mate in the 1948 presidential campaign, Senator Glen Taylor of Idaho, each toured the South while refusing to speak to segregated audiences and endured threats to their physical safety as a result.[96] Daisy Bates, a black Arkansan and key figure in the Little Rock school desegregation crisis nine years later, recalled listening to Wallace speak: "I had waited all my life to hear a white man say what he said."[97] Truman's campaign was able to publicize Communist Party support for Wallace as an effective method of reducing his popularity within a largely anti-Communist electorate.[98] But Wallace had at least articulated the antiracist convictions shared by a growing number of white Americans, helping in the process to push Truman toward the more liberal racial stand he took in 1948.[99]

The Wallace campaign pointed to one final issue of uncertain racial and national identity that helps illuminate the unsettled relationship between race and diplomacy during Truman's presidency. African Americans of all political stripes had united during World War II in their opposition to colonialism and support for Asian and African independence. After the war they continued to view racial discrimination in the United States within that broader international context. But the onset of the Cold War between the United States and the Soviet Union forced them to choose between retaining an internationalist perspective that would leave them outside the bounds of mainstream debate in the United States by opposing America's European allies, or adopting a more nationalistic, anti-Communist stand that supported U.S. foreign policy while pursuing racial equality more narrowly at home. In a sense, Cold Warriors such as Truman and Kennan in 1946–47 implicitly raised the question of whether African Americans identified themselves primarily in racial or national terms. Did they represent a potential fifth column of the world's nonwhite majority within American walls, or were they loyal American nationalists fully committed to the country's dawning struggle against the forces of international Communism? It was a question, backed by a withering fire of political, social, and economic sanctions, that forced painful choices on black political leaders.[100]

Most African Americans in the political arena went with Truman and the Democratic Party. The president's unprecedented support of civil rights at home convinced them to tone down their criticism of American policies toward the colonial world to press on with the struggle for justice at home. Some were genuine anti-Communists, while most remained, on average, more doubtful than white Americans about the seriousness of a domestic threat of subversion; their experiences of power and prejudice in the United States left them unlikely converts to a campaign of repression. But they could read the writing on the wall. As the whole structure of the wartime Popular Front, uniting the Center and the Left, caved in under the weight of the Cold War, people like Walter White hustled out to the safe ground of the anti-Communist and increasingly antiracist president. Black leaders further to the left refused to leave that alliance structure to which they had committed their political lives and were destroyed along with it. Du Bois, Robeson, and William Patterson lost their passports for continuing to criticize American diplomacy and racial practices and had their careers crushed by federally sanctioned repression. A credible, coherent black Left sank below the surface of American political life, as the chilly waters of the Cold War closed over it.[101]

## Truman, Colonialism, and Africa

Western European and North American colonialism had long been charged with racial tensions and meanings, which inevitably complicated the Truman administration's policies toward decolonization. The essential problem for the White House was how to create as large and strong an anti-Communist, "free world" coalition as possible. The alliance had to be not only international but also multiracial, just as did the liberal anti-Communist political coalition Truman was assembling at home. The difficulty came in the conflicting axes of global tension that emerged after World War II: the East-West axis of the Americans and Soviets, and the North-South axis of the European metropolitan powers and their vast colonial territories. To keep both paler North and darker South on the Western side of the horizontal axis represented a major challenge for American foreign policymakers. In a report to the president in September 1948, the Central Intelligence Agency (CIA) underlined the "serious dilemma" of trying to forge close ties with the anticolonial new nations of the Middle East and Asia, while preserving good relations with European powers eager to retain their last colonial territories in Africa. Over it all hung the issue of color, the agency observed: the "deep-seated racial hostility of native populations toward their colonial overlords," caused by centuries of imperial exploitation.[102]

The situation facing the Truman administration abroad after World War II had certain similarities to the problems confronting the U.S. government after the Civil War. In both cases Washington had to figure out how best to reconstruct a defeated enemy, whether the Confederacy or the Axis powers, to mesh with a desired postwar order. In 1945 reconstruction included rebuilding war-torn Western European allies, whose economies depended greatly on the labor of nonwhite workers in their colonies—much like the South's dependence on African American labor in 1865. In both cases, the U.S. government had to decide whether to force white overlords to grant greater liberty to those workers—whether emancipation from slavery or independence from colonialism—and if so, how to reconcile that liberation with the rebuilding of needed white allies. Well aware that Jim Crow rather than full citizenship had ultimately followed emancipation, racial egalitarians three generations later sought to avoid either neocolonialism in Asia and Africa or a form of neosegregationism in the United States. Robert E. Lee was not Winston Churchill, Frederick Douglass was not Mohandas Gandhi, and the cotton plantations of Alabama were not the rubber plantations of Southeast Asia or the Congo, but the parallel dilemmas of Reconstruction and Cold War decolonization suggested the enduring character of race as a central problem for American policymakers across national boundaries.

Truman and his advisers hoped for a gradual but steady process of national independence spreading across the Third World, with power passing peacefully from retreating European colonial officials into the hands of pro-Western, anti-Communist indigenous elites. The ending of colonial rule had created the United States, after all, and anticolonial sentiment and conviction had endured through America's own rise to global power and acquisition of overseas territories. The economic advantages of greater American access to others' colonial territories—that is, free trade—dovetailed with traditional political principle. The Truman administration believed its own grant of independence to the Philippines in 1946 provided a model for the rest of the West.[103] The president was especially pleased when Britain arranged to withdraw from India and Pakistan a year later, a momentous step away from the old hierarchical empire and toward a new multiracial commonwealth.[104] Many in Britain and in other metropolitan nations resented American pressures for decolonization, particularly in light of Jim Crow's continued existence. Randolph Churchill, for example, asked visiting American journalist Walter Lippmann over lunch, "Why do you always worry about our niggers? We don't worry about yours."[105] But the U.S. government recognized the importance of self-rule in the colonial world for the successful waging of the Cold War. The Truman administration even occasionally used serious economic threats to promote that process, as when it forced the Dutch to de-escalate their war against non-Communist nationalist guerrillas in Indonesia.[106]

Sluggish economic revival in Western Europe and American fears of Communist advances in 1946 and 1947 diminished the Truman administration's concern with decolonization. The consolidation of a robust, integrated, anti-Communist Western Europe soared to the top of Truman's agenda, tightening the American embrace of colonial regimes in London, Paris, Brussels, and Lisbon and deepening Third World skepticism of American motives. The Marshall Plan and NATO aimed to bolster the economies and military forces of the metropolitan governments but also served to strengthen them in their quest to retain control of valuable colonies abroad.[107] Critics pointed this out at the time: Senator George Malone of Nevada told his colleagues that "the North Atlantic Pact simply guarantees the integrity of the colonial systems throughout Asia and Africa."[108] As the Dutch discovered regarding Indonesia, the results of American aid were not always that straightforward. But it was clear that the president's famous anti-Communist distinction in his Truman Doctrine speech—between a way of life "based upon the will of the majority" and one "based upon the will of a minority forcibly imposed upon the majority"—skipped over the most common form of minority rule in the world: colonialism.[109]

Race remained a crucial factor in the association of the United States with Western Europe.[110] The Soviets were swift to tell Third World listeners that the implementation of the Truman Doctrine would inevitably bring American racial discrimination in the wake of American dollars.[111] Scholars and journalists like Harold Isaacs and Richard Deverall traveled extensively in Asia after World War II, returning to report, in Isaacs's words, that "American racial discrimination is one of the facts that identifies us with colonialism in the Asian and African mind. They recognize it for what it is and relate it to their own experience."[112] The administration's own Psychological Strategy Board agreed that in colonial and newly independent areas, "the memory or actuality of domination by the white man is a far greater psychological reality than the Soviet menace."[113] While many African Americans protested Winston Churchill's Iron Curtain speech in 1946, delivered before Truman at segregated Westminster College and emphasizing the "special relationship" between English and Americans, most powerful white Americans applauded. Senator Richard Russell even took Churchill's suggestion of eventual "common citizenship" a step further by offering to invite England, Scotland, Wales, and Ireland (and perhaps Canada and Australia) to become American states—a construction of the whitest possible U.S. imperium.[114] Few democrats missed the irony of Dean Acheson, the undersecretary of state, promoting U.S. financial assistance for "freedom and democracy and the independence of nations" abroad to an audience of elite white planters in Cleveland, Mississippi, in May 1947, while just down the road the poorer allies of those planters were busy crushing a nascent voter registration drive by darker-skinned residents. "White Supremacy Is in Peril," declared the *Jackson Daily News,* asking its readers, "[Do] you want a white man's government, or will you take the risk of being governed by Negroes?" Acheson's pleas to help the administration support "human dignity, human freedom, and democratic institutions" worldwide had a peculiar ring in the Mississippi Delta in 1947.[115]

The racial element in U.S. tolerance of European colonialism showed up most starkly in regard to Africa. The centrality of race in U.S. policy toward that continent was due partly to the European tendency to contrast "black" Africa with "white" Europe, which mirrored the bipolar racial thinking typical in the United States, and partly to Africa's status as the last major area of European overseas control. Rapid postwar decolonization and Communist-led insurgencies in Asia made the Truman administration grateful for an area with little visible anticolonial or anticapitalist organizing. What the senior administration official with responsibility for Africa, Assistant Secretary of State George McGhee, called Africa's "situation of relative stability" preserved both the continent's significant contribution to the economies of Western Europe and American access to certain critical minerals there, particularly the uranium ore of the Belgian Congo and South Africa.[116]

With less previous involvement in Africa than on any continent besides Antarctica, American policymakers after World War II relied heavily on the European and white settler authorities of the region in dealing with its problems. This policy resulted partly from traditional diplomatic practice everywhere: governments deal mostly with governments. But it also reflected the political, cultural, and racial ties that American elites felt with their Western European counterparts. American diplomats and visitors had almost no significant contacts with Africans in the late 1940s, admitting privately their nearly total ignorance of what they called "native issues." Sympathetic with the white officials whose segregated society they shared there, white Americans tended instead to view Africa through European eyes.[117] Occasional exceptions startled and encouraged African nationalists, while exacerbating the latent fears of Europeans that the United States ultimately planned to replace them as the dominant force on the continent. Journalist William Attwood, later a U.S. ambassador in Guinea and Kenya, recalled the surprise of Guineans when he shook their hands during a 1947 visit. French officials had apparently encouraged Africans to expect no white American to touch a person with dark skin, and the more egalitarian style of some Americans like Attwood complicated the picture of a segregated United States, especially in light of the Truman administration's growing support for desegregation at home.[118] But the enduring closeness of white Americans with colonial authorities, along with the disenfranchisement of African Americans at home in the South, left uncertain the answer to the increasingly common African question, paraphrased by the U.S. ambassador to Liberia: "Does the U.S. favor rule 'of' the majority 'by' the majority in Africa as it does in Europe, the U.S., or Communist areas?"[119]

The Truman administration essentially answered this question, "Eventually, but not yet." That dawning of democracy was closely correlated to the density of white settler populations. Where European settlers were few, as in British West Africa and in North Africa outside Algeria, self-government would come soon. Where they were many—in the temperate areas of eastern and particularly southern Africa—their resistance to majority rule would slow the process of decolonization. In most of Africa, in other words, the presence of white people corresponded directly to the absence of democratic practices. This correlation created a conundrum for white American policymakers, who were accustomed to associating the influence of whites on the continent with Western civilization and material progress.[120]

For the best possible resolution of this dilemma, the United States looked again to Britain to provide a model of progressive, orderly decolonization that would not play into the hands of radicals or Communists. U.S. diplomats in Salisbury cheered the organizing of Southern Rhodesia, Northern Rhodesia, and Nyasaland into the Central African Federation in 1953, despite grave African doubts, as giving "the white man . . . a golden opportunity to really make his concept of a Free World work successfully."[121] That effort failed miserably over the next several years, however, demonstrating the limits of what metropolitan governments could or would do to restrain white settlers.[122] Meanwhile, the extent of African anger at colonial rule and European settlers became clear in British Kenya, where the Mau Mau rebellion broke out in the final months of the Truman administration. The chief American official in Nairobi recognized that a deep "racial division of wealth" lay at the heart of the conflict in Kenya, as whites there understood. But for a U.S. government primarily committed to containing Soviet influence and deep at war in Korea the bottom line on the anticolonial struggle in Kenya was how it worked "to the benefit of International Communism in creating another focus of unrest in the Western sphere."[123]

The most extreme version of the Truman administration's dilemma of how to fit diplomacy and race together unfolded in the Union of South Africa. The electoral victory of the Afrikaner nationalists in 1948 established the system of apartheid, as white South Africans rejected the postwar global trend toward racial equality. It was as though the Dixiecrats had won in the United States: absolute racial segregation and discrimination became the law of the land, and the evangelically racist government of Daniel Malan looked to spread its gospel beyond its borders. As the wealthiest and most powerful state in the region, South Africa became the core of a southern African white redoubt that utterly rejected the principle of human equality. While Communist totalitarianism rolled across eastern Europe, racial totalitarianism seeped into every corner south of the Limpopo River. Indeed, the rule of apartheid seemed a perfect model for how to drive Africans into the arms of the Communist Party, which remained the only political group open to all races and committed to complete racial equality. The injustices of anti-

Communist apartheid threatened to legitimate Communism as the only real defender of democracy in the region. Here was a terrible dilemma for American Cold Warriors.[124]

Strong common interests linked Washington and Pretoria. Historic alliances in both world wars and the Korean War, mutual anti-Communism, and growing trade patterns tied them together.[125] Strategic minerals proved even more important, with South African manganese, chrome, and uranium becoming crucial elements for the postwar American armaments industry.[126] Underlining these tangible concerns, Secretary of State Dean Acheson reminded U.S. officials to avoid "taking hold of glowing principles [of racial equality and majority rule] and dropping these other important considerations."[127] White Americans were also strongly inclined by tradition to identify culturally with white South Africans, whose European ancestry and frontier past seemed so like their own: bearers of Western civilization and Christianity to a continent inhabited by less technologically sophisticated, non-Christian, darker-skinned peoples. The racial character of this common identity was occasionally made explicit, as when State Department intelligence officers emphasized the importance for U.S. policy of South Africa's "having the largest white population on the African continent."[128] George McGhee, later recalled his own Texan heritage as a source of the "sympathy" he felt for South Africans "for their extremely difficult racial problem." Which South Africans he was referring to was no mystery: "It was unfortunate that I was not able, during my visit to Africa in 1950, to meet any of the African leaders."[129] Enduring habits of racial identification limited the understanding of American policymakers—even those of considerable goodwill, like McGhee—about who the vast majority of South Africans actually were.

The contrasting results of the 1948 elections in South Africa and in the United States indicated that the window of opportunity for a rising apartheid and a declining Jim Crow to embrace each other comfortably would not remain open forever. Unlike the Afrikaner nationalists, the Dixiecrats were resoundingly defeated by both major party candidates, who each supported greater racial equality. In South Africa there was no Supreme Court interpreting the Constitution in increasingly color-blind fashion. Dixie was only part of the United States; South Africa had no equivalent to the American majority beyond the Mason-Dixon line.[130] The governments of the two countries could still follow mutual interests into the same bed in the late 1940s, but growing tensions between the two over race relations began to point to the parting of the ways that the decline of the Cold War in the 1980s finally brought.[131] In the meantime, the Truman administration did its best to fend off critics who emphasized the parallels between apartheid and Jim Crow.[132] Liberal officials pointed to accumulating evidence of racial reform in the United States. Traditionalists like Acheson struck a more apologetic note while making the same point. He explained to the South African ambassador that the U.S. position regarding any UN discussions or investigations of apartheid "must of course necessarily be conditioned to an undetermined extent by complicating factors of our own domestic and public opinion situation."[133] In sum, South Africa had begun its lengthy term as the most awkward member of the multiracial alliance that the United States sought to maintain against the Soviet Union.

### Jim Crow on the International Stage

The elemental problem for America's first Cold Warriors in dealing with race was their inability to wall off white American racial attitudes and practices from the rest of the world and its nonwhite majority. The very idea of a containment of domestic racism cut directly against the grain of a major purpose of postwar U.S. foreign policy: to assert American leadership around the globe, thus exposing more rather than less of Americans and American culture to other nations. Jim Crow survived the inward turn of American society after World War I, but it fared much differently as an outrider on a sharply expanding American presence in the international arena after 1945. Competing with the Soviet Union in the postwar world meant, by definition, maximizing the amount that other peoples saw of American life. Hiding one's flaws was considered the telltale sign of a secretive, unfree country— precisely what American leaders in the late 1940s identified as the defining characteristic of a Communist nation.

The swift projection of American power onto every continent during World War II and Truman's assertion of U.S. leadership thereafter brought unprecedented international attention to American society. Other peoples had long been curious about this nation of immigrants, whose multicultural character connected it to almost every part of the world. The Cold War focus on the ideals of democracy and freedom assured that racial exceptions to the American practice of those principles would receive careful attention.[134] The long shadow of the Holocaust encouraged the postwar internationalism that also challenged unlimited national autonomy. This was the new era of the

United Nations and its Human Rights Convention for the whole world, a far cry from the American tradition of local government being solely responsible for the protection of citizens' civil rights. Acts of racial violence in obscure rural parts of Dixie changed almost overnight from events of mostly local interest to headlines splashed across newspapers around the world.[135]

The Soviet government and its allies, unsurprisingly, delighted in publicizing news of American racial discrimination and persecution. Racial events offered an irresistible opportunity to respond to American publicity about repression of individual liberties in the Soviet bloc. When Secretary of State Byrnes tried to protest the Soviet denial of voting rights in the Balkans in 1946, he was stumped by the Soviet retort that "the Negroes of Mr. Byrnes' own state of South Carolina" were "denied the same right"—"a checkmate of the first order," admitted a U.S. psychological warfare official. The U.S. Central Intelligence Group (precursor to the CIA) reported in 1947 that "the bulk of Moscow's criticism appears to be focused on U.S. discrimination against Negroes."[136] Moscow Radio framed U.S. military actions in Korea in terms of domestic American racism, calling bombing runs over North Korea and "the oppression of the colored people in the U.S. . . . links in the same chain."[137] Soviet propagandists zeroed in on evidence of double standards, such as the Voice of America's extensive coverage of the arrest of white South Carolinians accused of the 1947 lynching of Willie Earle, compared with its brief mention of their subsequent acquittal.[138] American diplomats in Moscow believed their hosts utterly insincere in these attentions to African Americans, but Soviet leaders consistently supported the overthrow of colonialism and the end of legislated racial discrimination. U.S. officials like Ambassador to India Chester Bowles admitted privately that the Soviets—despite their intense political repression at home and in Eastern Europe—in regard to racial equality "have done a better job than we."[139]

America's Western European allies found reports of racial persecution in the United States alternately scandalous and reassuring, offensive to their sense of decency but also helpful—especially to government officials—as they tried to fend off criticism of their own colonial practices. Some could not resist highlighting American double standards when the U.S. government issued anticolonial statements while allowing segregation to continue at home.[140] Certainly, though, the foreigners most interested in—even preoccupied by—what commentator Harold Isaacs called the infection of racism among white Americans were the nonwhite peoples of the new nations of Asia and the Middle East and the remaining colonies of Africa.[141] For them, the implications of how the world's most powerful country dealt with its own people of color were enormous. For them, the Klansman's knife, the police officer's baton, the senators' debates, and the president's actions had a particular immediacy. "Throughout the Pacific, Latin America, Africa, the Near, Middle, and Far East," the President's Committee on Civil Rights concluded, "the treatment which our Negroes receive is taken as a reflection of our attitudes toward all dark-skinned peoples."[142]

Truman and his foreign policy advisers were well aware of international attention to American race relations. Acheson in 1946 regretted with some annoyance being "reminded over and over by some foreign newspapers and spokesmen that our treatment of various minorities leaves much to be desired."[143] Two years later, Eleanor Roosevelt, a member of the U.S. delegation to the United Nations, called "our open discrimination against various groups . . . the one point which can be attacked and to which the representatives of the United States have no answer."[144] By 1950 Republican senator Henry Cabot Lodge was referring to race relations as "our Achilles' heel before the world," while the State Department noted that "no American problem receives more wide-spread attention, especially in dependent areas, than our treatment of racial minorities, particularly the Negro."[145] Not surprisingly, American policymakers sometimes tired of the issue and enjoyed turning the tables on critics such as South Asian Indians by pointing out their own color prejudices. Segregationists like Byrnes and Marshall were particularly inclined to respond in this fashion.[146] But the problem endured throughout Truman's presidency, as Bowles reminded an audience at Yale University in 1952: "A year, a month, or even a week in Asia is enough to convince any perceptive American that the colored peoples of Asia and Africa . . . seldom think about the United States without considering the limitations under which our 13 million Negroes are living."[147]

Perhaps nothing elicited world attention to American racial practices as effectively as direct appeals by African Americans to the international community.[148] Black Americans filed three major petitions with the United Nations during Truman's presidency, cataloguing the forms of discrimination under which they suffered and asking for assistance in pressuring American authorities to eliminate them. The appeals of the National Negro Congress in 1946, the NAACP in 1947, and the Civil Rights Congress in 1951 made clear that many Americans viewed civil rights in an international context.[149] These petitions were acutely embarrassing to the Truman administration; Attorney General Tom Clark publicly declared himself humiliated by such evidence that American citizens could not receive decent treatment in their own country.[150] There was little new in the petitions, even in the most scholarly and impressive one, *An Appeal to the World,* prepared by W. E. B. Du Bois for the NAACP. What was humiliating was the force with which they cut against the grain of U.S. foreign policy, exposing distinct racial limitations on the American campaign for freedom. *An Appeal to the World* appeared precisely in the midst of the administration's Cold War initiatives, with the president dividing the world into "free" and "slave" halves in the Truman Doctrine and bolstering the "free" half with the Marshall Plan and NATO. "It is not Russia that threatens the United States so much as Mississippi; not Stalin and Molotov but Bilbo and Rankin," Du Bois wrote. "This protest is a frank and earnest appeal to all the world" in hopes of inducing "the nations of the world to persuade this nation to be just to its own people."[151] It was hard to imagine a more pointed refutation of Truman's argument that the United States should now be going abroad to promote justice and freedom in other nations.

The Truman administration responded to the persistence of such critics who sought international assistance with two contrasting but complementary tactics. American policymakers deeply resented African Americans who encouraged foreigners to examine what they viewed as purely an internal matter. As the mercury of the Cold War thermometer plunged, the leftist associations of most of those critics made it easy for many government officials to assume they were trying to help the Soviet cause. The FBI, the State Department, the Justice Department, and Congress all contributed to the successful campaign to limit their audiences, publicly labeling them tools of the Soviet Union and canceling their passports.[152]

At the same time, the Truman administration sought to defuse these criticisms through a more positive approach. Most fundamentally, this meant emphasizing the president's own real commitments to racial reform and desegregation at home. Truman's advisers timed certain initiatives to counteract the negative publicity associated with the petitions: releasing the final report of the President's Committee on Civil Rights six days after the NAACP petition was published, and issuing the U.S. Information Agency's pamphlet "The Negro in American Life" partially in response to the Civil Rights Congress petition.[153] The boldest aspect of this approach was to send more conservative African Americans abroad to tell a different story than a Du Bois or a Robeson. Foreign critics of race relations in the United States could be most effectively rebuffed by the presence of visitors like Max Yergan and Edith

Sampson, who would not deny the continuing existence of racism at home but who would emphasize instead that the American system was steadily bringing greater equality to all.[154] The appointment of Edward R. Dudley as the first black American to the rank of ambassador (to Liberia) in 1949 represented a similar tactic.[155]

Beyond the ideologically charged arguments of Cold Warriors and leftist radicals, the bottom line for people of other nations evaluating American democracy along the color line was how the white American majority behaved. Actions in the South and around the country were important, while racial practices in Washington and New York and among Americans abroad often made the most dramatic impressions. Washington, the Justice Department argued before the Supreme Court, was "the window through which the world looks into our house."[156] What the world saw was no model of democracy: pervasive discrimination, widespread poverty, and the political disenfranchisement of all its citizens, an anomaly in the capital of a republic.[157] The District of Columbia was governed by congressional committees usually under the control of white supremacist Southerners like Theodore Bilbo, who vowed to preserve the nation's capital as a model of segregation. The city's *Evening Star* observed in 1946 that "it must be viewed as one of the ironies of history that the Confederacy, which was never able to capture Washington during the course of that war, now holds it as a helpless pawn."[158] Six weeks after Truman spoke to the nation and the world about the need to uphold freedom in distant capitals like Athens and Ankara, the executive secretary of his Committee on Civil Rights concluded: "As the nation's capital Washington is now a symbol of a failure in democracy."[159]

As the largest employer and landowner in the district, the U.S. government was not easily separable from the Jim Crow practices prevalent there. The State Department, despite its clear interest in improving domestic race relations, remained one of the most completely segregated federal agencies.[160] Foreign visitors to what was supposed to be the citadel of democracy could not avoid observing the prevalence of American racial discrimination, and visitors with dark skins often experienced the visceral dislike of many white Americans.[161] In contrast to the Dixie-dominated legislative branch, the president at least recognized the need to eradicate this highly visible stain on the nation's reputation. He could not control the political machinery of the district nor get his civil rights package through Congress, but he did order the elimination of racial discrimination in the federal civil service in July 1948.

Truman thus initiated the desegregation of Washington's public sphere, a process largely completed in the late 1950s.

The second major portal into the practice of American democracy was New York, the nation's largest city and the home of the new United Nations. Like Washington, New York received growing numbers of diplomats of color in the postwar years. But unlike the national capital, New York lay well north of the Mason-Dixon line, unencumbered by a firm legal tradition of segregation. Ruled not by segregationists in Congress, Gotham was instead part of one of the country's most liberal states and the heart of cosmopolitan America. None of these differences prevented dignified nonwhite foreigners from experiencing the humiliations of racial discrimination in the realm of public accommodations and real estate. The explicit commitment of all UN member states to racial equality, embodied in the 1945 UN Charter and the 1948 Universal Declaration of Human Rights, further highlighted the embarrassing gap between the host nation's words and practices.[162] U.S. officials had from the beginning feared potential UN involvement in human rights issues within the United States. Southerners and other conservatives in Congress refused to ratify the body's Convention on the Prevention and Punishment of the Crime of Genocide, owing to concern that American race relations might be put under an international microscope.[163] Diplomats from outside Europe varied widely in their overall views of American society and U.S. foreign policy, but they were nearly unanimous in their dislike of American racial practices.

The third demonstration of U.S. race relations was made by Americans traveling overseas. After 1945 they covered almost the entire globe, but certain areas were especially important. For all their colonial practices abroad, the more homogeneous Western Europeans were typically less racially discriminatory at home than the heterogeneous Americans, as the British had demonstrated in their welcome of African American soldiers during the war.[164] Violence by white Americans against their black countrymen, usually among military forces, troubled many Europeans, who resented such incidents happening in their countries.[165] Swedes, for example, were shocked in 1947 when white merchant marines with knives and razors assaulted black sailors at a dance hall in Malmoe City Park. The local paper *Expressen* regretted the damage to America's image by such "strange customs of intercourse among their citizens."[166] Less violent incidents were also troubling. Two officials in the U.S. embassy in Luxembourg refused to help or even be polite to the visiting Jubilee Singers of Fisk University in 1951, although the students were on precisely the kind of goodwill tour that the Truman administration was promoting. "We have been trained as Foreign Service Officers," one of the diplomats declared to the U.S. ambassador, "and we are not interested in negroes of any kind."[167]

Perhaps the most revealing demonstration of U.S. racial policies and practices overseas came in the Panama Canal Zone. Strict racial segregation there was the responsibility solely of the U.S. government, which ruled the canal zone without any local representation. Almost all whites in the zone were relatively wealthy U.S. citizens, while black workers came from Caribbean countries, had no rights of U.S. citizenship (nor could their children born there become American citizens), and enjoyed a much lower living standard. The dominant voices controlling the zone, as in the District of Columbia, were the Southern chairmen of the congressional oversight committees.[168] Unlike Washington, however, the canal zone was not surrounded by segregated Southern and border states. It sat squarely in the middle of another nation, whose darker-skinned majority resented American racial prejudices and the support lent to Panama's light-skinned elite.[169] Latin Americans throughout the region were concerned about U.S. sovereignty a thousand miles south of the Rio Grande, and Yankee racial discrimination was not reassuring. American rule along the Panama Canal seemed to represent a pure case of U.S. overseas imperial policy, directly analogous to European colonial policies abroad, and unlike in the Philippines, the Americans were not leaving anytime soon. Civil rights problems varied in other U.S. offshore holdings, from less pronounced tensions in the organized territories of Hawaii, Puerto Rico, Alaska, and the Virgin Islands to plainly exploitative relationships in Samoa and Guam.[170]

The largest multiracial group of Americans overseas in the Truman years was the armed forces. Racial policies in the U.S. military served as a lightning rod for domestic and foreign critics of inequality. Need rather than principle had created a temporary breach in the wall of military segregation during the winter of 1944–45, when the German counteroffensive at the Battle of the Bulge convinced General Dwight Eisenhower to allow volunteer black platoons to fill the gaps in larger white units. Their impressive performance under fire led to some minor postwar army reforms, but segregation—and rising African American resentment—remained the rule before the president's July 1948 executive order banning racial discrimination in the U.S. armed forces.[171] This was Truman's most significant action in favor of racial equality. The army and the marines, led by recalcitrant officer corps, resisted doggedly (in contrast to the navy and the air force), but the executive order provided the legal basis for what the war in Korea would make a military necessity two years later.[172] Desperate personnel shortages drove the process of desegregation in Korea, as American commanders seized on the efficiency gained by eliminating racial barriers. The president and his advisers embraced the political benefits of reducing discrimination in a multiracial force fighting in Asia. Both political and military leaders also recognized the controversy such policies tended to stir up at home, especially in Congress, and they tried to minimize domestic publicity about the process of Jim Crow's discharge from American ranks by discussing it with the press in only the broadest terms.[173]

The Korean War demonstrated the ways in which race continued to complicate U.S. foreign relations right through the final days of the Truman administration. Historic anti-Asian sentiments, which had reached the boiling point during the war in the Pacific a few years earlier, reemerged as North Koreans and Chinese began killing American soldiers on the battlefield.[174] U.S. commanders like General Douglas MacArthur radically underestimated the skill and tenacity of the Chinese People's Liberation Army, and young American men paid with their lives in the bloody retreat from the Yalu River. Disdain for China's military capacity stemmed in part from its lack of heavy artillery and air power and its primitive logistics, but it also reflected American racial thinking.[175] Captain Fred Ladd, an aide to MacArthur's chief of staff, recalled later how U.S. officers en route to the Korean peninsula "thought that they were going to go over there and 'stop the gooks'—just the same as in Vietnam. Just who 'the gooks' were, they didn't know, and they didn't want to know. You could have asked any American senior officer in Korea: 'Who commands the Korean 42nd division—ROK or Communist— and what's his background?' He wouldn't have known what you were talking about. A gook is a gook. But if the Germans had been the enemy, he'd have known."[176]

Establishing bases in a friendly, if occupied, Japan and having South Korean allies in the field required distinguishing "good Asians" from "bad Asians," but the fundamental inclination to view Asians in racial terms remained. Evidence of this attitude abounded at the UN's prisoner-of-war camp at Koje-do, where U.S. guards expressed their disdain for Chinese and

North Korean prisoners in explicitly racial language. Those prisoners also witnessed considerable conflict, sometimes armed, between white and black or Latino Americans guarding them.[177] The integration of U.S. forces and the presence of Asian allies did not eliminate overnight the entrenched habit among white Americans of seeing the world in racialized terms.

U.S. commanders court-martialed a disproportionate number of African American soldiers during the conflict and sentenced them more severely on average than their white counterparts.[178] An investigation by the NAACP's Thurgood Marshall suggested that white officials suspected black troops of "fragging"—murdering by stealth—their officers, who were typically white and often Southern.[179] One of the most basic fears of some white Americans in the early Cold War—that African Americans might serve more as a fifth column behind U.S. lines rather than as a loyal force—had evidently not been put completely to rest. This concern was amplified by stories of North Korean and Chinese "brainwashing" of American prisoners, which was blamed for the decision by some twenty-two U.S. prisoners of war, including three African-Americans, not to return home when offered their freedom after the war.[180]

One other complication along the color line showed up during the Korean War. The sexual relationships of American soldiers of all colors with Korean and Japanese women took various forms, and many veterans returned home with Asian wives. Accepted quietly in much of the United States, this development created serious problems when it involved white Southern men returning to their home region. The essential fabric of segregation appeared to be threatened, and state justice officials in Georgia and Mississippi refused to recognize the validity of the marriages.[181] This issue highlighted in acute form the ambiguity still surrounding the nexus of race and foreign relations in the United States at the conclusion of Truman's presidency. The Korean War had ended further efforts at domestic social reform, including civil rights legislation, and had revealed anew abundant white American prejudices against both Asians and blacks.[182] But the conflict had also hastened military desegregation, allowing white and black soldiers to live together in unprecedented closeness, and resulted in many white American men finding themselves undeterred by racial differences in the pursuit of their most intimate relationship. The experience of transcending distinctions of color, even in limited ways, helped lay some of the groundwork for the success of the coming civil rights movement. In the quintessential dilemma of postwar America, old habits of discrimination would continue to conflict with a growing disinclination to view the world though racial lenses.

BY DESTABILIZING THE social order, wars bring unexpected changes in their wake. The larger the conflict, the more extensive such alterations tend to be. As the greatest conflagration in human history, World War II left a swath of extraordinary destruction across much of the globe, while also creating the conditions for both reform and revolution. After 1945 the U.S. government faced a situation in which traditional hierarchies of power, especially racial ones, had been greatly disturbed in the United States and abroad. How these would be reconstructed was an open question.

Harry Truman presided over an administration riven by the tensions between older traditions and structures of discrimination and newer commitments to equality. On one side stood the segregated backgrounds of U.S. policymakers, the latent racial prejudice of most white Americans, the power of the white South in Congress, the political bent of the FBI and other segregated bureaucracies in Washington, and the colonialism of America's closest allies. On the other side were aligned the decline of scientific racism, the Holocaust's delegitimation of racial discrimination, African American demands for decent treatment, the rising tide of independence in the colonial world, and Soviet ideological and diplomatic competition. The tension between these two conflicting tendencies marked Truman's presidency from its first day to its last.

The gap between official U.S. rhetoric and actual American practices regarding human equality was vast in 1945 and remained marked in 1953. That it shrank in some significant ways between those years is a tribute, above all, to the persistence of people of darker hue who refused to accept discriminatory treatment; their resistance and pressure created the force to drive reforms. Truman himself bears a measure of credit as well for promoting certain changes, for a combination of reasons including political expediency, international pressure, and personal belief. It is perhaps worth remembering that the United States was hardly the only nation not living up to its international agreements regarding human rights after World War II. But because of its extraordinary position of power and its decision to take on the mantle of international leadership, what the United States government said and did mattered enormously for the course of post-1945 world history. Framing its foreign policy in terms of containing Soviet power and influence in order to promote and sustain a "free world," the Truman administration exposed itself to accusations of hypocrisy in an era of Jim Crow, colonialism, and apartheid.

Truman and his advisers strongly believed that the security of the nation and the world depended upon halting the expansion of Communist rule. The president and more liberal members of his administration also agreed that racial discrimination must end, but none of them viewed racism as a threat to American interests equal to Communism. Indeed, they had little patience with those who did—some leftists, many African Americans and other people of color, and most Third World revolutionaries—seeing them as naive at best and Soviet agents at worst. Like the white supremacists they opposed in the South and in southern Africa, such dissenters threatened the president's efforts to assemble a multiracial anti-Communist alliance at home and abroad. Antiracists and American policymakers shared the conviction that domestic happiness during the Cold War could no longer be separated from a sound and stable international order. Where they differed was in the designation of the foremost threat to that order.

Ultimately, much but not all changed along the color line in the Truman years. Progress at home included military desegregation, a Democratic Party increasingly supportive of racial equality, and federal judicial decisions against elements of discrimination. Abroad, it encompassed the independence of most colonies in Asia including the two most populous ones, India and Indonesia. Left still standing were a largely segregated America and an Africa yet under colonial control, with an expanding core of enthusiastic white supremacism at its southern end.[183]

# 3

## THE LAST HURRAH OF THE
## OLD COLOR LINE

STOPPING OVER IN FIJI on a return trip from Asia, U.S. Secretary of State John Foster Dulles donned swimming trunks for a dip at the beach. His bodyguard, Louis Jefferson, and a local black policeman watched. "Meestair Doolays, he is very white. Very, very white," the policeman commented quietly. "Yes, he is," agreed Jefferson. The policeman continued, "Some of you whites are whiter than others." The bodyguard acknowledged that was probably true. The policeman smiled: "You whites see us blacks as having many shades of black, brown, and so forth, in our color, but most of you do not know that *we* see *you* as having many shades of white. Many shades. It does help us to tell you apart."[1]

Dulles was indeed "very, very white," in his politics as well as his skin tone. He was representative of the administration of Dwight Eisenhower, which governed the United States from 1953 to 1961, a period of extraordinary change in race relations both in the domestic sphere and in the international system. It was the opportunity and the misfortune of Eisenhower to occupy the White House during the years when African Americans moved to the forefront of American politics and Africans initiated their final push for liberation from colonialism. Those twin struggles for racial equality, the American civil rights movement and the African quest for independence, caught most white Americans by surprise and challenged their simple assumptions about a world divided by Cold War tensions between East and West. America's new preeminence in global affairs in the 1950s meant that its traditional patterns of racial segregation and discrimination would not likely survive intact in a world of changing race relations. In the last week of the Eisenhower administration Chester Bowles, Connecticut congressman and soon-to-be undersecretary of state, emphasized in a *New York Times* article that in matters of race Americans "will appear [to the world] no better than we actually are. In this sense, as in so many others, the division between 'domestic' and 'foreign' policies no longer has meaning."[2]

Well prepared for dealing with most foreign policy issues and enormously popular at home and abroad, Eisenhower faltered in the face of challenges to the existing racial status quo. In the aftermath of *Brown v. Board of Education,* the epochal 1954 Supreme Court decision outlawing racial segregation in public schools, the former five-star general refused to exercise the leadership for which he was famous. Despite his administration's emphasis on America's proclaimed moral and spiritual superiority to Communist nations like the Soviet Union, the president and his advisers failed to recognize either the central moral issue involved in racial inequality or the significance of race relations in the modern world. The men of Washington tried likewise to sidestep the issue of African independence. They hoped above all to keep the inexorable processes of domestic desegregation and foreign decolonization quiet and gradual. They accepted only the slowest of changes toward greater equality, as they sought to bolster the international social order in which the United States had become the dominant force. Robert Burk, the most careful student of the administration's civil rights policies, has argued convincingly that Eisenhower was content with "the political containment of racial problems rather than their solution." And those racial problems were not merely domestic but also international.[3]

### The Eisenhower Administration, Black Americans, and Civil Rights

Dwight Eisenhower was a child of the nineteenth century. Born of a Southern mother in Texas in 1890, the year of the massacre at Wounded Knee, he grew up in Abilene, Kansas, not far from what contemporaries considered the "Indian frontier." He was six years old when the Supreme Court established in *Plessy v. Ferguson* the "separate but equal" doctrine of racial segregation as the law of the land. No African Americans lived in his hometown, nor did any attend the U.S. Military Academy at West Point with him. His military career before World War II took him to army posts almost exclusively in the southern United States, or in the Panama Canal Zone and the Philippines, where racial discrimination was at least as rigid as below the Mason-Dixon line. The U.S. Army remained segregated throughout his career in it, and his primary experience of people of color was in the role of servants. Few were surprised by his 1948 testimony to the Senate Armed Services Committee in opposition to desegregating the American armed forces. Never an explicit bigot, Eisenhower occasionally showed a dislike of raw prejudice. But he had neither experience nor models of egalitarian multiracial cooperation. He was a full generation older than Martin Luther King, Jr., and other civil rights organizers who would challenge the American social order he so cherished, and he remained essentially a man of his times.[4]

Eisenhower valued white Southerners and felt at ease in the segregated South. He had met his wife, Mamie, in San Antonio, and they considered retiring there. He vacationed frequently at the southern Georgia plantation of his secretary of the treasury, George Humphrey, playing bridge and hunting wild turkey while riding in carriages driven by old black servants. Georgia and the rest of the Deep South gained an additional tie to the president when the group of six millionaires who were his closest friends built him a vacation home on the segregated Augusta National Golf Course. While in the White House, Eisenhower enjoyed elaborating on his extensive Southern ties when negotiating with recalcitrant Southern senators. He was troubled by the Supreme Court's attention in the *Brown* decision to the inner feelings of black schoolchildren rather than to those of white Southern youngsters. He also resented the way the Court's decision strained his personal ties with white Southerners. Even in his rejection of Southern white violence against African Americans and Jews in a 1958 news conference, Eisenhower posed as the *real* defender of supposedly genteel Southern traditions against a wave of terror bombings by a group calling itself "the Confederate underground": "From babyhood I was raised to respect the word 'Confederate'—very highly, I might add—and for hoodlums such as these to describe themselves as any part or relation to the Confederacy of the mid-nineteenth century is, to my mind, a complete insult." These were not the words of a man much troubled by regional racial traditions, like the slavery at the heart of that honored Confederacy.[5]

If white Southern racial practices did not usually bother Eisenhower, the presence of blacks in any but subordinate positions did. By the late 1940s he was long accustomed to abundant black or Filipino servants, but he remained uneasy in social gatherings with prominent people of color such as the Nobel Prize–winning diplomat Ralph Bunche.[6] As president he did recognize the importance of African American voters, and he sprinkled a small handful of lower-level black appointees throughout his administration. But the relatively easy access of prominent black Americans to the White House under Harry Truman evaporated after the 1952 election. Only once in his eight years as president—years of momentous changes in American and world race relations—did Eisenhower even meet with black political leaders, in June 1958 for forty-five minutes.[7]

Eisenhower's most influential advisers rarely encouraged him to advocate racial equality. The strongest supporter of civil rights in the administration, Attorney General Herbert Brownell, resigned early in the second term, leaving only Vice President Richard Nixon as an occasional voice opposing racial discrimination. The most important figures on foreign affairs, Foster Dulles and his brother Allen, the head of the Central Intelligence Agency—descendants of South Carolina slave owners—showed little interest in racial matters. FBI Director J. Edgar Hoover viewed the mere advocacy of racial equality as a subversive act.[8]

What little openness to combating racial injustice existed in the administration ebbed further in the last few years of the decade, replaced by anger at what officials perceived as black ingratitude toward the president. Offended as early as 1956 by what they saw as a new aggressiveness among black Americans—especially, in the words of White House staffer Maxwell Rabb, "an ugliness and surliness in manner"—the president and his advisers maintained little real interest in civil rights. Even the notably polite early phase of the civil rights movement was apparently threatening to them. In February 1959 segregationist and Alabaman Wilton Persons replaced Sherman Adams as the White House chief of staff. Persons told Frederic Morrow, the sole black member of the White House staff, to speak with him about all issues except those regarding race and civil rights; the latter should be excluded, said Persons, for emotional reasons. Here was a revealing window on the racial blinders of the Eisenhower administration: the man controlling access to the president of the United States in 1959, in the midst of African decolonization and American civil rights activity, would not even *talk* with a black assistant about anything having to do with race relations.[9]

Morrow's tenure as a White House assistant provided a catalog of racial insensitivity and discrimination at the highest level of the U.S. government. His colleagues on the president's staff regularly ignored or made fun of him, from baiting him with "nigger" jokes to refusing to acknowledge his presence in social situations. He was forced to live in dilapidated housing in the still segregated city of Washington. On the campaign trail and on other travels for the Republican Party, he was frequently mistaken for a hired servant and harassed by hotel employees, who assumed he was surreptitiously luring white women into his room. Morrow accepted such indignities calmly because he believed that the symbolism of his presence in the administration was an important first for African Americans and because he considered Eisenhower a decent and admirable man. But he grew increasingly unhappy with his superiors in the president's second term, as their lack of commitment to racial justice was highlighted by rising white violence against blacks in the South. Morrow ultimately came to suspect that other blacks were right when they accused the administration of using his presence to pacify African Americans.[10]

Eisenhower's lack of concern for civil rights stemmed in part from his ignorance of the circumstances in which most Americans of color lived. His extraordinarily broad travels to every state and almost every continent had not included visits with darker and poorer people. He knew almost nothing of the appalling housing options and limited employment possibilities facing his fellow citizens of darker hue—what even Hoover, an inveterate opponent of racial equality, admitted in 1960 were "very trying conditions."[11]

But the president also chose to pay little attention to evidence of mounting white violence toward African Americans during his years in office. That wave of racial fury rose most ominously in the Deep South, typified by the murder of Emmett Till in 1955 and the lynching of Mack Parker in 1959. In Birmingham in 1957 six Ku Klux Klansmen randomly seized and castrated black war veteran Edward Aaron, taunting him in the process with the name of the Supreme Court chief justice associated with the *Brown* decision: "Look here, nigger! You ever heard of a nigger-loving Communist named Earl Warren?" Assaults on blacks knew no regional boundaries, however, as crowds of thousands in the South Deering section of Chicago turned out in August 1953 to harass the first black tenants of Trumbull Park Homes, a formerly all-white public housing project. Physical intimidation continued in the neighborhood for years thereafter. One of the more revealing indications of the conditions facing black Americans in the Eisenhower years was the title of a 1956 travel guide published by the American Automobile Association, listing public accommodations that served guests of all colors: "Vacation without Humiliation."[12]

Eisenhower believed that neither personal nor political benefit would accrue from his becoming involved in civil rights. He felt so uncomfortable with the issue that he simply avoided it. He disliked the words "discrimination" and "racial" and kept them out of his speeches. Refusing to meet not only with black leaders but also with Southern white ones at critical points, Eisenhower worked to confine race relations to courtrooms, statehouses, and school boards. Roy Wilkins, the director of the NAACP in the 1950s, concluded in retrospect: "President Eisenhower was a fine general and a good, decent man, but if he had fought World War II the way he fought for civil rights, we would all be speaking German today."[13]

Personally comfortable with segregation, the president viewed it as primarily a political rather than a moral issue. This approach required balancing the claims of all contestants, including white Southern voters whom he strove to bring into the Republican fold in large numbers for the first time. So Eisenhower refused all opportunities to wield his considerable moral authority by speaking out against racial injustice and in favor of racial harmony. He could not agree with Martin Luther King, Jr., that race was "indeed America's greatest moral dilemma." In contrast to 1948, when it had been a central part of the presidential contest, civil rights in the 1952 campaign barely showed up on the major parties' political radar. Eisenhower ran hard below the Mason-Dixon line, winning four states and more Southern votes than any Republican presidential candidate since Reconstruction. With the Democrats determined to avoid the party split over civil rights of four years earlier, nominee Adlai Stevenson chose the segregationist Alabama senator John Sparkman as his running mate. Not until after its second defeat by Eisenhower in 1956 would the national Democratic Party begin to shift toward a stance clearly in favor of racial equality. During his years in the White House, Eisenhower felt little pressure from his political opponents to stand up for racial justice.[14]

As president in some of the chilliest years of the Cold War, Eisenhower did recognize the need for at least symbolic improvements in American race relations. He was acutely sensitive to the image of the United States abroad and did not enjoy seeing it tarnished by the more extreme brutalities of Jim Crow. His conservative view of the role of the federal government in American society precluded significant federal intervention in matters of segregation, which he saw as falling under local and state jurisdiction. But one area in which Eisenhower did support some greater federal involvement was voting rights. He believed in the Fifteenth Amendment and understood that the denial of voting rights to African Americans, especially in the South, undercut the nation's claim to being a democracy. He also recognized that granting the ballot to blacks would not necessarily end social segregation, with which he and most other white Americans were still comfortable.[15]

The Eisenhower administration's greatest achievements in civil rights came in two highly symbolic areas of federal authority: the District of Columbia and the nation's armed forces. Washington's history as a Southern city controlled by Southern-dominated congressional oversight committees made it a peculiar liability in the Cold War competition for the goodwill of newly independent countries. The prejudice and humiliation experienced by nonwhite visitors to the nation's capital—unable to use public facilities like restaurants, theaters, and hotels—seemed to trumpet to the world American hypocrisy about freedom. Eisenhower recognized this problem even before taking office, and he eliminated racial barriers in public places in the district between 1953 and 1955. After the *Brown* decision of 1954, he moved swiftly to include public schools.[16]

While successful in removing the most egregious symbols of inequality in what the president called the citadel of democracy, the administration hardly transformed the district into a showplace of American egalitarianism. There was minimal progress during the 1950s in reducing extensive discrimination in employment and housing in Washington. Federal agencies and city departments remained segregated when Eisenhower left office in 1961, and massive white flight to the suburbs during the decade undermined the effort to integrate either schools or neighborhoods. The patterns of urban decay, poverty, crime, and discrimination that marked the nation's capital received little attention from the Eisenhower administration.[17]

The American armed forces, stationed throughout the world since 1945, served as an even more visible symbol of the United States than its capital city. Truman had ordered their desegregation in 1948, and the process was well under way when Eisenhower took office. By 1955 the American military had become an integrated institution in an otherwise still segregated society. The armed forces thus served as a laboratory for social change in the years before the rise of the modern civil rights movement. "In effect," historian Bernard Nalty notes, "the Department of Defense was operating a racially integrated society sealed off from nearby civilian communities, with its own stores, its own sources of recreation, and in many instances its own family housing." Military desegregation was not perfected in the 1950s, as many National Guard and reserve units remained all-white, and incidents involving civilian employees and black service personnel continued to fester. The scale of the problem was, after all, enormous: the massive institution of the American military had to make a 180-degree turn, from enforcing segregation in every detail of its collective life (as it had for most of two hundred years) to banning it completely. But the symbolism of the change could not be missed by foreign observers, as Eisenhower—like Truman—intended.[18]

Beyond these circumscribed areas of clear federal authority, Eisenhower believed that changes in race relations could only come slowly in the United States. He assured his "great friend" James Byrnes, the segregationist governor of South Carolina, over lunch in the summer of 1953 of "my belief that improvement in race relations is one of those things that will be healthy and sound only if it starts locally. I do not believe that prejudices, even palpably unjustified prejudices, will succumb to compulsion." Six years later he wrote to Atlanta newspaper editor Ralph McGill that "coercive law is, by itself, powerless to bring about complete compliance with its own terms when in any extensive region the great mass of public opinion is in bitter opposition." To those who insisted on the elimination of racial discrimination, he counseled—to their dismay—only greater patience. "No one," he told a skeptical group of black newspaper publishers in May 1958, "is more anxious than I am to see Negroes receive first-class citizenship in this country . . . but you must be patient." Whites, he believed, deserved more time to adjust themselves.[19]

Eisenhower repeatedly condemned what he called extremists on both sides of the civil rights issue, a calculus equating whites engaged in violence with polite, peaceful protesters seeking the fulfillment of their constitutional rights. He insisted that those "who want to have the whole matter settled today" were no different than those "so filled with prejudice that they even resort to violence." He rejected suggestions that he meet with civil rights leaders, arguing that he would then also have to meet with officers of the Ku Klux Klan. The president failed to grasp the elemental moral distinction between people of enormous courage, willing to sacrifice their lives for the highest principles of American life, and people of marked cowardice, eager to wound and even kill others while showing no willingness to risk their own well-being.[20]

In contrast to such "extremists," Eisenhower hewed to what he called "the center line, which is the only path along which progress in great human affairs can be achieved." He was sure that the passage of time would bring change in the hearts of white segregationists, and he believed that more observant African Americans recognized this. Speaking with Republican congressional leaders in the summer of 1956 about his administration's pending civil rights bill, the president repeated a story he had heard recently in Augusta from golfing legend Bobby Jones, of a black field hand supposedly saying, "If someone doesn't shut up around here, particularly these Negroes from the North, they're going to get a lot of us niggers killed!" Like self-described white moderates of the South, Eisenhower saw himself as a protector of the majority of moderate blacks, who were imperiled by "outside agitators" likely to provoke a violent white response. Ultimately, Dwight Eisenhower believed that he was the right man to lead all Americans responsibly along "the center line," including all black Americans.[21]

### Declarations of Liberty and Equality: Brown, Bandung, and Montgomery

The nineteen months from mid-1954 to late 1955 marked a sea change in American and international race relations. The U.S. Supreme Court declared racial segregation in public schools unconstitutional; leaders of color from around the world gathered for the first time in history, to declare their solidarity and to reject white supremacy; and the African American community of Montgomery began a boycott of segregated city buses that initiated the modern black civil rights movement. The Court's decision in *Brown v. Board of Education* in May 1954 was carefully limited: it addressed only schools, and it was to be enforced only "with all deliberate speed" rather than with any specific timetable. In fact, school desegregation took place so slowly that by the end of the Eisenhower administration almost seven years later, only 6.4 percent of black schoolchildren in the South were attending integrated classes. It would take ten years before Congress broadened the scope of that judicial decision by outlawing racial discrimination in all public places. But the symbolic significance of the case could not have been greater. By a unanimous decision that included three Southern justices, the nation's highest court reversed the political and moral context of race relations in the United States. Racial discrimination was no longer allowed by the laws of the land. What had previously been considered by most whites subversive—racial integration—acquired the full moral authority of the Constitution.[22]

The Court's logic in *Brown* was at least partly international. The Justice Department brief in the case, filed just weeks before Eisenhower took office, emphasized that "it is in the context of the present world struggle between freedom and tyranny that the problem of racial discrimination must be viewed." The Court's decision did not specifically cite the Cold War or the retreat of colonialism in the rest of the world, but the justices could not help being affected by the dominant political and social realities of their time. American racial segregation, so little questioned in legal circles even a decade earlier, carried much heavier baggage in a world now dominated by the United States but marked by the rapid decline of white supremacy.[23]

The Eisenhower administration certainly understood this reality. The Voice of America immediately beamed the news of the Court's decision around the world in thirty-four languages, along with background materials emphasizing the history of supposedly steady black advancement in the United States. Foster Dulles and the State Department were enthusiastic about the benefits of the decision for America's foreign relations. International reaction to the *Brown* decision was uniformly favorable, with the predictable exception of the South African government. Some African Americans resented the administration's emphasis on Cold War logic over genuine belief in the fundamental validity of racial equality. Sociologist Franklin Frazier, for example, argued that "the white man is scared down to his bowels, so it's be-kind-to-Negroes decade at last." But most blacks, including even some Communist Party members, were impressed by the Court's decision. Cold Warriors of all but the most racist stripe found cause for celebration. The black-owned *Pittsburgh Courier* agreed with the administration and with most other newspapers outside the South that "this announcement will . . . stun and silence America's Communist traducers behind the Iron Curtain."[24]

The administration as a whole, however, along with many other white Americans, seemed more sure of what they wanted the world to think of the *Brown* case than of what they thought themselves. Many local media outlets were silent, and Universal Newsreels declined to mention the case because of fears that it would prove too controversial. Eisenhower himself refused to endorse the Court's decision or to offer any leadership to the country—beyond a quiet agreement to desegregate Washington schools—as it grappled with the implementation of this monumental cultural change. The president also declined to speak of the case as one involving a moral issue. A few months before the Court's announcement, he had even gently lobbied Chief Justice Earl Warren on behalf of segregationists. "These are not bad people. All they are concerned about is to see that their sweet little girls are not required to sit in school alongside some big overgrown Negroes." Afterward, Eisenhower made clear in private his dislike for the decision, his fears of white Southern resistance, and his certainty that the Court had guaranteed a worsening of race relations in the South. Four years later he admitted publicly that he would prefer a slower version of school desegregation, to which NAACP chief Roy Wilkins could only respond that if the snail's pace of the previous four years represented swiftness, "then we certainly do not understand the word speed." Eisenhower's abdication of leadership on school desegregation would come back to haunt him in the 1957 crisis in Little Rock, before an international audience.[25]

Eleven months after the Supreme Court changed forever the shape of race relations in the United States, an event of comparable significance for international race relations unfolded in the Indonesian city of Bandung. There in April 1955 representatives from twenty-nine nations of primarily Asia, Africa, and the Middle East met in what host president Sukarno of Indonesia called "the first international conference of colored peoples in the history of mankind." The agenda was threefold: to promote cooperation among the nonaligned nations of the Third World; to deliberate about such common problems as colonialism and racism; and to advocate world peace. The gathering had an ecumenically ideological cast, mixing Communist, pro-Western, and neutralist states. What almost all the representatives shared, besides a non-European phenotype, was a common historical relationship of colonialism with the West. The conference therefore carried an implicit condemnation of the West that was bolstered by an explicit call for eliminating vestiges of colonialism and racial discrimination.[26]

Delegates at Bandung tended to hold a nuanced view of the United States. President Carlos Romulo of the Philippines noted the centrality of the doctrine of white supremacy in all versions of Western colonialism and underlined "the role played by this racism as a driving force in the development of the nationalist movements in our many lands." He urged Western nations to cut themselves free from the "albatross" of racial discrimination that still hung around many of their necks—an undisguised reference to Jim Crow practices in the United States and South African apartheid. But Romulo also noted the considerable amount of goodwill evident at Bandung toward the United States, stemming in part from such evidence of progress as the *Brown* decision. Sukarno observed in his opening speech on 18 April the anniversary marked by that date: Paul Revere's ride through the Massachusetts countryside, warning of the approach of British troops and helping precipitate the American Revolution, "the first successful anti-colonial war in history." Toward the United States, then, the new nations of color in the 1950s had mixed feelings.[27]

Few white Americans expected anything good to come out of the Bandung conference. The nonaligned position of the representatives regarding the Cold War made Dulles and his colleagues deeply suspicious. In contrast, the

Soviets and Chinese strongly supported the gathering, and the United States feared that their influence would subvert the neutralism of the new African and Asian nations. The Soviet Union was excluded from the actual meeting as a white, European nation, despite its claim to being part Asian. China, of course, was invited as an Asian nation, and the U.S. government worried about its impact on the others. As the National Security Council (NSC) noted a few years later, the People's Republic had "an important advantage" over the Soviet Union in the Third World: "They can put themselves forward as an under-developed country which has recently been freed from foreign domination." The Bandung conference was not likely to win much support in official Washington, a place dominated in 1955 by such figures as Texan Lyndon Johnson, the Senate majority leader, Georgia segregationist Walter George, the chair of the Senate Foreign Relations Committee, and segregationist sympathizer Dwight Eisenhower.[28]

The Eisenhower administration sent no greeting to the conference and did its best to ignore it or sabotage it. Foster and Allen Dulles agreed in January 1955 that Bandung likely portended an aggressive new Communist strategy in Africa. The secretary of state convened a meeting of the Southeast Asian Treaty Organization in Bangkok in February as a forum to condemn neutralism. Escalating U.S.-Chinese tensions in the Taiwan Straits that spring led to Eisenhower's public warning about American readiness to use nuclear weapons in the region; Navy Chief of Staff Robert Carney then leaked to the press American contingency plans for an all-out attack on China in case of war between the two nations. Administration officials hoped to discourage the consolidation of an African-Asian bloc in an effort to keep Africa more oriented toward the West, and they were careful not even to use the term "Afro-Asian group" without the adjective "supposed."[29]

Adam Clayton Powell, one of three black members of the U.S. House of Representatives, attended the conference in Indonesia as a journalist. With great fanfare he criticized U.S. foreign policy as insufficiently anticolonial, but he strongly defended American race relations. His presence in Bandung, he reported to Eisenhower afterward, gave "living proof to the fact that there is no truth in the Communist charge that the Negro is oppressed in America." Powell returned to the House to receive a standing ovation, a singular experience for a man generally resented by his colleagues, especially those from the South. Several months later Foster Dulles tacitly acknowledged the success of the gathering in Indonesia when he called privately for a "Bandung Conference in reverse" as a forum for colonial and ex-colonial powers to lay out an independence program "in a dramatic way": as a means, that is, for re-treating white powers to cut their ideological losses.[30]

African Americans in the cradle of the old Confederacy later that year fol-lowed the same logic as the Supreme Court and the Bandung delegates in de-claring their own opposition to the tradition of white supremacy. The *Brown* decision had set the Constitution squarely on the side of desegregation, and the black American press widely hailed the Bandung conference as, in the words of the *Baltimore Afro-American,* "a turning point in world history" and perhaps even the most important event of the twentieth century in its "clear challenge to white supremacy." The Montgomery bus boycott initiated the modern era of mass civil rights organizing in the United States. Lasting from December 1955 to its successful conclusion one year later, the boycott took advantage of the easing of the Red Scare that had dominated the American political landscape of the early 1950s and had made efforts at social change appear traitorous. The peaceful black protesters in Alabama, while framing their actions in patriotic language and while concerned primarily with local issues, also identified their cause with that of people of color abroad. King de-scribed the Montgomery movement as part of a global process in which "the oppressed people of the world are rising up" against colonialism, imperialism, and segregation. The retreat of Europeans from Asia and Africa seemed clearly to African Americans to be part of their struggle for racial justice.[31]

Despite its explicitly Christian style and commitment to nonviolence, the Montgomery bus boycott represented just the kind of social change "from below" that the Eisenhower administration hoped to avoid. The president himself simply sat it out, refusing to make any public comment on the issue. He ignored appeals from King and a variety of other Americans to support the boycotters in their quest for polite treatment on public transportation. Eisenhower confessed in his diary in November 1956 his disappointment in the Supreme Court's upholding of a lower court decision banning segrega-tion on intrastate buses: "In some of these things [I] was more of a 'States Righter' than the Supreme Court." Other Americans were pleased by the outcome of the boycott, finding in its peaceful, patriotic, and religious char-acter precisely the kind of affirmation of the American political system that the country needed in the Cold War. Even many white citizens of Montgom-ery seemed ready to accommodate themselves to some change in race rela-tions. On 21 December 1956, the first day of integration on the city's buses, one white man found himself—for the first time in his life—sitting behind a black man and piped up: "I see this sure isn't going to be a white Christmas."

His fellow passenger smiled back, "Yes, sir, that's right," and those within ear-shot laughed. Such good humor seemingly found little echo in the Oval Office that holiday season.[32]

Southern white resistance to the changes suggested by *Brown,* Bandung, and Montgomery tended to divide into two camps that differed in strategy and often in class origins but not in essential goals: the violent and, in the common phrase of the time, the "respectable." The first approach had an impressive pedigree in Southern history, renewed for a national and international audience in August 1955 by Roy Bryant and J. W. Milam of Money, Mississippi. Enraged at reports that a fourteen-year old black Chicago resident, visiting relatives nearby, had whistled at Bryant's wife, the two men kidnapped, tortured, and murdered Emmett Till. This was actually the fourth known interracial homicide of the year in Mississippi. The first three victims had been prominent black Mississippians engaged in voter registration campaigns. Those political assassinations had received some notice in the national press, but nothing like the enormous attention brought by Till's death. The difference had to do with his age, his being merely a visitor to the South, and his mother's insistence on an open casket at his funeral back in Chicago, which allowed press cameras to record the particular brutalities inflicted upon the young man. Bryant's and Milam's immediate acquittal by an all-white jury, despite eyewitness evidence against them (and, indeed, their later admission of guilt to a journalist paying them for their story), further inflamed opinion outside the white South and beyond the United States.[33]

Many white Southerners sympathized with the murderers of Emmett Till, seeing their action as a regrettable but understandable response to the *Brown* decision and to black Southern organizing, as well as to the supposedly ever present threat of black male lust for white women. One local white at the Bryant and Milam trial explained the realities of preserving the status quo to a Northern reporter with a nod toward the Tallahatchie River, where Till's body had been found: "That river's full of niggers." Some white Southerners dissented, like novelist William Faulkner of nearby Oxford, who argued that in 1955 to "be against equality because of race or color, is like living in Alaska and being against snow." Black Americans were disturbed, if not surprised, by what the NAACP called the "state of jungle fury" among white Mississippians. Foreign observers tended to share that estimation, in Europe as well as in the Third World, and the Eisenhower administration could not miss seeing how the Till case undercut the goodwill that the *Brown* decision had recently won for the United States abroad. The FBI, for its part, was certain that the only whites who cared about the Till case must have been Communists. Hoover could find no other explanation for Chicago mayor Richard Daley's protest against federal inaction in the case than that he had been duped by the Communist Party. Liberals used anti-Communist logic in a converse fashion, believing the jurors in the trial of Till's murderers deserved, in the words of NAACP chairman Channing Tobias, "a medal from the Kremlin for meritorious service in communism's war against democracy."[34]

"Respectable" defenders of the South's traditional racial hierarchy avoided the overt viciousness of Emmett Till's murderers but tapped into the same broad reservoir of resentment of black self-assertion in the second half of the 1950s. White moderates no less than white conservatives were uncomfortable with African Americans who did not defer to their wisdom and power. White anxieties escalated as the decade wore on and evidence piled up that Jim Crow was under siege: the founding of the Southern Christian Leadership Conference (SCLC) in 1957 as the political arm of the black church in the South; the rising alienation of some civil rights workers, like Monroe, North Carolina, NAACP chapter president Robert Williams, who spoke openly by 1959 of meeting "violence with violence"; and the growth of the Nation of Islam, which whites unanimously disliked for its unflinching rejection of white leadership and even white people. Like their president, most white Americans were not yet ready for social upheaval along the color line.[35]

White Southerners generally saw the *Brown* decision as a terrible mistake. Powerful U.S. senators like Strom Thurmond and Richard Russell believed that racial integration would subvert the fundamental social order of the United States. The civil rights movement was as great a threat to the national security of the country as the Soviet Union. They were determined that racial equality would not be, in the words of one South Carolina newspaperwoman, "rammed down our throats." Governor Herman Talmadge of Georgia argued that the Supreme Court had "violated the law" in the *Brown* decision and called for white Southerners as a "sovereign people" to now become "the Court of Last Resort."[36]

In the absence of support from Washington for the implementation of the *Brown* decision, "respectable" Southern resistance built up over the next two years, culminating in the Southern Manifesto of 12 March 1956. Almost every U.S. senator and representative from the South signed this Declaration of Constitutional Principles, as it was officially known, condemning the Court's decision as an unconstitutional "abuse of judicial power" that usurped states' control of public education. Several state legislatures in the former Confederacy had already passed resolutions declaring that *Brown* had no legal force within their borders. In the first week of March, the University of Alabama expelled Autherine Lucy, a black student whom federal courts had just ordered admitted. These developments were keenly watched abroad; American journalist Carl Rowan, traveling in India and Ghana, was struck by the intensely negative responses to these events that he encountered. The early spring of 1956 thus marked a high-water point of national division over whether or not the United States would join the rest of the world—outside southern Africa—in moving away from racial discrimination.[37]

In this period of crisis for the United States in determining its future as a society, the Eisenhower administration maintained a low profile. Having ducked the original Court decision, the president also avoided confronting subsequent Southern resistance until his hand was forced in Little Rock in the fall of 1957. Eisenhower responded publicly to the announcement of the Southern Manifesto by seeing the issue from the white Southern viewpoint: he emphasized that the Court had upheld segregation for the previous sixty years, and that white Southerners' "deep emotional reaction" would take time to moderate. Brownell's Justice Department was working quietly on some limited civil rights proposals regarding voting, but white Southerners kept a close eye on the White House. Governor Allan Shivers of Texas, a Democrat who had supported Eisenhower in 1952, defiantly tested the president in September 1956 by using state police to prevent court-ordered desegregation in two Texas cities. Eisenhower ducked again, evading reporters' questions and denying there was any federal role in the case. White Southerners understood the White House's message, and violence against blacks by both police and private citizens continued unabated. In January 1957 the Koinonia Community, a racially integrated Christian group of sixty people farming near Americus, Georgia, appealed directly to Eisenhower for protection from the barrage of physical harassment and destruction—shootings, burnings, and dynamitings—they faced daily. The administration replied that it had no jurisdiction in the situation. Two weeks later, the president flew to Thomasville—just one hundred miles south of Americus—to enjoy twelve days of white Georgian hospitality at the Humphrey plantation.[38]

The presidential election of 1956 demonstrated anew the tepidness of support for equality in the United States in the era of Dwight Eisenhower. African Americans who could vote split their ballots between the two candidates, finding little in either to arouse enthusiasm. In his continuing appeal to white Southerners, Eisenhower refused to let the Republican platform explicitly link his administration to the *Brown* decision. Unlike four years earlier, when the platform had called for the "liberation" of white "captive peoples" in Eastern Europe, the president's party avoided any inkling of support for the liberation of black Americans from the chains of Jim Crow. The Democrats again provided little pressure on their opponents to identify with the cause of equality. Presidential nominee Adlai Stevenson represented a party deeply divided along sectional lines by the issue of civil rights. He therefore hewed to the middle ground of advocating only gradual implementation of the Supreme Court's ruling on school desegregation, and he opposed the use of federal troops for that purpose. Leadership on the crucial issue of race relations did not come from within the traditional political leadership of the United States in the 1950s.[39]

With little enthusiasm, Eisenhower allowed his attorney general to continue developing proposed legislation bolstering black voting rights. Brownell was concerned by the increasing tension in the South between violent whites and organizing blacks; he hoped that the bill would appeal to moderates of all colors by focusing on voting rather than the more emotional issue of school desegregation. The purpose was to restrain further racial polarization in the South. Signed into law after considerable compromise with the Southern congressional leadership, the Civil Rights Act of September 1957 represented the first federal law of its kind in eighty years, but its course through Congress also revealed how little the president cared about it or lobbied for it. Two months earlier he had declared at a press conference that he did not understand parts of his own bill, the parts that were toughest on violators of black voting rights. Recognizing encouragement when they saw it, white Southerners seized the opportunity to amend further the legislation. Most Southern senators saw the weak final version as such a clear victory for their side that they were embarrassed by Strom Thurmond's unsuccessful last-minute filibuster. Civil rights advocates were equally dismayed at the law itself. King warned Nixon that any impact of such inadequate legislation depended on "a sustained mass movement on the part of Negroes"—precisely what the Eisenhower administration hoped to avoid.[40]

Like their domestic counterparts in the American South, defenders of the traditional international social order also resisted change in the mid-1950s. Just as white Southerners reluctantly gave up peonage, prison labor leasing, and frequent lynchings, so Western Europeans relinquished most of their direct colonial control of the Third World. But the imperialists abroad, like the segregationists at home, refused to retreat quietly. While white Southerners drew the line at school desegregation in 1956, the British and the French joined Israel in drawing their line at the Suez Canal that same year. Their co-ordinated assault on Egypt at the end of October after Gamal Abdel Nasser's nationalization of the canal confronted the Eisenhower administration with an international crisis that played out along racial lines. *Time* magazine noted that "the 'nonwhite' nations of the world lined up against Britain and France in a virtually solid front." Eisenhower told his advisers not to overemphasize the role of Nasser, as the British had, because the Egyptian president merely embodied the broader desire of Arab peoples for full independence and for "slapping the white man down."[41]

The assault on Suez represented precisely the kind of escalation of conflict between the First and Third Worlds that the Eisenhower administration sought to avoid. The president was furious with the precipitous action of the British, French, and Israelis, which he and Foster Dulles saw as such an egregious act of aggression that they had to condemn it. Eisenhower particularly resented his closest allies, the British, for forcing him to line up against them at the United Nations. His reaction would be the same a year later when white Southerners put him in a similar situation in Little Rock. The president and his advisers shared the dismay of one British Labour Party official who bemoaned the reversal of supposedly traditional racial roles: "Nasser's behaving like an Anglo-Saxon—we're behaving like Arabs." Henry Cabot Lodge, Jr., the U.S. ambassador to the UN and one of the most liberal members of the administration, reported to Eisenhower with relish "the enthusiastic reactions from Afro-Asian nations about your policy here in the Near East crisis"—forcing the British and French to withdraw from the canal—and other U.S. officials were also pleased by the positive responses from non-European countries. But the president discounted his novel, and brief, status as a hero in the Third World, criticizing instead what he saw as non-Europeans' hypocritical lack of concern with the contemporaneous, brutal Soviet occupation of Hungary. To Asians and other nonwhites, he complained to the British ambassador, "colonialism is not colonialism unless it is a matter of white domination over colored people." The president found few non-European governments that he could trust.[42]

White resistance to racial change in the Eisenhower years culminated in the desegregation crisis at Central High School in Little Rock in September 1957. There the violent and "respectable" streams of segregationism flowed together. Governor Orval Faubus and other Arkansas officials defied the federal courts first by using the Arkansas National Guard to prevent nine black students from entering the school and then, after the courts ordered them to halt such obstructionism, by openly encouraging the white mob that shut down Central High. Faced with blatant defiance of federal authority and apparent anarchy in the streets of Little Rock, a furious Dwight Eisenhower had no choice but to send in the U.S. Army. On the evening of 24 September, the joking young men of the Arkansas National Guard who had abetted the mob disappeared. They were replaced by a thousand unsmiling, steely-eyed paratroopers of the 101st Airborne Division, a unit whose experiences with the Nazi Wehrmacht and the Chinese People's Liberation Army left it unimpressed by civilian hooligans. They escorted the black students to school for the next two months. The president's years of sympathizing with segregationists had finally caught up with him, as white Southern extremism forced Eisenhower to become the first president since Reconstruction to use military might to protect black American citizens and their constitutional rights.[43]

Eisenhower responded to the situation in Little Rock much as he had to the crisis at Suez, with white Southerners in the role of the First World and black Southerners cast as the Third World. In each case he lost his patience with people with whom he usually agreed but who had finally gone too far by choosing violence rather than moderation. And in each case he seemed somewhat uncomfortable with the approval he received from anticolonialists and racial egalitarians, whom he saw as not much less extreme than the members of the hysterical crowd outside Central High. In a televised address to the nation on 24 September, Eisenhower explained his actions in Little Rock as a matter of preserving domestic order, not promoting racial justice. The issue was anarchy, not desegregation, he said. The president emphasized his "many warm friends" in the South and his own years of residence there, and declared that his personal opinion about the *Brown* decision had "no bearing on the matter of enforcement" of federal court decisions. Eisenhower felt personally betrayed by Faubus, who had backed out of an agreement with the White House not to obstruct the court order further. As David Halberstam observed, the former five-star general "did not look kindly on frontal challenges by junior officers." Insurrection, not integration, brought the crisis to a head for the man in the Oval Office.[44]

Little Rock displayed America's racial dilemmas to a fascinated international audience. Television cameras from around the world whirred as vicious white mobs taunted and assaulted the handful of orderly, well-dressed black schoolchildren behaving with great dignity. African American residents of the city were astonished and encouraged by the scope of world attention, including mail from well-wishers around the globe to the nine black students. The name "Little Rock" quickly became the foremost international symbol of American racism, with hostile crowds in Venezuela chanting it as they attacked Nixon's motorcade in Caracas in 1958. Rejecting American warnings about Communist influence in South Africa, Nelson Mandela declared that Africans "do not require any schooling from the U.S.A., which . . . should learn to put its own house in order before trying to teach everyone else." Moscow Radio mockingly included the Arkansas capital in its daily itineraries of cities passed over by Sputnik I, the world's first orbiting satellite launched just ten days after Eisenhower's dispatch of troops. Western Europeans emphasized the connection between American behavior at home and its leadership abroad. French commentators concluded, in the words of an administration summary, that "the United States could hardly hope to set world standards for morality in the face of such degrading spectacles." A white captain based at Little Rock Air Force Base asked the obvious question about U.S. foreign relations in a letter to the editor of the *Arkansas Gazette:* how could the peoples of Asia and the Middle East "have faith in our government when we so openly show hate for anyone outside the white race?"[45]

The Eisenhower administration again seemed more certain of how it wanted its racial policies portrayed abroad than at home. Once the president had dispatched U.S. troops, his advisers moved to ensure maximum propaganda benefit from the decision. His initial address to the nation was swiftly translated into forty-three languages, and the Voice of America broadcast generous details of the federal military intervention in an American state. The Eisenhower administration, as Moscow Radio enjoyed pointing out, showed more concern with the international repercussions of the events in Little Rock than with the actual violations of human rights and democratic practices there. The president himself refused to offer any hint of approval for the federal court decisions underlying the situation, emphasizing instead how "our enemies are gloating over this incident and using it everywhere to misrepresent the whole nation." Above all, he regretted how "it would be difficult to exaggerate the harm that is being done to the prestige and influence" of the United States abroad. For Eisenhower, white racial violence appeared to remain a strictly political rather than moral problem.[46]

## *Race as an International Issue for the United States*

Despite significant progress in the military and the schools and in popular sports and entertainment, racial discrimination remained a fact of American life. Indeed, it was even exported, to the fierce resentment of people of color abroad. In the private sector, this meant the establishment of segregated workplaces by American companies abroad, such as Firestone in Liberia, of which Eisenhower himself was fully aware. In the public sector, this included the often disdainful attitudes of American diplomatic personnel posted in various Third World countries. Not until 1956 did the State Department seem to realize how offended Africans were by the American practice in South Africa and Rhodesia of inviting only whites to Fourth of July celebrations at the U.S. embassies and consulates. Members of the U.S. delegation to the UN lobbied the U.S. government to change this tradition, especially in light of "the recent disgraceful race riots in Alabama" over the possibility of integrating the state university in Tuscaloosa. Dulles agreed in principle but refused to issue any specific orders on the matter. Those American diplomats abroad who refused to join all-white social clubs, such as Henry Ramsey in Madras, India, often felt the stinging resentment of colleagues who believed they had "gone Asiatic." The White House chief of protocol complained about having to invite "these niggers" from Africa to receptions, and African diplomats experienced enormous difficulties in finding decent housing both in Washington and in New York. The new states of Africa, swiftly passing legislation to ban racial discrimination, could not avoid knowing the deep American ambivalence about racial equality.[47]

Racial thinking influenced Eisenhower's evaluation of the two states he most feared, the Soviet Union and the People's Republic of China. With his advisers and friends, the president referred to the Chinese as "hysterical" and "fanatical" and warned, "we are always wrong when we believe that Orientals think logically as we do." Long-standing anti-Asian feelings among white Americans had been exacerbated by three years of war against the People's Republic in Korea, as old images of the Chinese as cruel, inscrutable, robotlike, and ultimately inhuman resurfaced. One American officer recalled Chinese soldiers' bravery in the face of withering U.S. firepower: "It was like dealing with mass lunacy." Those Americans impressed by the Chinese military performance showed no less surprise, like the administration official who exclaimed: "I was brought up to think the Chinese couldn't handle a machine.

Now, suddenly, the Chinese are flying jets!" Like many Americans, Eisenhower was angered by what he saw as Chinese ingratitude for all that Americans had done for their country. American frustration with the Chinese apostasy in rejecting the pro-American Chiang Kai-shek in favor of the Communist Party remained enormous in the 1950s. The convergence of the Yellow Peril with the Red Peril in the People's Republic helped China to surpass Russia in the 1950s as the enemy whom many Americans most loathed.[48]

The racial and ideological constitution of the Soviet Union was more ambiguous to Americans in the 1950s than that of China. Fresh from their revolution and from holding their own in Korea against the vaunted U.S. military, the Chinese openly encouraged the spread of anticapitalist revolution throughout the Third World. By contrast, the Soviets shifted after Stalin's death to a less confrontational stance toward the West. The Eisenhower administration appreciated this change. In contrast to the "hysterical" and "irrational" Chinese who did not seem to fear American nuclear threats, Russian leaders, according to the president, despite "all differences in culture and tradition, values or language, . . . were human beings, and they wanted to remain alive." Foster Dulles called the Russians "calculating" in their actions, while arguing that "emotion played a large part in [China's] conduct." Nevertheless, the inclusion of a vast swath of Asia and its peoples within the Soviet Union made many Americans unsure of the country's racial dependability. In its coverage of the Soviet occupation of Hungary in 1956, *Time* described the "big new tanks . . . protected by trotting groups of Asian-Russian infantrymen." Obsessed by racial categorization, Americans were not completely sure what to make of the Soviets.[49]

Cold War competitiveness with the Soviet Union highlighted the hypocrisy of American racism amid U.S. claims to leadership of the "free world." Eisenhower campaigned in 1952 on a platform calling for liberation of the "captive peoples" of Eastern Europe, and Congress joined him in proclaiming a Captive Nations Week in 1959. Such a narrow vision of who was not free omitted vast numbers of people south of the Mason-Dixon line and the Sahara. An editorial in *The Crisis,* the monthly journal of the NAACP, pointed this out: "The time has come for the 'Free World' to devote as much attention to liberating the 'enslaved peoples' behind the various bamboo and liana curtains of Asia and Africa as behind the Iron Curtain of Europe." African Americans denounced the discrepancy between their secondary status in their own country and the generous refugee programs established by the U.S. government for white aliens fleeing the 1956 invasion of Hungary. "The advocacy of free elections in Europe by American officials is hypocrisy," Martin Luther King, Jr., declared, "when free elections are not held in great sections of America." Africans, Indians, and other nonwhite foreigners were equally skeptical of U.S. policies favoring those with fairer skins, as numerous observers pointed out and as Eisenhower and Dulles privately acknowledged.[50]

The standard American explanation of racial discrimination in the South during the 1950s involved the doctrine of federalism and states' rights: the division of authority among federal, state, and local governments precluded federal interference into such matters as education and criminal justice, which were the states' responsibility. The awesome reach of the U.S. government around the globe, however, convinced many foreigners that such reasoning was either absurd or disingenuous. John Hope Franklin discovered this opinion at a scholarly seminar he attended in Salzburg, Austria, in the summer of 1958. A French participant told him: "It appears to the outsider that federalism stands in the way of nothing that the national government actually wants to do; but it is always used as an excuse for the national government's not protecting the rights of Negroes." A Yugoslav at the same conference noted the contrast between Eisenhower's ready dispatch of troops to Lebanon in 1958 and his great hesitancy in sending paratroopers to Little Rock a year earlier. The Eisenhower administration likewise refused at first to become involved in the 1958 North Carolina "kissing case," in which two black boys under ten were arrested and sentenced to indefinite terms in the state reformatory for kissing a white female playmate. The administration changed strategy, encouraging a swift release of the young "subversives," only after local black protests spurred extensive international media coverage of the case, which led in turn to major demonstrations at U.S. embassies throughout Europe.[51]

As Americans wrestled with issues of racial equality and Communist influence, the two most contentious problems of the 1950s, a debate emerged about their precise relationship to each other. Liberals and racial egalitarians argued that the Cold War competition with the Communist bloc required the United States to live up fully to its proclaimed ideals of freedom and equality for all. Otherwise, the Soviets would win over the world's nonwhite majority and the future of the globe would be theirs. Black labor leader A. Philip Randolph encouraged Eisenhower in 1953 to stand up for African independence; since Africans were now determined to be free, he wrote, the United States had to help them see that the Soviets were not "the only champions of revolutions for nationalism and revolt against landlordism, poverty, disease, illiteracy and tyranny." Congressman Adam Clayton Powell of New York called the arrests of black bus boycotters in Montgomery in February 1956 "another ghastly victory for communism" and urged federal intervention. Eisenhower's refusal to render any public judgment about the events in Alabama was, other critics noted, "exactly what the communists desire" and directly counter to what the United States had fought for in World War II. African American journalist Rowan learned on a 1954 tour of India how offended Indians were by domestic American racial practices and how effectively local Communists could make political points out of them. *Blitz,* a Communist Party newspaper, connected the antiblack riots in Chicago's Trumbull Park with Rowan's simultaneous State Department–sponsored lecture tour under the headline "ROWANS BABBLE WHILE NEGROES BURN."[52]

Conservatives and segregationists disagreed fiercely with the liberal conjunction of domestic and foreign racial policies. Their equally anti-Communist language targeted support for racial equality and integration as subversive of American freedom. Even as red-baiting in general declined in American politics after the end of the Korean War in 1953 and the Senate censure of Joseph McCarthy in 1954, white Southerners increased their use of anti-Communist rhetoric after the *Brown* decision as part of a strategy to equate integration with Communism. Governor Talmadge explained this position in *You and Segregation,* a 1955 book immensely popular among white Southerners: "Too many things are being done in this country and by our country because we keep looking back over our shoulders at the Communists. Who cares what the Reds say? Who cares what *Pravda* prints?" Talmadge and other prominent Southerners like Georgia senator Richard Russell believed liberals were being suckered by Moscow's Cold War rhetoric. Rather than try to satisfy Soviet demands, the United States should stand up proudly for its own traditions. If Communists supported racial integration, could there be any clearer sign of its immorality?[53]

The Eisenhower administration agreed with elements of each side in this debate about Communism and racial equality. The president and his advisers recognized the logic of not driving African states toward the Soviet bloc for assistance, but they shared an underlying assumption about the potential subversiveness of alienated African Americans. Dissatisfaction breeds dissent, and J. Edgar Hoover argued that the civil rights movement in the South, being angry and reformist, was thoroughly penetrated by Communist Party operatives. No one in the administration disagreed with the nation's chief policeman. The FBI responded to school desegregation incidents by investigating them for disorder and subversion rather than for the local obstruction of federal court orders. Accordingly, bureau reports were treated above all as "domestic intelligence" and were sent first to the Internal Security Division of the Justice Department and only later to its Civil Rights Section. Foster Dulles revealed the depth of the administration's distrust of black people in a 1953 lament about "the problem of getting colored people cleared by the FBI." As recorded by a note-taking assistant, Dulles said, "there was practically no negro, even Ralph Bunch[e], who could come through an FBI check lily white, because all of their organizations had been infiltrated at one time or another." Despite the White House's insistence on "getting lily white clearances on everybody" working for the government, the secretary of state concluded that "it is impossible to do this with negroes."[54]

Even with their uncertainty about the loyalty of black Americans, Eisenhower and his advisers recognized that accelerating changes in race relations abroad in the late 1950s would inevitably impact racial practices at home. Nixon returned from Ghana in 1957 to tell the president bluntly: "We cannot talk equality to the peoples of Africa and Asia and practice inequality in the United States." In a discussion of the 1959 lynching of Mack Parker with Governor J. P. Coleman of Mississippi, Eisenhower did not indicate any concern for the victim, but he made very clear his unhappiness with the damage such incidents were doing to the U.S. image abroad. The end of white supremacy in the rest of the world, journalist Isaacs observed, "made its survival in the United States suddenly and painfully conspicuous . . . It was like being caught naked in a glaring spotlight alone on a great stage in a huge theater filled with people we had not known were there." The increasing appearance of African diplomats in Washington and at the United Nations in New York, and their respectful treatment by white American policymakers who had never previously dealt with people of color as peers, signaled the decline of rigid racial hierarchies.[55]

For Americans of African descent, the liberation of Africa from colonial rule carried particular meaning. As citizens of a country that had long associated Africa with savagery and darkness, few black Americans had been able to embrace their African heritage without ambivalence. Some, like John Lewis, grew up cheering from segregated balconies for the African warriors in Tarzan movies; more probably agreed with Roger Wilkins that "to identify with the black clods of Tarzan's Africa never entered my mind." Malcolm X recalled, "we did not realize that in hating Africa and Africans we were hating ourselves," including the very features and hues of an African phenotype.

The appearance of proud, capable statesmen from the emerging independent African nations in the halls of the UN in the late 1950s changed that perception of primitive Africa with dramatic suddenness. Black Americans across the political spectrum shared a newfound enthusiasm for African culture and an admiration for black Africa's political leaders. The new civil rights movement drew encouragement from events across the Atlantic. Martin Luther King, Jr., repeatedly equated colonialism with segregation—"they are both based on a contempt for life, and a tragic doctrine of white supremacy"—and emphasized African Americans' awareness that their "struggle for freedom is a part of a worldwide struggle." Antiracist organizers understood at least as clearly as American policymakers that racial hierarchies in the United States and abroad formed a seamless web, and they correctly foresaw that independence in Asia and Africa would hasten the demise of Jim Crow.[56]

Many black Americans traveled to the new nations of West Africa in the first years of independence, from 1957 onward, searching for their roots in their ancestral continent. They were inevitably impressed by the sight of black people occupying all positions in a society, from the most menial to the most elite. They thrilled to the absence of racial harassment and humiliation. "Two whole months," one told an American journalist, "for the first time in my life, two whole months without incidents or insults." For most African American visitors, however, the intense feeling of racial familiarity was balanced by the reality of alienation from a vastly different African culture. Like all peoples traveling abroad, they tended to become aware of their own strong personal and cultural attachments—in this case, to the United States. Faced with African pride in hard-won independence over white colonial rule, black Americans were sometimes made to feel disadvantaged because of their still segregated American homeland. Some African Americans in West Africa found themselves in the unexpected position of defending the United States against African criticism. For most black Americans, the precise character of their renewed relationship with the ancestral continent remained open to negotiation.[57]

### Eisenhower, the Third World, and Africa

In contrast to his counsel of patience for people of color at home, Eisenhower seemed to understand that nonwhites abroad had gone too far down the road of change to wait any longer for gradual progress. Most of the peoples of Asia and the Middle East had achieved their independence from European rule before 1953, and Africa swiftly followed. As at home, the issue of race was crucial abroad. Colonialism had been grounded in racial inequality and discrimination, and the successful struggles for national liberation brought a new day of formal racial equality to the world's nonwhite majority. Eisenhower generally recognized the power of nationalist sentiment and commitment in the Third World. Within certain ideological boundaries, he tried to position the United States in support of the governments of newly independent nations. The U.S. government itself controlled a handful of largely nonwhite territories, most importantly Hawaii and Alaska. Unlike Southerners in Congress who opposed statehood for them because of the accompanying infusion of citizens of color, Eisenhower supported the two territories' bid to join the Union on an equal basis. He signed the bills designating them the forty-ninth and fiftieth states in 1959.[58]

Beyond a basic recognition of the inexorable character of anticolonial independence movements, however, Eisenhower and his secretary of state, Foster Dulles, knew little about the Third World. Like most white Americans concerned with foreign affairs in the 1950s, they were men of Europe. Eisenhower had forged close ties with the British government as commander of the European theater in World War II, links he further strengthened as NATO commander in the late 1940s. His most prominent biographer, Stephen Ambrose, notes that the Atlantic alliance was "the issue closest to his heart." With the exception of his work on the Japanese peace treaty, Dulles's extensive background in foreign affairs had focused primarily on Europe before 1953. The secretary of state's general opposition to European colonialism in the 1950s derived from his understanding of U.S. interests in the Cold War, not from sympathy with nonwhite liberation fighters. Even his differences with the Europeans over preserving formal colonialism sometimes blurred. In February 1956 he dismissed the Indian claim to the city of Goa—a tiny vestigial Portuguese colony surrounded by Indian territory—insisting instead that "all the world regards [Goa] as a Portuguese province." "The world" for the American secretary of state in the 1950s still meant Europe.[59]

The administration's thin veneer of anticolonialism masked not only a sturdy Eurocentrism but also a marked disdain for most non-European leaders, including even those with close ties to the West. White House assistant C. D. Jackson was plainly disgusted by what he called "the swirling mass of emotionally super-charged Africans and Asiatics and Arabs that outnumber us." Even Vice President Nixon, the administration's "liberal" on racial issues, who generally argued for greater U.S. attention to Africa, referred to the continent in a 1960 NSC meeting as "a horrible place." Foster Dulles's successor, Christian Herter, warned the president that Cuba's Fidel Castro was "very much like a child" who became especially "voluble" and "wild" when he spoke in Spanish; Eisenhower responded by recalling that India's Nehru "accumulated emotional frenzy" as he spoke. The image of Third World leaders as volatile children was especially enduring for the administration. Sounding remarkably like his white South African counterparts, Foster Dulles lamented in June 1958 the "tremendous surge in the direction of popular government by people who have practically no capacity for self-government and indeed are like children in facing this problem." Whether these "children" could mature remained uncertain to U.S. policymakers.[60]

Non-Europeans abroad were frequently skeptical of American foreign policy and occasionally demonstrated their displeasure in ways that further alienated U.S. officials. Crowds of angry protesters in Caracas, for example, assaulted and nearly killed Nixon on his would-be goodwill trip to Latin America in the spring of 1958. The Tokyo government canceled its invitation for Eisenhower to visit Japan in the summer of 1960, after enormous street protests broke out; a fierce attack by the crowds on the advance party of press secretary James Hagerty required U.S. marines to rescue him by helicopter. Even Third World peoples more admiring of the war hero president showed some ambivalence, like the sign visible in Rio de Janeiro during his stopover there in February 1960: "We like Ike; We like Fidel, too." Third World dubiousness about the administration's actions in Iran, Guatemala, Indochina, the Taiwan Straits, Lebanon, Indonesia, Cuba, and the Congo—often stridently expressed—exacerbated official American dislike for much of the world beyond Western Europe.[61]

The willingness of the Eisenhower administration to acknowledge the seriousness of nationalism in the Third World was undercut by its growing anxiety about Communist influence there. From 1955, with Stalin dead and postwar Europe mostly stabilized, the Soviet government under Nikita Khrushchev sought to expand its contacts with the new governments of Asia and the Middle East and the emerging nations of Africa. Mao Tse-tung's similar intentions provoked American fears that China's history as the largest nonwhite nation exploited by the West might position it to provide leadership to other similarly exploited countries in the Third World. Just as the FBI and other elements of the U.S. government assumed that African Americans in the South were naturally docile and could be organized only by subversive and usually white outsiders ("outside agitators"), Eisenhower and his advisers believed that dark-skinned, childlike leaders of non-European nations were vulnerable to the pernicious influences of subversive outsiders like the Soviets and the Chinese. In the steely light of the Cold War, American policymakers saw the dark hand of Moscow behind all challenges to a Western-dominated capitalist order.[62]

The Eisenhower administration found it difficult to convince Asians and Africans that the expansion of Soviet influence represented a new and more powerful form of colonialism. For most countries, European colonialism remained a far more clear and present danger than Communism. The close American relationship with the colonial powers of Western Europe and with South Africa, along with American racial practices at home, often brought U.S. rather than Soviet intentions into question. The National Security Council acknowledged this problem privately in March 1958: "African desires for self-government[,] as well as the racial policies of the Union of South Africa, make Soviet pretensions to be the champion of the oppressed colonies acceptable in some areas, so that Western attempts to picture Soviet Russia as a colonialist power itself have simply not been believed by African leaders." Later that year the U.S. Information Agency (USIA) warned the White House of the deteriorating image of the United States abroad. American influence in the world was being perceived increasingly as a form of cultural and military imperialism, it feared, with the creation and maintenance of states like South Vietnam, Taiwan, and South Korea—with their Christian, pro-Western leaders—as prime examples. The USIA paraphrased the Indian perspective: "We don't see the Russian fleet in Oriental waters. We see only the American fleet. We don't see the Russian Army in mainland China but we see a good deal of the American Army in Formosa, and Japan, and Korea, and Okinawa, and the Philippines." Worst of all, the USIA concluded that the United States was behaving exactly like one of the Third World nations that the administration disdained: "Our chief problem is to grow up psychologically." Boasting about "our richness, our bigness, and our strength, . . . we continue to act like adolescents."[63]

Fearful of Soviet influence and distrustful of the newly independent nations, Foster Dulles lashed out at those countries seeking to remain nonaligned in the Cold War. In a commencement address at Iowa State College in June 1956, the secretary of state declared that neutrality "has increasingly become an obsolete conception, and, except under very exceptional circumstances, it is an immoral and shortsighted conception." Even those in the

State Department more sympathetic to the Third World considered neutralism a product of "the strong irrational nationalist tendency" in those countries, ruled by people the NSC called "still immature and unsophisticated with respect to . . . the issues that divide the world today." An internal State Department study of the problem in 1955 did acknowledge, however, that neutralism was a complicated issue, as the United States had itself promoted its neutral position regarding other nations' conflicts for almost all of its history, most recently in the years 1914–1917 and 1939–1941. The study also emphasized that "color consciousness is closely linked to anti-colonialism," and that neutralism was often defended on the grounds that "the racial intolerance of the Western powers is just as bad as anything that might be practised by the Communist bloc." Despite Dulles's severe public words about neutralism, his department concluded privately that "this sensitivity about race is one of the chief obstacles to sympathy with the West."[64]

The success of independence movements in Asia and the Middle East in the Truman years meant that the problem of colonialism for the Eisenhower administration was confined increasingly to Africa. Africa's significance for the United States in the 1950s included economic, strategic, and political elements. This bright continent represented the world's last great frontier of natural resources, offering vast quantities of such critical minerals as gold, diamonds, columbite, cobalt, chromite, and uranium. "It is our Last Frontier," declared John Gunther in 1955 in his popular book *Inside Africa*. "Africa lies open like a vacuum, and is almost perfectly defenseless—the richest prize on earth." The American economic stake in the region, while smaller than in other parts of the world, still amounted to 3.5 percent of U.S. foreign trade. The continent's strategic importance for raw materials for modern weapons was amplified by its location astride major shipping lanes and its utility in wartime for military bases, as Eisenhower himself had learned in commanding forces along its northern shore in World War II. Africa's political significance to the United States lay mostly in its meaning to America's NATO allies. The Eisenhower administration acknowledged privately the pervasive African resentment of European economic exploitation and racial discrimination. "Should serious disorders develop in the area," the NSC warned the president in 1957, "there might be a further military and economic drain on some of the more important NATO powers." Worse, the current easy access to Africa's mineral wealth might be cut off. The NSC concluded that the United States therefore had "a very real interest in orderly political evolution in Africa."[65]

Uranium was the key to the American perspective on Africa at the start of the Eisenhower administration. The preeminent military might of the United States depended on its nuclear arsenal, and over 95 percent of the fuel for those weapons since the original Manhattan Project had come from the Shinkolobwe mine in the Belgian Congo. It would be difficult to overstate the strategic importance of this resource for the United States in 1953. The chairman of the U.S. Atomic Energy Commission, Gordon Dean, was careful to remind Foster Dulles of this in his first weeks as the administration's chief foreign policymaker. Just behind the Belgian Congo came the troubled land of apartheid, Dean told Dulles: "Within two to three years South Africa will be our most important uranium supplier." As the 1950s progressed, other sources of the crucial ore became available, from expanded operations in Canada and on the Colorado Plateau at home, while production at Shinkolobwe tailed off until the mine finally closed in 1960. But throughout the years of the Eisenhower administration, first the Belgian Congo and then South Africa held a unique place in American strategic planning.[66]

South Africa epitomized the problems that Eisenhower faced in Africa. Control of that nation's vast mineral wealth and strategic materials rested in the hands of its small white minority. By the mid-1950s the largest producer of uranium ore, South Africa also received the bulk of American investment and trade with the entire continent. His State Department superiors emphasized to Henry Byroade as he settled in as U.S. ambassador to Pretoria in 1956 that American relations with the apartheid state "are very friendly and harmonious. South Africa is strongly anti-Communist and pro-West" and looked increasingly to the United States rather than Britain as its closest ally.[67] But these same friendly white folks had already begun, as one State Department official reminded Foster Dulles, "to create a police state." The NSC privately agreed, regretting that South African "political development has been retrogressive." And the whites seemed immune to friendly persuasion. The next U.S. ambassador to Pretoria after Byroade, Philip Crowe, referred privately to Prime Minister Henrik Verwoerd as "a fanatic with a fanatic's absolute faith in his own righteousness," especially about racial issues. So while an earlier U.S. ambassador, Waldemar Gallman, had urged Dulles in 1953 to remember that "peace in the mines, in the homes and on the streets [of South Africa] is essential" to American security interests, other U.S. officials grew more worried as the decade progressed. Mason Sears of the State Department warned Dulles of the "contagious influence of racism" on neighboring African states, and many in the administration began to fear that the brutalities of anti-Communist apartheid might drive Africans into the arms of the Communist Party.[68]

The Eisenhower administration believed it could have little influence on the racial policies of the South African government. Following the ruling Nationalist Party's electoral victory in April 1953, Dulles directed Ambassador Gallman to suggest gently to the prime minister the virtues of some mild reforms. Gallman agreed with that approach, while warning Washington that the possibility of massive African organizing in South Africa was more imminent than he had previously believed. African National Congress (ANC) literature reflected increasing hostility toward the United States during the 1950s, as Washington preserved its close ties to Pretoria. One young ANC activist suggested African disillusionment with the United States: "I think America has lost African friendship. As far as I am concerned, I will henceforth look East where race discrimination is so taboo that it is made a crime by the state."[69]

South Africans, however, could not help noticing changes in American racial practices. In January 1955, the *U.S.S. Midway* docked in Cape Town for a shore leave; the American officers not only refused a South African request to keep sailors of color on board but also opened up the ship to South African visitors on a nonsegregated basis. Over 20,000 South Africans of all colors came aboard over two days to see the inside of an integrated American warship. In a quiet but revealing administrative shift, the State Department by 1956 moved its coverage of South Africa out of the Bureau of European Affairs and into the Bureau of Near Eastern, South Asian, and African Affairs. It was as though, for Washington, South Africa had disembarked from Europe and finally arrived in Africa. If this was true, then perhaps the African majority of South Africa would now show up more clearly on Washington's radar.[70]

The overall thrust of U.S. policy toward Africa in the 1950s was the same as the administration's policy toward civil rights at home: to avoid it as much as possible. The greater American interest in Africa by the end of the decade came only in response to decolonization, not in support for it. If top U.S. policymakers knew little about the world outside Europe in general, they knew almost nothing about Africa. Dulles devoted only two sentences to the continent in his initial speech as secretary of state. Blaming "Communists" rather than white authorities for any unrest in the area, he worried "*if* there should be trouble there"—indicating that the Defiance Campaign of Africans in South Africa against apartheid, the Mau Mau rebellion of Kenyans against British rule, the full-scale revolt in Madagascar in 1947, and the outbreaks of anti-French violence in Morocco and Tunisia had made little impression on the chief U.S. diplomat. Africa remained a future problem for the administration, one that it figured to avoid for now.[71]

At least until 1958, when accelerating African independence began to require the United States to establish direct political ties to most of the continent, Eisenhower and his advisers sought to leave African issues generally to the Western European colonial powers. Europe and Africa remained "fundamentally complementary areas," according to the NSC. Sounding much like a white American Northerner speaking of white Southerners and the need to preserve close ties to them, Henry Byroade—then an assistant secretary of state—emphasized in a 1953 speech the crucial importance of African interests to the Western European economy, "which we have contributed so much to support." The success of the Marshall Plan investment, in other words, depended to a great extent on Africa. Byroade warned that "a sudden break in economic relations might seriously injure the European economies upon which our Atlantic defense system depends." American policymakers believed that orderly progress toward African self-rule would develop best under European tutelage. The U.S. government itself depended in large part on European experts on Africa in the 1950s, owing to the dearth of such specialists in the United States.[72]

Official American policy toward colonialism in Africa changed little between 1953 and 1958. Independence was the eventual goal, but "premature independence" remained the great danger. "It is a hard, inescapable fact that premature independence can be dangerous, retrogressive, and destructive," Byroade declared in 1953 in the administration's first major statement on Africa. In a world populated by Soviet predators, there was no room for romanticizing about immediate liberation. "Unless we are willing to recognize that there is such a thing as premature independence," Byroade concluded, "we cannot think intelligently or constructively about the status of dependent peoples." Here was the key: while supporting the principle of "eventual self-determination," the United States implicitly claimed the right to determine when African peoples were "mature" enough for independence. The image of parent and child—and the reality of what Africans increasingly called neo-colonialism—could not have been more clear. In the administration's second major statement on Africa, George Allen sounded the same notes three years later. On the very cusp of the great turn in African history toward independence, the U.S. assistant secretary of state could only manage to call the Europeans in Africa "the so-called colonial powers" and attribute antiracist organizing in South Africa to "Communists."[73]

The Eisenhower administration did not intend this approach as a recipe for simply preserving the status quo. Gradual but steady preparation for eventual independence was crucial to avoid a rerun of the previous decade's events in Asia. In his report to the president on his 1957 visit to Africa for Ghana's independence celebration, Nixon spoke of his "distinct impression that the communist leaders consider Africa today to be as important in their designs for world conquest as they considered China to be twenty-five years ago." Many Americans in the 1950s were still traumatized by "losing" China to Communist revolution and hoped to prevent a similar development in Africa. Realizing that "the grandchildren of Dr. Livingstone's porters [now] go to Oxford," as John Gunther put it, they sought to make allies rather than enemies of the new nationalists taking power south of the Sahara.[74]

Beginning with the Suez crisis in the fall of 1956, several developments converged to move the administration to a position of greater support for African independence and even a limited openness to African neutralism in the Cold War. As black African independence began to unfold in Ghana in 1957 and in Guinea in 1958, civil rights also emerged as a major political issue at home with the Little Rock school desegregation crisis of 1957–58, while Vice President Nixon's ambitions for the White House in 1960 led him to push for a more active U.S. policy regarding Africa. By 1960, the year in which seventeen new nations emerged on the continent, Eisenhower himself could be heard at the United Nations declaring America's acceptance of African nonalignment. U.S. officials shifted ground to increase American influence with the new nonwhite majority in the UN General Assembly and its prominent political role in international affairs. Race relations were an important element in producing this change. Americans both inside and outside the government acknowledged that racial discrimination was "in many ways the heart of the colonial question," as Chester Bowles noted. At the same time, the rise of the civil rights movement in the United States was changing the domestic calculation in African policy. George Allen advised Dulles of the importance of a "multi-racial approach" to African problems: "Any other course of action would, in the long run, meet with such domestic opposition within the United States that it would be next to impossible to carry out." A new day was coming in American relations with Africa.[75]

## African Challenge and American Response

The white Southern challenge to desegregation that crystallized at Little Rock was soon eclipsed for the Eisenhower administration by the rising wave of African independence. That wave began to crest in Ghana in 1957 and buried most of the remaining European colonial ties to the continent in its thunderous crash from 1960 to 1963. Asian independence in the early postwar years had provided a crucial precedent, bolstered by the addition of three Arab north African states—Libya, Morocco, and Tunisia—by 1956. Most British and French efforts to prop up collaborative regimes in the Middle East failed during the decade; the 1958 revolution in Iraq was just one example. The outbreak of the lengthy Mau Mau uprising in Kenya in 1952 and the start of the protracted Algerian revolution two years later marked the spread of wars of national liberation to Africa. Severe British repression of the Kenyan rebellion highlighted the racial hostility present under colonial rule. Senator John Kennedy's July 1957 speech supporting Algerian independence signaled his new prominence in foreign affairs, while his future opponent in the 1960 presidential race, Vice President Nixon, worried instead about the actions of the minority of one million Frenchmen living in Algeria should the colony become independent. Racial polarization in much of Africa by the late 1950s was creating a similar problem for the Eisenhower administration to that represented by the crisis in Arkansas, as politically active black Americans were quick to note.[76]

Racial divisions in Africa stemmed above all from the resistance of white settlers to African liberation movements. Tensions rose in direct proportion to the number of white settlers in an area; South Africa, Southern Rhodesia, Kenya, and Algeria formed the strongest white redoubts, while West Africa moved most quickly to majority rule. Metropolitan administrations mattered, too: the British, moving steadily toward independence for their colonies, seemed more like moderate white Southerners, while the Portuguese and the South Africans, digging in for a last stand, appeared analogous to white "massive resisters" in the South. The administration was stumped by the question of how "to force the obdurate right wingers among the 'settlers' to become cooperative with the Africans," and feared that a mere "handful of . . . white die-hards" might spark an international racial conflict certain to damage the interests of the United States abroad, not to mention its domestic stability. The administration had precisely the same concern regarding violent white Southerners.[77]

In addition to apartheid in South Africa and insurrections in Kenya and Algeria, another manifestation of the white settler problem that coincided precisely with the tenure of the Eisenhower administration was the Central African Federation (CAF). Formed in 1953 out of the British territories of Nyasaland and the two Rhodesias, the federation was intended by Britain to tie the self-governing colony of Southern Rhodesia more closely to the rest of black Africa to the north, thereby discouraging the growing political orientation of Southern Rhodesia's white community toward South Africa. Apartheid might thus be contained at the Limpopo River. The British government framed the creation of the CAF as a step toward "racial partnership" in an eventually independent, multiracial state. But the actual effect of the federation was to increase white political and economic domination over Africans. Africans in the three territories had opposed the idea of the CAF from the beginning, and they resented the intensifying racial discrimination and harassment they experienced during the 1950s. The NSC acknowledged in March 1958 that "the hardening of European settlers' attitudes" was "undermining the principle of racial partnership" and thus destroying the "U.S. hope that the Federation would serve as an example for the development of multi-racial societies." African resistance to white rule in the CAF accelerated after 1957, leading to independence under majority rule for Nyasaland and Northern Rhodesia early in the 1960s. The more numerous and powerful whites of Southern Rhodesia, like their neighbors in South Africa and the Portuguese colonies, held out. As one boasted to an American visitor, "this country is like the American South at its best."[78]

The problem for the Eisenhower administration in dealing with Africa was that Africans across the continent saw white domination rather than Communism as their chief stumbling block. Ndabaningi Sithole of Southern Rhodesia spoke for most Africans in his widely read 1959 book, *African Nationalism,* which declared that "African nationalism is a struggle against white supremacy." Sithole and others argued that white rule in Africa was precisely analogous to Soviet control of Eastern Europe. Washington's anti-Communist prescription for dealing with unrest elsewhere in the world therefore was unlikely to work in Africa, as American policymakers reluctantly admitted. The CIA acknowledged that most African nationalists were political moderates "well-disposed by education (and sometimes religion) toward the West." In fact, the agency reported, "most of them have sought to avoid violence except as a last resort," and outside South Africa "none is a known Communist." The agency warned instead of increasing interracial tensions in areas of heavy white settlement. And an aide to Foster Dulles, returning from a tour of the continent in 1958, emphasized to the secretary of state the often savage character of white rule in African colonies. As a result, he said, "the black African's attitude toward the white man shades from universal envy through mistrust and fear to burning hate."[79]

At midnight on 5 March 1957, in a celebration rich in symbolic importance, Ghana became the first black African nation to declare its independence from European colonial rule. Africans, white settlers, and colonial officials alike knew this marked the beginning of the end of the Africa they had known. Events in Ghana encouraged nationalists elsewhere on the continent in their own struggles against white rule. African Americans also recognized the impact that events in West Africa could have on their movement for equality in the United States. Martin Luther King, Jr., had been unable to get an audience with Richard Nixon before the two met by chance in Accra at the independence celebrations; in that atmosphere, the astute vice president treated King with great respect and arranged to see him again at home.[80]

President Kwame Nkrumah of Ghana overnight became the leading political figure on the continent. Like Sithole, Nigerian journalist Nnamdi Azikiwe, and most other African leaders, Nkrumah had important personal and cultural ties to the West. He had spent ten years studying and working in the United States and recalled that period with affection in conversations with Nixon. But he also remembered his first experience south of the Mason-Dixon line, when the future world figure asked a white waiter in a bus terminal restaurant for a glass of water and was told with icy disdain: "The place for you, my man, is the spittoon outside." Nkrumah's determination to help lead all of Africa out of colonialism made him skeptical of Eisenhower's lukewarm approach to African independence. Events in the Congo in 1960 divided him further from the United States, and Ghana moved soon thereafter into a new and close relationship with the Communist bloc.[81]

After Ghana, independence came swiftly to most of the rest of the continent. Throughout 1958 African representatives gathered in a series of conferences to encourage the liberation of the remaining colonies. The All-African Peoples Conference that convened in Accra in December symbolized a reversal of the famous Berlin Conference seventy-four years earlier; where the delegates at Berlin had divided up the continent under European rule, those at Accra called for the departure of the remaining colonialists and the unification of the continent under African rule. Guinea declared its independence from France in October 1958, and by the end of 1960—the Year of Africa—

seventeen more nations had come into existence, with the rest outside southern Africa soon to follow. Prime Minister Harold Macmillan aligned the British government with these developments by traveling to the heart of white supremacy—Pretoria—and telling the South African parliament on 3 February 1960 that "the growth of national consciousness in Africa is a political fact and we must accept it as such." The leader of the greatest colonial power in Africa affirmed that "the wind of change" blowing through the continent was not to be denied.[82]

The U.S. government responded to the rise of neutralism in Asia and the Middle East and the growth of nationalism in Africa in part by emphasizing cultural diplomacy with the Third World. The State Department, for example, dispatched African American speakers to India and other nonwhite nations to explain the progress being made at home in eliminating racial discrimination. In 1956, the Voice of America began broadcasting jazz, an American music form wildly popular in much of the world. In the spring of that year, Louis Armstrong played before an enthusiastic audience of 100,000 in the Gold Coast, and trumpeter Dizzy Gillespie received State Department sponsorship to tour Asia and the Middle East with his racially mixed eight-piece jazz orchestra. Gillespie remembered afterward that he "wasn't going over to apologize for the racist policies of America," but he did enjoy dispelling some of his audiences' worst assumptions about the state of race relations in the United States. He recalled how being the black leader of a multiracial band surprised many foreign listeners: "They'd heard about blacks being lynched and burned, and here I come with half whites and blacks and a girl playing in the band. And everybody seemed to be getting along fine."[83]

The Eisenhower administration's strategy of using African Americans as cultural diplomats in the Third World undoubtedly helped create some goodwill abroad, but it also occasionally backfired. This was hardly surprising, given the ambivalence most black Americans felt about their country and its treatment of them. Gillespie and his band found that while they were shown off abroad by the U.S. government, they were often ignored or mistreated at home, as when they were harassed by police in the Atlanta airport for not waiting to board a plane until all white passengers were on board. The news of white treatment of black schoolchildren in Little Rock—and the initially hesitant response of the president—so angered Armstrong that he promptly canceled his much anticipated tour of the Soviet Union for the State Department. He was dismayed by Eisenhower's role in allowing the crisis to develop. When asked by the press about the Russian trip, Armstrong replied: "I'll do it on my own. The people over there ask me what's wrong with my country, what am I supposed to say?" Given the limits on the role black Americans could play in this administration's diplomacy, Henry Cabot Lodge, Jr., suggested to Eisenhower that high-ranking white officials "who are temperamentally so inclined" could be put to great use in Asian and African countries; they could demonstrate that white Americans, unlike Europeans, would not only work with people of color but also would "play with them and treat them as social equals." Lodge concluded that "a certain amount of sociable drinking, dining, dancing and laughing" by elite American policymakers visiting Third World nations would go a long way toward building goodwill for the United States.[84]

Lodge was one of a handful of influential Americans pushing the administration toward a more positive view of an independent Africa by 1956. Republican Congresswoman Frances Bolton of Ohio was another. She toured the continent at the end of 1955 and called for an immediate effort by Americans to overcome their "apathy or ignorance" regarding the continent. A third was the rising critic of the administration's African policy in the Senate, John Kennedy. The most important was probably the vice president, who returned from Ghana in 1957 to recommend paying much more attention to Africa and creating a bureau for African affairs in the State Department in recognition of the continent's new significance. By 1958 Nixon was arguing in the National Security Council for the United States to "take the initiative in encouraging neutralism, which the national independence movements favor, instead of assuming that a neutral is on the Soviet side." Nixon concluded that in place of military or political connections with the West for Africa, the United States should instead promote "educational and cultural ties." NSC note takers recorded the revealing argument of Eisenhower himself in August 1958 that "rather than slow down the independence movement," he would "like to be on the side of the natives for once."[85]

The president was articulating, in his own condescending fashion, the shift in American policy toward Africa that occurred in 1958. The new Bureau of African Affairs created that summer in the State Department initiated the idea of a unified U.S. Africa policy. No longer would the continent be understood primarily through its relationship with Europe. Career diplomat Joseph Satterthwaite filled the new post of assistant secretary of state for African affairs, and, despite his known sympathies for white South Africans and his subsequent ambassadorship to Pretoria, eschewed references to "premature independence" or the priority of America's NATO allies. Instead, the administration focused on countering the Soviet and Chinese diplomatic initiatives on the continent and preventing Communists from posing as the friendly alternative to colonialists. The NSC emphasized the need to avoid letting "thwarted nationalist and self-determinist aspirations" be turned to the Eastern bloc's advantage. The United States could no longer afford to remain behind the curve in its relations with Africa.[86]

On 30 October 1958 the administration signaled another change in its thinking about Africa by voting, for the first time, in favor of a UN resolution condemning South Africa's apartheid policies. Lodge had lobbied for a year in favor of this new position, arguing that the *Brown* decision and the Little Rock crisis had made it "even more important that we express ourselves positively on racial issues." Ambassador Byroade tried afterward to mollify an unhappy South African foreign minister, Eric Louw. When Louw suggested that the change in the U.S. position on apartheid resulted from the United States' anxiety about its own domestic racial conflicts, Byroade conceded that it could "hardly be denied that our problems at home had made more people aware of and think about racial problems than in years of the recent past." By 1959 the United States even voted for a resolution opposing the continuation of racial discrimination anywhere in the world—a remarkable stance in light of Jim Crow's abiding presence in the South at home.[87]

Africa's acquisition of a more positive policy from Washington after 1958 did not mean that Africans had won over the hearts and minds of the Eisenhower administration. Even as they established friendly relations with the new nations of the continent, white American policymakers could not hide their ambivalence about newly independent black people. A 1958 NSC report praised by Eisenhower captured the dilemma for many Americans: "The Spirit of 1776 was running wild," it said—showing American pride in being a model for other nations—but this phenomenon was "rather terrifying" in Africa. Other advisers to the president deplored the "juvenile delinquencies of these new nations," while admitting the need to "cheer for freedom." The NSC referred to "the contagion of the nationalist fever," a disease sure to spread even to the isolated and presumably healthy Portuguese colonies. Part of the problem, as one American official admitted, was the "serious and unnecessary handicap" that burdened the administration because it had "relatively little direct association with Africans, or knowledge of what they are thinking." That lack of information was a direct cost for U.S. foreign policy of the administration's willing participation in racial segregation, both at home and abroad: if one talks only with whites, one can know only what whites think. The extent of this ignorance of Africans among American policymakers as late as 1960 sometimes appeared unlimited: Nixon, the administration's strongest supporter of Africa, announced to a National Security Council meeting in March that "some of the peoples of Africa have been out of the trees for only about fifty years." Budget director Maurice Stans responded that his recent visit to the continent convinced him that "many Africans still belonged in the trees."[88]

While Britain, France, and even Belgium were easing themselves out of most of Africa by the end of Eisenhower's second term, the Portuguese dug in to stay. The U.S. government, as one American diplomat noted in 1955, was "well aware of the oppressive and medieval practices of the Portuguese" in Angola and Mozambique. The same NSC report that Eisenhower praised so highly emphasized how "badly governed and administered" the two colonies were, how common forced labor—that is, slavery—was, how rare educational opportunities of any kind were for Africans, and how "mercilessly" the Portuguese authorities exploited the resources of the area. None of this apparently troubled the president. Fresh from the disappointment of his canceled summit meeting with Khrushchev in Paris in May 1960, he stopped over in Lisbon to an enthusiastic welcome. There Eisenhower praised the "real progress" made by the dictatorship of Antonio Salazar, affirmed that officials from Washington and Lisbon "have worked together without a single difference of opinion," and called for even closer ties between Portugal and the United States in their mutual struggle against Communism. The *New York Times* report of the visit could not help noting the disappointment of Portugal's own persecuted democrats, who watched Eisenhower's appreciation for the Salazar regime provide cover for "the continuing lack of civil liberties, censorship, repression of political activity and police rule" at home in a member nation of NATO.[89]

The experiences of the growing number of African diplomats working and traveling in the United States indicated the tentativeness of the new U.S. warmth toward Africa in the last three years of the Eisenhower administration. High-profile visitors, like Nkrumah and Sekou Touré of Guinea, were carefully shielded by their American handlers from chance encounters with venomous white racism. Others were less fortunate, especially along the Maryland and Delaware sections of the corridor between New York and Washington. The eviction of Ghanaian finance minister H. A. Gbedemah from a Howard Johnson restaurant in Dover on 9 October 1957 received considerable publicity, coming as it did at the height of the Little Rock crisis.

Eisenhower acted swiftly to make amends by inviting Gbedemah to the White House for breakfast. But the ease with which any white American could embarrass the U.S. government in this way was striking. Whether in Baltimore, Charlottesville, Houston, or elsewhere, white American citizens frequently failed to hide the feelings they shared with their vice president and president about people of color and wound up insulting African visitors. The swiftness of the administration's response to such incidents mollified many black diplomats from abroad, but the contrast between Eisenhower's concern for the treatment of foreigners of color and his seeming indifference to the treatment of Americans of color raised doubts about his sincerity. African Americans were both amused and disturbed to see white officials suddenly fawning on dark-skinned foreigners while keeping mum on Jim Crow for the home folks.[90]

### 1960: The Challenge Intensifies

During Eisenhower's final year as president, three major challenges arose to the American hope for a multiracial, postcolonial Western alliance against the Communist bloc. The first was the Sharpeville massacre that completed the racial polarization of South Africa; the second was the crisis of national disintegration that followed the Congo's independence; and the third was the campaign of Cuban president Fidel Castro against U.S. leadership, waged partly along racial lines. All of these emerged against the domestic backdrop of the student sit-in movement that began on 1 February in Greensboro, North Carolina, and spread rapidly throughout the South. African American resistance to segregation at home thus increased hand-in-hand with the Third World struggle for racial equality. Phaon Goldman noted in the *Negro History Bulletin* in the fall of 1960 that much of the students' inspiration came from African nationalists "who recognize that the 'go slow' school of moderates didn't tell the Hungarians and Tibetans [in their rebellions against the Soviet Union and China] to 'go slow' and they don't want to hear it either." Four black residents of Haughton, Louisiana, distilled the problem for Eisenhower in a letter in January. Citing the denial of their right to vote and the campaign of terror against African Americans throughout much of the South, they told the president: "This country can no longer be a leader of the free world and speak for freedom when its citizens suffer as we do."[91]

On 21 March 1960 police in the small town of Sharpeville opened fire on a peaceful crowd protesting the apartheid pass laws for nonwhites, killing sixty-nine—many of them shot in the back—and wounding over two hundred. So began a major turn in South African history. The outraged black response led to the banning of political organizations opposed to apartheid. With all forms of protest against white supremacy now illegal, the ANC and other black groups went underground and took up weapons for the first time. U.S. ambassador Philip Crowe reported home that the radicalization of Africans in South Africa in the days after the massacre had created "a dangerous and explosive situation" in which African leaders "no longer are thinking of very gradual revolution some time in the future." CIA chief Allen Dulles shared with the National Security Council his discouragement about the increasingly remote prospects of a negotiated settlement of the South African racial conflict. He saw only trouble ahead: "Especially after the Congo becomes independent [in three months], there would be great opportunities for smuggling arms to the natives of South Africa."[92]

The confused response of the Eisenhower administration to the Sharpeville killings demonstrated its uncertainty about how to accommodate rising racial egalitarianism while protecting America's perceived interests abroad. Typically, the U.S. government avoided critical comment on internal events in other countries, especially friendly ones. But the slaughter at Sharpeville seemed too egregious for the United States to have "no comment." Without checking first with their superiors, State Department officials released a mild statement of "regret" at what had happened and of hope that Africans would be allowed to use peaceful means to "obtain redress for legitimate grievances" in South Africa. Many black South Africans and other opponents of apartheid were encouraged, believing that the world's greatest power was at last on their side. Lodge reported the "unanimous thanks" coming in at the United Nations from Asian and African delegates. But Eisenhower and Secretary of State Christian Herter, Dulles's successor, were furious. The president insisted on an apology to the South African ambassador—though "this action should be kept secret"—and told Herter that if it were his choice, he would fire the bureau chief responsible for the statement. Herter was especially troubled by such criticism "on a subject which not only has world-wide interest, but also involves domestic political factors." In a discussion with British prime minister Macmillan a few days later, Eisenhower emphasized his sympathy with white South Africans and their "difficult social and political problem"; it reminded the president of his good wishes for his "friends in Atlanta on some of their difficulties."[93]

In addition to having sympathetic feelings toward white South Africans and perceived vital economic and military interests, American policymakers believed pragmatically that the apartheid regime was not about to crumble in the face of rising dissent. When asked by an audience in Ann Arbor, Michigan, a few months earlier what he predicted for the future of South Africa, Kenyan labor leader Tom Mboya had responded simply: "Black." Washington's view would have been "black eventually, white for now." At the first NSC meeting after the news from Sharpeville arrived, Allen Dulles affirmed that South African authorities "would probably be able to maintain order for some time"—a period the CIA calculated as at least the next few years. An NSC analysis of Africa two months earlier had underlined the "resiliency" of the South African economy, with its vast gold reserves and industrial diversification. Confronted with this situation, and given U.S. strategic and economic interests in the region, including plans for a new missile tracking station on South African soil, the Eisenhower administration chose to maintain its close relationship with the masters of apartheid.[94]

The next crisis of 1960 with strong racial overtones unfolded three months later a little further north on the African continent. Belgium's unexpectedly swift withdrawal from the Congo left that vast new nation on the verge of disintegration after its 30 June independence ceremonies. The mineral heartland of Katanga province immediately seceded, under the leadership of anti-Communist Moise Tshombe and with considerable help from Belgian mining corporations, along with Belgian citizens and soldiers. Prime Minister Patrice Lumumba, a man of neutralist and socialist inclinations, stood firmly for national unity. He called for outside assistance—first from the UN, and later from the Soviets—in opposing the Belgian-backed effort to detach the wealthiest part of the brand new country. Eisenhower's goals in this crisis were twofold and somewhat contradictory: to preserve Western access to Katangan minerals (for which Tshombe was the best instrument), and to maintain a unified Congo with a central government oriented more to the West than the East (for which Lumumba was probably the best instrument). Belgium emphasized the first goal. The United States gave priority to the second, while keeping both options open. With the Soviets eager to intervene as a way to jump-start their influence on the continent, the Cold War thus came to Africa in the same year that the civil rights movement embarked on a newly mobilized campaign in the United States.[95]

The Eisenhower administration decided within two months of Congolese independence and the beginning of the political crisis there to remove

Lumumba from power. State Department officials were at first hesitant to adopt such a radical view of American needs in central Africa. Throughout July and well into August, U.S. diplomats in the Congo and their superiors at Foggy Bottom believed Lumumba was "an opportunist and not a Communist." They saw him as a neutral African nationalist. They were impressed with his leadership skills and believed there was "no better alternative on the horizon than a government built around him." But Lumumba was determined to drive out the Belgian forces defending secessionist Katanga, and his willingness to ask the Soviets for assistance after a slow initial response from the UN brought a sharp change in the United States' attitude. In late July Allen Dulles told Eisenhower that Lumumba was "a Castro or worse" who "has been bought by the Communists." The American ambassador in Leopoldville, Clare Timberlake, began referring to the "evil" Congolese prime minister as "Lumumbavitch." In the frigid Cold War climate of mid-1960, amid the Laos and Cuban crises, the downing of the American U-2 plane, and the cancellation of the Paris summit, the president was taking no chances. He apparently granted permission to the CIA in late August to try to eliminate Lumumba.[96]

The discussions within the Eisenhower administration that surrounded the decision to try to kill Lumumba revealed an array of American anxieties about this proud African nationalist. Foremost was white Americans' resentment of what they saw as the Congolese leader's ingratitude to the departing Belgians. The American press had reported favorably on Belgian rule in central Africa during most of the 1950s. "Nowhere in Africa is the Bantu so well fed and housed, so productive and so content as he is in the Belgian Congo," *Time* effused in 1955; thanks to Western technological improvements, "the sons of cannibals now mine the raw materials of the Atomic Age." Eisenhower's closeness to King Baudoin of Belgium made him unlikely to appreciate Lumumba's refusal to offer humble or even polite words at the new nation's independence ceremonies. "We are no longer your monkeys!" the prime minister declared. "We have known ironies, insults, and blows which we had to undergo morning, noon, and night because we were Negroes." This was precisely the kind of language that the American president was already hearing more than enough of across the American South in 1960. Lumumba concluded in that speech that the Congolese would not forget the deaths and imprisonment at Belgian hands of countrymen who resisted "a regime of injustice, suppression, and exploitation."[97]

This flagrant lack of appreciation for the benefits of Belgian colonial rule suggested to some in the Eisenhower administration that Lumumba might not even be mentally competent. This was a major question for American policymakers who dealt with the Congo. During Lumumba's visit to the UN on 26 July 1960, Lodge found him "a little flighty and erratic" but someone who "knows exactly what he is doing" and, overall, "not a bad man to deal with." Lumumba also made fairly positive impressions on several State Department officials in Washington and on Averill Harriman during the latter's tour of the Congo on behalf of presidential candidate John Kennedy.[98] But most of the administration viewed the Congolese prime minister differently. Undersecretary of State Douglas Dillon judged him "impossible to deal with" and "just not a rational being"; Herter agreed with Secretary General Dag Hammarskjold of the UN that Lumumba was "definitely a dope fiend"; Ralph Bunche declared him "crazy"; and Allen Dulles concluded that Lumumba's actions "indicate that he is insane." The leap from mental debility to witchcraft followed swiftly. Dillon agreed with the assessment of Pierre Wigny, the Belgian foreign minister, that Lumumba was "a sorcerer" who could entrance the Congolese parliament, and the U.S. ambassador to Belgium, William Burden, referred to an upcoming meeting with him as a seance. This was demonization in its most literal sense.[99]

Ingratitude and insanity combined with one other issue that stirred the men of the Eisenhower administration: sexual intercourse between black men and white women. During the first weeks of the Congo crisis, which was initiated by the mutiny of Congolese soldiers against their Belgian officers, reports began reaching the United States of Congolese troops raping white women, including nuns. Stimulated by press coverage of the reports and detailed accounts given to the UN Security Council by an outraged Belgian foreign minister, this issue became, in the words of a State Department memorandum, the "continuing preoccupation" of the White House and the State Department. The passion and fascination with which the subject was discussed within the administration finally drove one State Department official to remind his superior in writing that "the UN did not go into the Congo to save white women from being raped." Southern segregationists shared the horror of the administration and were explicit about where they thought desegregation would lead. Conflating Africans with African Americans, white supremacist organizer Leander Perez told a segregationist Citizens Council meeting in New Orleans that fall: "Don't wait for your daughter to be raped by these Congolese. Don't wait until the burr-heads are forced into your schools. Do something about it now."[100]

Suspected of being a dupe of the Soviets and nominally responsible for the apparent sexual atrocities of Congolese troops, Lumumba helped seal his fate with the Eisenhower administration during his one visit to Washington by asking his State Department liaison, Thomas Cassilly, to procure him a blonde companion for the night in Blair House. The request was turned over to the CIA, which satisfied it, and was duly reported to the White House. Eisenhower and his advisers were outraged. Sympathetic to the Soviets, antiwhite, ungrateful, probably insane, head of a nation of black rapists, and now lusting after blonde American women: Lumumba seemed to represent everything wrong about African independence. The extreme licentiousness of certain American political leaders, such as the Democratic presidential candidate that year, was not used as a standard for judging Lumumba—not when the issue was seen as race. The only historical analogy left for white Americans to call on in viewing the Congo leader was that of a slave revolt. Budget director Maurice Stans provided this comparison in an August NSC meeting when he argued that it was "the objective of Lumumba to drive the whites out and take over their property." The oldest and deepest fear of white Americans seemed to be coming true on the international stage in the midst of the Cold War: Patrice Lumumba was Nat Turner.[101]

Eisenhower liked Lumumba even less than Nasser, and he disapproved of the Belgians for creating a problem in the Congo similar to that of the British and French at Suez. The Congolese Force Publique mutiny had begun 6 July after Belgian officers made it clear that independence would have no effect on their control of the army. One general, for example, wrote on a black-board in front of his troops: "After independence = before independence." Once Belgium sent in military reinforcements to protect Belgian lives and defend Katanga's secession, Eisenhower reluctantly supported UN military intervention in the Congo to reestablish order, hasten the evacuation of Belgian forces, and end Katanga's would-be independence. Belgian behavior had called attention to the racial coding of the conflict in the Congo—just as white Southerners had done with their massive resistance campaign at home—and the administration was eager to avoid further racial polarization that could only hurt the West and benefit the Soviets. Eisenhower insisted that the UN troops going to the Congo not be white, but preferably African or at least Asian or Middle Eastern. Ambassador Timberlake reported from Leopoldville that some Belgian soldiers were shooting civilians in the streets without provocation. The Belgians, he concluded with dismay, "have become completely irrational and in many instances have behaved worse than the worst Congolese." Supposedly traditional racial roles were once again not holding up. American policymakers feared that Belgians determined to remain in an independent Katanga were opening another front in the white settler problem of Africa, like the situations in Algeria, Kenya, Rhodesia, and South Africa.[102]

Tensions along racial lines between First and Third Worlds in 1960 were pointed up by one other international incident: Fidel Castro's ten-day stay at Harlem's Hotel Theresa while attending the September session of the United Nations. The Eisenhower administration's initial view of the revolutionary Cuban leader and his associates as needing to be treated "more or less like children," in Allen Dulles's words, had darkened considerably by this point, as Cuba's relationship with the Soviet Union warmed. Castro responded to U.S. hostility in part by using race as a weapon. Though phenotypically "white" himself, his racially egalitarian government was popular with Afro-Cubans, who constituted a substantial minority of the island's population. Castro equated and denounced the racial prejudices of many of Cuba's counterrevolutionary elites and of white American Southerners, abetted by the U.S. government's disinterest. When the somewhat bohemian Cuban entourage met with hostile treatment at the plush Shelbourne Hotel in New York, the traditional lodging for prerevolutionary Cuban diplomats, Castro sought a public relations coup against the Eisenhower administration. He briefly considered camping in Central Park and then seized on the idea of staying in Harlem to highlight American racism and Cuba's greater commitment to racial equality.[103]

Castro's sojourn in Harlem proved a triple success in racial terms: it improved his standing among Afro-Cubans, black Americans, and Africans. Harlem residents, regardless of their views of the Cuban revolution, appreciated the global attention their neighborhood received, as world leaders like Khrushchev, Nehru, and Nasser came up to 125th Street to meet with Castro. Black Americans applauded the Cuban leader's opposition to racial discrimination and savored his explicit challenge to white American authority. They enjoyed the prominent place in the Cuban delegation accorded to the black army chief of staff, Major Juan Almeida, in an era when Americans could hardly dream of General Colin Powell's comparable stature thirty years later. Castro also met with Malcolm X and discussed their common support for Third World independence from white control. In his five-hour speech to the UN General Assembly, the Cuban leader stressed his country's support for Lumumba in the Congo crisis and for African self-rule throughout the continent. He emphasized the parallels between Cuba and the Congo, as both emerged from rule by racially discriminatory elites, whether pro-American white Cubans or colonialist Belgians. He and Lumumba also shared the unenviable status of being targeted for elimination by the CIA. In this widely publicized visit, Castro challenged the idea of U.S. leadership in a predominantly nonwhite world. By putting race at the center of his message, he pinpointed America's greatest weakness in the Cold War.[104]

FOR EIGHT YEARS Dwight Eisenhower presided over a nation undergoing, like the larger world around it, fundamental change in its race relations. Both at home and abroad, people of color mobilized in the late 1950s to overcome racial discrimination and colonialism. Most whites resisted this challenge to their traditional authority. Whether in the American South, in the settler communities of Africa, or in the metropolitan governments in Western Europe, they worked to build bulwarks against the rising tide of equality, independence, and desegregation. It was the unique historical opportunity of the Eisenhower administration to wield power at a turning point in national and global relations. How the administration performed in these difficult circumstances says much about Eisenhower's leadership and wisdom, as issues of race pervaded the politics and diplomacy of the 1950s.

The president and his advisers were astute, sophisticated men, as two decades of "Eisenhower revisionist" scholarship have now made clear. Recognizing at least some of the political costs of Western white racism in the Cold War, they took a few symbolic steps to accommodate the new realities of a changing global racial order, like desegregating Washington's public spaces and trying to avoid close identification with segregationism or colonialism. A few members of the administration, like UN ambassador Lodge, openly supported desegregation and swift decolonization. The administration as a whole was quicker to acknowledge change abroad than at home, as the reality of African independence forced its hand in a way that the still developing civil rights movement at home could not yet do. Most notable, American policymakers showed their frustration with short-sighted white resistance in the crises at Suez, at Little Rock, and in the Congo, which required the president to align himself—briefly and somewhat uncomfortably—with Third World and African American causes. These three incidents marked the high points of the administration's efforts to contain racial hostilities and co-opt demands for racial equality.

But Eisenhower and those closest to him also remained in part blinded by their nostalgia for the stability of the white-ruled era now slipping away. They consistently refused to demonstrate almost any sympathy for black Americans or Africans in struggles for liberation. Put off by even the supremely polite, respectful behavior of early civil rights organizers like King, they could hardly imagine the perspective of those promoting armed self-defense by the late 1950s, like Malcolm X of the Nation of Islam or Robert Williams of the Monroe, North Carolina, chapter of the NAACP. Yet those voices only grew louder and more numerous after 1960, as did those in southern Africa calling for armed struggle to overcome the entrenched forces of white supremacy there.[105]

# 4

# REVOLUTIONS IN THE AMERICAN SOUTH
# AND SOUTHERN AFRICA

THE BRIEF PRESIDENCY of John F. Kennedy spanned a period of intensifying change and conflict in race relations around the globe. Hard-won African independence rolled south from the Mediterranean Sea in these years, halting only at the Zambezi River by the time of the young president's death in 1963, while segregation in the United States faced unprecedented challenges. The epicenters of racial tension lay in the American South and southern Africa, as the expanding civil rights movement encountered increasingly violent white resistance in the United States, and armed insurgencies replaced nonviolent protests against white rule in Angola and South Africa. Faced with the beginnings of the final chapter in the world struggle against legal white supremacy, Secretary of State Dean Rusk acknowledged in 1961 that the Kennedy administration confronted the "historical problem of coming into some reasonable relationship with [the] non-white world."[1]

Previous presidents had largely been able to avoid the escalating racial conflicts at home and abroad. Much as he might have wished to, Kennedy did not have this option. "The time comes in the life of any nation when there remain only two choices: submit or fight," the African National Congress announced on 16 December 1961, as it initiated its campaign of sabotage against government buildings. "That time has now come to South Africa." Angolans had made the same choice ten months earlier, taking up weapons against their Portuguese colonial masters just three weeks after Kennedy took the oath of office. In the form of Freedom Rides and peaceful mass mobilizations across the American South, that time had also come to the United States in 1961. Both Africans and African Americans were determined

to make the U.S. government take sides in struggles that seemed to them utterly clear in their moral justice and world historical in their political
significance. This was their "Cold War" against racial inequality: replete with
the same full measure of righteousness and clarity that Kennedy and other
Cold Warriors saw in their own conflict with Communism. Just as anti-
Communists disdained or mistrusted neutralism regarding the Soviet Union,
antiracists, the Central Intelligence Agency reported to the White House,
saw "no room for nonalignment in this dispute."[2]

There was also little room for avoiding the dispute. Intensifying racial
conflict threatened a crucial tenet of Kennedy's foreign policy: what the State
Department called "the global U.S. strategy of fostering a cooperative community of free nations across the North-South dividing lines of race and
wealth." That strategy of preserving a unified "free world" alliance of the First
World and the Third World was integral, not peripheral, to the American
policy of containing Soviet and Communist influence in the early 1960s, as
Kennedy's unprecedented attention to the nations of the Third World indicated. Conversely, Rusk argued, Moscow would "make the most of its opportunity to develop divisions within the free world and to be the champion of
the colored races—the same old game." Since the death of Stalin in 1953 and
the start of European withdrawal from Africa a few years later, Soviet leaders
had begun to show greater interest in expanding their influence south of the
Mediterranean. The secretary of state concluded that any encouragement of
racial strife "would enhance Sino-Soviet Bloc opportunities in Africa" and diminish American unity at home.[3]

Kennedy entered the White House after campaigning on a platform that
supported domestic civil rights and African independence. After eight years
of Dwight Eisenhower's coolness toward their cause, antiracists greeted the
new administration with optimism. But Kennedy and his advisers had first to
carry out their primary mission: winning the Cold War. For that purpose the
president believed he needed the support of both black Americans and white
Americans, both Africans and Europeans. To secure this support, the administration pursued greater racial equality, but it tried to do so without alienating either side. Finessing their differences was the key, and compromise and
the diminution of conflict were the preferred tactics. While the new African
nations sought to "make us choose between Portugal and South Africa, on
the one hand, and the rest of Africa, on the other," White House aide Arthur
Schlesinger, Jr., reminded Attorney General Robert Kennedy, "we wish to
evade that choice." The strategy of evading the choice was precisely the same

at home, where civil rights workers in the South pushed the administration to support either them or their opponents. The president needed white Southerners as well as African Americans and their liberal white supporters in the Democratic Party, and he was determined to avoid having to choose between them.[4]

Southern Africa and the American South were the two places where the global problem of racial conflict was intensifying most dangerously in the early 1960s. The nations of the Third World, newly prominent in the United Nations and a central concern of the Kennedy administration in its competition with the Soviet Union, watched these two "Souths" for signs of the true intentions of the U.S. government. Would the United States and its new president lead as a multiracial model in a world arching toward greater racial justice? Or would they instead continue as a defender of white privilege in the international system? These questions went to the core of American national identity in a global community.

## The Kennedy Administration and Racial Change

Alone among Democratic presidents since 1945, John Kennedy entered the White House without strong personal feelings about civil rights and racial discrimination. The others—Harry Truman, Lyndon Johnson, Jimmy Carter, and Bill Clinton—all came from former slaveholding states, and in their different ways each wrestled with problems of race and took clear stands against Jim Crow before their ascension to the presidency. The lone Northern Democrat in the Oval Office during the Cold War, Kennedy came from a background of great privilege in nearly all-white Massachusetts. Like the rest of his family, he knew few African Americans and had little sense of the impact of the color bar on their lives. By 1961 the only black person he had spent significant time with was George Thomas, his personal valet.[5]

Inexperience does not necessarily imply prejudice, however, and Kennedy as president surprised many with his complete personal ease around people of color in social settings. The generational contrast with his predecessor in the White House seemed to show up here more clearly than anywhere else. While Dwight Eisenhower's attitudes had been formed earlier in the century, people of Kennedy's age were dramatically affected by World War II and the ways it delegitimated white supremacy. His own experience of prejudice against Roman Catholics may also have disinclined him to discriminate blindly against others. Civil rights activist James Meredith was not far from the mark in remembering later that, in personal terms, Kennedy was the first American president who was not a racist.[6]

Even so, he did not automatically take the side of antiracists in the political conflicts of the early 1960s. The president and his brother Robert shared a mistrust of moralistic idealism and of the liberals they associated with it; they saw themselves instead as cool-headed pragmatists. As he had done in the Senate, the president hoped to keep both black and white Southerners reasonably satisfied with him, while focusing on his higher priority of stopping Soviet expansionism around the world. This was a political strategy not much different, ironically, from that of Eisenhower. But the accelerating conflict in the South did not allow Kennedy to avoid the issue as much as his predecessor had, and by 1963 he was forced to take sides.[7]

The pattern was similar abroad. Kennedy had built a reputation in the Senate as a critic of European colonialism, even while staunchly defending America's alliance with Western Europe. As president he seemed to take a strong interest in the new nations and peoples of Africa, inviting twenty-eight heads of state from the continent to visit him in the White House. Africans appreciated his attentions—so much so that the National Security Council recognized that America's "one important asset" in dealing with Africa was "the President's status and personal relations" with leaders there, "on which we can draw heavily." Like the presence of unprecedented numbers of African Americans in his administration, Kennedy's ease with people of color abroad had great symbolic value. Thus he pursued close ties with both First and Third Worlds, working to mediate their differences just as he did those of white and black Southerners at home.[8]

What especially roused the president's ire about both segregation and colonialism was the hindrance they caused to the struggle against Communism. Such forms of racial discrimination were anachronistic and deeply irrational to a modernist like Kennedy: wastes of emotion, energy, and time. In a life-and-death struggle with the Soviet Union, and with the loyalties of the vast Third World in the balance, he had difficulty understanding the shortsightedness of white supremacists. Kennedy strongly hoped not to have to force desegregation on those who would resist it, but he considered such matters as sitting next to people of different skin colors a requirement of public civility in the modern world.[9]

The 1960 presidential campaign reflected these concerns. Kennedy had started out as the weakest Democratic candidate on civil rights, but he moved quickly to a more active stance. In doing so he represented the broader shift of the center of the Democratic Party away from an accommodation of its white segregationist Southern element, the latter having failed to put a dent in Eisenhower's two victorious campaigns. Republican candidate Richard Nixon took the opposite tack, moving to a less liberal civil rights stance with appeals to white Southern voters in a partial preview of his 1968 "Southern strategy."[10] Kennedy won a narrow electoral victory, in no small part by maintaining more effectively than Nixon a delicate balancing act about race. On one hand, he intervened to help get Martin Luther King, Jr., released from a Georgia prison and spoke repeatedly on the campaign stump about Africa, as a way to appeal to black and liberal voters in Northern cities without threatening white Southerners. On the other hand, he used the support of his running mate, Lyndon Johnson, and other white Southern officials to win back Louisiana and the key state of Texas, which the Republicans had taken in 1956.[11] The international context of this racially charged campaign was obvious to both camps, as Kennedy and Republican vice presidential candidate Henry Cabot Lodge, Jr., competed in calls for an end to racial discrimination to win the friendship of the new African nations. The awareness of the international arena had helped drive the effort to free King, whose sentence to months of hard labor for a minor traffic offense was, as Robert Kennedy put it, "making our country look ridiculous before the world."[12]

In his first press statement after the close election of 1960, Kennedy sought to pacify conservatives by announcing that the directors of the FBI and the CIA would continue in their positions. This gesture built into the bureaucratic structure of the new administration the staunch hostility of J. Edgar Hoover to the civil rights movement at home and of Allen Dulles to Third World nationalism abroad. Bureau agents in the American South and agency operatives in southern Africa proved extremely "soft" on racism in their common quest to root out Communist subversives. Their priorities made them insensitive to racism's corrupting influence on civil society. The CIA worked closely with South African security forces, and Hoover became obsessed by 1963 with discrediting the civil rights movement and especially King. The performance of these powerful security bureaucracies did not always satisfy Kennedy and his advisers, but their control of classified information about political activists and revolutionaries (and about the president himself) gave them considerable influence on a White House focused above all on the Cold War.[13]

The new administration respected Kennedy's long-standing ties to the white South and the power of its representatives in Congress, particularly the Senate. The political struggle in the South in the early 1960s over racial equality was essentially an intra–Democratic Party contest, and a Democratic president with a narrow margin of victory felt he had to work both sides of the street. From his Senate days Kennedy had personal links to white Southern leaders, like George Smathers of Florida, and was naturally inclined to see other prominent figures in his own party as reasonable people he could work with. Southern Democrats chaired the majority of congressional committees, exerting enormous influence on the legislative process; in combination with Republicans on many domestic issues, they functioned as the real majority party. Their control of federal funding created roadblocks even for such symbolic executive initiatives as desegregating the National Guard. From appointments of segregationist judges to the federal bench in the South to a refusal for more than two years to press for civil rights legislation, the president made real efforts to accommodate the rulers of Dixie.[14]

There were limits to that accommodation, of course, as his choice of a secretary of state showed. For an administration so concerned about foreign affairs and so vulnerable to criticism regarding American racial discrimination, there was no more symbolic appointment. Kennedy personally favored the chair of the Senate Foreign Relations Committee, J. William Fulbright, but the Arkansan's domestic segregationist voting record made him unacceptable—clear evidence of how much had changed in sixteen years, since South Carolina's more enthusiastically segregationist James Byrnes had been easily appointed Truman's secretary of state.[15] White Southerners with traditional racial attitudes were no longer qualified to represent the United States to an outside world that was mostly nonwhite.

The president instead pulled an end run around this dilemma, choosing a racial liberal from the Deep South whose grandfathers had both served in the Confederate Army, native Georgian Dean Rusk. Rusk wielded his geographical and cultural roots with aplomb, reminding Southern senators during a testy public exchange on racial discrimination's effects on American foreign relations that he was at least as "Southern" as they were. When Strom Thurmond asked, "Mr. Secretary, aren't you lending support to the communist line?" Rusk dissented indignantly, noting that he spoke as the American secretary of state. "Mr. Secretary," Thurmond persisted, "I'm not sure that you understood my question. I am from South Carolina." "Senator," replied Rusk, "I understood your question. I am from Georgia."[16] The secretary of state early on declared American racism to be "the biggest single burden that we carry on our backs in foreign relations," and he helped the president try to counteract it with symbolic gestures like sending the first black American ambassadors to European countries.[17]

While juggling competing loyalties to white Southerners and to civil rights supporters, the administration had to contend with a deep division between traditional, Eurocentric Cold Warriors, concerned with the fate of European colonial empires abroad, and advocates of greater attention to the emerging nations of the Third World. What the NSC called the "very bloody struggle" within the State Department between Africanists and Europeanists represented at an institutional level the president's own personal ambivalence about this problem.[18] Undersecretary of State Chester Bowles led the forces attuned to the Third World, and his replacement by Europeanist George Ball in November 1961 represented a turning point in the administration's orientation. Bowles had written the civil rights plank for Kennedy's campaign platform, and his supporters were dismayed at the signal that his removal would send both to nonwhite nations abroad and to racial liberals within the Democratic Party. White House civil rights adviser Harris Wofford warned Kennedy that this change would encourage the numerous racists in the State Department and undercut the president's own warmer policy toward Africa. "You need someone," Wofford concluded, "who, from the time he wakes up in the morning until he goes to sleep, knows that the Cuban invasion is wrong and that our new position on Angola is right."[19]

Instead, the administration began shifting its attentions away from the concerns of Third World nations, who had "names like typographical errors," in Ball's words, and whose leaders were "over-sensitive," according to the NSC's Robert Komer, or in the case of Arabs "rug merchants," as the State Department's William Bundy put it.[20] Removed from his influential position in the State Department and shunted off to the Third World as the president's special representative and adviser on African, Asian, and Latin American affairs, Bowles regretted that Kennedy's "principal advisers on foreign policy were heavily oriented towards Europe" and the Soviet Union.[21] This reassertion of Cold War thinking within policymaking circles encouraged the NSC in its argument that the continuing decolonization of Africa was now making Soviet-dominated Eastern Europe by far the largest bloc of unfree peoples in the world. Europe, not Africa, could now be the proper focus of world concern for national independence and self-determination.[22]

## *Kennedy, the Third World, and Africa*

John Kennedy's foreign policy combined a fierce anti-Communism with an unusual interest in the emerging nations of the Third World. His commitment to West Berlin during the wall-building crisis of August 1961 indicated the centrality of Western Europe in his strategic thinking, while his recognition of the power of nationalism and the weakness of colonialism marked his presidency as a time of change in U.S. relations with the world outside Europe. He and his advisers were determined to be both more successful in containing the expansion of Soviet influence and more sensitive to the nonwhite world's concerns than Eisenhower had been. "The great battleground for the defense and expansion of freedom today," Kennedy told Congress in May 1961, "is the whole southern half of the globe—Asia, Latin America, Africa, and the Middle East, the lands of the rising peoples."[23] The administration created the Peace Corps as a way of recognizing and addressing the growing importance of the North-South axis of tension in world affairs. This was a racially coded axis, as Sargent Shriver, the Peace Corps's first director and the president's brother-in-law, emphasized: a division "between the white minority and the colored majority of the human race."[24] The choice of Shriver for the position reflected Kennedy's awareness of the importance of race in American relations with the Third World, as Shriver had a long history of involvement in the national Catholic interracial movement and was the most liberal member of the Kennedy clan—"the house Communist," as others liked to call him on occasion.[25]

Real Communists, usually of the Soviet and Chinese varieties, created or exacerbated the most pressing problems in the Third World, according to the Kennedy administration.[26] One reason for establishing the Peace Corps, the president explained, was to counteract the overseas work of Eastern bloc professionals—doctors, engineers, nurses, teachers—who served as "missionaries for international communism."[27] Khrushchev and Mao seemed to compete with each other in their support for "wars of national liberation" in remaining colonial areas, to Kennedy's chagrin. The State Department warned that "the Communist Bloc will continue to fish in troubled African waters" and feared that the Chinese "may be in a particularly strong position [there] on grounds of race."[28] Kennedy worried that Beijing's efforts at promoting its leadership of the non-European world would intensify further with its imminent acquisition of nuclear weapons.[29] By contrast, racial considerations would not likely be a source of strength for the United States. American military commanders trying to stem the Communist-led insurgency in South Vietnam were leery of using U.S. combat troops in part because it might "stir up [a] big fuss throughout Asia about [the] reintroduction of forces of white colonialism" into Indochina, as Admiral Harry Felt explained to General Maxwell Taylor in October 1961.[30]

Kennedy's stiffest competition for African friendships may in some ways have come from a less likely source, much closer to home. Fidel Castro, like Kennedy in his presidential campaign, began courting African sympathies in 1960. Castro's personal challenge to Kennedy as another new world leader of youth, vigor, virility, athleticism, and idealism, but also anticapitalism, has long been noted. It has been less well remarked that the Cuban revolutionary's words and actions also challenged and, in fact, surpassed those of the American president on matters of racial equality and African independence.[31] The revolution's commitment to ending racial discrimination had made it especially popular among the island's large Afro-Cuban population. Castro's increasing attention to Africa may have been in part a way of gratifying Afro-Cuban supporters while sidestepping the difficult task of fully eradicating traditional white Cuban racism—based on precisely the same logic as Richard Mahoney's argument about Kennedy's attention to Africa during the campaign as a way to please African Americans while not provoking white Southerners.[32] Regardless of Castro's personal motivations, however, his pursuit of diplomatic ties with African nations and his enthusiastic support for Patrice Lumumba in the Congo and for antiracist guerillas in the white redoubt of southern Africa were warmly appreciated south of the Mediterranean. In Washington, such initiatives and his increasingly close relationship with Moscow were instead deeply resented.[33]

Revolutionary Cuba's identification with the cause of international racial equality deepened the hostility of Third World reactions to the failed invasion at the Bay of Pigs in April 1961. Few African or Asian delegates at the UN shared the Kennedy administration's view of the Havana government as illegitimate. On the contrary, they were generally pleased when Robert Williams, a U.S. Army veteran and civil rights activist, sent a telegram to the UN denouncing the contrast between U.S. actions in the Caribbean and inaction in the American South.[34] When Williams fled North Carolina five months later to avoid being lynched by a white mob, he was given asylum in Havana. There he began broadcasting a twice weekly radio program across the Florida straits under the clever title *Radio Free Dixie,* encouraging armed African American rebellion. Williams appears to have been one of the few observers of the early 1960s to highlight explicitly the parallel between black Americans in the Jim Crow South and Eastern Europeans under Soviet-backed rule. While in Cuba he also established close contacts with other antiracist liberation fighters such as the South African ANC representative Ambrose Makiwane.[35]

Despite his radicalism, Williams was not alone among black Americans in his reading of the racial meanings of the contest between Havana and Washington. A wide range of African American intellectuals and political commentators, in contrast to the anti-Cuban hostility that pervaded the white media, associated the Bay of Pigs invasion with racist elements in the U.S. government, particularly the CIA.[36] Just as Southern segregationists were especially enthusiastic in their loathing for Castro, South Africa was the sole African nation to support the U.S.-backed invasion.[37] Few observers could miss the racial symbolism that Cuba and its chief antagonist seemed to be acting out, even if they did not know of the CIA's ongoing efforts to assassinate Castro and simultaneous collaboration with South African security forces.[38] Here we find one of the roots of Cuba's assistance to Angolan rebels against South African invaders in 1975.

The relationship of the United States to Africa would ultimately be determined not by the actions of America's rivals like Cuba or the Soviet Union but by the United States itself. Kennedy was the first American president to face fully the new reality of African independence. It has long been observed that his administration initially paid considerable attention to the continent and sought to accommodate radical nationalism there, but that subsequently a less sympathetic anti-Communism and neglect came to pervade Kennedy's Africa policies as the Cold War heated up in Berlin, Indochina, and Cuba.[39] Kennedy undoubtedly created much goodwill among Africans for the United States. This had begun with his support for Algerian independence in 1957; it had continued with his attentions to the continent during the 1960 campaign; it was boosted by his appointment of a strong cadre of Africanists to staff the African bureau in the State Department, led by Assistant Secretary of State G. Mennen ("Soapy") Williams; and it was sustained by the president's personal attention to African diplomats and visiting heads of state, and by his growing commitment to civil rights.[40] Several times Williams toured the continent, where his declaration that "Africa is for the Africans" was not well received by white settlers and colonial officials. When asked about the statement at a press conference, Kennedy's response—"I don't know who else it would be for"—underlined the sense among many Africans that an American president was finally on their side.[41]

Nevertheless, the Kennedy administration's interest in improving U.S. relations with Africa never approached the level of its commitment to American political, strategic, and economic priorities in Europe and East Asia. South of the Sahara, there were no equivalents to NATO or to U.S. trade and investment relationships with Europe or the Pacific rim. The discovery of alternative sources had reduced American dependence on African strategic minerals since the Korean War, and U.S. trade with the continent remained relatively minor. "From a global perspective," Pentagon planners concluded in 1963, "Africa is not an area of primary strategic importance to the US, and we therefore have a strong interest in restricting our involvement" there. In other words, there would be no strategic airlifts, à la Berlin, to sustain the besieged citizens of Soweto in their struggle with totalitarianism, nor would there be any counterinsurgent campaigns, as in Indochina, to contain the expanding influence of apartheid in Southern Rhodesia.[42]

The degree of intimacy that the Kennedy administration developed with the new nations of Africa was ultimately limited by the differences between African and U.S. perspectives and priorities. For Americans in the early 1960s, Africa was what the State Department called "probably the greatest open field of maneuver in the world-wide competition between the [Communist] Bloc and the non-Communist world."[43] Not surprisingly, Africans did not tend to see their countries as an "open field" for anything. Instead, for all their differences, they were fully united on the need to bring an end to the continuing brutalities of racial discrimination on the continent. As Soapy Williams reminded Rusk, "there are no African 'moderates'" on the twin issues of apartheid and colonialism.[44] A group of U.S. ambassadors in Africa warned their superiors in Washington in 1961 that "the most highly-charged issues in sub-Saharan Africa today are the war in Angola and racial discrimination in the U.S."[45] These did not match up well with the Soviet Union, Cuba, and Berlin, the priorities of the men in Washington. The CIA acknowledged that south of the Sahara, the United States, despite Kennedy's personal popularity, was seen as a nation "which does not fully understand Africa's problems or fully support African aspirations."[46]

Lingering elements of racism and segregation within the U.S. government reinforced this perception. Africans appreciated Kennedy's efforts to include darker faces in his administration, but they could hardly fail to notice how white the overall visage of American foreign policy remained. Below the ceremonial level of certain ambassadorial appointments, desk officers in the State Department and the other bureaucracies involved in foreign relations were still all white in the early 1960s.[47] The close personal ties of top U.S. policymakers with European and even South African officials contrasted sharply with their nearly complete ignorance of African officials and southern African nationalist leaders.[48] The explicit racial prejudice of many older foreign service officers was an obvious problem, but insensitivity to ingrained racism was perhaps more pervasive. When the U.S. embassy in Ghana asked the State Department for a short film to use at its Fourth of July reception in 1961, it received *The Life of Theodore Roosevelt,* filled with images of San Juan Hill certain to remind viewers of the Bay of Pigs invasion—and, even worse, of Roosevelt in a pith helmet leading overburdened African porters through the bush on his 1910 safari in east Africa.[49]

There was no clearer reminder to Africans of American racism at the highest levels than the spectacle of Senator Allen Ellender, Democrat of Louisiana, touring Africa in the fall of 1962 and declaring in a press conference in Salisbury, Southern Rhodesia, that Africans did not have the ability to govern themselves.[50] The State Department labored mightily to separate the Kennedy administration's policies from the senator's sentiments, and observers of all colors knew that Ellender was not an intimate of Kennedy.[51] But the declarations of a senior U.S. senator from the president's own party, made in southern Africa—along with his assurances that he had "never seen any subjugation" in South Africa—only served to bolster long-standing African skepticism about the intentions of American leaders.[52]

The acid test of the Kennedy administration's relationship with Africa came in the region south of the Zambezi River, the most racially polarized place on earth in the early 1960s. There, the State Department observed, the southward sweep of anticolonial liberation had "finally rolled up against the last remaining redoubts of control by European settlers, investors and administrators."[53] With no apparent room for compromise between those committed to permanent white minority rule and those dedicated to majority rule, the two sides appeared to be digging in for a showdown. Each side was organizing alliances throughout the region, revealing how integrated the region had become and how inseparable would be the fates of South Africa, Southern Rhodesia (Zimbabwe), South West Africa (Namibia), Angola, and Mozambique. The State Department worried about the increasing consolidation of "the Welensky-Verwoerd-Salazar axis," which prompted other Africans to organize military support for the armed guerillas in South Africa and Angola.[54] "Our enemies fight collectively," Nelson Mandela reminded Africans all over the continent in January 1962, as he recruited them to do the same.[55] American hopes that Southern Rhodesia, at least, might be encouraged to start down the path of racial liberalization—that it might "move north" rather than "move south"—were dashed by white elections in December 1962 that brought the white supremacist Rhodesian Front to power.[56] Southern Rhodesia, Williams told Rusk, "is [the] new African time bomb."[57] In sum, the State Department warned that if current trends continue, "we may be faced with a major racial war."[58]

The stakes in such a scenario for the United States were perilously high. Policymakers varied in their predictions of whether the conflict would unfold in the form of continued guerilla actions within the southern African states or with actual invasions across international boundaries from the north.[59] But either would have what the State Department called "a direct impact on two of the major axes of tension in the world: the latent division between North and South along racial lines and the active East-West competition for world influence." If the new African nations believed they had to chose between cooperating with the West and helping liberate Africans in the southern end of the continent from white supremacist rule, the results could undermine one of the most basic elements of American foreign policy in the Cold War. "It could fatally compromise our over-all strategy of fostering a cooperative community of free nations," the State Department concluded.[60] The racial policies of southern Africa's whites were a cancer threatening to destroy the "free world" alliance from within.

The Kennedy administration therefore followed a policy of containment in southern Africa—the containment of racial conflict. "To mitigate the polarization of the races into two warring factions" was the goal, according to the State Department.[61] A policy designed not to alienate either side inevitably made neither fully happy, as American officials criticized apartheid and colonialism while resisting substantive sanctions against South Africa and Portugal.[62] The parallels to Kennedy's policies toward racial conflict in the American South were striking: rhetorical support for racial equality, combined with calls for restraint on all sides and an abiding sensitivity to the political power of white authorities in the region. Even the complaints of officials in Pretoria and Lisbon sounded like those from Montgomery and Jackson. Like Southern segregationists talking about African Americans organizing against Jim Crow, Portuguese and white South Africans argued that whatever African unrest existed in their territories was the result of outside agitators, including the meddlesome U.S. government itself.[63] With substantial interests on both sides in southern Africa, "we have sailed an improvised, often erratic course between the antagonists," the National Security Council noted three weeks before Kennedy's death. "Since we can't now bet on a winner, we should [still] be hedging our bets and buying time."[64]

To many observers, it seemed that the racial conflagration threatening to engulf the region had already begun in the Congo.[65] The secession of the mineral-rich southernmost province of Katanga (Shaba), under the leadership of the anti-Communist, pro-Western Moise Tshombe, undermined the new nation's independence from its opening moments in June 1960. The execution of popular socialist prime minister Patrice Lumumba in January 1961 at the hands of Tshombe's soldiers then deepened the crisis. Though black himself, Tshombe had close ties to Belgium and hired white mercenary soldiers—including hated South Africans and Rhodesians—to preserve his control of an independent Katanga, framing the Congo crisis in racial terms.[66] The white governments to the south viewed Katanga as a buffer against black majority rule. Foreign Minister Franco Nogueira of Portugal explained this to the U.S. ambassador in December 1962, noting that the imminent assault by UN forces on Katanga was eagerly anticipated by Angolan rebels working out of Leopoldville (Kinshasa), who planned to use a "liberated" Katanga as another base of operations against Portuguese forces across the border in Angola.[67] The State Department recognized that "the struggle between Leopoldville and Elisabethville [the respective capitals of the Congo and Katanga] has represented in many minds the opening round in the battle over Southern Africa."[68]

Despite some obfuscation by conservative whites, the racial coding of the conflict in the Congo seemed clear to most observers. Africans, African Americans, and antiracists around the world condemned Tshombe as a stooge of Belgian mining interests and were outraged by Lumumba's assassination, which they likened to an international lynching.[69] Tshombe's white American defenders included an array of prominent conservatives in both parties who appreciated his anti-Communism, openness to foreign investors, nominal Christianity, and general orientation toward the West. On a continent filled with Africans resentful of European colonialism and skeptical of American racism, the Katangan leader seemed a refreshing alternative. In contrast to Lumumba, who appeared to listen to the wrong whites (those in the Eastern bloc), Tshombe was eager for the advice and support of whites from the "free world." He seemed to represent a solution to the Congo crisis, which had convinced so many whites of the dangers of "premature independence." But the American Committee for Aid to Katanga Freedom Fighters was also conspicuous for the enthusiastic support it received from leading segregationists, who understood precisely what Pretoria and Lisbon saw in Tshombe: Africa's most prominent black champion of white colonial interests.[70]

As with the rest of southern Africa, the Kennedy administration sought a compromise position between the two sides.[71] Despite considerable sympathy toward Tshombe among leading Europeanists in the State Department and prominent senators of both parties, the president and his closest advisers understood the unacceptable racial implications of Katangan independence. Fears of Soviet influence in a balkanized Congo bereft of its wealthiest province have usually been cited as determining Kennedy's response, but it was racial polarization that Kennedy feared would provide the opening to any Communist incursions. Recognizing Tshombe as the Congo's "most determined agitator of racism," Kennedy broke with Eisenhower by clearly opposing Katangan separatism and supporting the UN's mission to reunite the Congo.[72] He hoped the UN could do so without a war, and he avoided committing American troops, but after the international army's swift rout of Tshombe's forces in January 1963, the president was pleased by African praise for his position.[73] In denying Tshombe a visa to visit the United States a year earlier, Kennedy had provoked a storm of protest from conservatives, including prominent journalist and old Kennedy family friend Arthur Krock, a mainstay of the famously all-white Metropolitan Club in Washington. The president underlined the racial politics of U.S.-African relations in 1962 by dryly suggesting to aides an alternative arrangement: "I'll give Tshombe a visa and Arthur can give him dinner at the Metropolitan Club."[74]

If some in the Kennedy administration feared that the conflict in the Congo might light a fuse leading south, others focused on the racially charged war in southern Africa that had already begun: across the border in Angola. The rebellion against Portuguese rule began in Luanda in early February 1961 and escalated sharply the following month, spreading across the country to the north.[75] In some ways colonial Angola represented a clearer choice for U.S. policymakers than the independent Congo, where Tshombe was at least black, and South Africa, where whites tended not to be colonial officials but rather descendants of settlers who believed they had nowhere else to go. Indeed, Kennedy again broke sharply with Eisenhower's precedent by voting against Portugal in the UN and openly supporting Angolan self-determination, to the delight of Africans.[76] But U.S. policy was complicated by having substantive interests on both sides in the conflict: the goodwill of Africa and American standing in the Third World versus continued access to the strategic Portuguese-controlled air bases of the Azores.[77] The administration again tried to straddle the fence in an effort to avoid antagonizing either side. Hedging its bets in the most literal sense, the U.S. government provided aid both to the Portuguese armed forces, in the form of weaponry for a NATO ally, and to the most pro-Western elements of the Angolan rebellion under the leadership of Holden Roberto, who was put on retainer by the CIA. The results were sometimes bizarre, as when rebels and civilians wounded by American bombs and napalm were treated with American medical and food supplies in refugee camps across the border in the Congo.[78]

American assistance to the dictatorship of Antonio Salazar, the only European government to reject utterly the goal of independence for its African colonies, created a potential public relations disaster for the Kennedy administration. The Portuguese counterinsurgent campaign was unrelentingly savage in its slaughter of civilians and other atrocities. Rusk worried that "Portuguese repression in Angola is even bloodier than has come to light," and that the United States might be identified with it.[79] Images of white soldiers and settlers murdering and sometimes torturing thousands of unarmed black Angolans in their quest to root out nationalist guerillas were precisely the kind of spur to racial warfare that the U.S. government sought to avoid. When a London newspaper reported in August 1961 that part of a bomb dropped on an Angolan village carried the clearly visible insignia "Made in America," Kennedy was not pleased.[80] NBC's televised report a month later of American-made napalm being used against Angolan civilians further complicated the administration's dilemma.[81]

No other issue divided the Kennedy administration as clearly between Africanists and Europeanists as Angola. The latter emphasized the strategic importance of the Azores and the NATO alliance and worried about Communist influences among the rebellious Angolans. The former focused on the harsh treatment of Africans by Portuguese authorities, including vast immiseration, lack of education, and the modified form of slavery known as forced labor.[82] Assistant Secretary of State Williams made these points most strongly within the government, arguing that "while most of the world understands clearly the issues in Portuguese Africa, Berlin by comparison is primarily a white man's power struggle." For many observers in the Third

World, the Cold War seemed more like an intramural contest within the industrialized North than the ultimate conflict of two opposing worldviews, as was the case in southern Africa. Williams reminded Bundy of the fundamentally different priorities of the U.S. government and most people of color abroad: "If we expect Afro-Asian understanding and support in the great crisis facing us in Berlin, then we must have shown them by our actions on Angola that our opposition to oppression does not have geographic or racial boundaries."[83]

Regardless of their differences in emphasis, none of the elite white men who made policy decisions in the Kennedy administration was entirely immune to long-standing prejudices and assumptions about Europeans and Africans. While acts of savagery characterized both sides in the terrible conflict unfolding in Angola, U.S. government observers clearly reported the vastly greater force that the Portuguese brought to bear on their opponents and especially on civilians. It was "state terrorism," though they did not use this term. When American diplomats spoke frequently of "the terrorists in Angola," however, they were referring exclusively to African guerillas.[84] Even Williams accepted this terminology, while arguing that the United States should still deal with the insurgents, as "today's terrorist is tomorrow's statesman."[85] American policymakers used precisely the same linguistic distinction for the South African government and the ANC: Nelson Mandela, not Hendrik Verwoerd, was the terrorist. White people in the early 1960s, it seemed, could be oppressive and unjust, but they could not be terrorists.

The Portuguese government's perspective on the war in Angola, while opposite that of the insurgents, created comparable problems for the Kennedy administration in its broader Cold War strategy. Lisbon's anti-Communism and NATO membership did not prevent it from emphasizing the North-South axis over the East-West one, just as its African opponents did. "As far as Portugal is concerned," Foreign Minister Franco Nogueira reminded Washington, "Angola is much more important than Berlin."[86] The parallel to the situation in the American South was again clear: both white supremacists and antiracists showed far greater concern for race relations and colonial relations than they did for the struggle against Communism. Calling the rebel leaders in Angola "Congolese" and "Communists" to identify them as outsiders and blaming the United States for creating Angolan nationalism where it had supposedly not existed before, Portuguese officials made no secret of their contempt for what they considered American meddling in their country's internal affairs.[87] Salazar himself reminded Rusk that in authoritarian

Portugal the Americans were not dealing with a Britain or a France, constitutional democracies that had willingly relinquished their African territories: "I cannot give in Africa what I cannot grant to my own people."[88] Limitations on liberty in the "free world" were not restricted solely to its Third World precincts.

The real danger of the Angolan war for the Kennedy administration was its potential for spreading the virus of racial conflict. The immediate threat was to the surrounding southern African region, but problems in the Portuguese colony might also link up with racial antagonisms across the Atlantic. The NSC warned in January 1962 that the Angolan revolt meant that "Portugal will now be regarded as vulnerable" in Africa, encouraging Angolans to persevere and Mozambican nationalists to take up arms as well. The domino effect of African liberation would speed this process, as Tanganyika's independence next door provided a sympathetic neighbor and possible rebel bases, much as the Congo was providing for Angola.[89] Two weeks before Kennedy's death, the State Department reported that the fighting in Angola was certain to bring a further "sharpening of racial antagonisms" and the increased involvement of Africans from outside the country.[90]

The other direction in which the Angolan problem might expand was into domestic American politics. Portugal's aggressive public relations campaign in the United States threatened to tap into segregationist and other conservative sentiments, bolstering a loose international white resistance front.[91] Such an alliance was symbolized by white Rhodesian admiration for Republican senator and likely presidential candidate Barry Goldwater, including delight at Goldwater's belief that he had relatives in Southern Rhodesia.[92] Sympathy for Portugal and its actions in Angola were by no means restricted to Republicans and white Southerners, however. Dean Acheson, stalwart of the northeastern Democratic establishment and key Kennedy adviser on Portugal and other NATO issues, made no secret of his disdain for the Africanist position within the administration. He told Williams that just because the former Michigan governor was from "the dark city of Detroit," Williams should not think that the United States had "to pander to the dark and delirious continent of Africa."[93]

Acheson's fears were put to rest by Kennedy's decision during 1962 to shift attention from Angola to the Azores, as negotiations for renewing U.S. base rights there approached. Official American criticism of Portuguese colonialism diminished, in accord with Bundy's and Rusk's strategy of not letting liberals like Adlai Stevenson, ambassador to the UN, and Williams "make too much of a moral issue of what is essentially a political problem."[94] Having chosen Lisbon's camp, the Kennedy administration was still annoyed at the shortsightedness of its European ally. Presidential aide Ted Sorensen captured the White House's sentiment that the Azores issue was "not unlike other U.S.-European problems, in which the United States is expected to endure pain and criticism from our allies in order that we might maintain the right to protect them from the Soviet Union."[95] Both European colonialists and African revolutionaries, like Southern segregationists and African American civil rights workers, kept placing their own struggles above the anti-Soviet one. Managing this ongoing brawl within the "free world" remained an enduring problem for Kennedy and his advisers.

The Kennedy administration faced the same dilemma in South Africa that it did in Angola. Seceding from the British Commonwealth and declaring itself an independent republic in May 1961, South Africa hardened its apartheid system by cracking down on all forms of dissent. It was in the Kennedy years that South Africa—the heart of the white-ruled southern African region, with the most powerful economy and the largest white population by far—became an effectively authoritarian police state.[96] In response, the U.S. government faced, as it had with Portugal, what the State Department called "an embarrassing choice between security requirements and basic political principle."[97] American security requirements no longer centered on access to South African uranium, as they had in the first decade after World War II, but they still included a variety of strategic minerals.[98] The republic's fine harbors and location astride the east-west shipping route remained important to U.S. military planners, especially in light of the recent closure of the Suez Canal in 1956.[99] South African gold continued to stabilize the global capitalist monetary system, and American traders and investors were profitably involved in the republic's economy.[100] The one new American security interest in the land of apartheid in the Kennedy years was the establishment of a missile and satellite tracking station at Grootfontein, outside Pretoria. The U.S. desire to preserve access to that facility undercut its ability to distance itself politically from South Africa's apartheid policies and the enormous backlash they were creating at the UN and throughout the Third World.[101]

Apartheid's greatest problem for the Kennedy administration was its potential for undermining African and other Third World support for the West in the struggle against the Communist bloc. The president and his chief advisers did disapprove of the brutalities of apartheid on moral grounds, and they occasionally made public criticisms of the South African government's failure to live up to the human rights provisions of the UN charter.[102] The racial attitudes of Kennedy and Prime Minister Verwoerd were, after all, nearly opposites: the American, a social moderate whose trajectory was moving him into the camp of those supporting full racial equality, versus the South African, a reactionary white supremacist. But the administration seemed at least as anxious about how the apartheid policies of an anti-Communist government were actually helping the Soviet Union and its allies in their quest for greater influence in the Third World. Anti-Communism associated with white supremacy, in other words, encouraged Communism. Conversely, the prominence of South African Communists in the anti-apartheid struggle tended to identify Communism with freedom for many Africans. Williams explained to British officials that apartheid served as "a breeding ground for communism" that made "U.S. relations with the rest of the continent very difficult."[103]

Unfortunately for the Kennedy administration, South Africa was well on its way to pariah status in the international community for another reason besides its internal racial policies. It was also a colonial power in South West Africa, and a particularly illegitimate one in the eyes of most of the world because of what the State Department called its "persistent disregard of its obligations under the old League of Nations mandate" establishing its control there in 1919. Pretoria's determination to share the fruits of apartheid with Namibians further enraged anticolonialists and antiracists around the world, placing the territory "in the forefront of Afro-Asian attention."[104] The convergence in South West Africa of colonialism and apartheid thus concentrated the frustrations of most Third World observers. Simultaneously, the publication in 1962 of Allard Lowenstein's popular book *Brutal Mandate: A Journey to South West Africa* increased American public awareness of the colony and of the white authorities' treatment of Africans there.[105] Third World delegates made South West Africa a frequent subject of discussion and controversy at the UN throughout Kennedy's presidency; unlike apartheid, control of a separate territory prevented the Verwoerd regime from arguing that this was strictly an internal South African concern.[106] Supporters of Angolan liberation around the continent, like Prime Minister Ahmed Ben Bella of Algeria, watched the spread of apartheid northward toward the Angolan border and declared their commitment to Namibian liberation next.[107]

The U.S. government's response to these troubling developments was to try to separate matters involving race relations from all other elements of its relationship with South Africa. Kennedy took a rhetorically tough stand against apartheid, while seeking to disturb the fruitful aspects of its ties with the republic as little as possible. Thus his announcement of a unilateral partial arms embargo on South Africa in August 1963 symbolically disassociated the United States from the land of apartheid, while undermining the UN campaign for a more severe embargo and not materially damaging Verwoerd's military strength.[108] Francis Plimpton, a U.S. delegate to the UN, could assert boldly that "how and when the South African Government will abandon its hateful racial policies we cannot know, but abandon them it will," while Kennedy rejected economic sanctions to bring substantive pressure on Pretoria.[109] Bundy could advise the president to risk losing access to the missile tracking facility by agreeing to some kind of arms embargo, while Rusk urged his colleagues to remember that South Africa was ultimately an ally in America's "total confrontation [with the Soviet Union] affecting the life and death of our own nation."[110] There was some room in the administration for differences of opinion that could be kept under the roof of a single policy—a policy, ironically, of "apartheid," the Afrikaans word for "separateness," in this case the separateness of race relations from all other issues. Rusk emphasized this point with South African foreign minister Eric Louw, as recorded for telegraphic purposes: "While US and SA cannot agree on matter race relations," there was "no need why this disagreement should infect total range our relations."[111] Apartheid represented a kind of viral outbreak that had to be sealed off—contained—to limit its damage to more important interests within the anti-Communist alliance.

The Kennedy administration's unwillingness to go beyond rhetorical condemnation of South Africa's racial policies reflected its reluctance to encourage any destabilization of the Pretoria government in light of the political alternatives in the republic. With white support for Verwoerd overwhelming and dissent banned, the ANC was forced to go underground and began its sabotage campaign under Mandela's leadership in December 1961.[112] American diplomats watched with foreboding the growing pessimism of the ANC's Albert Luthuli, winner of the 1962 Nobel Peace Prize, whose commitment to Christian nonviolence paralleled that of Martin Luther King, Jr. Luthuli lamented to the U.S. ambassador Joseph Satterthwaite that the South African government seemed to be closing off all avenues of change for Africans besides violence.[113] It was as though the Birmingham police had used machine guns rather than water hoses on demonstrators, and the federal government had just watched with satisfaction. Political repression was so thorough that the Defense and State Departments agreed, "the U.S. does not wish to assume a stance against revolution, per se, as an historical means of change" in South Africa. It was instead only "communist inspired, supported or directed subversion or insurgency" that had to be totally opposed. This truism of American Cold War strategy had a peculiar meaning in a realm of white supremacy where the South African Communist Party was closely allied with the country's leading opposition group, the ANC. The ANC thus qualified as an organization of unacceptable revolutionaries, because it, U.S. officials believed, was "dominated by the Communist Party at the leadership level."[114]

By refusing to understand the Communist Party's legitimacy in the eyes of Africans in South Africa, the Kennedy administration identified Mandela and his colleagues as dangerous enemies of the United States. Mandela himself was neither "a Communist nor a member of the CP," as he told the court during his 1964 trial on charges of sabotage, but an admirer of the British and American political systems who sought some form of socialism in his country. The lawyer-turned-guerilla reminded listeners that Communists both abroad and at home had been stronger opponents of apartheid than had non-Communists, with the result that many Africans "today tend to equate freedom with Communism."[115] To the U.S. government, however, ANC members were not freedom fighters but "subversives." For all their racial liberalism and their distaste for racist brutality, the president and his advisers shared the fundamental assumption of their White House predecessors that the South African regime was a legitimate government. The changes in racial consciousness that were just beginning among white Americans in the early 1960s were not yet far enough advanced to induce elite white policymakers to question that elemental understanding. Similarly, African Americans had not established themselves as an influential voice on U.S. African policy, as they would by the 1980s.[116] Anti-Communist racial totalitarianism may have been problematic and even abhorrent to American leaders, but it was not yet illegitimate.[117]

Perhaps the most intriguing piece of evidence for the continuing close ties between Washington and Pretoria in the Kennedy years was the role that the CIA apparently played in helping South African security forces arrest Mandela outside Durban on 5 August 1962. The defense and intelligence establishments of the two countries worked closely together. This relationship was reconfirmed by the 15 June 1962 agreement on a tracking station, which included arrangements for South African purchases of U.S. weapons.[118] South Africa's departure a year earlier from the British Commonwealth had meant a decline in British intelligence support, and Pretoria's relatively small intelligence forces were happy to receive help from the well-funded and experienced CIA. Their mutual anti-Communism and suspicion of Third World nationalists inclined them to a similar view of the ANC, and the agency had at least one source within Umkhonto we Sizwe (the Spear of the Nation), the ANC's military wing, which Mandela headed.[119] Thus, reports that emerged in 1990 of the CIA tipping off South African authorities to Mandela's whereabouts in August 1962 fit well with established relationships of the time, even if those reports have yet to be confirmed with documentation.[120] The pattern also accounts for the evident sympathies of the FBI with segregationists in the U.S. South at the same time. Abroad as at home, American security agencies tended to array U.S. power on the white supremacist side in racial conflicts, especially when the president and his chief advisers generally paid little attention to the details of southern African policy, focusing instead on priorities north of the equator.[121]

### Kennedy and the Civil Rights Movement in International Context

In John Kennedy's ideal world, there would have been neither Communists nor racists. Unfortunately for him, the real world had plenty of both. His presidency, he declared in his inaugural address, would be "a celebration of freedom," and indeed the early 1960s were a time of epic struggles to extend freedom. But there was a central conflict during the Kennedy years about what people most needed to be freed from or kept free from: Communism or racism. Anti-Communists looked mostly for freedom abroad, while antiracists focused on freedom at home. The president and his advisers believed firmly that the spread of Communism, by destroying free enterprise and the principle of political liberty, would remove the economic and political structures necessary for further social improvements.

Kennedy saw himself as the national and international leader with the clearest vision of the greatest threat to human liberty, and he tended to look at civil rights organizers as unruly followers inclined to jump out of line, run up to the front, and seize the spotlight for a less important cause. When confronted by Theodore Hesburgh, chair of the U.S. Civil Rights Commission and president of the University of Notre Dame, with problems like the absence of blacks in the Alabama National Guard, the president responded, "Look, Father, I may have to send the Alabama National Guard to Berlin tomorrow and I don't want to have to do it in the middle of a revolution at home."[122] Like Dwight Eisenhower, Kennedy grew frustrated with both sides in the conflict in the American South, as neither side seemed to him to be keeping its eyes on the ultimate prize of the Cold War and worldwide stability. Indeed, both civil rights organizers and those resisting them found race relations at home far more important in their daily lives than events in far-off Berlin or Vietnam. This was a perspective quite alien to the president.

The one way the civil rights movement could get the Kennedy administration's full attention was to clearly impact U.S. foreign relations. The president feared how easily another Little Rock crisis might happen, embarrassing the country before a global audience. Robert Kennedy explained the administration's international logic in his first speech on civil rights as attorney general, given at the University of Georgia. He argued that the graduation of the two African Americans just admitted there "will without question aid and assist the fight against Communist political infiltration and guerilla warfare."[123] John Kennedy disliked racial discrimination and understood the politics of symbolism, and he made highly visible gestures to diminish the nation's association with white supremacy: appointing dozens of blacks to important posts in the administration, desegregating the Coast Guard Academy, and hosting many more people of color at the White House than all of his predecessors combined. The contrast with Eisenhower, at the symbolic level, could not have been starker.[124]

Kennedy's primary concern about the civil rights movement was controlling it: moderating its tactics, channeling its demands, and limiting the social instability it stirred up in the South.[125] In this sense he fit King's famous description of "the white moderate" who agreed with the goals but not the direct action methods of the movement, "who paternalistically feels that he can set the time-table for another man's freedom," and whose greater devotion to order than justice, King believed, was blacks' "greatest stumbling block in the stride toward freedom."[126] Even in his symbolic actions Kennedy would go only so far. He refused for two and a half years the appeals from within and outside his administration to provide moral leadership to the nation on the issue of racial equality, despite widespread and extraordinary violence against American citizens throughout the South.[127] Indeed, the administration seemed determined to remain as neutral as possible in what increasingly looked like low-level warfare across the former Confederacy.[128]

The day before astronaut Alan Shephard lifted off on the first manned space flight on 5 May 1961, a group of young Americans set off to explore another new frontier of freedom, this one south of the Mason-Dixon line. The

Kennedy strategy of co-opting civil rights organizers to minimize racial polarization began with the Freedom Riders of the Congress on Racial Equality (CORE) and the Student Nonviolent Coordinating Committee (SNCC). While the Freedom Riders sought to force the Kennedy administration to uphold federal court rulings against segregated transportation, the White House desperately wanted to avoid such a confrontation with white Southern authorities. The timing was crucial: the president, embarrassed by the debacle of the Bay of Pigs invasion of Cuba a few weeks earlier, was about to meet Soviet chief Nikita Khrushchev for the first time at a summit conference in Vienna. The violence and terror that greeted the riders in Alabama, and the international attention they received, deepened the president's embarrassment and anger. The Freedom Rides, Assistant Attorney General Nicholas Katzenbach remembered, were seen in the White House "as a pain in the ass."[129]

By contrast, James Farmer and the other organizers of the rides believed they were on the front lines of the struggle for freedom. There was no more important business for the U.S. government, as they saw it, than the protection of the rights and safety of its own citizens, especially on the eve of any conference in which it would be posing again as the leader of the "free world." Focused on how the Soviets could use such violent incidents to demean the reputation of the United States abroad, Kennedy and his advisers did not see that for civil rights workers, the Deep South was like the Soviet Union in its negation of liberty and the rule of law and its determination to crush dissent. Here was a great irony: loudly anti-Communist Southern local authorities ruling a chunk of the "free world" in quasi-totalitarian fashion.[130]

The Kennedy administration was relieved to emerge from 1961 with no further major racial incidents, but the next year confronted the president with another version of Eisenhower's crisis at Little Rock. The vast, heavily armed throng of segregationists that tried to prevent James Meredith's enrollment at the University of Mississippi on 1 October 1962 was abetted by state officials all the way up to Governor Ross Barnett, and the riot that ensued brought precisely the kind of negative international attention Kennedy feared. Observers around the globe were stunned when members of the white mob killed a foreign reporter, Paul Guihard of the *London Daily Sketch,* along with another bystander, and wounded 166 federal marshals (28 of them by gunfire).[131] Like Eisenhower with Arkansas five years earlier, Kennedy was forced to send thousands of U.S. troops to Oxford to restrain white American savagery being displayed on television for a world audience. And like

Eisenhower, he was learning how treacherous the white Southern politicians of his party could be.[132]

The international context of the Ole Miss debacle was evident to many participants, though it was understood differently by different parties. The whites chanting "Go to Cuba, nigger lovers, go to Cuba!" at federal marshals captured the regional sentiment that the U.S. government should attend to the Cold War and leave Southern racial matters to the South, while the attorney general's half-joking question about photographs of Soviet missile installations in Cuba—"Can these things reach Oxford, Mississippi?"—suggested instead that the Cold War could no longer be fought effectively with people like Barnett in power. "The eyes of the nation and all the world are upon you and upon all of us," the president reminded Mississippians in a nationally televised address as the unrest escalated.[133]

Kennedy's tolerance for traditional Dixie mayhem across the color line ran out the following spring in Birmingham, "the Johannesburg of America." Brutality rained down with particular viciousness on the civil rights campaign that began there in early April and elicited for the first time a widespread and violent black response, across class lines.[134] Reporters and cameras from all over the country and the world poured into Alabama, capturing appalling scenes of police violence for a national and international audience. The international context was again crucial, as the founding conference of the Organization of African Unity (OAU) was meeting simultaneously in Addis Ababa, Ethiopia. Prime Minister Milton Obote of Uganda warned Kennedy that the "ears and eyes of the world are concentrated on events in Alabama," and a Nigerian journalist observed that the United States appeared to be becoming "the most barbarian state in the world."[135] The global attention encouraged civil rights activists, who were putting their bodies on the line in Birmingham. At the height of the crisis, King reminded antisegregation protesters that they were succeeding in forcing the U.S. government to take their side in the conflict because "the United States is concerned about its image. When things started happening down here, Mr. Kennedy got disturbed. For Mr. Kennedy . . . is battling for the minds and the hearts of men in Asia and Africa," who would no longer respect an America that allowed Jim Crow to survive.[136] One marcher turned the anti-Communist language of segregationists back against them with a sign reading, "Khrushchev can eat here—why can't we?"[137]

Full-scale street warfare and international opprobrium were too much, even for the cautious Kennedys. Disturbed by both the violence of local authorities and the willingness of so many blacks in Birmingham to fight back against the police, the president and his advisers recognized that the civil rights movement and American race relations stood poised on the brink of a more confrontational stage. Kennedy knew he must act forcefully to head off escalation; he had to provide leadership to the nation by framing the issue, for the first time, in moral terms.[138] He was not giving up on white Southern leaders, with whom he still had to work, but he was going to push them harder. He tried with Alabama governor George Wallace during a brief, shared helicopter ride from Muscle Shoals to Huntsville, but it was not a fruitful experience. Kennedy told the governor that for the good of Birmingham itself, the city must begin treating its black citizens more fairly if it was ever to be restored to social and economic health. Wallace responded with two of the oldest canards of white supremacists: the problem in Birmingham was "the influence of outside leadership," and King was "a faker" interested primarily in competing with Reverend Fred Shuttlesworth to see "who could go to bed with the most nigger women, and white and red women, too." Annoyed, Kennedy insisted on the seriousness of the black insurgency in Alabama and urged the governor to accommodate it.[139] Those present for the conversation could not have been surprised that it was the action of Wallace three weeks later, in symbolically attempting to prevent the desegregation of the last all-white state university in the nation, that finally moved Kennedy to seize the presidential bully pulpit on behalf of racial equality.

In his 11 June 1963 nationally televised address on the "moral crisis" facing the nation, Kennedy took sides as he had never done before. The atypical fervor with which he spoke reflected both personal revulsion at the violence inflicted on black Southerners and a determination to get new civil rights legislation passed by Congress in order—as Robert Kennedy put it—to get "people off the streets and the situation under control." The president made the international context for desegregation clear in his speech: "When Americans are sent to Vietnam or West Berlin, we do not ask for whites only." The struggle against Communism, he argued, now required the full racial integration of American public life. There would have to be more freedom at the heart of the "free world."[140] But the timing of the speech also suggested that the administration's view of the relationship between anti-Communism and antiracism might be changing, with the latter no longer merely an aid to the former. The day before, Kennedy had given a major address at American University calling for peace and a reexamination of American attitudes toward the Soviet Union. While perhaps coincidental, these two key speeches together pointed toward a future without either Jim Crow or the Cold War.[141]

Kennedy's call for full desegregation was intended for an international as well as national audience. Rusk instructed all U.S. ambassadors abroad to bear down on the task of countering the "extremely negative reactions" that racial incidents at home had elicited "from all parts of [the] world." The administration, he reminded them, was "keenly aware" of the impact of such incidents on the nation's image overseas, and the president's speech should be disseminated as widely as possible, as should the country's achievements to date in desegregation.[142] As hoped, Kennedy's civil rights bill was widely applauded in the Third World and especially in Africa, where newspaper pictures of police dogs attacking unarmed African Americans in the South—so reminiscent of apartheid and colonialism—had made a deep impact. Africans noted how different Kennedy's stand was from Eisenhower's, and some commentators even suggested comparisons to Abraham Lincoln.[143] But there was also a "strong note of skepticism" about how much progress was being made toward real equality in the United States, and State Department officials worried that the outlook for America's reputation in Africa was "likely to become worse" as reports of racial violence continued to mount.[144] The evidence along these lines was not encouraging: the most symbolic white Southern response to Kennedy's speech came a few hours later, when Mississippi NAACP leader Medgar Evers was gunned down in his front yard. The president himself had turned a corner, but whether he could pull segregationists around that corner with him remained an open question.[145]

African Americans, meanwhile, were moving rapidly down the road away from that corner, leaving the Kennedy administration to straddle a growing racial divide. The president's success in channeling the March on Washington in August into support for his civil rights bill marked the apex of the peaceful, integrated stage of the civil rights movement.[146] But antiracist organizers were increasingly disillusioned by the failure of the federal government to protect the lives and safety of American citizens in the South from the predations of local authorities. For a growing number of SNCC and CORE activists and their supporters by late 1963, the Kennedy administration was beginning to seem almost as much the enemy as the Ku Klux Klan and local law enforcement officers. One elderly black woman in Albany, Georgia, captured this rising sentiment in her response to a plea from activist attorney C. B. King not to lose patience with Washington: "You know what, lawyer, the Federal government ain't nothing but a white man."[147] The president, never enamored of civil rights organizers to begin with, reciprocated the feelings, privately referring to SNCC members as "sons of bitches" with an "investment in violence."[148]

White Southerners would have been pleased to know of such sentiments in the White House, for they deeply resented Kennedy's new support for civil rights legislation. The sharp increase in Republican voters in the South in the 1962 congressional elections, encouraged by the crisis at the University of Mississippi, had offered early evidence of the white backlash developing against greater national Democratic Party support for racial equality.[149] Dissenting Southerners vied with Kennedy to preempt the meaning of the language of the Cold War. While the president reprimanded segregationists' inadequate commitment to anti-Communism—"Why can a Communist eat at a lunch counter in Selma, Alabama, while a black American veteran cannot?"—George Wallace argued the opposite, insisting that the federal government that now sought "to persecute the international white minority" was filled with "the same people who told us that Castro was a 'good Democratic soul' [and] that Mao Tse Tung was only an 'Agrarian Reformer.'"[150] Segregationists noted accurately enough that racial egalitarianism in the South was a subversive idea, and one supported by those other subversives: Communists. "Some of these niggers down here would just as soon vote for Castro or Khrushchev," Sheriff Z. T. Mathews explained to reporters after intimidating a voter-registration rally in Terrell County, Georgia, in July 1962.[151] That Kennedy acted like a Soviet dictator seemed obvious to those white Mississippians who, after the Ole Miss crisis, put on their cars the license plate legend "Kennedy's Hungary" in reference to the Soviet Union's brutal repression of the revolution in Budapest in 1956.[152] The slogan that best captured segregationists' views of the connections between foreign affairs and the American South was the sign greeting Robert Kennedy along the road into Montgomery in April 1963: "No Kennedy Congo Here."[153] Many white Southerners believed they were not just like whites in Eastern Europe but even more like embattled white settlers in Africa, facing an onslaught of imminent black political participation and perhaps revenge with the support of the meddling U.S. government. Gus Noble, president of the Canton Citizens' Council, warned that equal rights in Mississippi would lead to the same horrors that had supposedly happened in former African colonies of Britain and France: "Those natives were not prepared for self-government. They were unstable. They ate each other."[154] By the end of his presidency, in sum, Kennedy found himself increasingly alienated from elements on both ends sides the growing racial divide in the South, even as he committed himself to ending racial discrimination in the United States.

## Africans and Jim Crow

People of the Third World had long been interested in how people of color were treated in the United States, but it was only in the Kennedy years that significant numbers of Africans began viewing events on television or coming to America as diplomats and finding out some of the answers for themselves. Many African visitors were skeptical of the explanations offered for the continued widespread racial discrimination in the leading nation of the "free world." U.S. officials most often cited the federal system of government, with its reserved rights for states and local communities, as restricting the national government's ability to ensure racial equality. Most Third World observers, along with many Europeans, found this argument less than convincing, especially in light of the awesome power of the U.S. government to project military might around the globe.[155] If true, were white supremacists in the United States even more powerful than the extraordinary figure of the president himself? Outspoken internationalist and civil rights advocate Robert Williams, who was engaged in an increasingly violent conflict with the Ku Klux Klan in Monroe, North Carolina, tweaked Kennedy's nose on precisely these grounds in 1961. In his famous telegram read aloud at the UN by the Cuban ambassador during debate on the American role at the Bay of Pigs, Williams said that in light of U.S. aid to those fighting tyranny abroad, "oppressed Negroes in [the] South urgently request tanks, artillery, bombs, money, and the use of American airfields and white mercenaries to crush the racist tyrants who have betrayed the American Revolution and Civil War." There was considerable applause among the darker-hued delegates in the General Assembly, just as there was appreciation for the suggestion of Kwame Nkrumah of Ghana that Africans might offer a Reverse Peace Corps to teach respectful human relations to Americans.[156]

Africans in the early 1960s continued to experience the United States primarily through New York and Washington. Since the spring of 1960, the State Department had been deeply concerned about how UN delegates from the new nations south of the Sahara would be treated by New Yorkers. Rusk and Adlai Stevenson were well aware of "the problem posed by representatives of African nations seeking suitable housing and office accommodations." That the presence of foreign diplomats in the nation's most cosmopolitan city should pose a "problem" indicated how clearly the Kennedy administration understood that racial discrimination remained a national rather than a Southern phenomenon. The U.S. mission to the UN went to great efforts to prepare the city's hotels, restaurants, and real estate agents for the novel experience of large numbers of nonwhite foreigners arriving with expectations of dignified treatment. The administration even arranged for private funding to hire a "trilingual specialist" to help African diplomats and their families find suitable housing arrangements while shielding them from white American racial prejudice—a kind of house hunting without humiliation. The contrast to the degree of federal government concern about dark-skinned Americans' experiences of discrimination in Manhattan and elsewhere was difficult to miss, especially for African Americans. The Cold War was the key to unlocking the Kennedy administration's concern about racism, and African independence had created a vast new source of potential embarrassment that the president and his advisers sought to preempt.[157]

Washington was a Southern town with a strong Jim Crow tradition, and diplomats of color were even more anxious about being posted there than New York. In a precise mirror image of how most American diplomats viewed positions in Africa, African ambassadors and their families and staffs found the American capital—the nerve center of the "free world"—to be a true "hardship post." Well aware of white racial violence in the South, Africans not only worried about finding decent housing but even feared being assaulted on the streets of Washington. Some African officials bound for the First World sought to be posted instead to Europe, which they considered much safer.[158] Eisenhower's desegregation of public accommodations in Washington, combined with the Kennedy administration's presence and concern, had in fact created a limited oasis there. But most African diplomats came to Washington by car from New York, and once they crossed the Delaware River on Route 40, they quickly discovered how unwelcome they were. In Delaware and Maryland they were regularly refused service in restaurants, humiliated, and harassed. Washington, surrounded by segregationist states, seemed to be for African visitors what West Berlin, surrounded by Communist East Germany, was for Western visitors: an isolated citadel deep in hostile territory, safely reachable only by air or by two restricted highways off which one dared not venture.

An important part of the logic of American Cold War strategy had been the belief that the more that new nations learned about the principal antagonists, the more they would prefer the United States over the Soviet Union. The first wave of Africans to test this theory found the results mixed. The Malian embassy in Washington passed along to Pedro Sanjuan, the assistant chief of protocol for the State Department, three letters it had received in 1961 from the American Nazi Party and included an analysis of the situation facing African diplomats who wished to travel in the United States. Malian officials found that "movements of African diplomats assigned to New York and Washington, are reduced, for these two cities, to a corridor constituted by Route 40 and the New Jersey Turnpike, which link the two cities. And their movements are free only if they do not get out of their automobiles." Excursions by airplane were generally safe, they continued, but trips from Washington of longer than a day "cannot be made if one chooses to travel by automobile unless one has a trailer." If one "wants to enjoy a rest on the beach, he is greeted on the beaches with hostile cries of 'No Negroes here!'" as happened to their ambassador "all along Chesapeake Bay" on an excursion on 4 September. The overriding sensation was not one of freedom but rather of hostility, which "causes African diplomats to consider the United States the most difficult post."[159]

The problems facing Africans in the United States were not entirely news to Kennedy, as the situation had been developing since 1957, and his own Senate staff had sometimes been involved in finding housing for insufficiently pale visitors from abroad.[160] But the frequency of such unhappy incidents increased during his first months in the Oval Office, along with media coverage of the confrontations, and the president quickly grew frustrated and sought ways to manage the problem. He continued Eisenhower's practice of mollifying insulted diplomats by inviting them to the White House for a personal audience, just as many governors and mayors across the country invited African visitors into their homes after similar occurrences in their own jurisdictions.[161] Kennedy also ordered the State Department to work on a solution, and the Special Protocol Service Section was set up under diplomat Pedro Sanjuan's enthusiastic leadership to buffer African diplomats from negative treatment. Sanjuan led a lobbying effort to desegregate public facilities along Route 40, first through partially successful persuasion and then through a change in Maryland state law. Sanjuan's zest for ending racial discrimination won him great affection among Africans but sometimes went further than his cautious superiors had expected. When he even encouraged CORE activists in their plans to help the desegregation campaign by picketing segregated restaurants along Route 40 in the fall of 1961, the president and his top advisers—whom CORE's role in the Freedom Rides a few months earlier still rankled—were not pleased.[162]

Still determined to move slowly on civil rights to avoid alienating white Southerners, Kennedy understood that the eradication of Jim Crow was the best strategy for improving U.S. relations with Africa.[163] He was pleased by the goodwill Sanjuan was creating for the administration among Africans. His civil rights legislation was widely applauded on the continent, as was his dispatch of federal troops to the University of Mississippi. In a typical conversation at the State Department two months after the latter incident, leaders of the South West Africa Peoples Organization pointed to Kennedy's actions at Ole Miss as evidence of the "great role" the U.S. government could play in ending racial totalitarianism in southern Africa as well as in the American South. Deputy Assistant Secretary of State Wayne Fredericks demurred, noting that Washington could act within U.S. borders in ways it could not abroad, but he did underline the American "hope that other countries will see this resolve [that we have shown]" on this issue.[164] Even Congress, while still unable to pass a civil rights bill over Southern opposition, indicated some willingness to accommodate the desire of people of color everywhere not to be gratuitously insulted; in 1963 it passed legislation purging "nigger" from all names applied to geographic features on U.S. maps.[165]

While the well-publicized appearance on American shores of a new wave of Africans in positions of authority created problems for many white Americans and for the U.S. government, it had a different impact on black Americans. Inspired by the respect accorded these dark-skinned diplomats, African Americans could not help comparing their own circumstances and struggles with the speed with which Africans had gained their independence and eliminated white supremacy in most of the continent. Students and other young civil rights activists were especially attentive to this contrast, which reduced their patience with white resistance. "Frequently I hear them say," King wrote in the *New York Times* in September 1961, "that if their African brothers can break the bonds of colonialism, surely the American Negro can break Jim Crow."[166] King himself vented the same frustration a year and a half later in his "Letter from a Birmingham Jail": "The nations of Asia and Africa are moving with jetlike speed toward gaining political independence, but we still creep at horse-and-buggy pace toward a cup of coffee at a lunch counter."[167] The growing presence of African students at black colleges in the United

States further heightened younger black Americans' awareness of their ancestral continent, as did the ties of some of their families to Africa, like that of SNCC's Julian Bond.[168]

The melee in the visitor gallery that interrupted Adlai Stevenson's first major address to the UN on 15 February 1961 revealed the rising international consciousness of black Americans. Some sixty African Americans struggled with guards while protesting the murder of Patrice Lumumba and the UN role in the Congo crisis. Removed from the building, they and hundreds of other supporters marched through midtown Manhattan chanting "Congo, Yes! Yankee, No!" James Reston of the *New York Times* observed these events, noting the intensity of black frustration, and concluded, "It is obvious that something is seriously wrong." Reston went on in a thoughtful analysis to suggest that "the young intelligent American Negro . . . has been identifying the battle for freedom in Africa with his own struggle for equality within the United States" far more than most white Americans realized. Here was "an event of momentous importance," Reston concluded: "a confluence of the world struggle for freedom in Black Africa and the struggle for equal rights in the Negro communities of America."[169] The Kennedy administration also acknowledged this confluence, as Wofford pointed out a month later in a public address: "Our pace [in civil rights] is in considerable part being determined by events abroad—by the emergence of Africa—by the establishment of a clear colored majority in the United Nations."[170] In their first appearance in the United States in significant numbers since the days of the slave trade, Africans were clearly bad news for Jim Crow.

There were limits on the extent of black American identification with Africa in the early 1960s. Cold Warriors had for the previous fifteen years wielded anti-Communism as an effective tool for repressing the anti-colonialist, internationalist perspective of the black Left, represented by such figures as W. E. B. Du Bois and Paul Robeson.[171] The domestic civil rights struggle that had spread like wildfire through the American South since the Greensboro sit-ins of February 1960 demanded the near total attention and energy of American antiracists during the Kennedy years—a point the president specifically remarked on with his advisers in discussions of U.S. policy toward southern Africa.[172] Such initiatives as the creation in mid-1962 of the American Negro Leadership Conference on Africa, representing most of the major civil rights organizations, demonstrated the real black interest in the continent, but the conference's limited influence and brief life span reflected its constituents' overwhelming concern with the cause of equality at home.[173] Even for those African Americans who identified strongly with the cause of African independence, their personal experiences with Africans often pointed up their "Americanness" more than their "Africanness." Black Peace Corps volunteers, for example, found that African responses to their presence tended to undermine any quest they may have been pursuing for a transnational racial identity as "black." Africans instead referred to them more frequently as "white," "European," "Westerner," or "foreigner," or at most "black white woman," "suntanned white woman," "black European," or "native foreigner."[174] The ties of African Americans to Africans were real and growing during the early 1960s, but they were also complicated and limited.

"CHRIST, YOU KNOW it's like they shoot this guy in Mississippi," John Kennedy complained to House Speaker Carl Albert on 12 June 1963, the day after Medgar Evers's murder. Racial tensions, he went on, had infected all politics: "I mean it's just in everything. I mean this has become everything."[175] By the end of his presidency, the civil rights movement and white resistance to it had indeed come to dominate the government's attention. The African American determination to end discrimination once and for all was captured by the speaker at a March 1963 mass meeting in Birmingham who declared, "There will be no nigger any more. It will be *Mister* nigger."[176] Simultaneously, the waves of African independence from the north crashed against the bedrock of apartheid and colonialism in southern Africa. A budding alliance among Pretoria, Salisbury, and Lisbon created a wall of white resistance, provoking the first efforts of the liberation campaigns that would ultimately wipe the last realm of white supremacist rule from the face of the earth.[177] In the southern parts of North America and Africa, racial polarization threatened to destroy the multiracial unity that the Kennedy administration believed crucial for its own political success at home and for American victory in the anti-Soviet struggle abroad.

Particularly troubling to the president and his advisers was the possibility that the struggles against racism on the two continents would get intertwined. Africans and black Americans recognized the two as parts of the same global problem, as did some Africanists within the U.S. government.[178] But for an administration determined to contain the political damage of racial conflict—and confident of its ability to manage crises—such connections were to be minimized. Only the Soviets would benefit from associations of Johannesburg with Birmingham, or Angola with Mississippi. International criticism of racial discrimination in the United States, in particular, was to be avoided. Thus Kennedy and Rusk succeeded in persuading King to cancel his scheduled UN testimony on apartheid in June 1963, to avoid "the danger that our domestic racial policies will be made the focus of attention."[179] African independence sent African diplomats in growing numbers to Washington and New York in the early 1960s, however, and there was no way to avoid black Americans' awareness of them or their experiences of American racial discrimination.[180]

Having substantial interests on both sides of the racial divides in the American South and southern Africa, the Kennedy administration sought to finesse the problem by avoiding choosing one side over the other. The president offered Africans and African Americans the extraordinary novelty of an administration studded at the top with believers in racial equality: Rusk, Bowles, Williams, and other Africanists in the State Department; Burke Marshall, John Siegenthaler, and Robert Kennedy in the Justice Department; Wofford in the White House; Shriver in the Peace Corps; and, above all, John Kennedy himself. The contrast with the Eisenhower administration was stark. And despite his initial resistance to leading publicly on the issue of civil rights, President Kennedy did ultimately come out strongly in favor of ending racial discrimination. The grief of many darker-skinned residents of both continents on 22 November 1963 was therefore definitely real, as was the satisfaction of many of their paler neighbors.[181] At the same time, the president bent over backward to avoid alienating the white authorities of Dixie and southern Africa. After much initial attention to African concerns, Kennedy and his chief advisers retreated to a generally less critical position regarding the staunchly anti-Communist white rulers of Angola and South Africa.

The actual policies of the Kennedy administration toward white supremacy in Africa and the United States thus moved in opposite directions between 1961 and 1963. Initially tough on racism in southern Africa and guardedly sympathetic to those seeking to end its sway, the president and his most important advisers shifted over time to a more neutral stance in which they worked to limit criticism of the white authorities there. Distracted by crises elsewhere, they revealed their traditional Cold War and European priorities and took positions that were, to paraphrase their own anti-Communist language, soft on racism. Conversely, Kennedy began his term aware of his political need for white Southern support in Congress and eager to avoid civil rights confrontations at home. By the end of 1963, however, disillusioning experiences with men like Alabama governors John Patterson and George

Wallace and Mississippi governor Ross Barnett had helped move him to a strong public stand in support of outlawing racial discrimination. Initially soft-pedaling racism at home, he became more outspoken over time. Ultimately, preserving social order within the fifty states was more immediately important to an American president than events at the far tip of Africa, and the Southern civil rights movement—aided by the viciousness of its opponents—managed to change Kennedy's political calculations and perhaps even his core attitudes in ways that the ANC and other insurgents south of the Zambezi River could not yet do. Their days of altering U.S. policy still stood more than two decades off in the future.

# 5

# THE PERILOUS PATH TO EQUALITY

THE YEARS OF Lyndon Johnson's presidency marked both the apex of legislative racial equality in the United States and the culmination of racial violence in American cities and in Vietnam. From the great heights of the Civil Rights Act of 1964 and the Voting Rights Act of 1965, the political landscape fell away precipitously to terrifying uprisings in Los Angeles, Newark, Detroit, and more than a hundred other cities at home and a full-scale war between Americans and Asians abroad. For most American soldiers in Vietnam, the devastating combat took place increasingly along racial, rather than political, lines: the enemy was not just Communists but the Vietnamese. Moreover, rotating U.S. forces brought with them the sharpening racial tensions from home, so that black and white soldiers were often openly at odds with one another, even while fighting a single enemy. The Johnson administration confronted a downward spiral of racial antagonism and polarization rather than the era of racial progress and unity that it had worked so hard to promote. This pattern of racial crisis emerged between 1964 and 1968 not only in the United States and in Vietnam but also in southern Africa, forcing American policymakers to pursue a largely unsuccessful strategy of containing racial conflict both at home and abroad.

In the United States as well as in the Third World, Johnson tried to keep civil rights activists and anticolonial nationalists identified with the liberal, Western reformist model of his Great Society. He struggled to isolate them from the twin siren songs of Soviet Communism and nonwhite (black, African, or Asian) nationalism. As the most energetic proponent of racial equality to occupy the White House, Johnson hoped to become the *real* leader of the civil rights movement as well as of the non-Communist world. He also labored to blunt the impact of the white backlash in the United States against civil rights achievements and in southern Africa against the wave of independence ending colonial rule. Such vestiges of white supremacy, he knew, hindered his effort to promote a racially egalitarian Western alliance as a more attractive alternative to the Third World than Soviet or Chinese Communism. As a moderate man of the political center, Johnson believed that he occupied the middle ground between black and white extremism, and he sought to co-opt the energies of both.[1]

### Lyndon Johnson, Civil Rights, and the Third World

Lyndon Johnson had experienced poverty as a child in the raw Texas hill country, but he entered the White House as one of the wealthiest presidents in U.S. history. His trajectory to political and material success represented the elemental American dream, and he was determined to embody national unity as the president of all Americans. His interest in the welfare of working people of all colors and his dislike of barriers to equal opportunity were legendary among those who knew him.[2] The liberalism of the Great Society involved helping those who were less fortunate. For Johnson such an approach was deeply genuine—and profoundly paternalistic. He craved love, appreciation, and recognition from those around him and from the public at large. As long as those receiving his assistance were sufficiently grateful to their patron and deferential to his power, his system worked.[3] But ingratitude and opposition from those he was trying to help dismayed Johnson and shriveled his generous instincts. By 1967 he would recite to his staff his civil rights achievements and lament: "I asked so little in return. Just a little thanks. Just a little appreciation. That's all. But look at what I got instead. Riots in 175 cities. Looting. Burning. Shooting. It ruined everything."[4] After 1965 the beleaguered president felt swamped by ingratitude from every direction: rioting African Americans, intransigent Vietnamese nationalists, and rebellious antiwar liberals who derailed his reelection. "How is it possible," he asked, "that all these people could be so ungrateful to me after I had given them so much?"[5]

Johnson knew little of other cultures. He had traveled abroad only rarely before becoming vice president. Like many of his generation, he assumed unquestioningly that American values were universal. He expected other peoples to admire the achievements of the United States and to aspire to similar affluence. On an official visit to Senegal's independence ceremonies in April

1961, he toured a small rural community and told the village chief: "I came to Kayar because I was a farm boy, too, in Texas. It's a long way from Texas to Kayar, but we both produce peanuts and both want the same thing: a higher standard of living for the people."[6] He let his enthusiasm fill in for cultural sensitivity when abroad, plunging into crowds to shake hands and kiss babies and ignoring advisers' warnings about dirt, disease, and diplomatic dignity. Although he had once announced that the trouble with foreigners "is that they're not like folks you were reared with," he treated them as if they could become so.[7] Johnson's vision of racial inclusiveness showed in his physical enthusiasm for African, Middle Eastern, and especially Asian crowds—"little brown people . . . packed as close as you could pack sardines"—whom he viewed as the salt of the earth.[8] By contrast, Scandinavians and other white northern Europeans often struck him as stuffy and unreceptive.[9] It was almost as though his dislike for northeastern elites and greater ease with Southerners and Westerners in the United States were mirrored abroad in an uneasiness with Europeans and a warmer feeling for people of the Third World.

As with people of color at home, however, Johnson expected his relationship with Africans and Asians to be that of a generous patron. In contrast to John Kennedy, who hated even to have to talk about agricultural policy, Johnson loved animals and the ranching and farming life. He believed that all farmers, whether in West Africa, Texas, or Vietnam, were essentially alike. He spoke frequently of building another Tennessee Valley Authority for the Mekong River, reflecting his desire to export the benefits of the New Deal and the Great Society for which he had worked so hard at home.[10] He was therefore mystified when the Vietnamese did not seem to appreciate his largesse. He once exclaimed to his aide Bill Moyers, "My God, I've offered Ho Chi Minh $100 million to build a Mekong Valley. If that'd been [American labor leader] George Meany he'd have snapped it [up]!" Robert Komer, Johnson's assistant to the national security adviser, remembered that Johnson "felt no particular need to delve into what made Vietnamese Vietnamese—as opposed to Americans or Greeks or Chinese."[11] In contrast to Ho, those South Vietnamese officials who emulated Americans made sense to the president. His compliment to the much shorter General Nguyen Cao Ky upon meeting him in Honolulu in February 1966 suggested his paternal delight: "Boy, you speak just like an American."[12]

Johnson's chauvinism had the peculiar flavor of his home state. His favorite historical analogy was that defining piece of Texan pride and nostalgia, the Alamo. "Vietnam," he asserted more than once, "is just like the Alamo. Hell, it's just like if you were down at that gate and you were surrounded and you damn well needed somebody. Well by God, I'm going to go—and I thank the Lord that I've got men who want to go with me, from McNamara right on down to the littlest private who's carrying a gun."[13] He was intensely proud of his two sons-in-law and their service in Vietnam. But the rising toll of American casualties there appalled and grieved him, even as he made decisions that further increased their numbers. He seemed less and less able to relax as the war to preserve a non-Communist South Vietnam continued. He gave up drinking his favorite Cutty Sark whiskey and, unable to sleep, appeared frequently in the White House operations room in the middle of the night to check on American casualties. Unlike many domestic opponents of the war who began to sympathize and even identify with the victims of the American war in Vietnam and with other Third World peoples, Johnson continued to focus on American lives. His attorney general, Ramsey Clark, recalled about the president: "I never sensed any concern for the other side. How many did the Vietnamese lose? How many were killed in the village? How many South Vietnamese, how many North Vietnamese, how many Vietcong? It was *our* lives, *our* country; and they didn't figure, those people."[14] As the war in Vietnam slipped away from him, Johnson seemed less and less engaged with those "little brown people" he had originally hoped to help.

In Africa there were no Alamos. Unlike most Americans in the early 1960s, Johnson did not derive his ideas of Africa from Tarzan movies and exotic animals in *National Geographic*. He had visited the continent once and at least thought of it in terms of people. In his sentimental but sincere fashion, he reflected on his trip to West Africa as vice president: "You know, in Senegal, when I looked into the eyes of the mothers there, they had the same look as the people in Texas, the mothers in Texas. All mothers want the best for their children, and the mothers in Senegal were no different from the white mothers in Texas."[15] If his great humanity allowed him to ignore skin color and cultural differences more than most Americans of his generation, Johnson's relentless political calculations ensured that he would avoid any new American engagement in an area of political turmoil and limited strategic significance to the United States. Domestic politics were his love, and Vietnam his distraction and eventual obsession. Crises in the Dominican Republic, the Middle East, and Europe took what little other time he and his advisers had, and Africa remained—as it had been for all his predecessors—the lowest priority in, literally, the world. Angered at a State Department spokesman's public acknowledgment of the new combat role of American personnel in Vietnam in the spring of 1965, Johnson made clear his version of diplomatic and political irrelevance: "He'll be giving his future briefings somewhere in Africa!"[16]

Both Africans and Vietnamese had reason to doubt Johnson's interest in them when he took the oath of office in November 1963, and most African Americans were also skeptical about their new president. Black Justice Department official Roger Wilkins remembered that "he was a Texan, and to me Texas was South, and he sounded South, and that's where my enemies were, more than in the Soviet Union, more than in North Korea." Other black leaders, including Martin Luther King, Jr., suspected that their strongest white allies might well be "converted" Southerners. As political strategist and Johnson adviser Louis Martin put it, "a reconstructed Southerner is really far more liberal than a liberal Yankee."[17] Freed from the segregationist white Texan constituency to which he had long bowed on racial matters, Johnson swiftly jettisoned his previous record of accommodating segregationism. "You know segregation is absolutely crazy," Attorney General Nicholas Katzenbach recalled the president telling him. "Eighty percent of the world is not white, and we have to live in this world as we have to live with everybody else in it."[18]

In his ascent from the South, Johnson cut himself loose from close ties with segregationist Southern Democrats in Congress. A product of their base in the American version of one-party states, Southern Democrats' disproportionate seniority and power in Congress had long mocked the idea of equality before the law in the United States. As vice president and then president, Johnson knew their power but grew to despise the virulent racism of such men as Mississippi senator James Eastland and that "runty little bastard," Alabama governor George Wallace. Johnson loved to mimic and caricature Eastland in private: "Jim Eastland could be standing right in the middle of the worst Mississippi flood ever known, and he'd say the niggers caused it, helped out some by the Communists."[19] Johnson understood that "if you can convince the lowest white man that he's better than the best colored man, he won't notice you picking his pocket. Hell, give him somebody to look down on, and he'll empty his pockets for you."[20] Johnson's anger about the dangerous demagoguery of Southern leaders boiled over after a frustrating December 1966 meeting at his Texas ranch with Southern Democratic governors who complained of his betrayal of his regional heritage: "Niggah! Niggah! Niggah! That's all they said to me all day. Hell, there's one thing they'd better know. If I don't achieve anything else while I'm President, I intend to wipe that word out of the English language and make it impossible for people to come here and shout 'Niggah! Niggah! Niggah!' to me and the American people."[21] To no small extent, he succeeded in that endeavor.

The Southerner who may have bothered Johnson the most was his former senatorial ally and chairman of the Senate Foreign Relations Committee, J. William Fulbright of Arkansas. Fulbright's anger at Johnson's misleading representation of events during the American occupation of the Dominican Republic in 1965 blossomed into an early public dissent from the administration's policies in Vietnam. The segregationist senator became identified with concern for nonwhite peoples in Southeast Asia, while the integrationist president called down a war of destruction on the Vietnamese people. Johnson resented this obvious irony and preferred a different interpretation of the two men's views on race and Vietnam: all Fulbright "thinks about is England, the Marshall Plan or Europe. He doesn't give a damn about Asians because they're brown."[22] The president believed that he understood the Alamo analogy and that Ho Chi Minh and Southeast Asian Communists—latter-day equivalents of Santa Anna and the Mexicans—represented a clear threat to American national security. "Now, Fulbright and Mansfield and Lippmann and RFK don't see this," he argued, "because they think of the South Vietnamese as yellow people not worth protecting."[23] The White House staff unsuccessfully sought ways to use Johnson's professed racial liberalism as a means of undercutting Fulbright's authority on foreign relations with the nonwhite Third World.[24]

Leaving behind most white Southern leaders, Johnson constructed close alliances with the heads of the major civil rights organizations. Roy Wilkins of the NAACP had the greatest access to the president, grounded in their shared belief in legislative lobbying, litigation, and voter registration as the paths to racial equality. A. Philip Randolph of the Brotherhood of Sleeping Car Porters and Whitney Young of the National Urban League were close seconds. African Americans like Young and Reverend Leon Sullivan of Philadelphia earned the appreciation of the president and his advisers for their determined efforts at improving the daily lives of urban black Americans combined with their refusal to criticize the war in Vietnam. The administration was delighted with the election of such mainstream black Democratic politicians as Carl Stokes as mayor of Cleveland. White House staffer John Roche referred to Stokes's victory as "the kind of 'black power' we need in the Democratic Party."[25]

Johnson put much less trust in the younger, grassroots activists of the Student Nonviolent Coordinating Committee and the Congress on Racial Equality, and he grew increasingly skeptical about—and hostile toward—Martin Luther King, Jr., and the Southern Christian Leadership Conference. The ultimate political insider, Johnson rejected mass public demonstrations in favor of the careful application of interest group pressure on members of Congress, the source, he believed, of real social change. "You cannot find one minority group," he told a gathering of black candidates for elective office in October 1966, "that wasn't able to ultimately overcome its oppression by the ballots, by learning to use its power, P-O-W-E-R, capital at the polls, P-O-L-L-S."[26] In the later years of his administration, as many younger civil rights workers rejected liberalism in favor of black power and Marxism and as impoverished black communities in the North erupted each summer in riots, Johnson struggled to understand those developments. He listened carefully to extensive FBI reports on black radicals, and he sent advisers to tour burned-out areas and talk with residents. But Vietnam swallowed his attention, and for all his goodwill, the president could not fully comprehend the changing mood of black America. White House aide Sherwin Markham reported back to him that staying in the black neighborhoods of Chicago "was almost like visiting a foreign country—and the ghetto Negro tends to look on us and our government as foreign."[27] After visiting Baltimore, Bill Moyers agreed: "We didn't even speak the same language."[28] James Farmer of CORE remembered how Johnson "was much better able to understand" the courteous, middle-class representatives of the NAACP and the National Urban League than he could "the angry young blacks who would tell it like it is, and call him an MF [motherfucker]." Farmer emphasized the paternalism of Johnson's older Southern manner, which did not "jive very well with angry young black militants."[29]

Johnson was a most unusual Cold War era president. "I do not want to be the President who built empires, or sought grandeur, or extended dominion," he told the nation in a televised address in March 1965. His heart was set instead on regenerating America itself, by eliminating poverty and racial discrimination at home in order for the United States to realize more fully its promise as a model society for the world.[30] He took office in November 1963 on the heels of Kennedy's assassination, during a lull in international tensions due to the recent resolution of the Cuban missile crisis and the nuclear test ban treaty, which offered an opportunity to focus on domestic matters. Warning aide Richard Goodwin, "Those civil rightsers are going to have to wear sneakers to keep up with me," Johnson moved swiftly to make "that moral commitment" to racial equality which he had urged John Kennedy to do in the summer of 1963. He had told Kennedy and his advisers that "the Negroes are tired of this patient stuff and tired of this piecemeal stuff." It was time, he had said, for the president to proclaim the immorality of racial discrimination, and it would be best to do it in the South while looking white Southerners right "in the face."[31] Johnson did exactly that in a rousing October 1964 campaign speech in New Orleans.[32]

Johnson knew that he was trying to ride the back of the tiger of the civil rights movement. The laborious, dangerous work of black Southerners had created the unusual opportunity he now seized to push civil rights legislation through a reluctant Congress. He believed it was time for a sympathetic administration to take over the leadership of the forces of change in the country, guiding them into responsible legislative reform. Johnson and his advisers also considered it crucial to minimize what they saw as extraneous mass demonstrations that provoked the fears of white conservatives and increased opposition to Great Society programs. In shepherding through the limited civil rights bills of 1957 and 1960 as Senate majority leader, he had sought to coopt the energies and demands of the rising civil rights movement. So again, in 1964 and early 1965, he championed more substantial civil rights measures partly because he believed they were the right thing to do, but partly to siphon off the energies of the now much larger civil rights constituency. The president knew how much his support for racial equality would cost him and the Democratic Party in terms of white votes, especially in the South, and he was determined to contain further black political demands that would exacerbate that white backlash.[33]

Johnson's success in eliminating legal barriers to racial equality in the United States was embodied most dramatically in the Civil Rights Acts of 1964 and 1968 and the Voting Rights Act of 1965. The president wielded his particular skills—as a Southerner, as the preeminent legislator of his generation if not of the century, and as the recent master of the Senate—to make use of the opportunity provided by the national grief over the posthumously revered Kennedy.[34] He also appointed more African Americans to executive branch positions than the combined total from all previous administrations and pushed through comprehensive immigration reform in October 1965 to eliminate the racially discriminatory national origins system.[35] The international mood encouraged Johnson's reforms, as Africans and others paid close attention to American race relations and were disturbed by ongoing discrimination and violence against blacks, incipient race riots, and the developing white backlash represented by Republican nominee Barry Goldwater in the 1964 presidential campaign. Secretary of State Dean Rusk of Georgia emphasized in December 1963 the central importance for American foreign relations of a national commitment to racial equality: "We are looked upon as a leader . . . and when we fail to meet our commitments, this has a major impact on other countries."[36] The Johnson administration hoped that its leadership in civil rights would restrain criticisms of the U.S. government by people of color both at home and abroad. Black Americans, who ranged from conservative to radical, and the Third World might thus be maintained as parts of a large, liberal, "free world" alliance, which could outmaneuver threats from both the Communist left and the white supremacist right.[37]

### Promoting Equality and Restraining Polarization

By the summer of 1964, just eight months after the new president took the oath of office, events in the United States and abroad began to strain his strategy of limiting and defusing racial conflict. Johnson signed the Civil Rights Act on 2 July, in the midst of a season of extraordinary violence by the Ku Klux Klan in Mississippi. A week earlier, three civil rights workers had disappeared in Neshoba County, Mississippi, victims of the forceful response of white residents of the Magnolia State to "the Invasion," as some called the Mississippi Summer Project to register black voters. Sixteen days after the Civil Rights Act became law, the first major race riot of the decade ignited in Harlem, signifying a rejection of white liberalism and its gradualist approach to solving problems of racial discrimination and poverty. Writer and black nationalist Julius Lester observed that the riveting news from Mississippi slipped from the front pages "when Harlem held its own summer project to protest the murder of a thirteen-year-old boy by a policeman. Summer projects, northern style, usually involve filling Coke bottles with gasoline, stuffing rags down the neck, and lighting them."[38] White resentment of such actions—dubbed "Goldwater rallies" by gloomy Democratic Party strategists—fueled the Arizona senator's nomination that same month.[39]

Trouble abroad quickly added to trouble at home. In early August Congress passed the Tonkin Gulf resolution, granting Johnson a free hand in dealing with the situation in Southeast Asia. Civil rights workers listening to the president's radio announcement of air strikes against North Vietnam worried that the administration was embarking on another war before the struggle to liberate Mississippi and the rest of the South was won.[40] The very next day, 5 August, rebels in the Congo captured the city of Stanleyville, provoking a crisis in central Africa that quickly led to the use of white mercenaries, American planes, and Belgian paratroopers to free white hostages held by African forces. The Johnson administration's aspiration to manage and control the forces of racial polarization represented an uncertain prospect, but the president believed, with reason, that his best days were still ahead.

The American response to the Congolese rebellion derived from the Johnson administration's determination to avoid entanglements in Africa. Outside South Africa, whose anti-Communist white government seemed firmly in control, the continent held little economic or strategic significance for Americans. Anti-American rhetoric from such radical nationalists as Ghana's Kwame Nkrumah made Johnson wary. Even the explicit efforts of the People's Republic of China and the Soviet Union to increase their influence there did not deeply trouble the administration, given the combination of Africans' poverty and strong nationalism. Unlike Southeast Asia, this was one part of the world to which American officials did not simplistically apply the domino theory. Africanists in the State Department generally lacked influence with Johnson, Rusk, and National Security Advisers McGeorge Bundy and Walt Rostow, while Defense, Commerce, and Treasury Department officials were far more concerned with South Africa than the rest of the continent. Key power broker George Ball, the undersecretary of state, had strong Europeanist inclinations that undergirded his determination to stay close to the British and avoid any other potential Third World morasses like Vietnam.[41]

In addition, by 1963 the initial romantic enthusiasm for African independence of many white American liberals, both in and out of government, had begun to ebb. The corruption, economic failings, and one-party rule of many new governments on the continent were helping drain away the interest in newly independent Africa evident in the Kennedy years.[42] Liberals in the Johnson administration no longer seemed so confident about making an analogy to the United States in 1776, in which Africans were seen as doing what white Americans had had to do two centuries earlier. Indeed, liberals worried more about the version of that analogy promoted by conservatives, who viewed Africans not as the white Americans but rather as the Native Americans, with white settlers in southern Africa seen instead as the true spiritual kinfolk of American pioneers.[43] This disillusionment with Africa coincided with rising militancy among elements of the civil rights movement and consequent white liberal dismay. Black folks everywhere, it seemed to whites like Lyndon Johnson, were getting harder to deal with.

African leaders were disappointed by the Johnson administration's lack of interest in them. They admired the president's commitment to civil rights legislation, but racial violence in Birmingham, Selma, Harlem, and elsewhere and the white backlash symbolized by Goldwater troubled them. They missed Kennedy and his greater interest in their continent, and they resented the American use of white mercenaries in the Congo and ongoing U.S. ties to the white minority regimes to the south.[44] The close American relationship with NATO partner Portugal did not improve the American image among Africans. In May 1964, for example, two deserters from the Portuguese army surfaced in the Congo to denounce the Lisbon government for its indiscriminate slaughter of civilians across the border in Angola, while the U.S. ambassador to Portugal toured Angola during the same month and publicly praised Portuguese colonial practices.[45] Robert Komer of the NSC optimistically summarized the problem for the president. The Azores base (which the U.S. leased from Portugal), he wrote, "makes it hard to be anti-Portuguese, while the UK's economic stake in Rhodesia and South Africa makes us reluctant to push them too hard." Since Africans could not ignore these concerns, he concluded, "to the extent that we can stay slightly ahead on these issues instead of being reluctantly dragged toward the inevitable, we can keep our African affairs in reasonably good repair." Staying only slightly ahead of white supremacy did not, however, represent the kind of leadership that Africans hoped the United States might provide.[46]

In the Congo in the summer of 1964, the American government quickly fell behind on an issue of great symbolic importance to much of Africa. After the withdrawal of UN peacekeepers from the country in June and the return of Moise Tshombe from exile in fascist Spain as the new prime minister on 5 July, much of the huge, unintegrated nation rose up in simultaneous but uncoordinated rebellions. Tshombe had made himself into perhaps the most hated black political figure in Africa through his leadership of the unsuccessful Katanga secession of 1960–1963, his ready use of white mercenary troops against fellow Congolese, his intimate ties with colonialist Belgian enterprises, and, above all, his responsibility for the murder of the Congolese independence leader and first prime minister Patrice Lumumba.[47] With a third of the country falling quickly into rebel hands, the Central Intelligence Agency warned Johnson that the pro-Western Tshombe's odds of political survival were only "about even." "Should Tshombe fall," the agency warned, "the prospects are dark. Extremists would be likely to gain increased influence in Leopoldville, secessionist regimes might break off and disorder would spread."[48] The Johnson administration's primary concern was to avoid the dissolution of this centrally located African nation, especially at the hands of leftist rebels. This was no time for "another Cuba." Johnson himself had long appreciated Tshombe as an African who openly admired the United States and disliked Communists, and the president failed to recognize the depths of African loathing for a man so closely identified with colonialist interests.[49]

The American response to the crisis in the Congo was to have the CIA organize a private air force to bolster Tshombe's government forces while working with him and the Belgians to hire a mercenary army of some seven hundred white South Africans, Rhodesians, and Europeans to quell the uprisings.[50] Having helped change the odds in favor of the government forces, the problem for the Johnson administration became one of managing the political fallout on the rest of the continent. George Ball either betrayed nearly inconceivable ignorance of American actions or simply deceived journalist Walter Lippmann in a conversation on 25 August, claiming that the United States was not involved at all in the Congo. Ball's metaphor aptly revealed the American view of the continent: the administration recognized, he said, that it "should not get bogged down in the African swamp." The undersecretary of state identified the ongoing problem for Washington officials regarding African affairs as the limits on "our ability to control" the Congolese and other governments there. Working in the "swamp," it seemed, was perilous, unpredictable, and not very rewarding. It should be strictly a last resort.[51]

The Congo in 1964 represented the first use of mercenaries as a direct instrument of U.S. policy in Africa. The white supremacist attitudes of South African and Rhodesian soldiers of fortune created obvious problems for an American government seeking to promote the appearance of a racially egalitarian alliance against leftist influences worldwide. British mercenary leader Mike Hoare explained to a white comrade that "we have a great mission here. The Africans have gotten used to the idea that they can do what they like to us whites, that they can trample on us and spit on us."[52] His attitude mirrored that of an increasing number of white Americans in late 1964 regarding African Americans. It seemed in one sense that the Johnson administration was colluding with the white backlash in Africa at the same time it was fending off the domestic version of that backlash in the United States. Journalist David Halberstam suggested the irony of the situation by noting that hiring

South African mercenaries to bring peace to the Congo was like the mayor of New York City bringing in the Mississippi Highway Patrol to halt riots in Harlem.[53] The Johnson administration's obtuseness about African sensitivities and realities surfaced again with the selection of Charles W. Englehard to represent the United States at Zambia's independence celebrations on 24 October. A major financial contributor to Johnson's campaigns, Englehard was well known in Africa as the largest American investor in South Africa and an intimate friend and enthusiastic supporter of the apartheid regime in Pretoria. The editors of the journal *Africa Today* declared him "no more fit to speak for the U.S. in Africa than is Governor George Wallace or the Grand Dragon of the Ku Klux Klan."[54]

In November Congolese rebels in Stanleyville seized two thousand white foreigners, mostly Belgians but also several Americans, as a hostage shield against an approaching force of mercenaries and Congolese government troops. On 24 November American planes flying from a British base on Ascension Island in the South Atlantic dropped Belgian paratroopers in a largely successful mission to rescue the hostages, although a few dozen were executed at the last minute by their captors. That same day the mercenaries also reached Stanleyville, and the combined mercenary and Belgian forces made swift and brutal work of the rebels and many civilians. As Bundy had warned Johnson a week earlier, an American role in the operation would carry with it "real political costs in the Congo" and in Africa generally, but the storm of criticism that followed seemed to dissipate quickly over the next few months.[55]

Africans objected to the rescue operation because they saw it as a reassertion of external white control over the sovereignty of an African state. They were appalled by Tshombe's use of white mercenaries against fellow Congolese, especially as they learned of what even the CIA admitted were the mercenaries' tactics of terrorizing civilian populations through robbery, rape, beatings, torture, and murder. While *Life* magazine described them as resembling "rough-hewn college boys," the mercenaries' attitudes were more accurately encapsulated in the answer Wally Harper, a South African, gave to a journalist's question regarding how he felt about fighting and killing people in the Congo: "Well, I've done a lot of cattle farming, you know, and killing a lot of beasts; it's just like, you know, cattle farming, and just seeing dead beasts all over the place. It didn't worry me at all."[56] Africans intensely resented both Western actions and news reports that valued white lives more highly than black lives. A Kenyan delegate at the UN Security Council re-

jected American claims that the hostage rescue was a humanitarian operation: "Where is this humanitarianism when the white mercenaries are allowed full license to murder innocent African men, women and children? . . .
Where is this humanitarianism when American Negroes are brutally done to
death in Mississippi and elsewhere?"[57] African American leaders across the
political spectrum shared this skepticism, from Martin Luther King, Jr., with
his mild but firm criticism to Malcolm X and his searing denunciation. Returning to New York from his second trip to Africa on the very day of the
Stanleyville rescue, Malcolm called Tshombe "the worst African on earth"
and the American policy of supporting him "insane." He warned that Africans were beginning to recognize the common ground in the U.S. government's apparent disregard for black lives in both the American South and the
Congo.[58]

White Americans saw matters differently. The Johnson administration, the
media, and the predominantly white public all overlooked the atrocities committed by the mercenaries against Congolese civilians. They focused exclusively on the white hostages and abuses by the rebels, and they were disgusted
by African condemnations of the rescue effort as "imperialist aggression."
The scenario of white hostages tormented by "savage" kidnappers touched a
deep nerve in the American psyche, stirring emblematic memories of generations of violent European–Native American conflict, refreshed and distorted
by the Hollywood westerns of the post–World War II era. This scenario also
touched old fears of plantation slave revolts and potential black rapists, especially in the white South. Coming so soon after another summer of well-publicized white brutality against nonviolent blacks in the American South, the
Congo involvement pushed many politically moderate Americans, whether
reluctantly or eagerly, toward the more traditional color-coding of savagery in
the American national narrative. The U.S. ambassador to the UN Adlai
Stevenson accused African critics of "black racism," and *Time* magazine highlighted reports of rebel cannibalism and sexual mutilation of European nuns
and priests. Citing the selfless medical work of American missionary physician Paul Carlson among the Congolese poor, *Time* put his picture on its
cover and argued that his murder proved "that Black African civilization . . .
is largely a pretense." The magazine blasted African criticisms of the rescue
operation in revealing fashion: "The sane part of the world could only wonder whether Black Africa can be taken seriously at all, or whether, for the
foreseeable future, it is beyond the reach of reason."[59]

Here, ultimately, was the problem: the West was "sane" and Africa was not, at least for now. Grounded in a fanciful depiction of the Congolese rebellion and its aftermath, one intended by its proponents to justify the CIA's actions, *Time*'s conclusion about black Africans echoed claims of black immaturity long promoted by white Southerners to justify black subjugation. Bundy chose the paternalistic image of disobedient children in explaining the problem to Johnson in January 1965. Citing Africans' "willful misunderstanding of our paratroop rescue," the national security adviser recommended some careful, parental management of African feelings in the new year.[60]

As the political and racial crisis deepened in the Congo in the summer and fall of 1964, Johnson was confronted at home with the spreading dissatisfaction of African Americans with Democratic Party leadership.[61] A sharp split became evident at the party's national convention in Atlantic City in August, where simmering tensions between civil rights activists and the Democratic Party boiled over. Organizers in the South had for years faced violence and danger on a daily basis as they tried to register blacks to vote. They had operated in conditions often similar in many respects to those of a war zone. They perceived their opponents as the local Democratic Party elites, with the Ku Klux Klan as their enforcers.[62] The slow pace of change in the South and the persistence of white brutality were fraying the commitment of many organizers to nonviolence, especially among the less religiously motivated SNCC workers.[63] The violence of the white response to the Mississippi Summer Project further deepened their alienation, as did the ongoing failure of the federal government to protect civil rights workers.

When Johnson and the national Democratic Party then rejected the bid of the Mississippi Freedom Democratic Party (MFDP) to be seated in Atlantic City as the only democratically elected delegation from that state, accepting the all-white party regulars instead, many civil rights workers had had enough. With Washington's dominant party seemingly on the side of white Southern authorities, America itself appeared to many as no more than Mississippi writ large. They found it increasingly hard to disagree with Malcolm X's advice that "the best way to stop the Ku Klux Klan is to talk to the Ku Klux Klan in the only language it understands, for you can't talk French to someone who speaks German and communicate." The road to black power was opening up, and SNCC's Stokely Carmichael would soon conclude about the Democratic Party that it was "as ludicrous for Negroes to join as it would have been for Jews to join the Nazi Party in the 1930s."[64]

Like Africans abroad, African Americans at home were proving difficult for the Johnson administration to manage or control. During the fall presidential campaign, CORE and SNCC refused the administration's request through Roy Wilkins and civil rights activist Bayard Rustin for a moratorium on demonstrations to avoid encouraging further negative white reactions. The crux of Johnson's problem with the MFDP at Atlantic City had been its rejection of his compromise offer of two at-large delegates, as the president's forces refused to allow any possible dissenters to mar his renomination triumph.[65] Johnson believed he had to preserve the support of white Southerners for his reelection, and they had threatened to walk out of the convention if the black Mississippians were seated. Frustrated by televised pictures of MFDP pickets protesting the seating of the regular Mississippi delegates, the president seized his phone to order the top official of one of the national television networks, "Get your goddamn cameras off the niggers out front and back on the speaker's stand inside, goddamn it!"[66] Even his stalwart supporter Wilkins had to admit that Johnson's display of political power in defeating the MFDP, eased by access to FBI wiretaps of MFDP strategy sessions in Atlantic City, "wasn't one of his finest hours." "The lasting sense of grievance," Wilkins noted, caused "terrible damage to relations between white liberals and black organizers."[67]

Johnson's black support was beginning to slip away on the left at the same time as whites were starting to abandon him on the right. Much of the civil rights movement clearly had different perspectives and goals than the White House: social transformation of America from below versus gradualist leadership from above; distrust of rigid anti-Communism versus global leadership of the non-Communist world; and rejection of the legitimacy of Jim Crow versus respect for Southern officials. Perhaps the most crucial difference came in their views of the white Southern leadership. For civil rights workers, white supremacists like George Wallace and Jim Eastland were dire enemies in a struggle for control and direction of the American South. Black organizers were appalled that the U.S. government could send enormous armies halfway around the globe to defend the "free world," while refusing to order even one American soldier into the South to protect the legal right of American citizens to vote. For the White House, however, segregationist officials were an obnoxious but crucial part of the power structure of the federal and state governments and the Democratic Party—undoubtedly stubborn and backward-looking, but part of the respected leadership of the United States. Like the white authorities in southern Africa, they were in no way an enemy against whom the U.S. government should use force. For better or worse, Johnson believed, they were a part of "us."[68]

Despite these differences with the civil rights movement, the Johnson administration managed through 1964 to fend off most of the forces of racial polarization and keep its liberal coalition moving forward. Johnson's leadership in passing the landmark Civil Rights Act had been superb, and he succeeded in keeping the American role in Vietnam out of the fall presidential campaign. A landslide 61 percent of the voters—including almost all blacks casting ballots—elected him in November, sweeping into office as well a large Democratic majority in Congress more liberal than any in thirty years. Goldwater carried only his native Arizona and five states in the Deep South. While this portentous shift of white Southern voters away from a fellow Southerner and toward the Republican party suggested eventual trouble, for now Johnson savored his mandate for continued liberal reform, especially in the area of his starkest difference with Goldwater: civil rights. White supremacists in South Africa confirmed that reading of the election, registering their dismay that Goldwater did not symbolize what one representative of apartheid had anticipated as a "triumph of conservatism in the West," which would have allowed the United States to shake off its "sickly humanism."[69]

An explosion of racial violence in Alabama four months later, on 7 March 1965, shocked the American people and provided Lyndon Johnson with his greatest opportunity to demonstrate his leadership of the nation. Viewers of the Sunday evening ABC television movie *Judgment at Nuremburg* were treated to the irony of a news flash showing home-grown, state-supported storm trooper activity right in the United States. Heavily armed Alabama state troopers and Dallas County sheriffs viciously assaulted a line of peaceful, unarmed civil rights marchers at the Edmund Pettus Bridge outside Selma. Television cameras captured the ferocity of the beatings for a national and international audience. Having just been reassured a few months earlier that the events in Stanleyville showed racial savagery to be a problem of Africans (and perhaps their descendants), Americans and their Texan president were dismayed by the most brutal repression yet of any civil rights demonstration. No surreptitious act of night riders, this was a full-scale riot by the uniformed authorities of an American state.[70]

What did the events at Selma mean? For most white Alabamans, the police action saved them from the indignity of hundreds of black Americans marching symbolically down the Jefferson Davis Highway to Montgomery, the capital of the old Confederacy. The Alabama state legislature passed a resolution charging the marchers with conducting sexual orgies, leading several nuns in the group to joke about their lost reputations. SNCC chairman John

Lewis responded to the questions of the press: "These white segregationists always think about fornication. That's why you see so many shades of brown on this march."[71] For Vice President Hubert Humphrey and some others in the administration, the issue was not carnal but ideological: they believed Communist agents among the Selma demonstrators had successfully provoked a violent confrontation.[72] For FBI Director J. Edgar Hoover the problem was one of both sexual and political subversion, but he also understood that the strong national reaction against the police violence meant the ending of an era of quiet FBI alliance with Southern authorities in the defense of Jim Crow.[73] Perhaps the most illuminating evidence of the nature of the Alabama conflict appeared in the symbolism of flags: black Selma high schoolers in the march carried both the Stars and Stripes and the blue flag of the United Nations, while state patrol cars bore Confederate flags on their front license plates, and the capitol dome in Montgomery flew the Confederate flag above the Alabama state flag. Displaying the only American flags in sight and proclaiming their connection to a larger international community, young black Alabamans in their own state seemed to be walking through a foreign country.[74]

The events in Selma unfolded in a troubling international context. On the day after state troopers assaulted African American and white civil rights activists in Alabama, the first 3,500 U.S. marines waded ashore in South Vietnam to defend the Danang airbase. With his skull fractured by a police baton, John Lewis declared angrily, "I don't see how President Johnson can send troops to Vietnam [and] the Congo . . . and can't send troops to Selma, Alabama." Lewis and others could not believe that democracy deserved greater defense abroad than at home.[75] Harris Wofford, the associate director of the Peace Corps, flew to Montgomery on 8 March to join a second march because after "two years in Africa, I knew afresh that America's relationship with the world depended on how speedily and fully we ended racial discrimination at home."[76] That same day Bundy warned Johnson that "U.S. prestige and influence on the African Continent have never been lower," endangering American strategic, economic, and political interests there. The problem, Bundy said in language again implying a parental analogy, was that Africans were not convinced that anyone at the highest level of the U.S. government cared about them, while diplomats from China and the Soviet Union lavished public attention on them.[77] Events like those in Selma did little to improve African confidence in the United States and its leadership in a multiracial world. In a public meeting about American ties to South Africa, CORE's

James Farmer argued that "the fight against aggression and for equality is essentially the same struggle in South Africa and in Selma."[78] The Johnson administration would not have disagreed, but its primary concern was not swiftly achieving racial equality but avoiding friction and instability. In speech notes made three days after the Selma incident, Johnson defined America's mission in Africa as "[a]verting racial conflicts between [the white-ruled] parts of Southern Africa and the rest of the continent."[79]

Domestically, Johnson seized the opportunity arising from the national outrage about what came to be called Bloody Sunday in Selma to make a preemptive strike against further racial polarization. Aware that many younger African Americans agreed with SNCC's James Forman—"If we can't sit at the table of democracy, then we'll knock the fucking legs off"—the president delivered the most famous speech of his career to a joint session of Congress on 15 March.[80] "We have already waited a hundred years and more" since equality was promised, he pronounced in his most serious tone, "and the time for waiting is gone." With a determination unusual even for this forceful man, the president demanded that Congress pass a national voting rights bill to guarantee finally the most basic right of citizenship to all Americans. Selma marked a turning point in the nation's "unending search for freedom," he said, just as surely as Concord, Lexington, and Appomattox had done generations earlier. In a final twist that shocked even his most sympathetic listeners, Johnson seemed to identify himself, the U.S. government, and the American people for the first time fully with the cause of the civil rights movement. Pausing for emphasis, he declared: "And we . . . shall . . . overcome!" Stunned, the audience sat silent for an instant as one Southern congressman murmured, "Goddamn." Then the room erupted in a sustained standing ovation.[81]

Martin Luther King, Jr., watching the speech on television in a Selma living room, began to cry, something his aides had not seen before. Roy Wilkins, who was sitting in the audience on Capitol Hill that night, remembered that "at that moment, I confess, I loved L.B.J." At this high-water mark of the movement for racial justice in the United States, Lyndon Johnson was in the lead. He followed through by sending federal troops to protect the reconstituted marchers in Alabama and by pushing the Voting Rights Act through Congress with remarkable speed despite a Southern filibuster.[82] His assistants made certain that the international audience did not miss the significance of the stand he had taken, sending copies of his speech to the leader of each African nation.[83] In a graduation address at Howard University on 4 June, Johnson went further in his support for African Americans by laying out the logic of what would become known as affirmative action: "You do not take a person who, for years, has been hobbled by chains and liberate him, bring him to the starting line of a race, and then say you are free to compete with all the others, and still just believe that you have been completely fair." He "spelled out the meaning of full integration for Negroes," the noted black novelist Ralph Ellison recalled, in a way no other president ever had.[84]

### Trouble in Vietnam, Los Angeles, and Rhodesia

The spring of 1965 marked the turning point in the Johnson administration's journey from great success to deep failure. From the moral heights of leading the campaign for national voting rights legislation at home, the president and his advisers tumbled toward the boggy ground of the Southeast Asian quagmire, the troubled waters of urban violence at home, and the swamp of white supremacy in southern Africa. The administration's growing international involvements, first in the brief occupation of the Dominican Republic in late April and then in the shift to a full-blown ground war in Vietnam in July, brought an end to most of its impressive domestic achievements in the areas of economic and racial justice.

The issue of race was never far below the surface for American policymakers dealing with Southeast Asia. General Maxwell Taylor, the U.S. ambassador to South Vietnam, laid out for the Joint Chiefs of Staff his strong reservations about committing American ground combat troops to the country: "The white-faced soldier, armed, equipped and trained as he is, is not a suitable guerrilla fighter for the Asian forests and jungles."[85] Administration officials on both sides of the debate about further involvement in Vietnam feared what dissenter George Ball called "the appearance of a white man's war."[86] Johnson's appointment in July of Major Hugh Robinson as the first black military aide to a U.S. president seemed no coincidence in this regard.[87] McGeorge Bundy advised the president to reject Ball's recommendation to withdraw from Indochina, but not before receiving "pretty tight and hard analyses of some disputed questions like the following . . . What are the chances of our getting into a white man's war with all the brown men against us or apathetic?"[88] The Johnson administration believed it could not afford to pull out of Vietnam, even as it acknowledged the likely racial character of a deeper involvement in the war there.

— 191 —

Bundy's "brown men" did seem particularly dubious about Johnson's new war. To preserve its precarious diplomatic balance in Africa, the administration had to resist the temptation to respond strongly to vocal critics like Ghana's Kwame Nkrumah.[89] Dissent grew quickly among black Americans, beginning with the speech of SNCC's Bob Moses at the first large antiwar demonstration on 17 April in Washington and accelerating among civil rights workers in the South that summer. A leaflet issued by a group of activists in McComb, Mississippi, in July urged resistance to the draft by connecting racial issues at home and abroad: "No Mississippi Negroes should be fighting in Viet Nam for the White Man's freedom, until all the Negro People are free in Mississippi . . . No one has a right to ask us to risk our lives and kill other Colored People in Santo Domingo and Viet Nam, so that the White American can get richer . . . [W]e don't know anything about Communism, Socialism, and all that, but we do know that Negroes have caught hell here under this *American Democracy.*"[90] Most Americans in 1965 still supported their government's anti-Communist stance abroad, but younger African Americans were sliding toward agnosticism on this issue. More moderate civil rights leaders opposed efforts at draft resistance, but that same month King also condemned Johnson's quest for a military victory in Vietnam and called for a negotiated settlement.[91]

The antiwar views of Moses and other SNCC staffers invited segregationists to identify them as traitors. U.S. Congressman Joe Waggoner of Louisiana seized the opportunity to condemn them as a "mob" with no students, "only radical, Communist-infiltrated gangs of agitators." Historian C. Vann Woodward tried to remind readers of the *New York Times* in August that the hearts of SNCC activists were "in Mississippi or Harlem, not in Moscow or Peking."[92] The FBI, however, was not buying any excuses for what it saw as subversive activity. With the concurrence of Johnson's Justice Department, on 15 June Hoover ordered a wiretap of the office phones of SNCC because it was "the principal target for Communist Party infiltration among the various civil rights organizations."[93] Going to war in Asia was clearly splitting the White House and civil rights workers further apart.

Thus far Johnson had been able to count on the commitment of most black civil rights activists to nonviolence as the key to limiting racial polarization in the United States, despite continuing white violence and a growing white political backlash. But the situation began to change in the summer of 1965 in ways that suggested the president's task as a keeper of national unity would soon get much harder. *Newsweek* and the *New York Times* both reported in August the growing popularity among Southern blacks of the Deacons for Defense and Justice, a group begun in Louisiana to provide armed security for civil rights workers and African American neighborhoods threatened by white violence and unprotected by local white police. The Deacons' effectiveness was clear in Bogalusa, Louisiana, where in April they had ended the traditional Saturday night entertainment for certain whites of shooting up the black section of town. Deacon leader A. Z. Young explained how: "Three rednecks [with rifles] got out of a car and began shouting in the middle of the night. About a dozen of us [with guns] come out from the bushes, from driveways, from dark houses. We ringed 'em around, and then, well, we talked to them a little. You know, they got mighty polite. They was all smiles. It was 'yes, sir' and 'no, sir' and so we let 'em go, and they ain't been back." Bogalusa had become "an armed camp" and a symbol of the Johnson administration's limited influence on the African American quest for equality and dignity.[94]

Small-town Louisiana provided merely a prelude, however, to the racial crisis that ignited in the Watts neighborhood of Los Angeles on the night of 11 August. Over the next six days, arson, looting, and gunfire left thirty-four people dead, over a thousand injured, and $40 million in property damage.[95] On a scale far larger than the disturbances of the previous summer, the Watts uprising was the first of the decade's insurrections in impoverished black urban neighborhoods to gain major national attention.[96] Most ironic and telling of all, the violence began just six days after Johnson signed into law the Voting Rights Act, probably the most effective single piece of legislation in promoting racial equality in the twentieth century. And it came only two weeks after he ordered over a hundred thousand American troops into Vietnam. As the United States entered into war abroad, national guardsmen patrolled the decimated streets of black Los Angeles in a scene that looked an awful lot like war at home.

Competing explanations of the violence quickly filled the national news, with responsibility assigned variably to black unemployment and poverty, white racism, black immorality and disrespect for the law, police brutality, and Johnson's coddling of African Americans.[97] The president himself reacted with shock, sorrow, and anger. The Voting Rights Act had been, he later told Doris Kearns, "a triumph for freedom as huge as any victory that has ever been won on any battlefield."[98] Expecting gratitude, he instead received the news of the Watts riot as a personal affront: "How is it possible after all we've accomplished? Is the world topsy-turvy?"[99] He literally did not know what to do at first, staying at his ranch in Texas where he had been vacationing and refusing for three days even to accept his assistants' calls from Washington—the only time he was ever so out of touch as president. After recovering his political instincts, he arranged for Republican John McCone to chair a state investigation of the riot, to defend his right flank: "An ex-CIA Director, conservative, if he says no communist conspiracy and describes the [awful] conditions in Watts, we'll be able to help those Negroes out there." Johnson feared that by increasing white resistance, Watts and any further disturbances might undermine future Great Society legislation and perhaps even threaten the liberal gains already made.[100]

In just five months, the dominant image of African Americans in the national media had changed from the hymn-singing, flag-bearing marchers of Selma willing to suffer for the cause of justice to uncontrolled hooligans reveling in random violence. Equating rioters with Klansmen, the president revealed his concern that Watts might be a prelude to a black return to savagery, perhaps like that of the African rebels in the Congolese jungle. "Negroes," he told his aide Joseph Califano, "will end up pissing in the aisles of the Senate" and making fools of themselves as they had after the Civil War a century earlier. The younger, Northern-born John Kennedy had not imbibed the Reconstruction myth of black depravity in its most racist form, and as president his experiences with white Southerners led him to doubt the traditional white view of post–Civil War history. His successor, raised in the segregated South, labored mightily to mold a nation that would not discriminate. But deep down, Johnson apparently still feared that beneath a thin veneer of civilization, primitive instincts lurked in the hearts of Americans of African descent.[101]

In the midst of these rising tensions, in October 1965, Congress passed Johnson's new Immigration Act, which abolished the long-standing national origins quotas and put all countries on an equal basis for the first time as potential providers of new Americans. The old system of ethnic and racial discrimination, with its strong preference for northern and western Europeans, had fit a segregated society. But the experience of World War II as well as the end of legal segregation made that vestigial structure an embarrassment to a multiracial nation at the head of the non-Communist world. By eliminating that system, the American government removed a major irritant to nonwhite nations in their dealings with the United States. The change would lead in subsequent decades to an unexpected new wave of immigration, especially from Asia, but in the fall of 1965 the new law's significance lay in its symbolism of a sharp break with the past: the United States would no longer legally seek to preserve an identity as a homogenous white society. There was little coincidence in this change being enacted in the wake of both the civil rights movement and the dispatch of American troops into war with an Asian enemy. The Johnson administration was determined to minimize racial conflict on all fronts.[102]

A few weeks later, the white backlash the Johnson administration had worked so hard to restrain at home erupted overseas. On 11 November Prime Minister Ian Smith of Southern Rhodesia issued a unilateral declaration of independence (UDI) from Britain. In an age of African states gaining their freedom from European colonial control, the UDI represented an exceptional form of decolonization: shifting power from the metropole not into the hands of representatives of the majority but into those of the tiny minority of white settlers and their descendants. The 95 percent of Rhodesia's population that was African held no political power and earned only 5 percent of the country's income, leaving white Rhodesians with one of the highest per capita incomes in the world. White Rhodesians had no intention of waiting for the continent's rising tide of racial equality and self-rule to reach their shore. They had observed recent events in the rest of Africa with dread, from the Mau Mau uprising in Kenya in the early 1950s to the Congo disorders since 1960. They had received thousands of British and Belgian refugees from those lands who bolstered their assumptions about Africans beyond white control as "savages." White Rhodesians were appalled that by 1964 Britain had granted full independence under African rule to Northern Rhodesia (Zambia) and Nyasaland (Malawi), the two other colonies of the former Central African Federation, while refusing to allow the same to their government in Salisbury, which had been self-governing since 1923. They had also been deeply impressed by Moise Tshombe's success in using a few hundred white mercenaries to gain control of huge portions of the Congo. "We have struck a blow for the preservation of justice, civilization and Christianity," Smith declared in his UDI speech, emphasizing his view of southern Africa as "the ultimate bastion against communism on the African continent." Equating the ending of racial hierarchies with Communism was part of a language familiar to American listeners: the language of the Dixiecrats, the Southern white segregationists. By setting its face against the tide of modern history, the Smith regime had chosen to follow the South African model, and in doing so it created a whole new front of racial polarization for the beleaguered Johnson administration.[103]

The British government refused to use force to restore its sovereignty, to the chagrin of Africans, who found themselves promoting British colonial control for the first and only time. London turned instead to the United Nations to promote diplomatic isolation and economic sanctions for Rhodesia as a way to pressure Smith.[104] African and Asian states reacted angrily to the UDI. Having just emerged from decades and centuries of European rule, they were appalled by the idea of a small number of whites trying to reverse the tide of anticolonial liberation. Africans condemned the unwillingness of Britain to use force against whites in Rhodesia, especially in light of its ready military response against rebellious nonwhites in other colonies like Malaya and Kenya. Even the governments of South Africa and Portugal responded to the Smith regime with some ambivalence, considering the renewed international condemnation it was sure to bring to all of the white-ruled states in the region.

African leaders spoke threateningly of possible race war. The Ivory Coast ambassador to the UN, Arsene Usher, warned the Security Council that if Belgians, British, and Americans had the right to rescue white hostages at Stanleyville, then Africans had the same right "to free their brothers taken as hostages by white rebels under a regime condemned by you and considered by world public opinion as illegal."[105] The CIA worried that in "exposing Africa's impotence before the world, the [Rhodesian] crisis has awakened bitter feelings of frustration, humiliation and racial inferiority which may lead to extreme, and sometimes irrational actions against Western interests."[106] A commentator in the *Christian Century* observed that Africans and other Third World peoples saw Rhodesia as "a touchstone of the moral integrity not only of Britain but also of the white world as a whole as they grapple with the injustice of racial discrimination."[107]

The Johnson administration in 1965 believed its record on racial discrimination was quite strong, and it had no interest in besmirching that reputation by a high-level engagement with the racially explosive situation in southern Africa. The timing of the UDI, just months into the new American involvement in a ground and air war in Vietnam, ensured that Washington officials would be distracted. Already battling Communists abroad and the forces of white conservative reaction at home, Johnson had no taste for fighting foreign racists in a region of low strategic priority. The American obsession with the war in Vietnam until 1973 and then with avoiding other such involvements for the rest of that decade would coincide precisely with the years of civil war in Rhodesia that ended in the establishment of Zimbabwe in 1980.

The Johnson administration followed Britain's lead in eschewing the use of arms and confrontation with either South Africa or the Portuguese rulers of neighboring Angola and Mozambique, while at the same time condemning the UDI and imposing sanctions on the Salisbury regime.[108]

The debates within the Johnson administration about how to respond to the UDI reveal the range of options policymakers could imagine. At one end stood White House aide Jack Valenti, who warned Bundy of the importance of the West resolving the Rhodesian problem rather than avoiding it: "A crisis faced now can return Rhodesia to legal rule, influence Portugal in a liberal sense, isolate South Africa and weaken its stand over S[outh] W[est] Africa, and keep alive in the rest of Africa distrust of Communism and belief in the West." Sidestepping the issue, he argued, would instead encourage Africa to turn away from the West and would produce "greater risks of bloody racial conflict" in Rhodesia and elsewhere in southern Africa in the long run. Valenti dismissed most supporters of the Smith regime as immigrants from Europe who "went to Rhodesia not to pioneer but to get sun, servants, no taxation and no welfare state"—not tough, self-reliant farmers supposedly comparable to white Americans' ancestors. He reminded Bundy sharply that there "*is* a contradiction between fighting to give South Vietnam the right to choose its own government and doing little or nothing about the rights of four million Rhodesian Africans. It perpetuates the Communists' cry that all rules are broken when white interests are at stake—a dangerous cry for a world in which the white man is outnumbered four to one." In the wake of the Watts riot, Valenti and others feared the impact of televised images of a potential Rhodesian race war on an American society increasingly marked by racial polarization and violence.[109]

At the other end of the spectrum of advice in the administration stood Dean Acheson, former secretary of state, original Cold War "wise man," and informal adviser to Johnson. Acheson strongly supported the Smith regime in Salisbury as well as the apartheid government in Pretoria, and he abhorred the UN sanctions against Rhodesia. He considered the sanctions a form of pandering to "the international juvenile delinquents" of the Third World and "the Black Mafia" of African ambassadors to the UN.[110]

Rusk and Bundy fell somewhere between Acheson and Valenti in their views of southern Africa. Unlike Acheson, neither the secretary of state nor the national security adviser had much personal sympathy for white supremacists. But Bundy seemed as concerned with avoiding American identification with "hot-headed Africans" as with the white government in Salisbury.[111] And Rusk declared flatly a year later, "The problem cannot be settled by force. The thought of using U.S. troops is appalling." For the vast majority of Rhodesians, of course, that same thought might instead have been encouraging, which raises questions about why, more precisely, the idea seemed so unthinkable to the secretary of state. Was Rusk simply reflecting the unavailability of U.S. forces already deployed in Southeast Asia? Was he also demonstrating the ongoing tendency of even racially liberal white Americans to identify with other whites abroad? From a key supporter of sending hundreds of thousands of American troops into Vietnam, such sensitivity about settling problems by force sounded false.[112]

While the Johnson administration struggled to avoid the issue of white Rhodesian independence as much as possible, the responses of other Americans demonstrated the chasm between opponents and defenders of the UDI. This gap reflected fundamental differences in definitions of "the West" and "Western values," as well as the widening split between mobilized African Americans and their segregationist countrymen. While the UDI did not generate much attention among the general public in the United States, civil rights workers and racial liberals strongly opposed the creation of what seemed to be another apartheid state. Martin Luther King, Jr., called on black Americans to monitor closely U.S. ties with the southern African states, and he condemned the considerable American investments in South Africa as undercutting Washington's verbal condemnations of apartheid and the UDI.[113] Even National Urban League director Whitney Young weighed in with the State Department to urge uncompromising opposition to Ian Smith. Young reminded George Ball that he had never discussed Vietnam publicly and had discouraged his colleagues from doing so, but that unlike Vietnam, Rhodesia was "purely a racial matter."[114] Opponents of Rhodesia argued that long-term American access to valuable Rhodesian minerals, especially chrome, would best be served by closer identification with that country's vast African majority than with its fleeting white rulers.[115]

The Rhodesian lobby, by contrast, represented a marriage of anti-Communism and white supremacy. White Southern senators and representatives like Strom Thurmond and James Eastland saw the Salisbury and Selma crises as closely related challenges to white authority that had to be resisted. Eastland complained bitterly in the Senate that, in contrast to U.S. nonrecognition of Rhodesia, "Every time a group of partially educated, half-savage tribes has constituted an alleged government and declared its country free and independent, we have been pressured by an increasing fear of world opinion into recognizing that government."[116] Anti-Communists like Barry Goldwater loathed the idea that the United States was expanding trade with the Soviet Union and China while cutting off economic ties with a government that was openly anti-Communist, pro-Western, Christian, and prosperous. After all, the Soviets and Chinese were aiding America's enemies in Vietnam while the Rhodesians spoke openly of sending troops to fight *with* the American forces there.[117]

For many white Southerners, the Rhodesian experiment represented a successful Western version of how the otherwise chaotic Third World ought to be run. U.S. Representative Joe Waggoner of Louisiana proclaimed that "Rhodesia has become the cornerstone of this nation's tenuous foothold in the entire Afro-Asian world."[118] If the Rhodesian government fell, the American group Friends of Rhodesian Independence argued, "both South Africa and Portuguese Africa will inevitably fall like dominoes, leaving the entire continent in anti-Western hands."[119] Here, then, was the heart of the conflict between Americans on opposite sides of the Rhodesian issue. Did Ian Smith have his finger in the dike, staving off a flood of savage African madness, or was he an unwelcome obstructionist, holding the door shut against simple representative government? Both defenders and opponents of the Salisbury regime believed they were promoting the values and security of the West against its worst enemies, but they differed dramatically in how they understood the West and their own country. Thus did the civil rights movement and the white backlash clash on international as well as domestic issues.

The international focus on Rhodesia brought renewed attention to the Republic of South Africa, the powerful hub of the white redoubt of southern Africa. In the first months of 1966, both SNCC and Senator Robert Kennedy increased their criticisms of American coziness with apartheid. SNCC members staged a sit-in at the South African embassy in Washington, while Kennedy traveled to the University of Cape Town to deliver the strongest anti-apartheid speech yet by a major American political figure. Within a year such pressures led to a new U.S. military policy of unofficially boycotting South African ports for refueling or shore leave.[120] Martin Luther King, Jr., accepted two invitations to speak in South Africa during 1966, but the South African government refused to grant him the necessary visas. Instead, he led a march in July by civil rights demonstrators seeking an end to residential segregation in Chicago, in which participants carried signs reading "End Apartheid in Real Estate." The response of white Chicagoans, gathering in crowds of thousands to throw bottles and rocks and shout obscenities at the peaceful marchers, only served to underline the parallels between racial discrimination in South Africa and that in the United States.[121]

Johnson faced an obvious dilemma in South Africa. A president so committed to ending racial discrimination could hardly have approved of apartheid, yet the United States continued to have substantial economic and strategic ties to South Africa. Along with Japan, South Africa had the fastest growing economy in the world in the 1960s. As one U.S. government study put it, "US private investment is continuing at a high rate in South Africa because of unusually favorable returns."[122] As the world's largest supplier of gold, the apartheid state had unique importance for the global economy and particularly for the economy of America's closest ally, Great Britain. The CIA emphasized that South Africa was "a major supplier of minerals to the free world" and that "consuming countries would have difficulty finding alternative sources."[123] Both the Defense Department and the National Aeronautics and Space Administration (NASA) operated space tracking stations within South Africa that they considered crucial for American space and missile programs.[124]

Nevertheless, South Africa was a growing political problem for the Johnson administration. International condemnation of the apartheid government was escalating, symbolized by the country's being banned from the Olympic Games in 1964. Undeterred, the Pretoria government by 1965 had crushed the initial black efforts at armed insurgency that had marked the first half of the decade, since the Sharpeville massacre of 1960, and had created a more ruthless, efficient version of a police state. "The rule of law has been set aside by arbitrary arrest and detention," observed the NSC, and "apartheid [is] now being drastically extended."[125] White liberal dissent virtually disappeared, with the opposition United Party even trying on occasion to "race-bait" the ruling Nationalists as insufficiently supportive of white rule in the region.[126] South Africa was, in fact, busy building additional facilities near its northern borders and in South West Africa better to project its military power into the surrounding area.[127] Meanwhile the Rivonia trial of 1964 resulted in life imprisonment terms for Nelson Mandela and eight other top leaders of the African National Congress who, as officials in the Johnson administration admitted privately, were "the leaders of the *moderate* African opposition in South Africa."[128] "Having been barred from all peaceful courses of action," the NSC noted, black South Africans were turning toward radicalism and "black consciousness," a movement that would parallel black power in the United States.[129] State Department emissary Charles Fahy warned Secretary of State Rusk upon returning from a fact-finding tour of South Africa that "for every Mandela there are 20 to take his place."[130]

South Africa's defiance of world opinion inevitably spilled over to roil its relations with the United States. A particular source of tension was South African treatment of nonwhite American officials. Rusk reacted with great anger to the apartheid state's efforts to prevent Ric Haynes, a young African American on the NSC staff, from visiting the neighboring British High Commission territories.[131] Haynes himself responded with humor to an invitation to a reception at the South African embassy in Washington two years later, telling his boss, Robert Komer, that it was probably a clerical error but that "nevertheless I think it's important I put in a brief appearance if only to prove the point that some of my best friends are South Africans, but I wouldn't want my daughter to . . ."[132] Administration officials in South Africa found their South African counterparts increasingly arrogant and even paranoid. The U.S. ambassador to South Africa, Joseph Satterthwaite, a man known for his sympathy for white South Africans, essentially gave up on talking with the dogmatic prime minister, Henrik Verwoerd. Lewis Douglas—prominent American businessman, former ambassador to England, investor in South African mining companies, and self-described "friend" of South Africa—spoke with the prime minister on a visit to the country in 1964 and, in Satterthwaite's words, "about reached [the] conclusion that Verwoerd is a psychopath."[133] If the South African leadership appeared insane to its friends, it looked much worse to those less at ease with apartheid.

While Johnson administration officials debated privately how best to respond to the deteriorating situation in the land of racial totalitarianism, the international community and civil rights leaders in the United States demonstrated what the NSC called "a growing dissatisfaction with our ambivalent policies toward South Africa."[134] Preoccupied with Vietnam and awash in conflicting advice about the need to alienate neither South Africa nor the independent black African nations, Johnson sought to muddle through and fend off domestic critics of his policies toward Africa. On 26 May 1966, two and a half years into his presidency, he gave his first speech about Africa and the importance of majority rule on the occasion of the third anniversary of the founding of the Organization of African Unity. White House aide Bill Moyers underlined the speech's importance not only for Africans but also as a way to trump two domestic critics: civil rights workers and Robert Kennedy. For the former, "it is a cheap way to keep them quiet on at least one issue." For the latter, "it will . . . make it difficult for Bobby to get far ahead of you" on the issue of political liberty for black Africans.[135] Anticipating that an imminent World Court decision would declare South Africa's control of South West Africa illegal, Johnson told the NSC on 14 July 1966 that perhaps a compromise statement by the United States would "relieve some of the pressure [on us] which will arise. We should try everything. Even a blind hog may find an acorn." The search for that acorn of compromise remained a Herculean task, however, as militant white supremacy in South Africa converged with that in neighboring Rhodesia, while both African Americans and Africans grew more skeptical of the motivations of the rooting American hog.[136]

## The Escalation of Dissent

Racial polarization and antiwar dissent accelerated in the United States during 1966 and 1967, undercutting the Johnson administration's popularity and effectiveness. On 6 January 1966 SNCC became the first major civil rights organization to declare its opposition to the American war in Vietnam and to encourage resistance to the draft. One of its staff, Navy veteran Sammy Younge, was murdered for attempting to use a "white" restroom in Tuskegee, Alabama. Partly in response, SNCC's executive committee issued a statement condemning the U.S. government for being "deceptive in its claims of concern for the freedom of colored people in such countries as the Dominican Republic, the Congo, South Africa, Rhodesia, and in the United States itself." The war in Southeast Asia seemed to SNCC workers a demonstration of hypocrisy by liberal American politicians who declared their support for democracy around the world while tolerating undemocratic practices right under their noses in the American South. Strongly opposing violence as a means to liberation in the southern United States, those same political leaders were now unleashing extraordinary violence to prevent the apparent liberation of the South Vietnamese. Civil rights organizers were moving from a narrow critique of a double standard to a broader rejection of an American role in Southeast Asia. They increasingly connected the disenfranchisement of black rural Southerners with the disempowerment of Vietnamese peasants, and laid the blame for both at the U.S. government's doorstep.[137]

The predictable torrent of criticism that greeted SNCC's announcement emanated from whites of almost all political loyalties and from such mainstream civil rights organizations as the NAACP and the National Urban League. The Johnson administration cut off most of its contacts with SNCC, and the organization's white Southern opponents seized the opportunity to portray it as clearly subversive. SNCC's long-standing policy of not excluding Communists or anyone else willing to work for its goals made it vulnerable to red-baiting, especially now that it had moved beyond issues of racial equality to express opposition to an American war against Communists. SNCC worker Jimmy Garrett explained to a reporter that SNCC was actually "subverting" any Communists who might be working with it, as "we're more revolutionary than the Communists."[138] That insight did little to overcome the prevalent American assumption in the Cold War years that any organization not excluding Communists would soon come to be dominated by them. Even the Christian faith of many SNCC workers failed to bridge the growing gap between them and the anti-Communist mainstream in American life. When John Lewis, the SNCC chairman and a devout Baptist minister, was granted the first conscientious objector status of any black in Alabama history as a result of Justice Department intervention, his local draft board chairman complained, "But *we're* all Baptists and *we're* not C.O.'s."[139] Former SNCC staffer Julian Bond won election to the state legislature of Georgia in June 1965 but was temporarily prevented from occupying his seat in January 1966 because of his new would-be colleagues' outrage at SNCC's opposition to the draft. As if to emphasize the gap between America and the Third World on this issue, African diplomats at the UN hosted Bond with a luncheon in his honor.[140]

Despite their new pariah status in American politics, SNCC staffers were not alone in their skepticism about the expanding war in Vietnam. If Johnson could dismiss SNCC as a subversive organization, he faced a more formidable foe in William Fulbright. Beginning on 28 January 1966, the chair of the Senate Foreign Relations Committee held six televised hearings on the war in which emerged his doubts and those of other critics about American policies. Among civil rights groups, CORE moved in a similar trajectory to that of SNCC, declaring its opposition to both the war and the draft in July 1966. Southern Christian Leadership Conference staff shared most of that same perspective, and Martin Luther King, Jr., increased the mild but steady criticisms of American war policies he had begun in 1965. King refused to condemn Julian Bond or the SNCC statement against the war. As the cost of the war effort skyrocketed, he became increasingly disillusioned with how military spending was replacing funding for the poor at home. King hesitated for another year before giving up completely on the Johnson administration, but by the close of 1966 he had ended personal communication with the president. King, SNCC chair John Lewis noted, was no longer Johnson's "head nigger when they [civil rights leaders] come to the White House."[141]

SNCC remained at the cutting edge of African American disillusionment with the White House and with white Americans in general. Stokely Carmichael's defeat of John Lewis in the May 1966 election for SNCC chair marked a watershed for the organization, as it shifted to a less religious and integrationist, more rhetorically militant and nationalist position. SNCC's earlier denunciation of the Vietnam war blossomed into the angry rhetoric of "black power," beginning with Carmichael's effective use of that phrase during a 16 June march in Greenwood, Mississippi. Whites responded with dismay to this new language of confrontation and its rejection of the nonviolent style of the integrationist phase of the civil rights movement. These "angry children of Malcolm X," as Julius Lester called the new black radicals, had come to agree with Malcolm's assertion that "I believe in the brotherhood of all men, but I don't believe in wasting brotherhood on anyone who doesn't want to practice it with me."[142] King rejected the language and style of black power but, as civil rights struggles shifted from the rural South to the urban North, he acknowledged, "You can't communicate with the ghetto dweller and at the same time not frighten many whites to death."[143] The wave of white violence that met King's open-housing demonstrations in Chicago less than a month later left no doubt just how large the racial divide in America remained. Rising black anger and greater white hostility fed directly off each other.

SNCC had long been the least acceptable civil rights organization to the Johnson administration. By mid-summer 1966, SNCC members were calling Johnson a murderer of Vietnamese civilians and were arguing that white liberals were no better than Southern racists on matters of human equality. For Johnson, who had staked his reputation on the importance of precisely that distinction, this accusation was appalling. Carmichael's plan to protest the Vietnam war at the wedding of Johnson's daughter, Luci, on 6 August made their conflict more personal. When King, Wilkins, and other civil rights leaders appealed to the SNCC chairman not to go through with a demonstration "in [such] extremely poor taste," Carmichael responded with a withering blast at "your boss" Johnson's napalming of Vietnamese and scheduling of the wedding on the anniversary of the atomic bombing of Hiroshima.[144] Julius Lester registered his disgust with the NAACP and the National Urban League and their condemnations of black power, stating, "as sure as the cavalry always comes to rescue the settlers, here come Roy Wilkins and Whitney

Young riding across the plains, yelling, Here we is, white folks. Let's get them niggers. Even Tonto didn't *join* the damned cavalry."[145] Moreover, Carmichael and other black power advocates began broadening their discussion of racism and its causes to include capitalism as the fundamental problem in America. For many whites in Washington and elsewhere, this meant that J. Edgar Hoover's suspicions about the subversive nature of parts of the civil rights movement no longer seemed quite so preposterous.[146]

Lyndon Johnson's strategy of containing the direction and militancy of black political energies in the United States was faltering. The young radicals of SNCC by no means represented a majority of black America, but they seemed to be its most outspoken edge and thus perhaps its future. By the end of 1966 they had begun to switch allegiances: no longer Americans who believed in their government, they considered themselves domestic allies of Third World revolutionary forces like the National Liberation Front of Vietnam, fighting the American empire from within as a fifth column while the guerrillas did so from outside. Along with an increasing number of young white antiwar radicals, they rejected Johnson, insulting his family, even threatening to shoot his wife, and identifying with his enemies in Cuba, China, Algeria, and North Vietnam.[147] This shift was accelerated by travels to Africa and other parts of the Third World, which SNCC members had begun as early as 1964.[148] They knew the significance of Martin Luther King's journeys to Ghana in 1957 and India in 1959, and they realized the importance of Malcolm X's visits to Africa in 1959 and the Middle East in 1964 in shaping his understanding of, and identification with, the Third World.[149] Confronted with diminishing white support for substantive social change, ongoing black poverty and racial discrimination, and an expanding war in Vietnam, politicized young African Americans were trading white liberal allies at home for what they believed was membership in an international struggle for liberty by people of color everywhere.[150]

One of the most important ways in which black radicals identified their situation with that of Third World revolutionaries was, by 1966, through the growing use of the analogy of colonialism. "Black people in the United States have a colonial relationship to the larger society," Carmichael declared. Gone was the hope of a few years earlier that whites' personal prejudices could be changed through education; the problem had become a deeper one of social and economic structures that benefited whites over blacks.[151] By March SNCC staffers in Atlanta were speaking openly of white civil rights workers as analogous to "the white civil servants and missionaries in the colonial countries who have worked with the colonial people for a long period of time and have developed a paternalistic attitude toward them."[152] SNCC's James Forman pointed to the nation's capital to demonstrate the colonial relationship between black and white in the United States: a mostly black Washington citizenry was ruled directly by the white federal government without such democratic mechanisms as elected representation.[153]

The colonial analogy went hand-in-hand for many young African American radicals with a growing attraction to violence, or at least to the rhetoric of violence. Increasingly disdainful of King's nonviolent, religious, and integrationist vision, they turned to the writings of secular Algerian revolutionary Frantz Fanon, who saw violence as a "cleansing force" that liberates the colonized person from "his inferiority complex and from his despair and inaction; it makes him fearless and restores his self-respect."[154] The scale of American violence against people of color in Southeast Asia helped convince these radicals of the futility of continuing to try to convert white Americans through self-sacrificing love. King himself was moving toward a more radical critique of American society. By January 1966 he was referring to urban slums in the United States as "a system of internal colonialism" comparable to the traditional European relationship with the Third World.[155]

The turn to black power and the Third World by younger black American radicals and nationalists represented a defeat for the Johnson administration's efforts to create a unified and racially integrated America that would stand behind his war in Southeast Asia. "UHURU, LIBERTAD, HALAGUA AND HARAMBEE!" one black nationalist wrote to his local draft board in Detroit: "When the call is made to free South Africa . . . to liberate Latin America . . . to free the black delta areas of Mississippi . . . TO FREE 12TH STREET HERE IN DETROIT!: When these calls are made, send for me," but he would not fight against "my oppressed brothers" in Vietnam.[156] While King, Wilkins, and other civil rights leaders condemned the summer riots in black urban areas during the Johnson years, black power advocates cheered them on as signs of what they hoped might be a growing revolutionary consciousness among poor African Americans. After a riot in Cleveland, Carmichael announced: "When you talk about black power, you talk of building a movement that will smash everything Western civilization has created."[157]

If Johnson's attempts at channeling black political energies were failing, other white Americans stood ready with less friendly responses. White Southern segregationists had tapped into intense white resentment of the civil rights movement in the 1964 Democratic presidential primaries, where George Wallace had shown surprising popularity even in the North. A few months later, home in Alabama, Wallace had condemned the approaching Selma march as similar to the Communist "street warfare" that "ripped Cuba apart, that destroyed Diem in Vietnam, that raped China—that has torn civilization and established institutions of this world into bloody shreds."[158] The Alabama governor's description of the peaceful phase of the civil rights movement seemed, ironically, to match (albeit with different adjectives) Stokely Carmichael's version of what black Americans should now aspire to. The fantasies of the white right and the black left appeared to converge, far from the moderate middle ground of Lyndon Johnson and the rest of America, black and white. The election of race-baiter Lester Maddox as governor of Georgia in the fall of 1966 indicated that white racism was rising in step with black power.[159] Already angry about the decline of Jim Crow, Southern segregationists watched the Supreme Court strike down the last state antimiscegenation law in 1967 and then were dismayed in November 1968 to see Captain Kirk of *Star Trek* engaging in television's first interracial kiss with Lieutenant Uhuru. Senator Richard Russell of Georgia articulated their sexual anxieties by arguing that the new civil rights laws could be used to "compel [a black's] admittance into the living room or bedroom of any citizen."[160]

Southern segregationists in his own party siphoned off some of Johnson's potential support, but the real power of the white backlash showed up in the Republican Party. Goldwater's 1964 nomination and his support in the white South offered early evidence of this shift. The urban riots of the next three summers accelerated the trend: a growing number of white Americans saw these disorders as evidence of continuing black lawlessness and violence despite civil rights gains and federal government antipoverty programs. White demands for a reinstitution of order and severe punishment of rioters fed the Republican critique of Johnson as "soft" on crime, just as the GOP had condemned Harry Truman as "soft" on Communism twenty years earlier.[161] By 1966 some whites were taking to the streets in their own hostile response to civil rights protests and black riots. In Baltimore, a White House aide reminded Johnson, "Italian, Polish and other white minorities bellicosely marched into the Negro districts proclaiming 'white supremacy'" and other white racist groups held public rallies.[162] Another presidential aide thought "it would have been hard to pass the emancipation proclamation in the atmosphere prevailing this summer."[163] In November the Democrats lost forty-seven seats in the House of Representatives—more than they had added in the 1964 landslide. Johnson's liberal majority was gone.

While continuing to work for such legislative reforms as an open housing law, Johnson himself tacked closer to the prevailing political winds in his last two years in office. He spoke more about crime and less about civil rights.[164] The war in Southeast Asia commanded more and more of his attention. One other important force in the white backlash helped push him to the right: the FBI. Personal and bureaucratic racism encouraged Hoover and his agents to continue their long-standing vendetta against King ("the burrhead," as Hoover typically called him) and the civil rights movement as a subversive threat to the middle America they saw themselves defending.[165] Obsessed with the Communist Party, the FBI viewed the radicalization of the civil rights movement and the violence in Northern black ghettoes as further evidence of the essential subversiveness of African Americans and their vulnerability to Communist influences. "Communist," Hoover told his agents, "should be interpreted in its broadest sense."[166] Building on its already extensive spying on King and other black leaders, the FBI in 1967 launched a new counterintelligence program to disrupt and discredit black antiwar advocates and supporters of the black power movement.[167] Hoover fed Johnson a steady diet of information about King's sex life and friendships with leftists and supposed Communists. Already alienated from King, SNCC, and CORE, Johnson merely enjoyed the first kind of information but paid close attention to the second, which he found damning, especially in light of the war against Communism in which he was engaged in Vietnam. The president was skeptical of Hoover in some ways, but he also feared being identified with civil rights leaders should Hoover ever leak his information. With the cooperation of Johnson and his administration, the FBI thus helped further distance the White House from all but the most conservative civil rights leaders by the last years of Johnson's presidency.[168]

Lyndon Johnson's hopes for an America and a world undivided by race and united behind his leadership continued to spiral downward in 1967. Deepening American involvement in Vietnam, the largest race riots of the decade in Newark and Detroit, and the shift of Martin Luther King, Jr., to active public opposition to the war led the way. King's commitment to non-violence had moved him to oppose the American war in Vietnam in a quiet way since its initial escalation in 1965. His dismay at military spending replacing antipoverty funding had deepened steadily since then. An encounter with photographs of napalmed Vietnamese children in the January 1967 issue of *Ramparts* magazine pushed him over the edge into active opposition and thus complete isolation from the Johnson administration. While the president remained tightly focused on American casualties, King's more internationalist perspective helped him count all the bodies in the war. On 25 February in Los Angeles he gave his first public speech against "a war that seeks to turn the clock of history back and perpetuate white colonialism" in Southeast Asia.[169] A month later in Chicago he helped lead his first antiwar march, and on 30 March he explained to a reporter that "the heart of the administration is in that war in Vietnam"—the opposite interpretation from Johnson's later claim that "that bitch of a war" had kept him from "the woman he loved," the Great Society. That same day King told the Southern Christian Leadership Conference board that in regard to Vietnam "the evils of capitalism are as real as the evils of militarism and evils of racism."[170] To Americans like J. Edgar Hoover—and Lyndon Johnson—this sounded awfully close to the language of Moscow or Hanoi.

On 4 April King gave his most significant address on the war at Riverside Church in New York City, assuring it much greater publicity than his previous antiwar statements. He condemned the U.S. government as "the greatest purveyor of violence in the world today" and its war in Vietnam as "an enemy of the poor." Just as the cost of the war was draining resources from impoverished Americans, the United States was siding with "the wealthy and the secure [the Saigon regime] while we create a hell for the poor" of Vietnam. King cited his Christian ministry and the commission to recipients of the Nobel Peace Prize (which he had been awarded in 1964) to work for "the brotherhood of man" as factors preventing him from viewing the war in Vietnam from an American nationalist perspective. Publicly opposing the war, he declared, was "the privilege and the burden of all of us who deem ourselves bound by allegiances and loyalties which are broader and deeper than nationalism and which go beyond our nation's self-defined goals and positions." Those allegiances and loyalties set King and others in the civil rights movement at odds with the militaristic nationalism of Lyndon Johnson.[171]

The Johnson administration now considered King beyond the pale. The president was particularly concerned with how King's new high-profile stance against the war and the draft might provoke further conservative backlash against Great Society programs already in place. Johnson suspected more strongly than ever that Communists were manipulating King. White House aide John Roche reported to him that King's speech was "quite an item" and indicated "that King—in desperate search of a constituency—has thrown in with the commies."[172] Infuriated at assertions by King that the Vietnam war was "a result of racist decision making" and by the general defection of a section of the civil rights movement from his liberal agenda, Johnson sought evidence from the FBI of a Communist conspiracy among radical black American leaders, a quest he renewed after the outbreak of violence in Newark and Detroit that summer.[173] Hoover was pleased to reply: "Based on King's recent activities and public utterances, it is clear that he is an instrument in the hands of subversive forces seeking to undermine our nation."[174]

The mainstream media responded to the Riverside Church address in similar fashion, rebuking King for his audacity in connecting the domestic issue of racial discrimination to foreign affairs. The *Washington Post* condemned him for doing "a grave injury" to "his natural allies," white liberals. *Life* was more direct in lambasting King's efforts at linking domestic and foreign developments: "He goes beyond his personal right to dissent when he connects progress in civil rights here with a proposal that amounts to abject surrender in Vietnam."[175] Such criticisms implicitly recognized the potential power of King's dissent in trying to link the civil rights and antiwar movements, and rejected such a rethinking of America's actions at home and abroad. King, prominent journalists said, was a civil rights leader and should remain just that. The NAACP board agreed, calling the Riverside Church speech "a serious tactical mistake."[176] Roy Wilkins argued that "you cannot serve the civil rights struggle at home by involving it in a struggle abroad." King had decided that the administration's determination to fight Communism abroad was squeezing out its interest in battling poverty at home, while the NAACP and the National Urban League continued to believe that the two wars could be conducted simultaneously.[177] During the early 1960s, King had commanded widespread, if often grudging, respect among the majority of Americans, white as well as black. But as he sailed into uncharted and unfriendly waters, responses to his voyage suggested the deepening split in American society. By 1968 younger black militants were dismissing him as an "Uncle Tom" while at the same time most whites feared him for his more militant and structural critique of American society and the war in Vietnam.

In the summer of 1967, black rage in Northern cities surged past dissent against the war as a challenge to the Johnson administration. Beginning on 12 July, Newark exploded in rioting, arson, and sniping that led to 26 deaths and over 1,500 injuries. Eleven days later Detroit erupted in the worst civil disorder of the century, leaving at least 40 dead and 1,300 buildings destroyed. Mayor Jerome Cavanaugh described the aftermath: "It looks like Berlin in 1945."[178] Touring the city at night for the Johnson administration, Justice Department official Roger Wilkins would not forget the impact of the military checkpoints: "There is no experience quite like being stopped at gunpoint by armed and uniformed men in the middle of an American city."[179] In the midst of increasing call-ups for the war in Vietnam, 4,000 paratroopers had to be diverted to Michigan to restore order in the city, the first such use of federal troops in a quarter of a century. Johnson was dismayed by the necessity of ordering mostly white National Guard and army units to occupy black ghettos, in part because he feared the increasingly frequent analogies between racial confrontations at home and abroad. He told Cyrus Vance, the top federal official in Detroit, "I'm concerned about the charge that we cannot kill enough people in Vietnam so we go out and shoot civilians in Detroit."[180]

Few Americans were pleased by the events in Newark and Detroit, but a small number of black radicals hoped they were witnessing the start of a revolution in America rather than merely ephemeral expressions of anger by the poor. H. "Rap" Brown, Carmichael's militant successor as SNCC chair, emphasized this distinction in a speech in Washington while Detroit was still burning: "Black folks try to loot when they should be shootin'. If you are gonna loot, loot you a gun store."[181] Brown called Johnson a "white honky cracker, an outlaw from Texas," and Carmichael, speaking at a press conference in Havana, where he was attending a conference of Latin American revolutionaries, urged African Americans to seek vengeance against Johnson, Rusk, and McNamara for their crimes in Vietnam: "we will kill first and we will aim for the head."[182]

The real violence in Newark and Detroit and the revolutionary rhetoric from some younger black leaders appalled white Americans as well as most African Americans. "Niggers with guns, niggers with guns" had been the muttered response of some white bystanders in Sacramento as thirty Black Panthers paraded through the California state capitol building with shotguns and rifles in May, and that thought was being murmured more widely by August.[183] When Carmichael announced on Havana Radio, on the second anniversary of the Watts riot, a call for African Americans to overthrow the "imperialist, capitalist and racialist structure of the United States," Senator Goldwater spoke for more than a few white Americans in urging Attorney General Ramsey Clark to arrest Carmichael and try him for treason, subjecting him to the death penalty.[184]

Johnson himself was pained and frustrated by the riots. He again sensed black ingratitude, for just a month earlier he had nominated the first African American ever for a seat on the Supreme Court, Thurgood Marshall. His leadership on behalf of racial equality seemed unappreciated either by younger, more militant black Americans or by white voters, who continued to shift toward the Republican Party. Public opinion polls after the riots showed sharp racial polarization. More than six times as many whites as blacks blamed the riots on outside agitators with Communist support. Conversely, two-thirds of blacks polled said police actions had contributed to the violence, while only one-sixth of whites agreed that police brutality even existed.[185] Congress reacted swiftly with harsh antiriot legislation and the defeat of such pending administration bills as the Rat Extermination Act for rodent eradication in urban slums, which opponents gleefully lampooned as a "civil rats bill." The riots led to a sharp drop in the president's public approval ratings, and Republicans emphasized how civil disorders had spread rapidly during his years in the White House.[186]

While opposition from white conservatives was intensifying on one side, liberal and black support for the administration was falling off on the other. Claiming that the riots were "caused by nice, gentle, timid white moderates who are more concerned about order than justice," King announced that he would go "all out" to prevent Johnson's reelection in 1968 and bring the war to an end. Senator Fulbright declared in the *New York Times* that the United States was fighting and losing "a two-front war" in Vietnam and in American cities. "The connection between Vietnam and Detroit," he argued, was in their conflicting demands on America for an "imperial role abroad" and "freedom and social justice at home."[187] Johnson created the National Advisory Commission on Civil Disorders (known as the Kerner Commission, after its chair, Illinois Governor Otto Kerner) to investigate the causes of the disorders, but he suspected that they had been instigated by a well-planned conspiracy of "Communist elements" and black nationalist agitators. He was unconvinced by the failure of the FBI and the intelligence services to find evidence of foreign funding of either the riots or black radical groups.[188]

Escalations of racial conflict abroad in the late summer of 1967 matched those at home. Despite some apparent victories on the ground in Vietnam, Johnson agreed in July to a significant escalation in the number of U.S. troops there. In southern Africa in August, African guerrillas crossed back into Rhodesia from neighboring Zambia, and suddenly white Rhodesian troops encountered their first pitched battles and suffered their first significant casualties. The war the UDI had invited had begun. The regional nature of the racial conflict also became evident that same month, as black insurgents of the South African ANC began working openly in Lusaka with their counterparts from Rhodesia. The Pretoria and Salisbury regimes responded in kind. South Africa declared in a "Monroe Doctrine for southern Africa" that its security frontier would now be the Zambezi River (the northern border of Rhodesia) rather than the Limpopo River (the northern border of South Africa).[189] The CIA's assurances to Johnson that Chinese and Soviet influence in the region was minimal and that the odds of a Communist government coming to power were "practically nil" did not alter the fundamental reality of a nascent race war developing on the southern end of the African continent.[190]

### Toward Race War Abroad and Polarization at Home

In Lyndon Johnson's last year in the White House America descended to its worst levels of racial violence and conflict of the entire post–World War II era. From the My Lai massacre to the assassination of Martin Luther King, Jr., to the election of Richard Nixon, 1968 marked a grim season along the color line. On 8 February police gunfire killed three black students and wounded thirty more from South Carolina State College during a protest rally at an all-white bowling alley in Orangeburg. Such ready violence when Southern white officers found people of color in their cross hairs coincided with furious fighting in Vietnam, where the Tet Offensive had been launched nine days earlier by the North Vietnamese and the National Liberation Front.

The American forces in Southeast Asia were not all white, of course. In the Vietnam war for the first time the U.S. military was fully racially integrated in combat. Not surprisingly, racial tensions were common in rear areas, but more striking in some ways were the innumerable interracial bonds developed under fire on the front lines. *Time* observed accurately in 1967 that "black-white relations in a slit trench or a combat-bound Huey are years ahead of Denver and Darien, decades ahead of Birmingham and Biloxi."[191] Even some members of the Ku Klux Klan had such transformative experiences as being rescued and befriended by black comrades.[192] Whites accompanying fellow black GIs into off-base restaurants and bars at home in the South learned from a different perspective the meaning of "Hey! We don't serve niggers here!"[193] And African American soldiers likewise learned, most for the first time ever, to deal with whites as friends and peers.[194] The capacity of joint combat experience to erase color prejudice and even color consciousness emerged vividly in one black private's explanation to an African American reporter of why black soldiers tended to segregate themselves. Sitting next to a white friend with a pronounced Southern accent in a Saigon bar, he concluded: "White people are dull. They have no style and they don't know how to relax." When his friend objected, he cut him off: "Shut up. I'm not talking about you, nigger. I'm talking about white people."[195]

As the war ground on, however, and as draftees increasingly replaced career soldiers and overall morale declined, racial tensions within the American forces escalated. Blacks were at first disproportionately represented in combat units and thus in casualty figures, a result of lower socioeconomic status, fewer deferments or alternate service options, and higher reenlistment rates.[196] They resented the easier life available in the whiter rear areas like the huge base at Cam Ranh Bay, away from the front lines. To some it seemed there were really two different wars, one a multiracial affair in the combat zones and the other an almost all-white, country club scene in the support areas.[197] Johnson's Committee on Equal Opportunity in the Armed Forces had concluded in 1964 that one of the most powerful influences of white American troops on foreign countries was their racial prejudice, which forced local proprietors of businesses near American bases to adopt segregationist practices they had never used before: "The nationals of these countries themselves do not practice discrimination or segregation. At points distant from the bases Negro and white servicemen are treated alike. The local proprietors are mainly led to follow a pattern of segregation near our bases by what they understand to be the attitudes of our own service personnel." It seemed that white American soldiers often had to *teach* other peoples how to be sufficiently prejudiced. Racial discrimination, in other words, was apparently a standard but unfortunate American export.[198] In Vietnam, racial fights grew more common, especially in bars, over issues like interracial couples (still a troubling sight for many white American GIs) and musical choices (soul versus country-western). Japanese and other Asians hosting American troops on leave from Vietnam also witnessed the rising frequency of conflicts between black and white GIs.[199]

When not buffered by the distraction of incoming fire, race relations among American troops in Vietnam followed the same general pattern as those at home in the United States. As black power, urban riots, and the white backlash ascended, civility declined. Confederate flags, racist graffiti, and Ku Klux Klan organizing grew more common in U.S. barracks by 1968, while younger black draftees proved much less willing to accept such provocations quietly. Incidents of fragging, especially of white officers by black soldiers, increased sharply. King's assassination in April 1968 greatly exacerbated an already deteriorating situation, with hostile attitudes hardening on both sides of the color line. Even experienced African American officers with a professional commitment to the military were disturbed by the rise in open white racism among the ranks. Eddie Kitchen, a thirteen-year veteran, wrote to his mother in 1968 about the prevalence of Confederate flags around him: "We are fighting and dying in a war that is not very popular in the first place and we still have some stupid people who are still fighting the Civil War." Americans' efforts to change the world outside their borders were stumbling over their inability to bridge their own nation's deepest divide.[200]

Racial tensions and hatreds among Americans in Southeast Asia paled, however, in comparison to the actions of U.S. forces, both white and black, against the people of Vietnam. Massive, continual bombing and defoliation of the country made homelessness and death the largest products of the United States' efforts in Vietnam. Air Force General Curtis LeMay told Bundy and Johnson bluntly, "we should bomb them into the Stone Age."[201] The White House tended to conflate Vietnamese and Chinese Communists. When the president argued that the real enemy in Southeast Asia was "the deepening shadow of Communist China," LeMay urged that he go to the heart of the matter and solve the problem by "nuking the Chinks."[202] The war was supposed to be about ideology, about defending democracy or at least capitalism against Communism. But the difficulty of estimating potential enemies' ideology simply from their appearance was further complicated for American GIs by their tendency to see all Vietnamese as looking alike.

The result was what psychiatrist Robert Lifton has called "an atrocity-producing situation," specifically, "a counterinsurgency war undertaken by an advanced industrial society against a revolutionary movement of an underdeveloped country, in which the revolutionary guerrillas are inseparable from the rest of the population."[203] Defense Secretary Robert McNamara described the problem to Johnson in May 1967: "The picture of the world's greatest superpower killing or seriously injuring 1,000 noncombatants a week, while trying to pound a tiny backward nation into submission on an issue whose merits are hotly disputed, is not a pretty one."[204] But it was the strategy of attrition and the policy of the "body count" that most encouraged

American soldiers to kill Vietnamese regardless of their political beliefs. "[I don't] want anymore of your _____ prisoners. I want a body count," one colonel told soldier Robert Kruch in mid-1969. Whose bodies? "We were in a free fire zone," Kruch remembered being instructed, "and anybody we saw that was over 12 years of age that we thought was a male, was to be considered the enemy and engaged as such." Novelist and veteran Philip Caputo explained the impact of this policy: "Our mission was not to win terrain or seize positions, but simply to kill: to kill Communists [ideally, but] . . . 'If it's dead and Vietnamese, it's VC,' was a rule of thumb in the bush."[205]

Washington's preparation of young American men for this mission began in basic training, where Vietnamese were referred to as "gooks" or "dinks" and where women and children were understood to be potentially as dangerous as men in a guerrilla war.[206] Dehumanizing one's enemies in war is not unusual, but American troops in Vietnam dehumanized their allies as well. "Gooks" were not just Communists but all Vietnamese, and indeed all Asians. The other common meaning of "gook" as liquid slime suggests the esteem in which most Americans held Vietnamese. Images of Vietnamese as children, homosexuals, Indians, deer, or gophers abounded. GIs typically encountered the people of Vietnam as often resentful servants: cooks, launderers, bartenders, and prostitutes. The only Vietnamese most American soldiers did not see as weak and pitiful were, ironically, the soldiers of the National Liberation Front and the North Vietnamese army. The generally poor fighting record of the South Vietnamese army increased GIs' resentment, for they seemed to be fighting and dying for a people who would not fight for themselves. Hateful anti-Asian epithets tumbled readily from many American mouths, underlining the growing sense that the entire Vietnamese population rather than the National Liberation Foundation or the North Vietnamese was the enemy. The T-shirt favored by some American soldiers made this clear: "KILL THEM ALL! LET GOD SORT THEM OUT!"[207]

The Johnson administration's evident lack of respect for the South Vietnamese government helped contribute to the broad American confusion about whether Vietnamese Communists or perhaps all Vietnamese were the problem. Johnson, for example, visited American bases in Vietnam while president but did not bother to consult with his Saigon allies while in their country. By contrast, it is impossible to imagine Franklin Roosevelt avoiding Winston Churchill were he to have visited U.S. bases in England in 1944. Comments to Johnson like that of the racially liberal McGeorge Bundy about South Vietnamese head of state Nguyen Khanh as "very Asian and devious politically" reveal Washington officials' often unconscious disdain for those they were supposed to be fighting for.[208] Even opponents of the war sometimes contributed to the dehumanization of the people of Vietnam. Walter Lippmann, for example, explained in a September 1965 column that they "do not value their material possessions, which are few, nor even their lives, which are short and unhappy, as do the people of a country who have much to lose and much to live for."[209]

The administration's lack of respect for the Vietnamese, both allies and enemies, helps explain the ready use of the "quagmire" metaphor by commentators in the United States. Reimagining American forces as bogged down in some form of quicksand allowed the land of Vietnam itself to be seen as the treacherous aggressor and the Americans there as its victims. In this construction, not only the real American role in the war but also the actual Vietnamese people disappeared from the story. There was a parallel here to Africa, where the indigenous people were equally obscure to most Americans, and the landscape stood out as dark and perilous jungle—or, in the words of Undersecretary of State George Ball, "the African swamp" that the United States "should not get bogged down in." The invisibility of the enemy in Vietnam to most Americans was noteworthy: no television story during the war, for example, examined in depth the history, politics, or program of the North Vietnamese.[210]

American soldiers of color faced a painful dilemma about how to understand their role in a war that appeared increasingly racial in its essential conflict. Many, if not most, black, Latino, and Native American GIs used the same dehumanizing language as their white comrades about the Vietnamese. In fact, even some English-speaking Korean soldiers fighting on the U.S. side could be heard referring to Vietnamese as "gooks." Traditional American patriotism and the traumatic and unifying experience of being under fire from National Liberation Front and North Vietnamese forces help explain this apparent oddity.[211] These nonwhite GIs resisted National Liberation Front efforts to demoralize them through racial appeals, such as signs left in the jungle reading in precise English: "They call us gooks here and they call you niggers over there. You're the same as us. Get out, it's not your fight."[212] Similarly, some Vietnamese would point to American Indian soldiers' skin color and hair and then to their own, pronouncing them "same."[213]

Despite their patriotism and identification as Americans, many nonwhite GIs—like many white GIs—began to suspect that this really was not their war. Some even started to wonder if they might have as much in common with the "enemy" as with their white colleagues. They feared being used as pawns in an effort by their superiors to demonstrate that the war was not simply a conflict between white and nonwhite. Like black radicals back home, they began to speak of the Vietnamese as their "brown brothers."[214] Interviews indicated that black veterans, on average, held more positive views of the people of Vietnam than did white veterans.[215] This deepened the shame that some of them felt about their actions in the war. "We did to yellow people what whites do to us," one African American soldier explained in 1968.[216] A Native American veteran recalled resettling Vietnamese civilians as "just like what the whites did to us. I helped load up ville after ville and pack it off to the resettlement area. Just like when they moved us to the rez [reservation]. We shouldn't have done that."[217] Black soldiers were encouraged in their growing doubts about the war by rising opposition to the conflict among prominent African Americans at home, including such figures as boxer Muhammad Ali, comedian Dick Gregory, guitarist Jimi Hendrix, and singer Diana Ross.[218] Noting frequently that "no Vietnamese ever called me nigger," some even wondered if they should be fighting instead in southern Africa against "the white colonialist honkie."[219]

By 1968 the combination of the intensity of the fighting and the anti-Vietnamese fury of American commanders and soldiers led some U.S. forces down the dark path to full-blown racial savagery. On 16 March the 105 young American men of Charlie Company, burning with frustration and rage at the recent loss of several comrades, destroyed the entire village of My Lai, raping, torturing, and slaughtering some 500 unarmed women, children, and old men. Loose in what they repeatedly called "Indian country," American soldiers carried on as their predecessors had done on earlier frontiers in places like Sand Creek and Wounded Knee, as well as the Philippines at the turn of the century. One member of Charlie Company later recalled discussions just before the massacre of "wiping the whole place out" and "the Indian idea . . . the only good gook is a dead gook."[220] That nearly half of Charlie Company was black and its commander, Ernest Medina, was Mexican American did not lessen the murderous rage that led to the obliteration of the village.[221]

The tragedy at My Lai suggested that the Johnson administration had lost control of the racially focused furies of its soldiers abroad. The final report of the Kerner Commission published the same month brought more bad news for the White House. Concluding that "our nation is moving toward two societies, one black, one white—separate and unequal," the commission—made up of moderate national leaders chosen by Johnson—blamed white racism for "the explosive mixture which has been accumulating in our cities" and called for massive new federal spending on the nation's cities to avoid worse disorders in the future. The report implied that the Johnson administration's five years of work on race and poverty had fallen far short of solving America's urban problems, and it gave the president no explicit credit for his considerable efforts. Offended by what he saw as black and liberal ingratitude and not eager to provoke disgruntled whites further, Johnson coldly refused to receive the report in person and ignored most of its recommendations. In a nation of deepening divisions, the president was increasingly isolated.[222] Deeply disappointed by developments in America and Vietnam since the height of his popularity in early 1965, and facing serious opposition within the Democratic Party as manifested in antiwar candidate Eugene McCarthy's surprising strength in the New Hampshire primary on 12 March, Johnson decided he had had enough. On 31 March he announced to a stunned nation that he would not be a candidate for reelection in the fall.

The remainder of 1968 brought mostly bad news of a nation deeply divided by race and the war in Southeast Asia. King's assassination unleashed the greatest wave of urban violence of the decade. Looting, sniping, and arson in over a hundred American cities, combined with police gunfire, left 46 dead, over 3,000 wounded, 27,000 arrested, and $45 million in property destruction. More than 700 fires burned in Washington, D.C., alone, as army units in full combat gear took up battle positions around the Capitol and the White House. Leading antiwar presidential candidate Robert Kennedy was murdered in early June. The Poor People's Campaign planned by King before his death continued under the leadership of Ralph Abernathy, bringing several thousand impoverished Americans to camp on the grounds of the nation's capital in May and June to publicize their condition. At the climactic rally of 50,000 people on 19 June, Abernathy condemned the administration's record on race and poverty as a five-year string of "broken promises." Johnson, who had just pushed through national legislation banning racial discrimination in housing, watched bitterly as his support continued to fall away.[223] In August massive demonstrations and a police riot marred the Democratic Party's national convention in Chicago.

On 29 August a race riot at the Long Binh jail (nicknamed LBJ) in South Vietnam marked the worst prison riot in the modern history of the U.S. Army. Severe overcrowding, radically disproportional numbers of black inmates, and blatant racial discrimination by white military police led to a takeover of the stockade by 217 African American and 3 Puerto Rican inmates, resulting in 1 death, 34 injuries, and a month-long stalemate. The holdouts, as *Newsweek* described the scene, "proceeded to shed their uniforms and to don white kerchiefs and African-style robes that they made out of Army blankets," while "beating out jungle sounds on oil drums." Here in the jungles of Vietnam, Johnson's hopes for a racially integrated and progressive America seemed to have reached rock bottom, as black American soldiers rejected the white authority and culture they found so racist in favor of a separatist cultural style looking toward Africa.[224]

The road to Richard Nixon's election was open. The Republican candidate chose Maryland Governor Spiro Agnew for his vice presidential running mate as part of the "Southern strategy" of appealing to whites of that region. By October Agnew was declaring on the campaign trail that "the civil rights movement went too far the day it began."[225] The white backlash, already manifest in the independent candidacy of George Wallace, had found another voice. In the wake of King's death and the rise of black power, the civil rights leadership was divided and many of its constituents deeply alienated. Burke Marshall of the Justice Department noted that loss of unity in the fall of 1968, observing that the black community "wouldn't pay any more attention to Roy Wilkins than to George Wallace, maybe less."[226] In a contest between Nixon and Hubert Humphrey, Johnson's vice president and for two decades one of the strongest supporters of civil rights in the Democratic Party, Stokely Carmichael and Rap Brown suggested African Americans "go fishin'" on election day rather than vote for "either of the honkies."[227] Most black voters rejected that advice and supported Humphrey, but the halcyon days of liberal victory in 1964 seemed a distant memory as the Republicans regained the White House.

FOR ALL HIS IMPRESSIVE legislative achievements in the pursuit of ending racial discrimination, Lyndon Johnson could not hold back the tide of racial polarization that swept through the United States in the 1960s. He had "made the goddamnest commitment to the civil-rights cause I had ever heard" from a president, Roger Wilkins remembered, but Johnson was put on the defensive by the rise of black power, the onset of urban racial violence, and the growth of the white backlash.[228] Most African Americans still quietly supported the president, but younger radicals increasingly seized the spotlight. Already alienated from the Johnson administration by frustrating experiences in domestic civil rights organizing, they now linked their cause directly to that of revolutionaries abroad, from Vietnam to South Africa. One of the best remembered examples was the black power salute of champion sprinters Tommie Smith and John Carlos on the Olympic victory stand in 1968 in Mexico City, in protest of both racism in America and U.S. ties to South Africa and Rhodesia.[229] These younger radicals, often unknowingly, were reviving a critique of America's role in a white-dominated international system that had been articulated a generation earlier by African American leftists like W. E. B. Du Bois and Paul Robeson.

Like black radicals in the United States, nonwhite revolutionaries abroad such as those in the National Liberation Front and the African National Congress dismissed the paternalistic liberalism and the preference for gradual reform of the Johnson administration and much of the white West. Ho Chi Minh, like Martin Luther King, Jr., or Stokely Carmichael, remained well beyond the control of the American president. The freedom struggle in southern Africa also carried on beyond the circle of White House power, owing to the radical inappropriateness of gradual reform in the lands of apartheid and the UDI—the lands of the ultimate white backlash. The efforts of U.S. policymakers to contain the virus of domestic segregationism were more effective, although they had the ironic effect of helping to create a new conservative Republican majority in American politics. In southern Africa, the white backlash seemed to be consolidating its power, at least for the near future. Both abroad and at home, the Johnson administration's struggle to restrain strife along the color line and to channel the political aspirations of people of color in liberal, pro-Western directions broke apart on the shoals of racial polarization.

# 6

# THE END OF THE COLD WAR AND

# WHITE SUPREMACY

LYNDON JOHNSON'S PRESIDENCY marked the climax of the close, complicated relationship between changing race relations and American foreign policy during the Cold War. The convergence of civil rights reform, racial polarization, and an anti-Communist but increasingly racially charged war in Southeast Asia made the Johnson years unparalleled: so much hope, so much achievement, and so much disappointment. After 1968 the story of how these two themes intersected retreated from center stage in American politics.[1] Racial reform in the United States shifted from the moral high ground of desegregating the public sphere to the more ambiguous and less visible terrain of eliminating discrimination in hiring and housing. Violent racial conflict did not disappear after 1968, but it never again reemerged in the sustained form of the summer uprisings of the Johnson years. And the Cold War itself rapidly grew less intense after the election of Richard Nixon, with the new policy of détente pointing the way toward the eventual deescalation of the Soviet-American conflict by the late 1980s and the ultimate dissolution of the Soviet Union in 1991. The twin erosion of American segregation and international colonialism (with the exception of southernmost Africa) by 1968 relieved the U.S. government of much of its self-inflicted burden of trying to promote a "free world" abroad while maintaining racial hierarchy at home.

## Richard Nixon and the Politics of Race at Home

At the Gridiron Club dinner of 14 March 1970 Washington's policymaking elite gathered for the annual bipartisan event. Hosted by prominent journalists, the occasion both honored and roasted the president. Democratic Senator Edmund Muskie provoked much laughter with a speech noting that the Republican Party's three problems were the war in Vietnam, inflation, and what to say on Lincoln's birthday. Indeed, the party of the Great Emancipator had a century later become the party of the white backlash against civil rights. Richard Nixon had boldly gone where no previous successful Republican presidential candidate had dared—explicitly wooing white Southern voters by playing to their antiblack sentiments—and he had won the White House. Just a few months later, Neil Armstrong and Edwin Aldrin fulfilled the age-old dream of reaching the moon and actually walking upon its surface, planting an American flag in the process. Even as American technological prowess seemed to portend an unlimited future, American racial politics appeared to be regressing into a too familiar past. The author of this Southern strategy surely did not anticipate Frank Wills, the African American watchman at the Watergate complex who would notice a suspiciously unlocked door one night in June 1972 and notify the police. But Nixon had his eyes wide open as he halted the momentum that the civil rights movement had acquired within the federal government since 1960, and ended Johnson's use of the symbolic and substantive power of the presidency to disavow racism as an acceptable part of American life.[2]

Ironically, Nixon's record before the 1968 campaign placed him among his party's most prominent supporters of greater racial equality. There is little evidence of notable prejudice in his upbringing in small-town southern California—for his family a difficult period of economic stress and the tragic early deaths of two of his brothers—or in his early political career. As vice president in the 1950s, he supported civil rights legislation and limiting the Senate filibuster used to defeat it. He traveled to West Africa in 1957 to represent the Eisenhower administration at Ghana's independence ceremony and came home to promote greater U.S. attention to that continent. Such positions earned him considerable black political support, including that of Martin Luther King, Jr., at the beginning of his unsuccessful 1960 bid for the presidency. He was even granted an honorary membership in a California chapter of the NAACP. If one can be known by one's enemies, it is worth noting that Nixon was regarded by Southern segregationists as the second worst figure in the Eisenhower administration, after Attorney General Herbert Brownell. Throughout the 1950s, he surpassed not only Eisenhower but also Kennedy and Johnson as a supporter of civil rights. In the 1960s, however, he moved in the opposite direction of his Democratic predecessors in the White House: while they emerged as stronger defenders of racial equality, Nixon tapped into the widening stream of white racial resentment.[3]

Nixon's electoral and governing strategies were rooted in a realistic appraisal of rising white resentment of African Americans. Traditional prejudice was exacerbated by several factors in the late 1960s: the summertime riots coming so swiftly on the heels of civil rights legislation, suggesting to many observers ingratitude; the antiwhite rhetoric of some black nationalists; the beginnings of school desegregation and the use of busing to achieve it; and growing anxiety about unemployment and inflation.[4] Anger about the failure of the American effort in Vietnam, and at nonwhite peoples more generally, also alienated many whites from an understanding of black political struggles. The leading newspaper in Greensboro, North Carolina, responded to a 1969 civil rights protest by Dudley High School students with the logic of U.S. officials blaming National Liberation Front successes on North Vietnam and China: the protesters, it editorialized, must have been "outsiders" engaged in "guerilla warfare" to manipulate a "terrorized majority."[5] In his inaugural address, Nixon spoke of overcoming these divisions, of bringing "black and white together, as one nation, not two."[6] But he understood better than most how resentment can serve as the engine of American politics. He positioned himself as the champion of aggrieved whites against what they saw as the special pleadings and privileges of African Americans.[7] By 1971, Spiro Agnew could declare publicly that "dividing the American people has been my main contribution to the national political scene since assuming the office of vice president . . . I not only plead guilty to this charge, but I am somewhat flattered by it." Some of that dividing was between young and old, left and right, protesters and war supporters. But a great deal of it was between black and white.[8]

The massive riots that had rolled through the nation's cities after King's assassination in April had set the tone for the 1968 presidential campaign. Riots dovetailed with increasing crime rates and antiwar protests to stimulate new fears of social instability among whites. Nixon had seized on these anxieties by running on a platform of "law and order." He generally avoided making explicit connections between race and social disorder, as white voters already associated the two from the urban uprisings of previous summers. But Nixon occasionally let down his guard, allowing code words to be replaced by plainer language. After taping a television advertisement attacking the decline of law and order, he said enthusiastically, "It's all about law and order and the damn Negro–Puerto Rican groups out there."[9]

Nixon won all but five Southern states to put him over the top in November's election. His key ally was Senator Strom Thurmond of South Carolina, the former 1948 Dixiecrat presidential candidate who had switched to the Republican Party in 1964. No one had stronger segregationist credentials, and no one could better convince white Southerners of Richard Nixon's commitment to their interests—especially slowing the process of school desegregation. It would have been hard to create a clearer contrast between Nixon's alliance with Thurmond and the Democratic candidate, Vice President Hubert Humphrey: Humphrey had led the successful civil rights campaign at the 1948 Democratic convention that had driven Thurmond and so many of his Southern colleagues out in rebellion. Nixon's ardent wooing of white Southern voters was a typical case of his savvy political calculations: "hunting where the ducks are," in Goldwater's phrase. There were at least twice as many whites as blacks in the South as a whole, and the white backlash was not limited to the region south of the Mason-Dixon line. "Remember, this isn't South Africa," one Republican strategist had remarked a few years earlier. "The white man outnumbers the Negro 9 to 1 in this country." No one understood that better than the Republican candidate.[10]

More dangerous to Nixon's Southern strategy than Humphrey was the independent candidacy of segregationist George Wallace. The former Alabama governor appealed explicitly to racial fears in showing how powerful a force white resentment could be. His running mate, retired Air Force General Curtis LeMay, was perhaps best known for his enthusiasm about the use of nuclear weapons. Wallace and his staff had, in fact, coached him extensively to stay away from the subject with the media during the campaign. But at the October press conference in Pittsburgh announcing LeMay's place on the ticket, the general could not resist a journalist's question about whether to use nuclear weapons in Vietnam: "I have to say that we have a phobia about nuclear weapons," he responded, and continued on at length, to the dismay of Wallace's staff.[11] Seizing victory abroad at whatever cost thus went with reasserting white authority at home. "On November 5, they're going to find out there are a lot of rednecks in this country," Wallace predicted: 9.9 million of them, in fact, constituting 13.5 percent of the total votes cast, and even 8 percent of votes outside the South.[12]

Nixon's choice of Agnew as his running mate marked the first payoff to the white South for its support of him in the primaries. The Maryland governor was best known by the late summer of 1968 for his tough response to the five-day Baltimore riot after King's death. At a well-publicized meeting with one hundred of the city's moderate African American leaders, most of whom had worked days and nights to calm angry black residents, Agnew stunned his listeners by denouncing them for not having condemned ahead of time young militants like Stokely Carmichael and Rap Brown—"the circuit-riding, Hanoi-visiting, caterwauling, riot-inciting, burn-America-down type of leader." Eighty of them got up and walked out of the meeting.[13] Together, Nixon and Agnew vied with Wallace during the fall to portray the Democrats as the party of failed liberal permissiveness—of welfare, crime, anti-American protesters, and favoring of blacks over whites. Just three years from the apex of Great Society legislative success, the Democrats now struggled against an image of not defending adequately the interests of most white Americans at home, while also failing to win the war in Vietnam and thus uphold the nation's interests in the Third World.[14] Nixon had replicated the Republicans' agreement of 1877 some ninety-one years later: winning the presidency by agreeing to end the "second Reconstruction" of civil rights, just as his predecessors had retained the White House by sloughing off their remaining commitment to equality and walking away from the first Reconstruction.[15]

As president, Nixon participated in the casual racism common among white Americans of his generation. He lacked the obsession with African Americans and their sexuality that characterized true race-baiters, but he did not spare the Oval Office references to "niggers," "jigaboos," "jigs," and "jungle bunnies."[16] News of a scholarship program for black students elicited this reply: "Well, it's a good thing. They're just down out of the trees."[17] That he had offered the same observation in an NSC meeting on Africa in the late 1950s suggested how little he had apparently learned from the ferment in race relations during the intervening decade. The president's instruction to White House chief of staff H. R. Haldeman that "we take a *very* conservative civil rights line" was grounded in what historian Hugh Davis Graham has called Nixon's unambiguously negative opinion of black Americans.[18] He informed aide John Ehrlichman more than once that blacks were genetically inferior to whites, while complaining several times that there were too many African American waiters in the White House.[19] His ease with the notion of white biological superiority was no doubt bolstered by similar theories from a handful of academics like Arthur Jensen of the University of California, reported to him by aide Patrick Moynihan as part of a "rather pronounced revival—in impeccably respectable circles—of the proposition that there is a difference in genetic potential" between the races.[20] The president's disdain for African Americans was no secret to them and was frequently reciprocated: Clifford Alexander noted in 1971, for example, that "blacks feel that it is hopeless to deal with Nixon. And they're right, because the man's a bigot."[21]

The significance of Nixon's attitudes toward people of darker hue can be clarified by noting his casual anti-Semitism. Like his views of blacks, the president's prejudices against Jews were more thoughtless than virulent. Indeed, several of his advisers were Jewish, including speechwriter William Safire and Henry Kissinger, who served both as national security adviser and as secretary of state. But the president shared the negative stereotypes of most gentiles of his generation, tending to see American Jews as a powerful, cohesive group committed to Israel's interests above all else. He enjoyed needling Kissinger to accentuate his vulnerability in this regard; after Kissinger had given an opinion on the Middle East in one Cabinet meeting, Nixon looked around the room and asked, "Now, can we get an American point of view?"[22] Nixon's attention to power above all else helps explain his greater respect for Jews than for blacks: while Jews had real economic and political clout, blacks generally did not. For Nixon the latter were weak and unorganized, able to get attention only by rioting.

For Nixon, African Americans were one of an array of domestic issues that he found ultimately boring and insignificant in comparison to the magisterial business of conducting international diplomacy. He often expressed the view that the Congress could run the country on the domestic side, while the president's job was to take charge of foreign affairs.[23] Like most white Americans, he associated blacks with bothersome domestic issues like welfare. At one point in the 1960 presidential campaign, he conceded to his staff that he would have to do a speech on "all that welfare crap." When aide Herb Klein gently suggested referring to the issue instead as "meeting human needs," Nixon replied, "I don't care. It *is* crap."[24] His interest in affairs within the United States picked up when they were likely to help his electoral chances; it was the politics rather than the substance of domestic policies that intrigued him. From 1968 on, black Americans were not part of his electoral strategy and therefore had little influence within his administration.[25]

Taking their lead from the president, Nixon's advisers demonstrated little concern for the interests of African Americans. Secretary of State William Rogers's support for civil rights since his days in the Justice Department under Eisenhower made him an exception, but one with little real power within the administration. Vice President Spiro Agnew's growing hostility to black militants earned him great popularity in the white South. Roger Morris covered African issues for the NSC staff and remembered ubiquitous racist humor about apes and smells; as Morris entered meetings, General Alexander Haig "would begin to beat his hands on the table, as if he were pounding a tom-tom." En route to a White House dinner for African ambassadors, Kissinger bumped into Arkansas senator J. William Fulbright, headed to the same event, and reportedly offered this greeting: "I wonder what the dining room is going to smell like?"[26] J. Edgar Hoover found fresh encouragement from Nixon's presence in the White House for his long-standing campaign against black militancy and black political organizations more broadly. The FBI director took the Black Panther Party at its word about planning "an armed black revolution" and viewed the Panthers as "the greatest threat to the internal security of this country." He sharply increased FBI surveillance of black communities nationwide during the Nixon years. Historian Kenneth O'Reilly has observed that Hoover had more in common with this president than with any of his six predecessors, under whom the bureau director also served.[27]

The racial inclinations of Nixon and the men around him matched those of many white Americans, but they did not create the racially polarized atmosphere of 1969. Four years of war in Vietnam and uprisings in black urban neighborhoods, plus the limits of civil rights gains and rising anger on both sides of the color line, had done that. Nixon sought advantage from a polarization between black power and the white backlash that he had inherited rather than manufactured. The United States' continuing destruction of much of southern Vietnam alienated more and more Americans, while younger African American militants increasingly identified with nonwhite revolutionaries in the Third World—including designated enemies of the U.S. government like Castro and Ho. Black nationalists began to call for Palestinian self-determination, a cause that a non-European majority supported in 1975 with a UN General Assembly resolution declaring Zionism "a form of racism and racial discrimination," even as white Americans were shedding some of their anti-Semitism and identifying with Israel as a bastion of "Western civilization" within the non-European world.[28] Moynihan warned Nixon not to underestimate the determination of African Americans to establish what he called their own "self-identity," the same issue motivating so many revolutionaries in the Third World: "Consider what those half starved, malaria ridden, pajama clad Viet Cong have done to the armies of the American Republic."[29]

Regardless of the accuracy of Moynihan's description of the National Liberation Front forces, there was no doubt by 1969 that those armies of the American Republic shared in the broader racial polarization of American society. This stemmed partly from the broader loss of morale among U.S. troops still involved in a losing struggle. Drug abuse began to reach epidemic proportions, and fragging escalated sharply. Racial conflict among American soldiers tended to disappear under fire, where the imminent threat of death and dismemberment bonded them tightly together. But away from the front, commanders could not prevent the suspicions and hostilities that pervaded American society at home from seeping into military life as well. Beyond dealing with discrimination from many of their white colleagues, African American GIs particularly resented the absence of blacks from positions of authority. In 1971, while blacks made up 11 percent of the American population and roughly 20 percent of military personnel, they accounted for only 2.3 percent of officers. A sometimes explosive tension developed between younger black soldiers, with a strong race consciousness and no longer willing to accept discrimination, and some white soldiers resentful of increasing demands for black recognition and parity. At Camp Lejeune in North Carolina, for example, a series of racial attacks and muggings in the spring and summer of 1969 culminated in a deadly brawl between black and white marines on 20 July.[30]

These conflagrations along the color line within the American forces were exceeded only by the racially coded violence of Americans against their perceived Vietnamese enemies, as had already become evident during Johnson's presidency. The slaughter of Vietnamese civilians forced its way into the consciousness of Americans at home in the fall of 1969. The initial cover-up of the destruction of the village of My Lai a year and a half earlier at last leaked to the press, and military authorities decided Lieutenant William J. ("Rusty") Calley was to blame. The very language of the indictment revealed the racial thinking of U.S. commanders: Calley was charged with the premeditated murder of at least seventy "Oriental human beings," a phrase eventually dropped by the prosecutors after repeated criticism but still used by the judge in his final instructions to the jury a year and a half later.[31] Calley was the only person found guilty of some of the hundreds of deaths at My Lai, as U.S. officials emphasized what they called the aberration of American behavior there. Some American soldiers took a different view. One of the hundred honorably discharged Vietnam Veterans against the War noted simply, "We all belong to the unit Lieutenant Calley belonged to."[32] Another GI in the same division as Calley told a reporter in Vietnam, "The people back in the world don't understand this war. We are here to kill dinks. How can they convict Calley for killing dinks? That's our job."[33]

The public response in the United States to the news about My Lai included outrage at the atrocity but focused mostly on how the tragedy affected the American soldiers involved. The mother of one member of Calley's Charlie Company spoke for many: "I gave them a good boy, and they made him a murderer."[34] Calley, seen by many as a scapegoat for higher officials, received an outpouring of public support after his conviction and sentencing at Fort Benning, Georgia. Governor Jimmy Carter of Georgia organized an American Fighting Man's Day, calling on Georgians to drive with their headlights on to "honor the flag" in solidarity with Calley.[35] Nixon added his own peculiar ethnic slant to the mix of responses to My Lai. Unhappy with the media attention being paid to the massacre and with the growing public opposition to his Vietnam policies, Nixon privately blamed the editors of moderate to liberal newspapers like the *New York Times:* "It's those dirty rotten Jews from New York who are behind it."[36]

Race remained to the very end a powerful yet ambiguous category for American thinking and behavior in Vietnam. Growing numbers of Americans were neither white nor black, but of Asian descent, and some of them fought in the war. One Japanese American GI, Scott Shimabakuro, remembered how his sergeant had told him not to marry his Vietnamese girlfriend "because she was a gook, which struck me as kind of funny because I was a gook also."[37] There was increasing slippage between "Americans" and "gooks": the former mostly killed, but sometimes married and sometimes even *were,* the latter. The final hours of the evacuation of the last U.S. personnel from Saigon on 29 April 1975 nevertheless suggested the continuing racial classification of "Americans." After checking the U.S. embassy parking lot one last time, administrative counselor Henry Boudreau reported with relief, "Didn't see any white faces out there."[38]

As president, Nixon implemented policies on racial matters in line with his campaign promises. He had confided to a supporter before the election, "If I am president, I am not going to owe anything to the black community."[39] "You received (probably) the lowest proportion of Negro votes of any President in history," Moynihan reminded him in his first months in office.[40]

Sensing the likely course of the president's policies, Jackie Robinson—former Nixon supporter, former baseball superstar, and conservative African American Republican—wrote to him in January 1969, "I sincerely hope you will forget the fact that the Black community . . . hardly had a role to play in your election."[41] For a man as focused on the maintenance and exercise of political power as Richard Nixon, this was unlikely. The advice of White House aide Patrick Buchanan made more sense: "The second era of Reconstruction is over; the ship of integration is going down; it is not our ship . . . and we cannot salvage it; and we ought not to be aboard."[42] The Nixon administration instead spoke for the white South: it urged Congress to slow court-ordered school busing and to weaken fair-housing and voting rights enforcement; it nominated two Southerners who supported a strict constructionist position on the Constitution for the Supreme Court; it hampered the civil rights offices of the Justice Department and the Department of Health, Education, and Welfare; and it fired officials seen as too eager to implement integration guidelines. Complaints about responsible enforcement of existing integration directives elicited this presidential command to John Ehrlichman: "tell them to *knock off this crap.*"[43] Nixon found his occasional meetings with black leaders useless and tiresome; to aides after one he sent a memo declaring, *"No More of This!"*[44] With Agnew as his point man, Nixon's popularity in the South continued to rise. George Wallace told NBC's *Meet the Press* in the fall of 1969, "I wish I had copyrighted my speeches. I would be drawing immense royalties from Mr. Nixon and especially Mr. Agnew."[45]

Unlike previous presidents who had opposed racial reform, Nixon faced novel limits on his ability to roll back gains for black equality. His administration had the sworn duty of executing federal law, including the 1964–65 civil rights bills and the Supreme Court's decisions requiring specific school desegregation plans. His solution to this dilemma was a clear instruction to aides to "do what the law requires and not *one bit* more."[46] Even his occasional initiatives at promoting black capitalism revealed ulterior political motives. The Philadelphia Plan, originally a Johnson-era Labor Department proposal to require minority preferences in hiring by federal government contractors—an early version of affirmative action—also served to drive a wedge between key Democratic constituencies: organized labor and African Americans.[47]

Nixon used Supreme Court appointments and school busing as his highest-profile demonstrations of sympathy with white Southerners. After the

Senate rejected his first choice, Clement Haynsworth of South Carolina, in part owing to evidence of segregationist attitudes, the president instructed his aides to look "farther South and further right" for another candidate.[48] In Florida they found G. Harrold Carswell, whose undistinguished legal career was matched by his prominence as a promoter of white supremacy. The administration's own private disdain for Carswell's qualifications suggested that his nomination was a calculated insult to Nixon's political opponents. Nixon turned a second Senate rejection to immediate political advantage in Dixie, declaring after the Senate's negative vote on Carswell: "I understand the bitter feeling of millions of Americans who live in the South about the act of regional discrimination that took place in the Senate yesterday."[49] Nixon's years in the White House were a time of considerable school desegregation in the South, effected through federal court rulings. But the administration made sure the courts, not the president, would be identified with that process. Nixon consistently opposed busing as a means of integrating schools and even had the Justice Department side with the state of Mississippi in its unsuccessful efforts to delay submitting desegregation plans. Few doubted where the president's sympathies lay.[50]

Nixon's position on civil rights issues helped lay the groundwork for his impressive reelection in 1972. "Go for Poles, Italians, Irish . . . don't go for Jews and blacks," he told Haldeman.[51] Winning forty-nine states to crush liberal Democratic candidate George McGovern, the president continued the Southern strategy of four years earlier. For the first time ever, the Democrats—the historic party of the South—won not a single Southern state. Nixon's real competition there would have come from George Wallace, who won a string of primary victories across Dixie before being partially paralyzed in an assassination attempt. With Wallace not in the running this time as a third-party candidate, Nixon sailed to victory. The Committee to Reelect the President had little need to engage in such dirty tricks as the Watergate break-in or its covert effort to weaken the early leading Democratic candidate, Senator Edmund Muskie of Maine, in the critical, nearly all-white New Hampshire primary. The latter took the form of late-night calls to white voters, with the person on the line claiming to be from a "Harlem for Muskie Committee" and informing them that Muskie had promised to do his best to help African Americans if elected.[52] The extent of Nixon's connection to black America in 1972 seemed to be summed up at the Republican convention in Miami, where conservative black performer Sammy Davis, Jr., hugged the president on stage after singing the anthem of the white South, "Dixie."[53]

## The Nixon Administration and Race Relations Abroad

The Nixon administration's foreign policy focused on power, not race. The president and Henry Kissinger prided themselves on their realpolitik perspective: discounting ideology and pursuing American interests abroad based on the actions rather than the rhetoric of other nations. Hemmed in by a disastrous commitment in Vietnam, declining relative economic power, and new Soviet nuclear parity, Nixon and Kissinger renegotiated relations with the two greatest enemies of the United States. Opening links with the People's Republic of China led swiftly to détente with the Soviet Union. This new respect shown to China by a president long known for his disdain for the Communist government in Beijing indicated the priority of power over ideology. China had become a nuclear power in 1964, and its economic and political potential was vast. For a practitioner of realpolitik like Nixon, old anti-Asian and anti-Communist sentiments were not as important.

China was an exception by dint of its size and power, real and potential. The Nixon administration had little interest in the rest of the nonwhite Third World. There an absence of power dovetailed with darker skins and different cultures to put off the men of Washington. Kissinger was sometimes quite blunt about this lack of interest. He told Foreign Minister Gabriel Valdés of Chile, "Nothing important can come from the South. History has never been produced in the South. The axis of history starts in Moscow, goes to Bonn, crosses over to Washington, and then goes to Tokyo." Valdés interjected, "Mr. Kissinger, you know nothing about the South." The national security adviser answered, "No, and I don't care."[54] From the White House's perspective, no continent wielded less military and economic power than Africa, and, of course, no continent was more clearly marked by skin color as nonwhite.

For Nixon, Africans in the international system were similar to African Americans at home: a minority with little power or influence. Haldeman recalled the president telling him that "there has never been an adequate black nation, and they are the only race of which this is true."[55] Early in his first term, Nixon instructed his staff to reduce the number of visiting African statesmen he had to host.[56] The president's lack of interest in Africans was echoed by Americans living in white-ruled southern Africa, where only one out of ten U.S. businessmen surveyed in 1969 objected to apartheid. "I didn't mix with them in the States," said one manager at a Ford plant, "and I don't mix with them here."[57] "Them" were, apparently, the same: black Americans and Africans. Several hundred white Americans fought as mercenaries with the white government against black nationalist guerillas in the civil war in Rhodesia. The Nixon and subsequent Gerald Ford administrations were untroubled by Rhodesian recruitment efforts using American agents, despite such events as Rhodesia's widely publicized slaughter of black civilians at the Nyadzonia refugee camp in August 1976. Historian William Minter explains the significance: "If a black group in the United States or Britain had been actively recruiting for an African government that had just massacred over five hundred white civilians, a similar lack of reaction would have been unimaginable."[58] Nixon summed up his perspective on the importance of Africans in a phone call he made to Kissinger, intended to soothe the latter's jealousy at positive press coverage Secretary of State Rogers had received for a recent trip to Africa: "Henry, let's leave the niggers to Bill and we'll take care of the rest of the world."[59]

Nixon and Kissinger presided over a shift in American policy toward southern Africa that aligned the United States more closely with its white rulers. Their focus on powerful nations and their lack of interest in weaker ones meant that Africa would always rank low in their priorities, but it also meant that South Africa—the only industrialized state on the continent with a modern military force—would be given special consideration. Their geopolitics and their racial prejudices fit neatly together. The Nixon administration could take this position for its first five years, in part because of relative stability in the region. Until the coup in Portugal in 1974 that led to independence for Angola and Mozambique, the white authorities seemed in control. African nationalists had finally taken up arms in each territory in the 1960s in response to the refusal of the white regimes to move toward democracy, but they could not yet effectively challenge white power. Similarly, American supporters of color-blind democracy in southern Africa were not yet organized and powerful in the way they would become by the mid-1980s. The Congressional Black Caucus was not formally founded until 1971 and focused primarily—like most American race reformers—on domestic policies. Private organizations like the American Committee on Africa remained small. Younger black nationalists paid increasing attention to Africa, but their opinions were hardly welcome in the White House. Not until the presidency of Jimmy Carter did the voices of supporters of African liberation become more influential.[60]

The Nixon administration's tilt toward whites in southern Africa also reflected ignorance of African affairs and politics at the highest levels of the

U.S. government. In a December 1969 NSC meeting, for example, Agnew spoke at length about "South African independence" in 1965 and its similarity to American independence in 1776, in regard to blacks not having the vote. Nixon finally had to interject, "You mean Rhodesia, don't you?" The vice president paused, checking his notes, and agreed that he did.[61] This shift in policy took institutional form in the National Security Study Memorandum 39 (NSSM 39) of 1969, which claimed famously that "the whites are here to stay and the only way that constructive change can come about is through them."[62] Instead, within five years the Portuguese were withdrawing from Angola and Mozambique, as the white-ruled redoubt at the tip of the continent began to crumble. NSC staffer Roger Morris was involved in assembling NSSM 39 and recalled later how the process of putting it together "unearthed in the bureaucracy an often appalling ignorance of the history and politics of southern Africa."[63]

This tilt toward the white regimes reflected the administration's strategy of supporting the anti-Communist, pro-capitalist status quo in the region, as well as the lobbying of key agencies, allies, and individuals. The CIA wished to preserve its close links to the regimes in Salisbury, Pretoria, and Lisbon; the Conservative Party came back into power in Britain in June 1970, with a more sympathetic view of whites in the region; and influential former secretary of state Dean Acheson pressured Nixon and Kissinger to support the white governments. Acheson warned against what he called—in peculiarly revealing language for an American statesman—the "subjugation of Rhodesia to majority rule." He argued that southern Africa was "the most stable portion of an otherwise disturbed, indeed turbulent, continent," and that only the Soviets would benefit from changes there.[64] Few in the American business community or the Commerce Department wished to disrupt the benefits of links with South Africa: its vast gold production, the favorable U.S. trade balance there, and what NSSM 39 called the "highly profitable return" on private U.S investments in the apartheid state.[65]

In Rhodesia, the Nixon administration did not take the lead in drawing closer to the white minority regime. Instead, it allowed Rhodesia's enthusiasts in the American South, the U.S. Congress, and the business community to shift the terms of the bilateral relationship. Nixon did reluctantly follow Britain's lead by closing the U.S. consulate in Salisbury in March 1970, after Rhodesia cut its last ties with London. This action disappointed those Americans—particularly white Southern segregationists—who approved of the Ian Smith regime, including more than one out of every six members of Congress. Most of them emphasized the common American and Rhodesian commitments to anti-Communism and free enterprise and the shared history of declaring independence from England. Some questioned Nixon's simultaneous efforts to open relations with what they considered a more clearly "illegal" regime in Beijing, and some demanded that Britain close its consulate in Hanoi. Others were more blunt about the racial contours of the problem. Newspaper publisher Charles Jacobs of Brookhaven, Mississippi, informed the president that white Rhodesians "have no intention of turning their country over to the semi-civilized black Africans," who would only return it to "the savage conditions" prevailing on the continent wherever whites were not in control. Jacobs went on to note with some accuracy the extensive parallels in the two nations' development. For Rhodesia to engage in color-blind democracy—that is, democracy—"would be very similar [to] if in a fit of moral righteousness we turned America back to the Indians." Other than the reversed demographics of the two situations, this was true—and precisely what such Native Americans as those involved in the American Indian Movement were beginning to advocate.[66]

Other Americans supported Nixon's decision to close the Salisbury consulate. They framed their arguments around the simple fact that Rhodesia was retreating into greater racial discrimination and hierarchy at precisely the same time that the United States and the rest of the world were moving in the opposite direction. The State Department emphasized the global unanimity on this issue: not even Portugal or South Africa had granted diplomatic recognition to the Smith regime.[67] The Congressional Black Caucus urged the administration not to slide back into any kind of formal relationship with the Rhodesian segregationists, and to abide by UN mandatory sanctions on trade with the territory.[68] Forty-three Americans working with the Peace Corps next door in independent Malawi wrote to Nixon of the enormous symbolism involved. "We can assure you from our first-hand observations of Rhodesia and Rhodesians," they concluded, that current Rhodesian society "stands diametrically opposed to the history-shaping demands of equal dignity and equal opportunity for all men."[69]

The real turn in Rhodesian policy in the Nixon years came with the passage of the Byrd Amendment in 1971. Named for its sponsor, segregationist Senator Harry Byrd of Virginia, this measure opened up an exception for chrome ore in the previous U.S. policy of adhering to all UN economic sanctions on the illegal government in Salisbury. While providing critical cash for Rhodesia, the measure was defended as essential to avoiding American dependence on the Soviet Union—the other leading exporter—for chrome ore for steelmaking. A law grounded apparently in anti-Communism thus bolstered the forces of white supremacy, to the delight of several white Southerners in Congress. Until the Byrd Amendment's repeal in early 1977 under the Carter administration, the United States was the only nation in explicit legislative defiance of its UN obligations regarding sanctions—and a de facto partner with South Africa and Portugal in trading with Rhodesia.[70] The White House largely avoided the Byrd Amendment by adopting a neutral stand. Supporters of Rhodesia already knew the president's leanings, and there was no political advantage for the president in alienating Salisbury's opponents at home or in Africa. Nixon and Kissinger were happy to let Congress lead, with white Southern members providing a disproportionate amount of the political muscle to support their segregationist brethren across the South Atlantic—just as they had succored Moise Tshombe in Katanga ten years earlier during the Congo independence crisis.[71]

Portugal's withdrawal from Angola and Mozambique in 1975 led Kissinger to one last shift in policy toward Rhodesia. Nixon had resigned the presidency over the Watergate scandal, but his successor, Gerald Ford, preserved the essence of his antibusing position at home and his tilt toward the white authorities in southern Africa. Still secretary of state, Kissinger recognized that Portugal's retreat altered the entire political calculus in the region. The anti-Communist white-ruled states were now down to two—South Africa (including Namibia, which it controlled) and Rhodesia—and the fresh victories over white supremacy in Angola and Mozambique encouraged the liberation forces fighting in Rhodesia. Aid from the Soviets and Cubans had been crucial for the final outcome in Angola, and Kissinger feared the creation of a whole string of radical, pro-Soviet regimes, with Salisbury being the next domino to fall. "What is required, then," he agreed with his aides, "is a preemptive strategy" to take the momentum away from the Soviets and Cubans.[72] With this aim Kissinger toured Africa in April 1976 and declared in Lusaka that America supported majority rule in neighboring Rhodesia, touting "racial justice" as "a dominant issue of our age" and "an imperative of our own moral heritage."[73]

Africans were surprised at such words from the originator of NSSM 39 and dubious about the extent of his moral conversion, but they were pleased with the novelty of the U.S. government's support. Southern white Americans were a good deal less happy and used the concurrent Republican primaries to express their opinion. Standing in front of the Alamo in San Antonio, presidential candidate Ronald Reagan told a campaign rally that Kissinger's Lusaka speech could lead to a "massacre" of whites in Rhodesia and had "undercut the possibility of a just and orderly settlement there." White Texans responded to the symbolism of massacres of brave, embattled white folks and gave Reagan a resounding victory over Ford in their presidential primary a few days later. Kissinger's staff reacted by serenading him, bleakly, with "The Eyes of Texas Are upon You." Nevertheless, over the next several months, Kissinger's shuttle diplomacy in the region helped lay some of the groundwork for the eventual settlement of the civil war in 1979 and the creation of the new state of Zimbabwe out of the shell of Rhodesia.[74] The task of preventing further expansion of Soviet influence in southern Africa continued to conflict with the sympathies of some white Americans for the increasingly embattled rulers of the region. As Zambian prime minister Kenneth Kaunda told an American journalist in 1968, Zimbabweans were like other oppressed peoples such as the Czechoslovaks: they would eventually fight for their freedom. If the West would not help them, they would accept aid from the East. By the brutality of its actions and the accompanying rhetoric of anti-Communism, Kaunda concluded, Salisbury was actually inviting Communist influence.[75]

The key change in Africa during the Nixon-Ford years was the Portuguese withdrawal, following years of armed nationalist struggle and the 1974 overthrow of the authoritarian regime of Marcello Caetano in Lisbon. The departure of the last European colonial power on the continent intensified the pressure on the remaining white settler states, especially neighboring Rhodesia.[76] Nixon had supported Portuguese authority in Africa to the end of his presidency; earlier, in 1963, he had even visited Lisbon as a private citizen and told the foreign minister that independence was "not necessarily the best thing for Africa or the Africans."[77] Kissinger's and Ford's decision to support one of the three competing Angolan factions in the civil war that broke out in 1975 emerged from the particular political circumstances of the spring of that year: the final North Vietnamese defeat of South Vietnam, with the last Americans fleeing for their lives, and the ongoing congressional investigations of CIA covert operations. Kissinger's response was typically global in its conception: he was determined to show the Soviets that despite events in Vietnam and the debacle of Watergate, the United States would still effectively oppose leftist revolutions around the Third World. He and the State Department considered it "essential to the credibility of our policies throughout the world" to prevent the victory of the Soviet-backed faction in Angola.[78] After U.S. policy failed and the Marxist Movimento Popular de Libertação de Angola (MPLA) took power at the new nation's independence late in 1975, Kissinger was asked by reporters if it might not have been better to leave the Angolan issue to Africans to sort out. "You may be right in African terms," he answered, "but I think globally."[79]

Congress responded in an almost opposite manner to events in Angola. The critical context for many senators and representatives was not just the loss in Vietnam, but also the ongoing congressional investigations of CIA covert operations. Disturbed by tales of agency assassination attempts abroad, leading Democrats were determined to restrict further foreign adventures that might turn out like Vietnam. They were upset to discover in the fall of 1975 how poorly the White House had kept them informed of American assistance to the Frente Nacional de Libertação de Angola (FNLA) and the União National para a Independência Total de Angola (UNITA), and how little clear ideological difference there was between those two factions and the MPLA. Newspaper reports of South African forces fighting with UNITA deepened their disillusionment, as it became clear that few Africans would support the American position. In December the Senate Foreign Relations Committee approved the Clark Amendment, which ended U.S. aid to any combatants in the Angolan civil war—the first time Congress had specifically banned a covert operation.[80]

Once Portuguese forces had withdrawn, the struggle throughout 1975 in Angola seemed at first to have little racial significance. All sides were Angolan. But the South African intervention on behalf of UNITA and the FNLA radically altered the equation, as did the Cuban troops flown in at the MPLA's request. What had initially seemed a conflict among Angolans involved Cubans and South Africans killing each other by November, with the support of their respective superpower allies: the Soviets and the Americans. For many Americans including President Ford and his advisers, the South African endeavor was legitimate because it opposed the expansion of Soviet influence; the troops of the hated Fidel Castro were seen not as liberators but as mere tools of Moscow and spreaders of Communism in Africa. Their presence seemed to call for containment of the Soviets and the Cubans, and the South Africans were the only folks in the neighborhood for the job.[81]

For almost all Africans, however, the meaning of the Angolan conflict was the opposite. Attitudes varied about Communism and about the Soviet Union, but not about South Africa. The apartheid state had for Africans the same meaning that the USSR held for Americans: the ultimate institutionalized form of evil. For people newly freed from centuries of white domination, the sight of white South African troops pouring across the border from Namibia into Angola was analogous to Americans viewing Soviet troops invading West Germany. The same Cuban state that appalled most Americans impressed citizens of African nations, where Castro had long been an ardent supporter of struggles for national independence. The contrast with South Africa could not have been more obvious, as the Cuban troops defending the MPLA were overwhelmingly black. The State Department privately admitted the racial coding the conflict had taken on: "The South African involvement on the side of FNLA/UNITA creates a dilemma for us. It . . . risks bringing discredit by association upon the US." Indeed, many African states that had originally been inclined to support the FNLA or UNITA reversed themselves and recognized the MPLA government instead. The Americans and the Soviets seemed to have their proxies engaged in a war about Communism but also about race relations, with the United States represented by the forces of white supremacy.[82]

As NSSM 39 made clear, the willingness of the Nixon and Ford administrations to be associated with South Africa reflected geopolitical calculations about the near-term future of the region. The whites were apparently "here to stay"; South Africa's economy had grown impressively during the previous decade; and "Nixon's personal sympathies were with the South Africans," as one of his NSC staffers put it.[83] It also reflected a lack of close attention to South African domestic conditions inherited from the Johnson administration, along with sympathy among Southerners in Congress for the Pretoria regime.[84] But the U.S. government lagged behind the broader international community, whose views of South Africa shifted sharply between 1969 and 1976. Condemnation of apartheid and the continued occupation of Namibia led to concerted efforts to expel South Africa from the UN, which was prevented only by the vetoes of the United States, Britain, and France. The UN's 1975 resolution condemning Zionism as racism reflected similar international anger at what was seen as another unjust "white settler" state in the Third World (and the United States defended Israel much as it did South Africa). South African prime minister John Vorster noted the parallel, referring sympathetically in a 1971 interview to Israel's "apartheid problem" of governing Palestinians in Gaza and the West Bank.[85] Black schoolchildren in Soweto highlighted the problems of the U.S. government's tilt toward Pretoria on 16 June 1976, when they began vast street protests against the South African government's orders that half of their classes be taught in Afrikaans rather than English. The police opened fire as they had at Sharpeville fifteen years earlier, but the massacre of dozens this time did not end the protests, which rolled on and set the stage for the final phase of the struggle against apartheid. Just as Angolans and Mozambicans had proven American policymakers wrong about the strength of Portuguese rule, black South Africans now demonstrated, at terrible cost, that the internal stability of even the region's sturdiest white state was no longer guaranteed.[86]

Nixon's Southern strategy had turned out to have an international reach, incorporating whites in southern Africa as well as the American South. The NSC acknowledged how racial issues crossed national borders. "Because of the multiracial character of our society and our own racial problems," NSSM 39 concluded, "other countries tend to see our relationships with southern Africa as reflections of domestic attitudes on race."[87] Lyndon Johnson's mantle of inclusive paternalism regarding racial equality did not fit well on Richard Nixon, who seemed to have little real feeling for the experience of racial discrimination, but he occasionally tried it on. As Kissinger drafted Nixon's first foreign policy address to Congress, the president instructed him, "Make sure there's something in it for the jigs, Henry"; a few minutes later in the conversation, he circled back to the same point: "*Is* there something in it for the jigs?"[88] Similarly revealing was Nixon's performance with Agnew in a supposedly self-mocking skit at the Gridiron Club dinner on 14 March 1970. Seated at adjoining pianos and bantering (Agnew in mock Southern accent) about their Southern strategy, Nixon would start playing various tunes only to have Agnew drown him out each time with a manic version of "Dixie." The elite, bipartisan, nearly all-white crowd roared with laughter.[89] "There is no documentary evidence that this [kind of] racism was the decisive influence in Kissinger-Nixon policies in Africa, Vietnam, or elsewhere, policies for which there were other arguments and reasons, however questionable," Roger Morris concluded later. "But it is impossible to pretend that the cast of mind that harbors such casual bigotry did not have some effect on American foreign policy toward the overwhelming majority of the world which is nonwhite."[90]

Ultimately, Nixon and his closest advisers were neither ideologues nor people of deep commitments about race.[91] The president sought political power above all, which could mean playing different sides of racial issues in different circumstances. "Hunting where the ducks are" at home translated into courting Southern whites, while abroad it required seizing the initiative by courting the very heart of the "yellow peril," the Chinese. Indeed, Nixon enjoyed playing the racial egalitarian in contrast to Soviet leaders, whose growing hostility toward Beijing in these years included occasional displays of anti-Asian racism—in remarks like "those squint-eyed bastards!" and "those yellow sons of bitches!"[92] The White House was delighted, similarly, with news from the FBI of a Black Panther Party member angered by experiencing racial discrimination on a visit to Cuba: more fodder for dividing antiracist opponents at home and abroad.[93] The administration's pursuit of political and diplomatic opportunities led to a focus on the most powerful nations, which could translate into political success at election time. Africa, by contrast, seemed to offer few rewards, and the NSC recommended simply keeping issues there "manageable."[94] Both at home and abroad, Nixon officially opposed "systems based on racial discrimination" while refusing to put more than a token element of Washington's power behind eliminating them.[95]

### Jimmy Carter and the New American South

The election of Jimmy Carter in 1976 offered a potentially sharp reversal of the Nixon-Kissinger obsession with power politics and disregard for matters of race relations. The first U.S. president from the Deep South and one dramatically affected by the civil rights movement, Carter entered the White House in the aftermath of the nation's bitter experience in Vietnam. His familiarity with the lives of African Americans was unprecedented in the Oval Office, and his commitment to racial equality was unquestioned by those who knew him. He promised to match this commitment with a reorientation of the nation's foreign relations, away from the anti-Communist focus of his predecessors and toward a novel attention to what he called "the newly influential countries in Latin America, Africa, and Asia."[96] The Carter administration sought to drop Washington's long-standing "zero-sum" view of international relations, by which political changes abroad had to be calculated as favoring either the Soviet Union or the United States. The budget of the covert operations arm of the CIA—long a bulwark against change in the Third World—was reduced to less than a tenth of its size a decade earlier, while congressional oversight of the agency was strengthened.[97] This shift toward a restrained diplomacy more favorable to social change in the Third World eventually faltered in the renewed Cold War that emerged in the administration's last two years, 1979 and 1980. But for at least their first two years, Carter and his advisers brought racial justice to the forefront of U.S. foreign relations, with a particular concern for southern Africa.

No other occupant of the Oval Office in the Cold War era grew up with Carter's intimacy with African Americans. His father, a successful farmer and businessman in Plains, Georgia, employed as many as two hundred and sixty black workers at a time. His mother worked as a nurse, and he and his siblings were cared for by a black nanny who worked for the Carters for twenty-one years. When Jimmy's parents left Plains for adult vacations, he stayed with an African American couple employed by the family. His first playmates were the children of his father's farmhands, and they remained his best friends until the segregating effect of the school system slowly pulled them apart. This was, of course, a limited, Jim Crow kind of intimacy, one embedded in the larger hierarchy of color of the 1920s and 1930s. Carter's wife, Rosalynn, recalled how, on their honeymoon in the North Carolina mountains in 1946, she had glimpsed a white domestic servant on a wealthy estate: "It was shocking to me. In Plains, Georgia, I had never seen a white woman doing yard labor or housework for a white person."[98]

Carter's racial attitudes as an adult and in his early political career reflected, in part, the contrasting influences of his parents. Earl Carter's perspective on African Americans was typical of his time and place: he was an old-fashioned racist and segregationist, though one capable of generosity to individual blacks in his employment. Lillian Carter held far more egalitarian views than did the bulk of her peers, especially in southern Georgia. Indeed, she even served in the Peace Corps in rural India from 1966 to 1968, when she was in her sixties. Jimmy's personal attitudes were close to his mother's. As an aspiring businessman and politician in the 1950s and 1960s in Plains after his return from the Navy, however, he chose not to rock the boat about race relations. He largely accepted the reality of segregation, even during a term as chair of the Sumter County school board in the years immediately following the *Brown v. Board of Education* decision. By character Carter was a conciliator rather than a confrontational person. He sought to get along with everyone, as he built both his peanut farming and warehousing business and his reputation as a man of integrity and industry. No aspiring politician willing to work within the Southern system in the 1950s could afford to denounce segregation. For white Georgians, one old friend remembered forty years later, "integration back then was about like child molestation is today."[99]

The overthrow of the traditional racial order of Dixie that unfolded in the two decades after 1954 left no Southerner untouched. With his spiritually driven seriousness about moral issues and his pragmatic sensitivity to changing political winds, Carter stood out for his determination to be a leader in the "New South." Other whites in Plains knew that he had different beliefs from most of them: he refused to join the archsegregationist White Citizens Council in 1954, and he tried unsuccessfully to integrate his own Baptist church in 1962. Three factors pushed him further down the path to racial egalitarianism: his deepening Christian faith, his service in the military, and his witnessing of the civil rights movement in Georgia. The extraordinary integrated Christian farming community of Koinonia, just seven miles from Plains, had been established in 1942. While unwilling to identify too closely with Koinonia's rejection of Jim Crow as it faced terrorist bombings and shootings by the Ku Klux Klan in the late 1950s, Jimmy and Rosalynn clearly respected the community's ideals and worked discreetly to mitigate some of the hostility it experienced. Carter served as an officer on an integrated Navy submarine a few years earlier, and he had supported his crew's unanimous rejection of an invitation to a party for only its white members by British officials in the port of Nassau. Finally, he was appalled in 1963 by the intensity of white hatred and violence against peaceful African American protesters in Americus, just nine miles from Plains. Few who knew him well were surprised that by the late 1960s, Carter had deepened not only his Christian identity also his commitment to a broader emphasis on social justice for the least powerful, particularly the poor and those with darker skins.[100]

Carter's term as governor of Georgia from 1970 to 1974 demonstrated both his ambitious political pragmatism and his commitment to a new era in Southern race relations. Believing it necessary for success, he campaigned to the right during 1970, appealing specifically to "the people who voted for George Wallace" for president in 1968 and "the ones who voted for Lester Maddox," the archsegregationist current governor of Georgia who could not by law succeed himself in office. Carter and his staff cast his major opponent in the Democratic primary, former governor Carl Sanders, as a liberal who was by implication too close to the integrationist national Democratic Party. Carter's campaign was careful: he avoided explicitly racial language in its messages to white voters, and he also appealed discreetly to black voters. This strategy led to a surprising upset of the better-known Sanders, who won 93 percent of the black vote in the primary. In the general election in November, African Americans decided to stick with the Democratic candidate, helping sweep Carter into office.[101]

He then surprised most Georgians with a clarion call for whites to accept a new racial order. In his inaugural address in January 1971 Carter declared, "I say to you quite frankly that the time for racial discrimination is over. Our people have already made this major and difficult decision." The *New York Times* covered the speech on its front page, as the national media took note of Carter as a spokesman for the New South. He governed Georgia carefully in regard to race, trying to win over conservative whites while turning the state toward an integrated future. Thus he remained opposed to school busing, while doubling the number of blacks in the state government. His symbolic gestures had particular impact, especially integrating the highway patrol and the walls of the state capitol itself by hanging a portrait of Martin Luther King, Jr., there. In a state where the feelings of most whites toward the recently martyred civil rights leader still ranged from doubt to hostility, this was not an easy step to take. Black Georgians rewarded the governor with strong support.[102]

African Americans across the nation then provided the crucial votes for Carter's extremely narrow victory in the presidential election of 1976. His record as governor won him the enthusiastic endorsement during the Democratic primaries of black leaders like Martin Luther King, Sr., and U.S. Congressman Andrew Young, who had been a close assistant to Martin Luther King, Jr. In the general election against Gerald Ford, Carter won more than 90 percent of the black votes, which, as Carter acknowledged, provided the critical margin in several of the states that put him over the top in the electoral college.[103] This was precisely the opposite situation of Nixon in 1968. The *New York Times* noted the apparent irony of a "south Georgia white man with a mint julep drawl" being sent to the White House by the "grandchildren of slaves."[104] But black Southerners, like white Southerners, tended to appreciate Carter's rural Southern background and his evangelical Protestant faith.[105] Indeed, in the election of 1976 many white and black Southerners voted for the same presidential candidate for the first time.

Carter ran for president by positioning himself as an outsider to the federal government. He campaigned not so much against Ford as against Nixon and Kissinger and the shrewd and seemingly amoral politics and diplomacy they represented. Untainted by associations with Washington, Carter promised to promote the decency of the American people and restore the national government's moral standing after the debacles of the Vietnam war and the Watergate scandal. He did not emphasize specific issues. Rather, he asked voters to have faith in him as a person and as a leader. Many people of influence, especially within the Democratic Party, lacked such faith; they were deeply skeptical of a man they knew little about, whose identity in rural Southern culture seemed foreign to them. Many African Americans and white liberals from outside the South distrusted his anti-Washington stance, which they associated with conservatism and segregationism—the forces that would be sympathetic to the next anti-Washington president, Ronald Reagan.[106]

But the man who won the Oval Office in the bicentennial year did not fit easily into existing political categories. His concerns for efficiency and budget balancing in the federal government, reflecting his own background in business and the military, were matched by an often stubborn determination to follow the more compassionate elements of the Christian gospel as he understood them. "I owe the special interests nothing," he declared repeatedly on the campaign trail, and indeed traditionally powerful political and business elites were anxious about the new Georgian candidate.[107] In an impromptu speech to a group of wealthy Hollywood liberals at actor Warren Beatty's elegant apartment in August 1976, Carter made his populist inclinations clear: "If we make a mistake, the chances are we won't actually go to prison, and if we don't like the public school system, we put our kids in private schools. But the overwhelming majority of the American people" had no such options. Suggesting that his allegiances had shifted away from people of privilege, he concluded—with a glance at the California governor, a primary opponent who had just entered the room—that "public servants like me, and Jerry Brown, and others have a responsibility to bypass the big shots, including you and people like you and like I was, and make a concerted effort to understand the people who are poor, black, speak a foreign language, who are not well educated, who are inarticulate," and to run the government in a way that delivers the services they desperately needed.[108] In cultural terms, Carter felt closer to Southern populist George Wallace than to any of the other Democratic presidential candidates of 1976. Only on matters of race did the two Deep South neighbors differ sharply.[109] This was crucial: Carter was a president whose concern for people with fewer economic assets and darker skins might make him unusually well suited for dealing with a mostly nonwhite world.

Carter sought to place human rights at the center of his new diplomacy. Rejecting the amoral, realpolitik calculations of Kissinger and Nixon, the new Democratic administration believed that the United States needed to reclaim its own ideals by reemphasizing moral decency in its relations with the rest of the world.[110] In place of CIA operatives undermining Third World nationalism Carter envisioned evenhanded support for justice for all people. The State Department created in 1977 an independent Bureau of Human Rights and Humanitarian Affairs, headed by a new assistant secretary of state, Patricia Derian, whose political reputation had been forged in civil rights work in Mississippi.[111] This shift reflected a national desire in the mid-1970s for a more humane diplomacy, evident particularly among younger members of Congress.[112] Demanding human rights within Communist countries was not novel in Washington, of course. What Carter added was an equal imperative for the protection of human rights among non-Communist nations. He believed such an approach was necessary for the building of what he called the global community—a world less scarred by the brutalities of political repression.[113] Because Carter also remained committed to restraining the growth of Communist influence abroad—he had no illusions about political liberty within the Soviet bloc—he was taking on a most difficult task. His willingness to preserve close ties with such noted anti-Communist tyrants as the shah of Iran earned him pointed rebukes about the true meaning of "human rights." Despite such exceptions and limitations on the administration's humanitarian priorities, including the return to a fierce anti-Communism in 1979, Carter's concern for political prisoners and social justice around the globe—particularly in Africa and Latin America—did contrast sharply with the explicitly political calculations of his Republican predecessors.[114]

Carter's identity as a Southerner sharpened his emphasis on human rights. The civil rights struggle of the decades leading up to 1976 had transformed Southern race relations. White people of conscience like Carter were deeply affected, as they had learned with sometimes terrible clarity the necessity of protecting the lives and liberties of all human beings. Carter spoke of how as governor of Georgia he had cringed at the firestorm of international criticism aimed at the United States for the violence and discrimination of whites against African Americans in the South, and for American support of "racist regimes" and "dictatorships" in southern Africa. "I used to shrink up and dread the day each fall when the United Nations General Assembly began its deliberations," he told the Congressional Black Caucus, "because I knew that my country, which I love, would be the target of every attack, and the butt of every joke among two-thirds of the nations on earth."[115] The election of a white president from south Georgia with overwhelming black support symbolized the political reintegration of the South with the rest of the nation. It marked the end of the nation's acute vulnerability regarding the treatment of its nonwhite citizens.[116] What Carter called "the cancer of racial injustice" would no longer weaken the country's body politic nor pollute its relations with the rest of the world.[117]

### The Carter Administration, Race, and Africa

Jimmy Carter believed that his mandate from the American people was to help heal the nation's wounds from Watergate, the war in Southeast Asia, and the social divisions that had emerged in the late 1960s. A conciliator, his personality seemed to fit the nation's need. His egalitarian inclinations showed immediately in his choice to walk rather than ride in his own inaugural parade. Gone were most of the limousines that marked the White House fleet, and gone was Nixon's love of the pomp and ceremony of the Oval Office. Carter was particularly determined to lead the nation symbolically toward greater racial and gender equality. He appointed unprecedented numbers of blacks and women to high federal offices; he and Rosalynn enrolled their daughter, Amy, in a desegregated public school in the District of Columbia; he spoke of racial discrimination as a disease comparable to polio; and his Justice Department worked quietly but diligently to enforce desegregation laws. Coretta Scott King praised him personally for "the new spirit of reconciliation which you and your Administration are causing in this nation."[118]

By the mid-1970s the battle for legal racial equality had been won. Struggles against discrimination now moved to the trickier ground of practice rather than law. Structures and habits of preferring whites over nonwhites in areas like employment, housing, and education represented less visible but more difficult barriers to overcome in many ways. One response to those deeply ingrained patterns of discrimination was affirmative action, articulated initially by Lyndon Johnson as a way of helping people of color overcome structural preferences against them. Affirmative action reached the Carter administration in the form of the suit filed by Allan Bakke against the University of California at Davis, charging that preferential treatment of less qualified minority applicants had resulted in his rejection for admission to the medical school there. The case went all the way to the Supreme Court, with Bakke's lawyers arguing that racial preferences of any kind were unconstitutional—that they represented "reverse discrimination" against white people.

The Bakke case became a lightning rod for contention about American race relations in the late 1970s. For many white Americans, Bakke's situation represented their growing frustration with what they believed was a new kind of racial discrimination against them. Roman Catholics and Jews remembered too clearly how a system of quotas had been used to limit their access to opportunities a few decades earlier. But for many African Americans and their white supporters, the Bakke case instead served as a litmus test of the nation's determination to remedy, rather than just talk about, the ongoing effects of past discrimination. For a seeker of national reconciliation like Carter, the case created a no-win situation. After extensive internal arguments, the Justice Department in September 1977 filed an amicus curiae brief with the Supreme Court that strongly endorsed the principle of affirmative action. Troubled by the idea of racial preferences in any form, the Carter administration nonetheless took the position that some kind of preferential consideration of race was necessary, owing to the damaging legacy of past discrimination and the continuing reality of covert discrimination. The Court agreed in its mixed decision of June 1978: actual racial quotas for admission were not constitutional, but taking race into less specific consideration as one of several admissions criteria was permissible. Carter himself did not take the opportunity of the Bakke case to make a ringing declaration of support for the principle of affirmative action, as his critics noted. His support was clear but quiet, as he sought to avoid alienating white voters.[119]

The Bakke case symbolized the broader post–civil rights dilemma of how to deal with persistent but unofficial racial discrimination. This was not a small problem for Americans of color. Discrimination shaped how the death penalty was administered, and it showed up in explicitly racial sentiments against Japanese expressed by white auto workers and even a Michigan congressman, frustrated by competition with Japanese car companies.[120] It included police brutality against Latino Americans in southwestern cities and at least one Klan kidnapping of a Latino outside San Diego, who was then delivered to the Border Patrol for deportation to Mexico—a vivid demonstration of the ongoing tendency of some white Americans to identify citizenship with phenotype.[121] It even encompassed the highest law enforcement officer in the Carter administration, Attorney General Griffin Bell. Bell's reluctance to resign from two whites-only country clubs and his conservative record on desegregation cases as a federal judge moved one early hero of the civil rights movement, Aaron Henry of Mississippi, to call him "just not a good man."[122] Discrimination even followed Americans of color abroad. Carter appointed Ric Haynes, an African American foreign service officer and former NSC staffer under Johnson, as U.S. ambassador to Algeria. Ambassador Haynes arrived in time for the 4 July 1977 party at the embassy in Algiers, only to overhear the spouses of two U.S. diplomats whispering about him, "Have you seen what Washington sent?"[123]

African Americans generally supported Carter throughout his presidency, but many of them grew disappointed as his term in office progressed. Most blacks remained confident that the president's heart was in the right place regarding matters of equal treatment and discrimination. What troubled them were his priorities, which increasingly focused on defense spending, balancing the budget, and fighting inflation. These left little room for promoting or even defending federal social programs, to the disappointment of members of the Congressional Black Caucus.[124] Regardless of his strong personal convictions about racial equality and his vocal defense of human rights abroad, the president chose not to use the bully pulpit of the White House to call the nation, as Lyndon Johnson had, to a greater commitment to civil rights at home.[125] Hemmed in by economic problems and political limitations at home and distracted by crises abroad, especially in Iran and Afghanistan, Carter did not provide as much leadership on civil rights as some wished to see.[126]

Carter's most significant step regarding race and foreign relations was his appointment of Andrew Young as ambassador to the UN. The sending of an African American for the first time to represent the United States to the world community at the United Nations carried considerable symbolic weight. Young's background in the Southern freedom movement and his strong support for the ongoing liberation struggles in southern Africa indicated that the new administration would part ways with its predecessors. Young served as a leader of the "regionalist" forces regarding Africa: those in the administration, including Secretary of State Cyrus Vance, who were inclined to understand African problems as essentially separate from the Cold War. While the UN ambassador did not hold the authority of either Vance or the national security adviser Zbigniew Brzezinski, Young's close relationship with the president helped focus American attention on the problem of human rights abuses in Africa to an unprecedented extent. Africans and other people of color around the world appreciated the sharp contrast between the politics of Andrew Young and those of Henry Kissinger, as human rights moved from the periphery to center stage. Brzezinski credited Young with "transforming American isolation in the Third World into American friendship."[127]

Part of Young's success in warming relations between Africa and the United States stemmed from his informal but effective style of diplomacy. Like his boss in the Oval Office, who arranged the Camp David accords between Egypt and Israel, Young was a conciliator by both nature and commitment— a man eager to bridge the gaps between conflicting positions and bring opponents together. In the civil rights movement his role had often been one of negotiating with white officials rather than receiving blows from police batons on the front lines. While unstinting in his pursuit of racial equality, he was no economic radical. He actively pursued the interests of American businesses in building trade with Africa, and he viewed American corporations operating in South Africa as a potentially liberalizing influence on apartheid. Even as the high-profile ambassador to the UN, Young had no immunity from enduring white attitudes about African Americans: headed into the garage at the Waldorf Towers in New York one day while dressed in a jogging suit, he encountered a white tourist who asked him to fetch his car. "There I was riding high being the ambassador and all," he recalled, "and this guy assumed I was the car hop. To him I was just another nigger." But such encounters did not deter Young's commitment to seeking racial reconciliation in American diplomacy.[128]

In contrast to most diplomats, Young was famously frank about his opinions. Depending on their politics, others found this alternatively refreshing or troubling. At various points, the ambassador argued publicly that Cuban troops brought "a certain stability and order to Angola"; identified the South African government as "illegitimate"; labeled the British government "a little chicken" on racial issues; called Nixon and Ford "racists"; and declared that there were "hundreds, perhaps thousands, of political prisoners [in jail] in the United States."[129] This was more than a simple breeze of fresh air in the U.S. government—it was a veritable gale of alternative perception. Carter was embarrassed by the barrage of criticism he received after each of these controversial assertions by his ambassador and friend, and more conservative Americans called for Young's removal from his prominent position at the UN.[130] Others, particularly Africans and their supporters in the United States, found Young's outspokenness bracingly accurate and encouraging. They considered it unarguable that apartheid rendered the South African regime illegitimate. They recognized Nixon's casual dislike for people of color and Britain's unwillingness to use force against rebellious whites in Rhodesia as it had against rebellious people of color in other colonies. They believed South Africa to be the real destabilizing force in Angola. And for people familiar with how the justice system in the American South had long served to incarcerate black organizers, including the ongoing case of the Wilmington Ten in North Carolina, Young's calculation about political prisoners seemed eminently plausible.[131]

Young was forced to resign from his position at the UN in August 1979 after meeting secretly with a representative of the Palestinian Liberation Organization (PLO), defying an administration promise to Israel not to do so. He was not the first administration official to meet with a PLO figure, and Carter himself had compared the PLO cause to that of the American civil rights movement.[132] Brzezinski had rejected Israel's proposed partial "home rule" for Palestinians in the West Bank and Gaza, comparing it to South Africa's "homelands" strategy for preserving white rule.[133] Few in American public life, however, were willing yet to negotiate with the PLO. And Young's firing ultimately reflected the feathers he had long ruffled with his frank diplomacy, the influence of American supporters of Israel, and the broader shift of the Carter administration to a more militarized and confrontational foreign policy. Young's refusal to think like a Cold Warrior conflicted with rising anti-Communism in the administration. The persistence of Cuban troops in Angola and their introduction into Ethiopia, in combination with the Nicaraguan revolution and insurgencies in other Central American states, raised concerns about leftist links between Africa and Latin America and about the expansion of Soviet influence on both continents.[134] Young's removal angered African Americans who considered him one of the primary symbols of Carter's commitment to black interests. It also exacerbated black-Jewish tensions in American politics, as blacks resented the influence of Israel's supporters and increasingly identified with Palestinians as struggling for self-determination against a more powerful "white" nation that discriminated against them.[135]

Before it tapered off in the renewed Cold War of 1979–80, the Carter administration's unprecedented interest in Africa arose from the confluence of several factors. The president himself was genuinely concerned about developments on the continent, on the basis of his early links to African Americans, his seriousness about social justice and human rights, and his interest in missionary work among the rural poor. He was, in fact, the first sitting American president to visit Africa, traveling to Nigeria in 1978. Carter's considerable involvement with development and health care issues in Africa in his postpresidential years has testified to these concerns.[136] The momentous political events in southern Africa in the 1970s had focused world attention on the region, especially the independence of Angola and Mozambique in 1975, the Soweto uprising of 1976, and the escalation of the civil war in Rhodesia/Zimbabwe. The withdrawal of U.S. forces from Vietnam allowed American liberals and leftists to shift their attention from Southeast Asia to the problem of white supremacy south of Zambezi River. At the same time the success of the civil rights movement in ending legal discrimination in the United States cast apartheid in a worse light than ever before for most Americans. Finally, more traditional security interests also increased U.S. attention to Africa, as Nigeria became the second largest provider of imported oil to the United States in these years, and Cuban troops in Angola and Ethiopia suggested a growing Soviet or at least Communist influence on the continent.[137]

Washington's renewed attention to Africa came only in the wake of changing race relations in the United States. By the mid-1970s the process of desegregation left little room in the mainstream of American politics for defending racial inequality and discrimination. Conservatives still vigorously defended authoritarian anti-Communist governments in places like Iran and Nicaragua, but fewer and fewer voices spoke up for the white supremacist rulers of South Africa, Namibia, and Rhodesia. "I believe very strongly in majority rule," Carter declared on his third day in the Oval Office." There was no clearer violation of the human rights that the new president touted than the forms of control exercised by the rulers of those three states. Indeed, the administration feared that continued white rule might so alienate the African majority in the region as to lead to eventual Communist revolutions there. Helping negotiate independence for Namibia and a settlement of the civil war in Rhodesia, Vance argued, provided the only "workable strategy for improving [U.S.] relations with black Africa and blocking the spread of Soviet and Cuban influence in southern Africa."[138]

The Carter administration's support for majority rule in southern Africa reflected as well the growing influence of African American organizations on U.S. policy toward the continent. "The politicians were frank. They used to call us niggers," Young liked to tell white audiences when he was a member of Congress in the early 1970s. "But when blacks in a community got 30 percent of the vote, we became nigras. Later on, at about 40 percent, we were Nee-grows or colored people. And when we got the majority, we became their black brothers."[139] As African Americans gained political power in the 1970s, their interests in Africa received greater attention. The newly founded Congressional Black Caucus became a major voice on African issues, as did the lobbying organization TransAfrica, created in 1976 in response to the

Soweto uprising.[140] The NAACP and the Reverend Jesse Jackson also lobbied the administration to take stronger stands against the white governments of southern Africa.[141]

Carter's Africa policy could never fully escape Cold War and defense considerations, and the movement toward renewed conflict with the Soviet Union inevitably reduced American attention to the issue of majority rule. The Soviet airlift of twelve thousand Cuban troops into Ethiopia in 1977 sharply increased U.S. anxieties. The invasion of southern Zaire by Cuban-trained Katangans from Angola in May 1978 exacerbated those concerns.[142] For its part, the Castro regime was determined to support leftist revolutionaries in the Third World, and the large percentage of Cubans who were of African descent shared a concern for developments on the continent. Ethiopia had long been a symbol of African independence from white rule, and Cuba's assistance helped it to stave off both Eritrean separatists and Somali efforts to seize the Ogaden region. Many Africans appreciated Cuba's support for the revolutionary regimes in Addis Ababa and Angola, especially in light of South African opposition to the Luanda government.[143] The slippage of U.S. policy back toward containing Communism reflected the rising influence within the administration of Brzezinski, who had earlier edited a book with a title suggestive of his primary concern regarding the region: *Africa and the Communist World*.[144]

The Carter administration's attention to South Africa followed the same trajectory from a strong initial stance to a tapering off by 1979 as crises elsewhere seized Washington's attention. In contrast to the aftermath of the Sharpeville massacre sixteen years earlier, black protest continued to build and roil South African society after the Soweto uprising of 1976. The recent Portuguese withdrawal from neighboring Mozambique and Angola made the apartheid state seem newly vulnerable to its opponents. Vice President Walter Mondale met in May 1977 in Vienna with Prime Minister John Vorster to warn that relations between the two countries would deteriorate sharply if South Africa did not move away from apartheid. Mondale even used the phrase "one man, one vote" to explain the new administration's goal for South Africa—an unprecedented public declaration by a U.S. official in support of democracy there.[145] When the apartheid regime escalated its repressive tactics in the fall of 1977, murdering black leader Steven Biko during a prison interrogation, banning opposition groups, and detaining an array of other anti-apartheid activists, the U.S. government responded swiftly. The House of Representatives, led by the Black Caucus, passed the first congressional resolution critical of apartheid. In a symbolic gesture revealing how much had changed since the Nixon era, Carter sent a senior State Department official to Biko's funeral.[146] Young voted for a mandatory arms embargo against South Africa by the UN Security Council, the first resolution ever requiring punitive sanctions be imposed on a member state.[147] White South Africans resented U.S. actions and placed the blame squarely on Carter and his convictions about racial equality.[148]

The Carter administration was not yet willing to go beyond symbolic disassociations with apartheid to the level of structural disengagement from South Africa. Economic sanctions, the ultimate weapon for pressuring Pretoria, were discussed but put off.[149] This approach reflected in part the probusiness orientation of men like Carter and Young, who were well aware of the highly profitable character of extensive U.S. trade and investment relations with South Africa.[150] They tended to agree with American business leaders who argued that U.S. companies in South Africa provided important models of decent treatment of black workers.[151] They were also reconcilers, who sought a negotiated solution to South Africa's civil strife to avoid a full-blown revolution and race war. Carter told his Cabinet early on that "South Africa is like the South fifteen years ago," implying that its race relations could be reformed from within.[152] The president and his advisers feared that economic sanctions might have the negative effect of making white South Africans more defiant and isolated, while leaving them powerful enough to rule the country.[153] The American desire for Pretoria's assistance in finding a negotiated solution to the Rhodesian civil war next door also inclined the administration to preserve channels of cooperation with the apartheid regime.[154] White South Africans and their American supporters argued that South Africa was "an integral and indispensable part of the West" and a critical bulwark against the "Soviet assault on southern Africa."[155] The Carter administration was less inclined to agree with these arguments than its predecessors had been, but it still tended to view white South Africans as part of the Western world. As American attention shifted northward to the crises in Iran and Afghanistan and a renewed confrontation with the Soviet Union by 1980, the administration's interest in challenging Pretoria waned. The resignations of Young (August 1979) and Vance (April 1980) punctuated the turn away from Africa. Public attention returned to the Cold War, and one poll in 1979 found that only 18 percent of the American public had even heard of apartheid.[156]

The other holdout of white supremacy reached its demise in the Carter years, as Rhodesia became Zimbabwe in April 1980. Similar in many ways to neighboring South Africa, Rhodesia previewed how a combination of internal struggle and external sanctions would finally end white rule in South Africa fourteen years later. The Carter administration inherited a rather different set of policies regarding Rhodesia than those for South Africa, grounded in the distinctive histories of the two states. South Africa had gained its independence from Britain in 1910, when white supremacy was still the norm in Europe and North America, and the Pretoria government was therefore considered unquestionably legitimate by most other governments. The white settlers of Rhodesia, a much smaller percentage of their state's population, instead declared their independence from Britain in 1965 to preserve their dominance in an era when white rule was receding from most of the African continent. Changes in global race relations meant that Rhodesia was received differently than South Africa had been. No state recognized the Ian Smith regime as legitimate. The United States followed Britain's lead in imposing economic sanctions on Rhodesia, where there was much less American investment than in South Africa.

Carter thus inherited a tougher policy toward Rhodesia than South Africa. He quickly patched the major hole in the sanctions system, through which Rhodesian chrome had been flowing for six years, by successfully pushing Congress to repeal the Byrd Amendment.[157] Young lobbied his former congressional colleagues for this measure, describing it as a "kind of referendum on American racism"—powerful rhetoric in post–civil rights America.[158] Carter also came into office with Smith having already conceded in October 1976 that white rule was coming to an end, another sharp contrast to South Africa. In the meantime, however, the ongoing civil war between Smith's troops and the guerrilla forces of the Patriotic Front under Robert Mugabe and Joshua Nkomo threatened to destabilize the entire region, and Britain and the United States were eager to promote a negotiated solution that would minimize further racial polarization.[159] Then the wily Smith complicated the situation by promoting an "internal settlement" that would bring moderate blacks into the government while excluding the more radical Patriotic Front, as a way of preserving as much white political influence as possible. His American supporters, led by twenty-six Southern and conservative U.S. senators like Jesse Helms, invited him to visit the United States in October 1978, where he and they lobbied the public and the rest of the government for an end to economic sanctions against Rhodesia, based on his agreement to hold multiracial elections in April 1979.[160]

Carter resisted the considerable pressure that built up for ending sanctions after the election of Methodist bishop Abel Muzorewa as the first black prime minister of Rhodesia. The president and his advisers recognized that however much they might admire Muzorewa's moderate politics and religious background, the real power among Africans in the country lay with the Patriotic Front, which had rejected the Smith-controlled elections. Congressional Republicans had long argued that the Patriotic Front was supported by the Soviet Union and that its politics were explicitly Marxist. They found the insistence of Carter and the British government on including the Patriotic Front in any final settlement incomprehensible: weren't these precisely the kind of revolutionaries Americans were supposed to oppose? Senator Robert Dole even compared the front to the PLO, arguing that since the United States supported Israel and refused to talk to Palestinian terrorists, it should similarly promote the Rhodesian "internal settlement" and exclude Mugabe and Nkomo.[161] Andrew Young, of course, agreed with the logic of this comparison, though he drew the opposite conclusion: if we can talk to the Patriotic Front, we should talk to the PLO. Strongly supported by Africans and African Americans, Carter rode out the storm of criticism and preserved U.S. sanctions until after the Lancaster House agreements in London in September 1979, which led to more inclusive elections and the creation of Zimbabwe with Mugabe as prime minister.[162] Averill Harriman then reported to Brzezinski and Carter from Zimbabwe's independence ceremonies in April 1980 that Mugabe was turning out to be quite pragmatic: friendly toward the West, inclusive of whites in his government, eager for Western investment, and hostile to the Soviet Union.[163] In a month when the administration was awash in criticism for its failed military effort to rescue American hostages in Iran, this was welcome news of a success story partly attributable to the principled actions of the president.

The Carter administration ultimately allowed its social justice priorities to be eclipsed in its last two years by renewed anxiety about political revolutions and instability, which it feared the Soviet Union was either instigating or benefiting from. A growing Cuban military presence in Angola and Ethiopia, revolutions in Iran and Nicaragua, and especially the Soviet invasion of Afghanistan in December 1979 convinced many Americans, including the president, that Communist forces were once again on the march, as they had been in the late 1940s.[164] Attention to human rights and to building a "global community" waned relative to this renewed concern with traditional national security issues.[165] The resignation of Secretary of State Cyrus Vance in April

1980 and the rising influence of national security adviser Zbigniew Brzezinski symbolized this reorientation. Domestic racial politics developed in parallel fashion. While most African Americans remained favorably inclined toward the president throughout his four years in office, Carter's emphasis on budgetary restraint and fighting inflation placed him increasingly at odds with black political leaders and the social programs they supported. Young's resignation tied together these shifts to the right in both foreign and domestic policy. Young was the leading advocate of closer ties with the Third World, including leftist governments there, and he was the most visible and influential black official ever in the U.S. government; his departure bitterly disappointed many African Americans.[166] Carter's personal commitment to racial and social justice remained firm, but his administration's determination to contain the expansion of Soviet influence took precedence. Relations with the Third World slid down the priority scale, occasionally revealing surprising ignorance in Washington. "What the hell is an 'Ayatollah' anyway?" Vice President Walter Mondale asked CIA director Stansfield Turner at an NSC meeting on the Iranian revolution in September 1979. Turner replied, "I'm not sure I know."[167]

Jimmy Carter governed the United States in a period of transition, both in race relations and in foreign relations. In response to the civil rights victories of the 1960s and to growing black political participation and power, the nation was moving toward the more conservative racial politics of Ronald Reagan in the 1980s. From the reconsiderations of the Cold War in the early 1970s—the antiwar movement, détente, and distrust of imperial behavior abroad—Americans were now edging back toward the anti-Communist enthusiasms that would break out anew in 1980. Constrained by these political trends and by the overwhelming reality of double-digit inflation at the end of his term, Carter struggled to pull Americans free of narrow anti-Communism and to enshrine human rights as the country's highest priority abroad. "Foreign policy no longer has a single or simple focus," he explained, urging Americans to try to understand instead "the complexity of interrelated and sometimes disturbing events and circumstances" abroad.[168] With Andrew Young as a key spokesman and with robust African American support, this peanut farmer and businessman from the Deep South made the pursuit of color-blind democracy in southern Africa a higher priority for the U.S. government than had any other president. Carter's return to the Cold War fold by his last year in office blurred that focus, but not before he had warmed considerably the relations of the U.S. government with both the Third World and African Americans.

### To the End of the Cold War and Beyond

After 1979 Americans seemed increasingly to agree about the evils of Communism and the Soviet Union and therefore the essential necessity of anti-Communism. Evidence of this abounds: from the popularity of Ronald Reagan for eight years in the White House, to the liberation of the Soviet empire and the implosion of the USSR itself, to the attention paid to recently declassified Soviet documents suggestive of extensive spying in the West during the Cold War. There were exceptions, particularly in the form of dissent against Reagan's support of right-wing governments and rebels in Central America. But overall, the transcendence of capitalist values and the delegitimation of socialist alternatives in the United States and indeed the world marked the last two decades of the twentieth century.

In the same period, the legitimacy in American public life of racial prejudice and discrimination continued to ebb. The epithet "racist" became a powerful rhetorical tool in politics, to an extent unimaginable a generation earlier. No demonstration of this trend could be clearer than the near universal condemnation of South African apartheid by the mid-1980s, including comprehensive economic sanctions against Pretoria passed by a Republican-controlled Senate. Again there were exceptions. Reagan vetoed those sanctions, requiring a congressional override, and George Bush played the race card successfully in the 1988 presidential campaign, while a broad white backlash dating back to the late 1960s helped end the federal welfare system and limit affirmative action. And prejudice and racial violence, of course, hardly disappeared. But explicit white supremacy as an avenue to mainstream political success was—like Soviet Communism—swept into the dustbin of history. A rising consensus in American life around racial equality and anti-Communism marked the final years of the Cold War.

Reagan rode to victory in 1980 on a wave of unhappiness with inflation, unemployment, and the seizure of American hostages in Teheran. His defeat of Carter carried racial significance. From his early years in Illinois and California, he had little experience with African Americans, like Kennedy, and he evidently demonstrated neither personal prejudice nor much interest in racial issues.[169] But his political ascendancy built from the Watts riots of 1965, as he was elected governor of California a year later as a proponent of law and order. His opposition to civil rights bills in the 1960s was well known.[170] In 1980 Reagan continued the Republican strategy of appealing to disaffected white Southern voters, in particular by rejecting affirmative action.[171] In implementing a Southern strategy Reagan even went so far as to open his campaign in Philadelphia, Mississippi, known primarily as the site of the infamous murder of three civil rights workers in June 1964. He made no mention of James Chaney, Michael Schwerner, and Andrew Goodman, declaring instead, "I believe in states' rights"—the precise language of those who had done the killing.[172] The Ku Klux Klan endorsed Reagan's candidacy, announcing that the Republican platform "reads as if it were written by a Klansman."[173] Twelve years earlier Martin Luther King, Jr., had too easily dismissed the California governor and aspiring presidential candidate as a "Hollywood performer lacking distinction even as an actor."[174] In 1980 and again in 1984, Reagan received the lowest percentage of black votes of any major party candidate in the twentieth century, but his brand of conservatism dominated American politics for a decade.[175]

The Reagan administration swiftly positioned itself as less sympathetic to the interests of African Americans than any administration since the 1950s. It appointed few blacks to top positions. Frustrated black foreign service officers eventually brought a discrimination suit against the State Department in 1986.[176] The Justice Department opposed affirmative action, narrowed the definition of racial discrimination, and supported federal tax exemptions for racially discriminatory schools. The administration's economic policies of favoring wealthier Americans and cutting social spending disproportionally hurt nonwhite citizens. Reagan appointed a raft of archconservative federal judges, including William Rehnquist as chief justice of the Supreme Court—despite Rehnquist's earlier record of sympathy for segregationist positions and his opposition to public accommodation laws outlawing racial discrimination.[177] The president's joke about differences within his administration regarding how tough to be with the Soviets— "Sometimes my right hand doesn't know what my far right hand is doing"— might have referred just as well to his civil rights policies.[178]

The Reagan administration's seeming indifference to African American conditions applied equally to the black majority in South Africa. "All Reagan knows about southern Africa is that he's on the side of the whites," Chester Crocker told a South African reporter a month before being named the administration's point man for African affairs.[179] American investors and foreign traders continued to benefit handsomely from their unparalleled position in South Africa's economy, but the president was not motivated primarily by such economic links.[180] He believed that instability under an anti-Communist government anywhere was caused by Communists. "Let us not delude ourselves," he explained in 1982. "The Soviet Union underlies all the unrest that is going on. If they weren't involved in this game of dominoes, there wouldn't be any hotspots in the world."[181] This simplistic view meant that, in South Africa, the banned African National Congress, which was allied with the banned Communist Party, was the source of trouble. As late as July 1986 Reagan blamed the ANC for a program of "calculated terror . . . designed to bring about further repression, the imposition of martial law, and eventually creating the conditions for racial war." The increasingly brutal repression of dissent against apartheid by the Pretoria government in the 1980s was, from the president's perspective, caused by its opponents.[182]

White South Africans were, of course, delighted at the good fortune dealt to them by American politics. They had been encouraged by the resurgence of anti-Communism in the late Carter administration, which gave them greater leverage against Western anti-apartheid pressures. Carter's assistant secretary of state for African affairs, Richard Moose, had noted in 1980 that "the apparent trend toward conservatism in the West also reinforces their world view."[183] But the contrast of Reagan's views on race relations and apartheid with those of Carter was stark and even more encouraging for them. The Pretoria government was almost euphoric at hearing the new U.S. ambassador to the UN, Jeane Kirkpatrick (unlike her predecessor, Andrew Young) defend apartheid against its critics by arguing that "racial dictatorship is not as onerous as Marxist dictatorship"—a rather bold opinion for someone who had lived under neither.[184] South African opponents of apartheid were dismayed. Reagan's policy of "constructive engagement" with Pretoria, Archbishop Desmond Tutu declared, was "immoral, evil, and totally unChristian."[185]

South Africa's severe crackdown on internal dissent in the early 1980s was matched by a series of military invasions to destabilize the neighboring "frontline" states of Mozambique, Zimbabwe, Namibia, and Angola, and thus weaken their ability and inclination to support ANC guerrillas.[186] A British Council of Churches delegation to Namibia in 1981 described the South African military occupation of that territory as a "reign of terror."[187] Congressional repeal of the Clark Amendment in 1985 allowed U.S. funds and weapons to flow again to the UNITA guerrillas in Angola, who were supported by South African forces in intense fighting against the Angolan government and its Cuban allies.[188] The CIA funneled military aid to UNITA through the Kamina air base in neighboring Zaire; the agency tried to keep this operation secret partly by using African Americans as ground personnel, in hopes that they would not be as conspicuous as whites.[189] Fidel Castro, for one, was not fooled. He reminded two visiting black U.S. officials in 1985 of the racial coding of the war in Angola: "We are the only country which has actually fought the South African racists and fascists."[190] Indeed, three years later Cuban forces finally halted the South African army's advance at a major battle at Cuito Cuanavale, setting the stage at last for a negotiated settlement of the political futures of Angola and Namibia. South Africa's regional offensive ultimately proved to be the final outward push of a cancer-ridden political system on the verge of internal collapse.

Apartheid was overcome primarily by the sustained resistance, at enormous cost, of black South Africans. The actions of Americans and other foreigners were secondary to developments inside the country. The dramatic upsurge in black protest in South Africa that began in 1984 did, however, affect American politics more directly than any previous African issue had been able to do. The South African government's declaration of a state of emergency in 1985 and its inability to halt massive protests made front-page news across the Atlantic. Best-selling books, popular films, and hit music albums in the United States focused on South Africa.[191] Archbishop Tutu's charismatic nonviolence and his winning of the Nobel Peace Prize reminded many Americans of Martin Luther King, Jr., a Nobel laureate two decades before. Indeed, the anti-apartheid movement that grew rapidly in the United States in the mid-1980s seemed to many of its participants to be a renewal of the American civil rights movement of the early 1960s. Under the leadership of TransAfrica and the Congressional Black Caucus, the movement focused with considerable success on two goals: getting American institutions to withdraw their investments from South Africa and from any companies engaging in business with South Africa, and moving Congress to enact broad economic sanctions on the apartheid state. Five years of "constructive engagement" yielded no evidence by 1986 of reform within the Pretoria regime, which instead continued to dig in its heels against change. The self-evident failure of the Reagan administration's policy opened the door to a new consensus in American politics on disengagement from South Africa.[192]

The comprehensive economic sanctions passed by Congress, including the Republican-controlled Senate, over Reagan's veto in October 1986, reflected the consolidation of a broad national agreement on the immorality of legal racial discrimination. The televised pictures and reports of police brutality in South Africa, based solely on the color of one's skin, dismayed American audiences. Despite the opposition of the president and of hard-line sympathizers with white rule like Jesse Helms, even most conservative Republicans decided to distance themselves from virulent white supremacy. Such long-time friends of the apartheid regime as Representative Newt Gingrich, soon to become Speaker of the House, began to put distance between themselves and apartheid's rulers.[193] For senators like Nancy Kassebaum of Kansas, the demands of black South Africans for the right to own property where they wished and to live free of government restriction and harassment seemed quintessentially American, even conservative. Political calculations were also part of the equation: Kassebaum and other Republicans feared losing congressional seats to the Democrats in the November 1986 elections if they were associated with human rights abuses in South Africa.[194] But even Reagan's own national security adviser, Robert McFarlane, was disgusted by the "hypocrisy" of Prime Minister P. W. Botha, whom he finally concluded was a "mean-spirited son of a bitch."[195] Secretary of State George Schulz decided that the domestic political costs of trying to work with Pretoria were increasingly not worth paying: the "flak factor" had gotten "completely out of hand."[196] The consensus against apartheid reflected, in part, the rising political power of African Americans and their votes, which also helped change the behavior at home of some formerly staunch segregationists. James Eastland gave the NAACP $500 shortly before his death; Strom Thurmond sent his son to an integrated school; and George Wallace was granted an honorary degree from the Tuskegee Institute.[197] The Reagan administration's hostility to the causes of domestic civil rights and southern African liberation, while important, was partially mitigated by the rise of the anti-apartheid movement and the tenacity of African American political organizing.

The election of George Bush in 1988 signaled, for the most part, a continuation of Reagan's policies regarding racial issues and foreign affairs. In contrast to Reagan, Bush came out of the more moderate, eastern tradition within the Republican Party, represented by his father, Prescott Bush, a U.S. senator from Connecticut. But like Reagan, he moved to the Sunbelt—Houston—early in his adult life and shifted politically to the right as his party did.[198] At heart a more cautious and less visceral conservative than Reagan, Bush adapted himself to the prevailing political winds of the 1980s and served as a loyal vice president for both of his predecessor's terms.

Like his early political patron, Richard Nixon, Bush took a much greater interest in international matters than in the intricacies of domestic governance. Indeed, his unwillingness to take actions to moderate a prolonged recession in the early 1990s contributed mightily to his failure to be reelected in 1992. With few African American supporters to sensitize him to the problems of discrimination, Bush viewed racial issues as only a minor aspect of the least interesting part of his job: domestic politics. Like Nixon, however, he proved adept at playing to whites' racial fears for political advantage. He allowed campaign manager Lee Atwater in 1988 to exploit fear of black rapists as a centerpiece of the campaign against Massachusetts governor Michael Dukakis. Republican advertising that fall focused on "Willie" Horton (a nickname manufactured to sound more "black"), a convicted criminal who committed rape and murder against a white couple while on parole from a Massachusetts prison. If the explicit message was that Dukakis was supposedly soft on crime, it required no great insight to see a calculated titillation of white racial and sexual fears.[199]

Once in the Oval Office, Bush continued Reagan's opposition to affirmative action policies. He responded to the May 1992 race riots that broke out in Los Angeles by blaming liberal social welfare policies that, he argued, had fostered dependency on the state and irresponsible personal behavior.[200] In a move seemingly almost as cynical as the "Willie" Horton campaign tactic, the president replaced retiring Supreme Court Justice Thurgood Marshall—a jurist of enormous reputation and dignity—with Clarence Thomas, a young nominee distinguished for such a position primarily by having conservative views and by being black.[201] The other African American to rise to prominence with the patronage of the Reagan and Bush administrations was General Colin Powell. Having served as Reagan's national security adviser in 1987–88, Powell became a household name as a result of his performance as chairman of the Joint Chiefs of Staff—the first black person to serve as the nation's foremost military commander—during the Persian Gulf war of 1991. Powell was a nonpartisan figure of widely admired strategic acuity and political skills. By the mid-1990s, in fact, he had become probably the most uniformly admired African American in the nation's history and was considered a possible presidential candidate in the mold of Dwight Eisenhower. He was no enthusiast for Republican racial politics and policies, however. "Even though Reagan and Bush are two of the closest people in my life," Powell recalled in 1995, "I've got to say that this was an area where I found them wanting."[202]

Two great epochs in international affairs came to an end while Bush was in the White House. One was the joint collapse of Communist rule in Eastern Europe in 1989 and of the Soviet Union itself in 1991. The other was the 1990 agreement of the last remaining white minority regime in the world first to grant independence to Namibia, arguably the world's last colony, and then to release political prisoners including Nelson Mandela and allow a free election in 1994 that would end apartheid. The speech by South African prime minister F. W. DeKlerk on 2 February 1990 announcing these decisions meant for legalized white supremacy what the fall of the Berlin Wall two and a half months earlier had signified for Soviet Communism: the final surrender.[203]

The Bush administration itself had little to do with these developments, which were driven primarily by indigenous actors in each region. The administration indicated little concern for events in South Africa, and the president's great caution regarding change in the Soviet bloc left the U.S. government mostly in the position of an observer.[204] But two more historic changes away from authoritarian rule of the many by the few would be difficult to imagine. The liberation of the last piece of Africa from white rule and the freeing of Eastern Europe and central Asia from Communist rule combined to close the curtain on the protracted process of decolonization, which had colored so much of twentieth-century world history. As the Cold War receded into history, contention over race relations was unlikely to exert as much influence again on international relations as it had in the era of African decolonization and America's civil rights struggle.

# EPILOGUE

AFTER THE FALL of the Berlin Wall issues of race and foreign relations continued to intersect, just as they had before 1945, but without the prominence that the Cold War had given them. Former Arkansas governor Bill Clinton won the presidency in 1992 and again in 1996 as a New Democrat, supportive of the interests of American corporations and less committed to his party's traditional backing of federal social programs. He stole much of the Republican Party's thunder by presiding over a period of dramatic economic growth, eliminating federal budget deficits, and ending the federal welfare system in 1996. He nevertheless built an exceptionally close personal and political bond with African Americans. They stood with him more reliably than any other group of Americans, even during his 1998 impeachment trial stemming from an affair with a White House intern. Clinton defended affirmative action ("mend it, don't end it"), appointed far more people of color and women to the Cabinet and the federal judiciary than had his predecessors, visited African American churches with relish ("He can sing the songs without even looking at the hymnal," black Congressman John Lewis noted), and had a black best friend (Washington lawyer and former National Urban League president Vernon Jordan). His roots in Arkansas help explain his connection to African Americans. As an eleven-year old fifty miles away in Hot Springs, he had been riveted and horrified by the 1957 school desegregation crisis in the state capital. "It was Little Rock that made racial equality a driving obsession of my life."[1]

Clinton similarly paid more attention to Africa than had previous presidents. He visited the continent twice to enthusiastic receptions, as he urged negotiated solutions to armed conflicts and promoted American trade and investment there. His administration's initial enthusiasm for peacekeeping missions involving U.S. personnel diminished, however, after eighteen American soldiers and more than five hundred Somalis died in an October 1993 firefight in war-torn Mogadishu, where George Bush had first sent marines a year earlier to establish safe routes for famine relief workers. When the genocidal slaughter of half a million Tutsis by Hutus in Rwanda broke out a few months later in 1994, the U.S. government and the other members of the UN Security Council failed to intervene to stop the killing. Later that same year, the Clinton administration did intervene in the much nearer black Caribbean nation of Haiti. Roman Catholic priest and social activist Jean-Bertrand Aristide had been elected president in 1991, only to be overthrown in a right-wing military coup. As the regime's repression sent thousands of Haitians fleeing toward Florida, Clinton used the threat of an American invasion to force the island's military rulers, despite long-standing links to the CIA, to abdicate and return Aristide to office.

Racial cleavages at home still occasionally wounded the reputation of the United States in the 1990s. Race riots engulfed south central Los Angeles in 1992 after a jury found police officers innocent of brutality in the filmed beating of black motorist Rodney King. A UN special investigator in 1998 found that a criminal defendant's race continued to be a crucial factor in determining who received the death penalty in the United States.[2] Los Alamos nuclear physicist Wen Ho Lee was fired, arrested, and kept largely in solitary confinement for seven months in 1999–2000 on suspicions of passing atomic secrets to China. Well before the Justice Department abandoned almost all of its case against Lee (bringing an extraordinary rebuke from the presiding federal judge, who believed he had been misled by prosecutors), a backlash developed against what many saw as racial profiling of the Taiwanese-born U.S. citizen. Even the head of counterintelligence at the Los Alamos laboratory agreed, accusing federal investigators of racial bias in assuming that Lee's ethnicity might incline him toward espionage on behalf of another country.[3]

America's multiracial demographic profile could also be wielded as a positive model for a world suffering fierce ethnic and racial conflicts after the end of the Cold War. President Clinton called the 1999 NATO air war against Yugoslavia, which aimed to end the slaughter of Muslims by Serbs in the province of Kosovo, a victory of ethnic diversity over the euphemistically named "ethnic cleansing." Praising a racially diverse crowd of three thousand service personnel at Whiteman Air Force Base in Missouri, Clinton declared: "I invite the people of this world today who say that people cannot get along across racial and ethnic and religious lines to have a good look at the United

States military, to have a good look at the members of the United States Air Force in this hangar today."[4] With segregation, colonialism, and the Cold War behind them, Americans claimed anew their diversity as an important feature of leadership in the contemporary world.

FROM THE atrocities of World War II to the emancipation of the majority of the world's people from colonial rule, race formed a prominent contour of world history during the second half of the twentieth century. Race relations particularly colored the development of the United States, as the most powerful nation in international affairs and as a society struggling with its own multiracial character. There was no greater weakness for the United States in waging the Cold War than inequality and discrimination. Other problems hindered American leadership abroad after 1945—U.S. economic needs, self-righteousness, parochialism, expansive definitions of national security—but none served to deny so blatantly America's Cold War promises of liberty and equality. To plumb the depths of American difficulties in providing international leadership after the World War II, the changing state of race relations inside and outside the nation's borders must be considered.

Confronted with the erosion of European colonial control of Asia and Africa, U.S. policymakers sought to contain the expansion of Soviet influence by building a multiracial, anti-Communist alliance of the West and the Third World. In pursuit of their goal of a capitalist and preferably democratic world order, American leaders worked to convince newly independent non-white nations of the superiority of American institutions and ideals to those of the Soviet Union. Both ends of the North-South axis of colonial tensions might thus be won to the Western side of the East-West axis of the Cold War. The strategy of wooing Asians and Africans bolstered the rising movement in the United States for desegregation and full racial equality. A key tactic was to limit racial polarization, both in the American South and southern Africa, by containing the forces of white racism and channeling the energies of race reformers along moderate lines.

What impact did racial considerations have on U.S. strategic priorities and decisions after 1945? With the question framed in this narrow fashion, the answer is relatively little. Race did not determine the main outlines of American policy toward the Soviet Union or U.S. plans for constructing a global capitalist order, although it did often affect how those priorities were pursued.

But if the question is cast more broadly to ask what the relationship was between the waging of the Cold War and the historic dissolution of global white supremacy, the answer is more complicated and more significant.

In the Third World and particularly southern Africa, U.S. Cold War policies served primarily to slow down the process of ending white rule over people of color. This was especially true from 1945 to 1960. American determination to reconstruct a vibrant, anti-Communist Western Europe translated into tacit support for often bloody efforts to preserve colonial rule abroad by the governments of France, Belgium, Portugal, and Britain. U.S. funding through the Marshall Plan and the NATO alliance contributed to the ability of European powers to wage counterinsurgent wars from Vietnam to Kenya to Angola. The precise overlap of apartheid (1948–1990) with the Cold War (1947–1989) reflected white South Africans' effective use of anti-Communism to preserve the U.S. government's support for their undemocratic rule. Such U.S. policies allowed the USSR, China, and Cuba to appear more supportive of the cause of national independence and racial equality. "The Soviets are probably just as racist as other white Europeans," one black Namibian pointed out, "but at least they support the right cause against South Africa."[5] Decolonization provided independence and formal equality for the nations of the Third World, much as emancipation had done for enslaved individuals a century before. In this largest of post-1945 struggles for liberty, the weight of the U.S. government initially came down on the side of the white powers.

This pattern began to shift after 1960. Colonialism had fallen in Asia and was collapsing in Africa, and African Americans across the South were launching the final phase of the civil rights movement at home. "Problems of race prejudice and discrimination are worldwide," observed the editors of the NAACP journal *The Crisis* in May 1960, as sit-ins spread throughout Dixie and as Africans marched for freedom in South Africa and fought for it in Algeria. "And so is the rebellion against these twin evils . . . We do not think anyone can deny the fact that the present global turbulence is a precursor of the worldwide collapse of white supremacy."[6] Within five years, all but southern Africa was free from white rule and civil rights legislation had erased Jim Crow's legal sanction in the United States. The Johnson administration responded with hostility to the formation of a new white-ruled nation of Rhodesia in November 1965. The contrasting support from Washington and other Western seats of power in 1910 for the creation of a white-ruled South Africa provided a measure of how much had changed in world race relations in the intervening decades. U.S. policy toward South Africa subsequently cooled under the pressure of a growing anti-apartheid lobby, leading eventually to the 1986 sanctions.

Even as it succeeded in Asia and progressed in Africa, the struggle for racial equality was buffeted in the United States in the immediate postwar years by the powerful downdraft of anti-Communist fervor. Truman's initial steps to desegregate the military and the civil service came at the cost of repressing a left-leaning anticolonialist movement in the United States. Only after 1954 did the easing of the Red Scare, the coalescing of a self-proclaimed Third World, and the rising visibility of the Southern freedom movement combine to bring race relations closer to the center of Cold Warriors' attention. "With the Communists reaching out to the uncommitted people of the Middle East and Africa and Southeast Asia," Senator Paul Douglas argued in 1957, "each housing riot in Illinois, each school riot in Kentucky, and each bombing of a pastor's home or intimidation of a would-be Negro voter in Alabama or Mississippi becomes not only an affront to human dignity here in this country, but a defeat for freedom in its tough world struggle for survival."[7] Despite stiff opposition from Southern segregationists, this liberal anti-Communist perspective eventually won out in American politics in the years of the Kennedy and Johnson administrations.

The far-reaching changes that swept through the American South in the second half of the twentieth century cannot be understood apart from the international context of the Cold War. The evolving civil rights movement fit into the larger story of decolonization and the Cold War struggle over world leadership and the meaning of "freedom." The scale of change in the former Confederacy was occasionally startling. Fifty years after his presidential candidacy as an anti-Communist, archsegregationist Dixiecrat in 1948, South Carolina senator Strom Thurmond could be found not only seeking and winning black votes at home but also smiling broadly arm-in-arm before the world's news media with South African president Nelson Mandela, the former anti-apartheid guerilla and Communist Party ally.[8] One need not deny the continuing reality of discrimination and de facto segregation in much of the South to acknowledge how different the region was at the end of the Cold War compared to the beginning. Out of the fires of those changes emerged Southern and border-state presidents who became the strongest supporters of racial equality in the postwar White House.

Among post-1945 presidents, regional background seemed the best predictor—even better than party affiliation—of their degree of enthusiasm for ending racial discrimination once in the White House. Non-Southerners displayed reticence: Dwight Eisenhower of Kansas, Richard Nixon of California, Gerald Ford of Michigan, Ronald Reagan of Illinois, and George Bush originally of Connecticut. Southerners, by contrast, led the way: Harry Truman of Missouri, Lyndon Johnson of Texas, Jimmy Carter of Georgia, and Bill Clinton of Arkansas.[9] The only Democratic president of this period not from below the Mason-Dixon line, John Kennedy, entered office with less clearly defined commitments on race than the others of his party; his shift to full support for civil rights legislation came only as a result of events during his presidency. Presidents who had grown up in the segregated South had been forced to confront racial issues and resolve their own racial uncertainties and commitments more clearly than their peers from outside the region. They were personally familiar with African Americans and the injustices that limited the possibilities of their lives. For Southerners who rose to the Oval Office, racial prejudice and discrimination were not distant problems that could mostly be ignored but personal issues that affected people they knew and the reputation of their own beloved native region.

The Cold War provided the context for the final resolution in American public life and in international affairs of the historic conflict between formal racial hierarchy and racial equality. That resolution frequently involved arms, bloodshed, and high personal costs, paid almost always by people of color. The destruction of white supremacy represented, in world historical terms, a more momentous achievement even than the conquest of Soviet Communism. Prejudice and discrimination and the violence they often spawned did not disappear entirely from American life, but they now had to survive without the support of law or majority opinion. While rarely standing at the front of the march for civil rights and decolonization, American leaders after 1945 accommodated themselves with varying degrees of enthusiasm to the new era of racial equality. By the end of the Cold War the United States had emerged as the multiracial leader of a multiracial world.

# NOTES

### Prologue

1. "Big Step Ahead on a High Road," *Life,* 8 December 1961, 32–33.
2. "Department Urges Maryland to Pass Public Accommodations Bill," *Department of State Bulletin,* 2 October 1961, 551–552.
3. Recent scholarship examining aspects of the relationship between race and U.S. foreign affairs includes Paul Gordon Lauren, *Power and Prejudice: The Politics and Diplomacy of Racial Discrimination* (Boulder: Westview, 1988); Richard

Drinnon, *Facing West: The Metaphysics of Indian-Hating and Empire-Building* (1980; New York: Schocken, 1990); John W. Dower, *War without Mercy: Race and Power in the Pacific War* (New York: Pantheon, 1986); Michael H. Hunt, *Ideology and U.S. Foreign Policy* (New Haven: Yale University Press, 1987); Brenda Gayle Plummer, *Rising Wind: Black Americans and U.S. Foreign Affairs, 1935–1960* (Chapel Hill: University of North Carolina Press, 1996); Penny M. Von Eschen, *Race against Empire: Black Americans and Anticolonialism, 1937–1957* (Ithaca: Cornell University Press, 1997); Gerald Horne, "Race from Power: U.S. Foreign Policy and the General Crisis of 'White Supremacy,'" *Diplomatic History* 23 (Summer 1999): 437–461; Renee Romano, "No Diplomatic Immunity: African Diplomats, the State Department, and Civil Rights, 1961–1964," *Journal of American History* 87 (September 2000): 546–579; Mary L. Dudziak, "Desegregation as a Cold War Imperative," *Stanford Law Review* 41 (November 1988): 61–120; Alexander DeConde, *Ethnicity, Race, and American Foreign Policy: A History* (Boston: Northeastern University Press, 1992); Thomas Borstelmann, *Apartheid's Reluctant Uncle: The United States and Southern Africa in the Early Cold War* (New York: Oxford University Press, 1993).

4. The phrase "Third World" emerged out of a 1955 conference in Bandung, Indonesia, to refer to those nations unaligned in the Cold War, almost all of which were peopled by non-Europeans (the capitalist West constituting the "First World" and the Communist nations the "Second World"). First used by a French journalist, it quickly became a term of self-designation for nationalists in Africa, Asia, and the Middle East, as well as revolutionaries in Latin America.

5. Lauren, *Power and Prejudice,* 155–156.

6. Roy Preiswerk, "Race and Colour in International Relations," in *The Year Book of World Affairs, 1970* (London: Stevens, 1970), 76, n. 65. On the North and West, see Steven Lawson, *Running for Freedom: Civil Rights and Black Politics in America since 1941* (Philadelphia: Temple University Press, 1991), 172.

7. Herbert Shapiro, *White Violence and Black Response: From Reconstruction to Montgomery* (Amherst: University of Massachusetts Press, 1988), 395–396 (emphasis added).

8. William Minter, *King Solomon's Mines Revisited: Western Interests and the Burdened History of Southern Africa* (New York: Basic Books, 1986); Robert Kinloch Massie, *Loosing the Bonds: The United States and South Africa in the Apartheid Years* (New York: Doubleday, 1997).

9. Henry F. Jackson, *From the Congo to Soweto: U.S. Foreign Policy toward Africa since 1960* (New York: Morrow, 1982), chap. 4.

10. Aldon Morris, "Centuries of Black Protest: Its Significance for America and the World," in *Race in America: The Struggle for Equality,* ed. Herbert Hill and

James E. Jones, Jr. (Madison: University of Wisconsin Press, 1993), 62–66; Harold R. Isaacs, *The New World of Negro Americans* (New York: John Day, 1963), 52; George M. Houser, "Freedom's Struggle Crosses Oceans and Mountains: Martin Luther King, Jr., and the Liberation Struggles in Africa and America," in *We Shall Overcome: Martin Luther King, Jr., and the Black Freedom Struggle,* ed. Peter J. Albert and Ronald Hoffman (New York: Pantheon, 1990), 179.

11. For extensive discussion of these themes, see Von Eschen, *Race against Empire,* and Plummer, *Rising Wind.*

12. Lauren, *Power and Prejudice,* 3; Dower, *War without Mercy,* 145–146.

13. Thomas McCormick, "Drift or Mastery? A Corporatist Synthesis for American Diplomatic History," *Reviews in American History* 10 (December 1982): 326, cited in Elizabeth McKillen, "Historical Contingency and the Peace Progressives," *Diplomatic History* 20 (Winter 1986): 124.

14. Van Gosse, "Consensus and Contradiction in Textbook Treatments of the Sixties," *Journal of American History* 82 (September 1995): 665.

15. The extensive bibliographies of two recent books on the movement suggest how little the international sphere has figured in the writing of civil rights history: Harvard Sitkoff, *The Struggle for Black Equality, 1954–1992,* rev. ed. (New York: Hill and Wang, 1993), and Thomas R. West and James W. Mooney, eds., *To Redeem a Nation: A History and Anthology of the Civil Rights Movement* (St. James, N.Y.: Brandywine, 1993).

16. See, for example, Walter A. McDougall, "President Fails as National Shrink: One Lesson of *Sputnik?*" *Reviews in American History* 21 (December 1993): 701–702; James Chace, *Acheson: The Secretary of State Who Created the American World* (New York: Simon and Schuster, 1998), chapter 17.

17. Isaacs, *The New World of Negro Americans,* xiv.

18. See Michael Omi and Howard Winant, *Racial Formation in the United States: From the 1960s to the 1990s,* 2d ed. (New York: Routledge, 1994), especially 60; Jonathan Marks, *Human Biodiversity: Genes, Race, and History* (New York: Aldine de Gruyter, 1995).

19. Lauren, *Power and Prejudice,* 6 (Plato); Ronald Segal, *The Race War: The World-Wide Conflict of Races* (Harmondsworth, Eng.: Penguin, 1967), 301 (Cicero).

20. Elazar Barkan, *The Retreat of Scientific Racism: Changing Concepts of Race in Britain and the United States between the World Wars* (Cambridge: Cambridge University Press, 1992).

21. David A. Hollinger, "National Solidarity at the End of the Twentieth Century: Reflections on the United States and Liberal Nationalism," *Journal of American History* 84 (September 1997): 567.

22. Harold R. Isaacs, *Scratches on Our Minds: American Images of China and India*

(1958; Westport, Conn.: Greenwood, 1973), 283–284; Ronald Takaki, *Strangers from a Different Shore: A History of Asian Americans* (Boston: Little, Brown, 1989), 298–299.

23. Beth Bailey and David Farber, *The First Strange Place: The Alchemy of Race and Sex in World War II Hawaii* (New York: Free Press, 1992), 139.

24. See, for example, R. Gordon Wasson, "Popular Fallacies about Russia," *U.S. News and World Report,* 16 March 1951, 30–33. For a wide-ranging discussion of the problems with such continental designations, see Martin W. Lewis and Kären E. Wigen, *The Myth of Continents: A Critique of Metageography* (Berkeley: University of California Press, 1997).

25. Numan V. Bartley, *The Rise of Massive Resistance: Race and Politics in the South during the 1950s* (Baton Rouge: Louisiana State University Press, 1969), viii.

26. F. James Davis, *Who Is Black? One Nation's Definition* (University Park: Pennsylvania State University Press, 1991), especially 12–13.

27. Davis, *Who Is Black?* 7.

28. Madeleine G. Kalb, *The Congo Cables: The Cold War in Africa—from Eisenhower to Kennedy* (New York: Macmillan, 1982), 40.

29. William Attwood, *The Reds and the Blacks: A Personal Adventure* (New York: Harper and Row, 1967), 188.

### *1. Race and Foreign Relations before 1945*

1. Edmund S. Morgan, *American Slavery, American Freedom: The Ordeal of Colonial Virginia* (New York: Norton, 1975), 6–18 (quotation at 13).

2. Gary B. Nash, *Red, White, and Black: The Peoples of Early America* (Englewood Cliffs, N.J.: Prentice-Hall, 1974, 1982); Drinnon, *Facing West;* Ronald Dale Kerr, "'Why Should You Be So Furious?' The Violence of the Pequot War," *Journal of American History* 85 (December 1998): 876–909.

3. Reginald Horsman, *Race and Manifest Destiny: The Origins of American Anglo-Saxonism* (Cambridge, Mass.: Harvard University Press, 1981), 1–6, 43–61, 208–229, 297; Thomas R. Hietala, *Manifest Design: Anxious Aggrandizement in Late Jacksonian America* (Ithaca: Cornell University Press, 1985), 10–54, 132–172.

4. Horne, "Race from Power," 443 (Stoddard); Lauren, *Power and Prejudice,* 54, 63–64; Isaacs, *The New World of Negro Americans,* 32–33; Hugh Tinker, *Race, Conflict, and the International Order: From Empire to United Nations* (New York: St. Martin's, 1977), 21; Gary Gerstle, "Liberty, Coercion, and the Making of Americans," *Journal of American History* 84 (September 1997): 549; Eric Tyrone Lowery Love, "Race over Empire: Racism and United States Imperialism, 1865–1890" (Ph.D. diss., Princeton University, 1997), 15.

5. Hunt, *Ideology and U.S. Foreign Policy,* 46–91, 116–117.

6. Peter Novick, *That Noble Dream: The "Objectivity Question" and the American Historical Profession* (New York: Cambridge University Press, 1988), 80–81.

7. James O. Gump, *The Dust Rose Like Smoke: The Subjugation of the Zulu and the Sioux* (Lincoln: University of Nebraska Press, 1994), 56.

8. Hunt, *Ideology and U.S. Foreign Policy,* 55.

9. Dower, *War without Mercy,* 151.

10. Walter L. Williams, "United States Indian Policy and the Debate over Philippine Annexation: Implications for the Origins of American Imperialism," *Journal of American History* 66 (March 1980): 810–831.

11. Dennis Hickey and Kenneth C. Wylie, *An Enchanting Darkness: The American Vision of Africa in the Twentieth Century* (East Lansing: Michigan State University Press, 1993), 19.

12. Alan M. Tigay, "The Deepest South," *American Heritage,* April 1998, 84–95.

13. Hazel M. McFerson, *The Racial Dimension of American Overseas Colonial Policy* (Westport, Conn.: Greenwood, 1997), 3. Over a century later, the one other possible exception is Puerto Rico, but it has not yet signaled a clear desire for statehood.

14. Thomas Pakenham, *The Scramble for Africa, 1876–1912* (New York: Random House, 1991), 28; Hickey and Wylie, *An Enchanting Darkness,* 8–13. On Stanley, see John Bierman, *Dark Safari: The Life behind the Legend of Henry Morton Stanley* (New York: Knopf, 1990). On the Congo Free State, see Adam Hochschild, *King Leopold's Ghost: A Story of Greed, Terror, and Heroism in Colonial Africa* (Boston: Houghton Mifflin, 1998).

15. Thomas G. Dyer, *Theodore Roosevelt and the Idea of Race* (Baton Rouge: Louisiana State University Press, 1980), especially 2, 19–20, 69–88, 114–115, 129–139; Hickey and Wylie, *An Enchanting Darkness,* 12–13. See also Michael McCarthy, *Dark Continent: Africa as Seen by Americans* (Westport, Conn.: Greenwood, 1983).

16. John Taliaferro, *Tarzan Forever: The Life of Edgar Rice Burroughs, Creator of Tarzan* (New York: Scribner, 1999); Hickey and Wylie, *An Enchanting Darkness,* 180–185.

17. Christopher Lasch, "The Anti-Imperialists, the Philippines, and the Inequality of Man," *Journal of Southern History* 24 (August 1954): 319–331.

18. Love, "Race over Empire," 83–84, 157–158, 162–164, 198; McFerson, *The Racial Dimension,* 2–3; Williams, "United States Indian Policy," 822.

19. Williams, "United States Indian Policy," quotations at 819, 825.

20. Ibid., 827–229; Dower, *War without Mercy,* 152.

21. Vicente L. Rafael, "White Love: Surveillance and Nationalist Resistance in the Colonization of the Philippines," in *Cultures of United States Imperialism,* ed.

Amy Kaplan and Donald E. Pease (Durham: Duke University Press, 1993), 185–186.

22. Drinnon, *Facing West,* 327–328 (quotation); Willard B. Gatewood, Jr., *Black Americans and the White Man's Burden, 1898–1903* (Urbana: University of Illinois Press, 1975), 261–279; Dower, *War without Mercy,* 152.

23. Drinnon, *Facing West,* 314.

24. Ibid., 309.

25. Lauren, *Power and Prejudice,* 61. For recent discussions of the German and Belgian cases and some of their continuing impacts, see Adam Hochschild, "Mr. Kurtz, I Presume," *New Yorker,* 14 April 1997, 40–47, and Donald G. McNeil, Jr., "Its Past on Its Sleeve, Tribe Seeks Bonn's Apology," *New York Times,* 31 May 1998, 3.

26. Anders Stephanson, *Manifest Destiny: American Expansionism and the Empire of Right* (New York: Hill and Wang, 1995), 104.

27. Gatewood, *Black Americans and the White Man's Burden,* 114–116, 129–153, 197–204, 241–245, 322–323; David S. Cecelski and Timothy B. Tyson, eds., *Democracy Betrayed: The Wilmington Race Riot of 1898 and Its Legacy* (Chapel Hill: University of North Carolina Press, 1998).

28. Bernard C. Nalty, *Strength for the Fight: A History of Black Americans in the Military* (New York: Free Press, 1986), 74–77; Willard B. Gatewood, Jr., *"Smoked Yankees" and the Struggle for Empire: Letters from Negro Soldiers, 1898–1902* (Urbana: University of Illinois Press, 1971), especially 3–6, 243–45; Kevin Gaines, "Black Americans' Racial Uplift Ideology as 'Civilizing Mission': Pauline E. Hopkins on Race and Imperialism," in *Cultures of United States Imperialism,* ed. Amy Kaplan and Donald E. Pease (Durham: Duke University Press, 1993), 441; Gatewood, *Black Americans and the White Man's Burden,* 183–186; Piero Gleijeses, "African Americans and the War against Spain," *North Carolina Historical Review* 23 (April 1996): 184–214.

29. Gatewood, *"Smoked Yankees,"* 199–200.

30. Stuart Anderson, "Racial Anglo-Saxonism and the American Response to the Boer War," *Diplomatic History* 2 (Summer 1978): 219–236 (quotation at 225); Thomas J. Noer, *Briton, Boer, and Yankee: The United States and South Africa, 1870–1914* (Kent, Ohio: Kent State University Press, 1978).

31. Anderson, "Racial Anglo-Saxonism," 229.

32. Isaacs, *The New World of Negro Americans,* 34–35; Pakenham, *The Scramble for Africa,* 470–486; Lauren, *Power and Prejudice,* 65.

33. Prasenjit Duara, "Transnationalism and the Predicament of Sovereignty: China, 1900–1945," *American Historical Review* 102 (October 1997): 1038.

34. Reginald Kearney, "Afro-American Views of the Japanese, 1900–1945" (Ph.D. diss., Kent State University, 1991), 34–64.

35. Lauren, *Power and Prejudice,* 67.

36. Walter LaFeber, *The Clash: U.S.-Japanese Relations throughout History* (New York: Norton, 1997), 80.

37. Roy Preiswerk, "Race and Colour in International Relations," in *The Year Book of World Affairs, 1970* (London: Stevens, 1970), 58.

38. Nell Irvin Painter, *Standing at Armageddon: The United States, 1877–1919* (New York: Norton, 1987), 364 (quotation); R. J. Vincent, "Racial Equality," in *The Expansion of International Society,* ed. Hedley Bull and Adam Watson (Oxford: Clarendon, 1984), 240–241; Lauren, *Power and Prejudice,* 69–71.

39. DeConde, *Ethnicity, Race, and American Foreign Policy,* 86.

40. Dimitri D. Lazo, "Lansing, Wilson, and the Jenkins Incident," *Diplomatic History* 22 (Spring 1998): 189 (quotation); David S. Foglesong, *America's Secret War against Bolshevism: U.S. Intervention in the Russian Civil War, 1917–1920* (Chapel Hill: University of North Carolina Press, 1995), 16; David S. Foglesong, letter to the editor, *The Society for Historians of American Foreign Relations Newsletter* 30 (June 1990): 17–25.

41. Hunt, *Ideology and U.S. Foreign Policy,* 115.

42. Herbert Shapiro, *White Violence and Black Response: From Reconstruction to Montgomery* (Amherst: University of Massachusetts Press, 1988), 145–157; Painter, *Standing at Armageddon,* 337–338, 363–365.

43. Isaacs, *The New World of Negro Americans,* 39 (quotation); Painter, *Standing at Armageddon,* 338.

44. Barkan, *The Retreat of Scientific Racism,* 57–59; Graham Smith, *When Jim Crow Met John Bull: Black American Soldiers in World War II Britain* (New York: St. Martin's, 1988), 17; Tyler Stovall, "The Color Line behind the Lines: Racial Violence in France during the Great War," *American Historical Review* 103 (June 1998): 737–769.

45. Lauren, *Power and Prejudice,* 106.

46. Steven A. Reich, "Soldiers of Democracy: Black Texans and the Fight for Citizenship, 1917–1921," *Journal of American History* 82 (March 1996): 1485–1486; C. Eric Lincoln, "The Race Problem and International Relations," *New South* 21 (Fall 1966): 6; Lauren, *Power and Prejudice,* 71; Smith, *When Jim Crow Met John Bull,* 7–17; Horne, "Race from Power," 450 (Wilson). On the generally respectful French treatment of colonial soldiers and its contrast to French hostility toward colonial workers in France during the war, see Stovall, "The Color Line behind the Lines."

47. Thomas A. Johnson, "Negro Veteran Is Confused and Bitter," *New York Times,* 29 July 1968, 14.

48. Wayne Addison Clark, "An Analysis of the Relationship between Anti-Communism and Segregationist Thought in the Deep South, 1948–1964" (Ph.D.

diss., University of North Carolina, 1976), 9–10 (quotation); Alexander Cockburn, "Beat the Devil," *Nation,* 3 May 1993, 582; George Frederickson, *Black Liberation: A Comparative History of Black Ideologies in the United States and South Africa* (New York: Oxford University Press, 1995), 140. Wilson worried that the "American Negro would be our greatest medium in conveying bolshevism to America." Melvyn P. Leffler, *The Spectre of Communism: The United States and the Origins of the Cold War, 1917–1953* (New York: Hill and Wang, 1994), 14.

49. Paul Gordon Lauren, "Human Rights in History: Diplomacy and Racial Equality at the Paris Peace Conference," *Diplomatic History* 2 (Summer 1978): 257–278; Lauren, *Power and Prejudice,* 82–98 (quotation at 93).

50. F. M. Carroll, ed., *The American Commission on Irish Independence, 1919: The Diary, Correspondence, and Report* (Dublin: Mount Salus, 1985), 37–38. Thanks to Rebecca Berens-Matzke for bringing this source to my attention.

51. Lauren, *Power and Prejudice,* 100–101 (quotation); LaFeber, *The Clash,* 123–124.

52. Kearney, "Afro-American Views of the Japanese," 87–116; Lauren, *Power and Prejudice,* 77–104.

53. Lauren, *Power and Prejudice,* 113.

54. Scott Ellsworth, *Death in a Promised Land: The Tulsa Race Riot of 1921* (Baton Rouge: Louisiana State University Press, 1982), 23 (quotation); Shapiro, *White Violence and Black Response,* 180–185.

55. Patricia Sullivan, *Days of Hope: Race and Democracy in the New Deal Era* (Chapel Hill: University of North Carolina Press, 1996), 27.

56. Gilbert C. Fite, *Richard B. Russell, Jr., Senator from Georgia* (Chapel Hill: University of North Carolina Press, 1991), 37–39, 166–168. See also Robert L. Zangrando, *The NAACP Crusade against Lynching* (Philadelphia: Temple University Press, 1980).

57. Kenneth O'Reilly, *"Racial Matters": The FBI's Secret File on Black America, 1960–1972* (New York: Free Press, 1989), 13–18; Theodore Kornweibel, Jr., *"Seeing Red": Federal Campaigns against Black Militancy, 1919–1925* (Bloomington: Indiana University Press, 1998).

58. Mae M. Ngai, "The Architecture of Race in American Immigration Law: A Reexamination of the Immigration Act of 1924," *Journal of American History* 86 (June 1999): 67–92; David M. Reimers, *Still the Golden Door: The Third World Comes to America,* 2d ed. (New York: Columbia University Press, 1992), 6–7; LaFeber, *The Clash,* 144–146; Lauren, *Power and Prejudice,* 110–111.

59. Alfred E. Opubur and Adebayo Ogunbi, "Ooga Booga: The African Image in American Films," in *Other Voices, Other Views: An International Collection of Essays from the Bicentennial,* ed. Robin W. Winks (Westport, Conn.: Greenwood, 1978), 350–357; Taylor Branch, *Parting the Waters: America in the King*

*Years, 1954–1963* (New York: Simon and Schuster, 1988), 54. See also Edward H. McKinley, *The Lure of Africa: American Interests in Tropical Africa, 1919–1939* (Indianapolis: Bobbs-Merrill, 1974).

60. Barkan, *The Retreat of Scientific Racism,* xi–xii, 2, 76–90; Frederickson, *Black Liberation,* 213–214; Vincent, "Racial Equality," 246; Ashley Montagu, *Man's Most Dangerous Myth: The Fallacy of Race* (New York: Columbia University Press, 1942); Lee D. Baker, *From Savage to Negro: Anthropology and the Construction of Race, 1896–1954* (Berkeley: University of California Press, 1999).

61. Lauren, *Power and Prejudice,* 123–128 (quotation at 128).

62. Ibid., 119.

63. John Hope Franklin, *From Slavery to Freedom,* 5th ed. (New York: Knopf, 1980), 422, cited in Kearney, "Afro-American Views of the Japanese," 119. See also Joseph E. Harris, *African-American Reactions to War in Ethiopia, 1936–1941* (Baton Rouge: Louisiana State University Press, 1994); William R. Scott, *The Sons of Sheba's Race: African-Americans and the Italo-Ethiopian War, 1935–1941* (Bloomington: Indiana University Press, 1993); and the nicely subtitled *African Americans in the Spanish Civil War: "It Ain't Ethiopia, But It'll Do,"* ed. Danny Duncan Collum (New York: G. K. Hall, 1992).

64. Frederickson, *Black Liberation,* 151, 155.

65. Text of Atlantic Charter, 14 August 1941, in *FRUS, 1941,* 1:367–369. See also *The Atlantic Charter,* ed. Douglas Brinkley and David R. Facey-Crowther (New York: St. Martin's, 1994).

66. Lauren, *Power and Prejudice,* 154.

67. Piero Gleijeses, *Shattered Hope: The Guatemalan Revolution and the United States, 1944–1954* (Princeton: Princeton University Press, 1991), 22–23.

68. C. Vann Woodward, *The Strange Career of Jim Crow,* 2d ed. (London: Oxford University Press, 1966), 131.

69. Fred Pollock and Warren F. Kimball, "'In Search of Monsters to Destroy': Roosevelt and Colonialism," in *The Juggler: Franklin Roosevelt as Wartime Statesman,* ed. Warren F. Kimball (Princeton: Princeton University Press, 1991), 127–157; Lloyd C. Gardner, "The Atlantic Charter: Idea and Reality, 1942–1945," in Brinkley and Facey-Crowther, *The Atlantic Charter,* 45–81; Warren F. Kimball, "The Atlantic Charter: 'With All Deliberate Speed,'" in Brinkley and Facey-Crowther, *The Atlantic Charter,* 83–114; Christopher Thorne, *Allies of a Kind: The United States, Britain, and the War against Japan, 1941–1945* (New York: Oxford University Press, 1978), 158–159.

70. Bailey and Farber, *The First Strange Place,* 20–25, 134–135, 152–157, 165 (quotation at 157).

71. Dower, *War without Mercy,* 176–177 (quotation); Thorne, *Allies of a Kind,* 6; Kearney, "Afro-American Views of the Japanese," 181–182; LaFeber, *The Clash,*

217. When asked by a U.S. official about the effectiveness of Japanese propaganda among African Americans, one Howard University professor responded by telling him about a white officer who had used the term "yellow bastards" in a pep talk to the Howard ROTC unit. This did not encourage patriotic feelings in the black students. "You know," he told the official levelly, "many of us are yellow bastards, second and third generation." Isaacs, *The New World of Negro Americans,* 30.

72. Leonard Dinnerstein, *Antisemitism in America* (New York: Oxford University Press, 1994), 105–149; Ronald Steel, *Walter Lippmann and the American Century* (1980; New York: Vintage, 1981), 372–373; David S. Wyman, *The Abandonment of the Jews: America and the Holocaust, 1941–1945* (New York: Pantheon, 1984), 6–15, 42–58, 103, 189–192, 305–340.

73. Barkan, *The Retreat of Scientific Racism,* 1, 334; Preiswerk, "Race and Colour in International Relations," 59; Sherie Mershon and Steven Schlossman, *Foxholes and Color Lines: Desegregating the U.S. Armed Forces* (Baltimore: Johns Hopkins University Press, 1998), 105–114; Novick, *That Noble Dream,* 348.

74. Morton Sosna, "Introduction," in *Remaking Dixie: The Impact of World War II on the American South,* ed. Neil R. McMillen (Jackson: University Press of Mississippi, 1997), xvi–xvii; Richard M. Dalfiume, *Desegregation of the U.S. Armed Forces: Fighting on Two Fronts, 1939–1953* (Columbia: University of Missouri Press, 1969), 49; Mershon and Schlossman, *Foxholes and Color Lines,* 77–78; Wallace Terry, *Bloods: An Oral History of the Vietnam War by Black Veterans* (New York: Ballantine, 1984), 145–147.

75. Richard Polenberg, "The Good War? A Reappraisal of How World War II Affected American Society," *Virginia Magazine of History and Biography* 100 (July 1992): 321; Dower, *War without Mercy,* 348; Spencie Love, *One Blood: The Death and Resurrection of Charles R. Drew* (Chapel Hill: University of North Carolina Press, 1996).

76. Carr to President's Committee on Civil Rights, "Puerto Ricans in the United States," 10 June 1947, President's Committee on Civil Rights—Committee Documents, box 17, HSTL; Phillip McGuire, *Taps for a Jim Crow Army: Letters from Black Soldiers in World War II* (Santa Barbara: ABC-Clio, 1983), 227–241; Mershon and Schlossman, *Foxholes and Color Lines,* 67.

77. "Because Their Skins Are Brown," *London News and Chronicle,* 8 May 1943, clipping in Philleo Nash Papers, box 17, HSTL; David Reynolds, *Rich Relations: The American Occupation of Britain, 1942–1945* (New York: Random House, 1995), 216–237, 302–324.

78. Reynolds, *Rich Relations,* 220, 223.

79. Ibid., 218.

80. Walter F. White, *A Rising Wind* (Garden City, N.Y.: Doubleday, 1945), 146;

Smith, *When Jim Crow Met John Bull*, 31–32, 85–87, 120–129; Reynolds, *Rich Relations*, 302–306 (quotation at 302).

81. Nalty, *Strength for the Fight*, 154–155; Smith, *When Jim Crow Met John Bull*, 138–151; Reynolds, *Rich Relations*, 319–320, 324 (quotation).

82. Harvard Sitkoff, "Racial Militancy and Interracial Violence in the Second World War," *Journal of American History* 58 (December 1971): 667–681; James Albert Burran, "Racial Violence in the South during World War II" (Ph.D. diss., University of Tennessee, 1977); Pete Daniel, "Going Among Strangers: Southern Reactions to World War II," *Journal of American History* 77 (December 1990): 886–911; Neil A. Wynn, *The Afro-American and the Second World War*, rev. ed. (New York: Holmes and Meier, 1993), 60–78; Neil R. McMillen, "Fighting for What We Didn't Have: How Mississippi's Black Veterans Remember World War II," in *Remaking Dixie: The Impact of World War II on the American South*, ed. Neil R. McMillen (Jackson: University Press of Mississippi, 1997), 93–110; Shapiro, *White Violence and Black Response*, 310–341; John Dittmer, *Local People: The Struggle for Civil Rights in Mississippi* (Urbana: University of Illinois Press, 1994), 16–17; Sullivan, *Days of Hope*, 136–137; McGuire, *Taps for a Jim Crow Army*, 201–203. Most racial conflicts involved whites and blacks, but the zoot suit riots in Los Angeles in June 1943, in which white sailors assaulted Mexican American youths, demonstrated that Latinos were also vulnerable to outbreaks of virulent white racism. See Edward J. Escobar, "Zoot-Suiters and Cops: Chicano Youth and the Los Angeles Police Department during World War II," in *The War in American Culture: Society and Consciousness during World War II*, ed. Lewis A. Erenberg and Susan E. Hirsch (Chicago: University of Chicago Press, 1996), 284–309.

83. Richard Polenberg, *War and Society: The United States, 1941–1945* (Philadelphia: Lippincott, 1972), 108, 117–118, 124, 128; George H. Roeder, Jr., "Censoring Disorder: American Visual Imagery of World War II," in *The War in American Culture: Society and Consciousness during World War II*, ed. Lewis A. Erenberg and Susan E. Hirsch (Chicago: University of Chicago Press, 1996), 46, 56–58, 64; W. E. B. Du Bois, *Color and Democracy: Colonies and Peace* (New York: Harcourt, Brace, 1945), 85–92; Mershon and Schlossman, *Foxholes and Color Lines*, 124–127; *Freedom to Serve—Equality of Treatment and Opportunity in the Armed Services: A Report by the President's Committee* (Washington: U.S. Government Printing Office, 1950), 34–35; Borstelmann, *Apartheid's Reluctant Uncle*, 20.

84. Lauren, *Power and Prejudice*, 140–141.

85. "Chinese Exclusion Act Is Keynote of Japanese Propaganda to Asia," 1943, Nash Papers, box 10, HSTL.

86. White, *A Rising Wind,* 152–154 (quotation); Tinker, *Race, Conflict, and the International Order,* 44.

87. FBI, "Survey of Racial Conditions in the United States" [1943–44], WHCF, box 21, HSTL; Gary Gerstle, "The Working Class Goes to War," in *The War in American Culture: Society and Consciousness during World War II,* ed. Lewis A. Erenberg and Susan E. Hirsch (Chicago: University of Chicago Press, 1996), 118–119 (quotation); Kearney, "Afro-American Views of the Japanese," vi; Dalfiume, *Desegregation of the U.S. Armed Forces,* 110–111; Isaacs, *The New World of Negro Americans,* 30; Polenberg, *War and Society,* 101; Lauren, *Power and Prejudice,* 131.

88. Roger Daniels, *Prisoners without Trial: Japanese Americans in World War II* (New York: Hill and Wang, 1993); Ronald Takaki, *Strangers from a Different Shore: A History of Asian Americans* (Boston: Little, Brown, 1989), 379–392; Polenberg, "The Good War?" 319; Tinker, *Race, Conflict, and the International Order,* 45.

89. Polenberg, *War and Society,* 62.

90. David Campbell, *Writing Security: United States Foreign Policy and the Politics of Identity* (Minneapolis: University of Minnesota Press, 1992), 191, n. 85.

91. Gary Y. Okihiro, *Margins and Mainstream: Asians in American History and Culture* (Seattle: University of Washington Press, 1994), 169. In what must have been the supreme irony of their service, Japanese Americans in the segregated 442d Regimented Combat Team—which became the most decorated unit in the entire U.S. Army—even helped to liberate the Nazi death camp at Dachau, while their own families were still incarcerated in American concentration camps. Daniels, *Prisoners without Trial,* 64.

92. Takaki, *Strangers from a Different Shore,* 396–403.

93. Dower, *War without Mercy,* 36, 104–105. On the absence of enemy corpse mutilation by American soldiers in the European theater in comparison with its presence in the Pacific, see Roeder, "Censoring Disorder," 52.

94. Polenberg, "The Good War?" 319.

95. Isaacs, *The New World of Negro Americans,* 4. See also Jonathan G. Utley, *Going to War with Japan, 1937–1941* (Knoxville: University of Tennessee Press, 1985), 103.

96. Tom Englehardt, *The End of Victory Culture: Cold War America and the Disillusioning of a Generation* (New York: Basic Books, 1995), 98; Dower, *War without Mercy,* 164–170 (quotation at 170); DeConde, *Ethnicity, Race, and American Foreign Policy,* 121; Takaki, *Strangers from a Different Shore,* 367–378; Isaacs, *The New World of Negro Americans,* 29.

97. Aimé Césaire, *Discourse on Colonialism,* trans. Joan Pinkam (1955; New York: Monthly Review Press, 1972), 14; Ndabaningi Sithole, *African Nationalism*

(Cape Town: Oxford University Press, 1959), 19–23; Pakenham, *The Scramble for Africa*, 673–674; Lauren, *Power and Prejudice*, 161; Borstelmann, *Apartheid's Reluctant Uncle*, 23–25.

98. Isaacs, *The New World of Negro Americans*, 30–31; Borstelmann, *Apartheid's Reluctant Uncle*, 38–52.

99. Du Bois, *Color and Democracy;* White, *A Rising Wind;* Rayford W. Logan, *What the Negro Wants* (Chapel Hill: University of North Carolina Press, 1944). See also Plummer, *Rising Wind*, and Von Eschen, *Race against Empire*.

100. Minutes of meeting of U.S. delegation to UN, 26 May 1945, *FRUS, 1945,* 1:894 (quotation); Robert L. Harris, "Racial Equality and the United Nations Charter," in *New Directions in Civil Rights Studies,* ed. Armstead L. Robinson and Patricia Sullivan (Charlottesville: University Press of Virginia, 1991), 126–148; Lauren, *Power and Prejudice*, 146–157.

101. FBI, "Survey of Racial Conditions in the US" [1943–44], WHCF, box 21, HSTL; McMillen, "Fighting for What We Didn't Have," 101 (quotation); Charles M. Payne, *I've Got the Light of Freedom: The Organizing Tradition and the Mississippi Freedom Struggle* (Berkeley: University of California Press, 1995), 30–31; Harvard Sitkoff, "African American Militancy in the World War II South: Another Perspective," in *Remaking Dixie: The Impact of World War II on the American South,* ed. Neil R. McMillen (Jackson: University Press of Mississippi, 1997), 70–92; Polenberg, "The Good War?" 321; Wynn, *The Afro-American and the Second World War,* 134–135; Lawson, *Running for Freedom,* 9.

102. Thomas J. Schoenbaum, *Waging Peace and War: Dean Rusk in the Truman, Kennedy, and Johnson Years* (New York: Simon and Schuster, 1988), 78; White, *A Rising Wind,* 15, 35–38, 123ff. African American historian John Hope Franklin discovered a similar sense of shifting attitudes in the Louisiana state archivist who sneaked him into the officially segregated archives in Baton Rouge on V-J day in 1945, letting him work while the rest of the town celebrated the end of the war. Peter Applebome, "John Hope Franklin," *New York Times Magazine,* 23 April 1995, 37.

103. McMillen, "Fighting for What We Didn't Have," 96, 103.

104. David W. Blight, "In Retrospect: Nathan Irvin Huggins, the Art of History, and the Irony of the American Dream, *Reviews in American History* 22 (March 1994): 184; Michael Wreszin, "Radical in Wisconsin," *Nation,* 1 January 1996, 31; Mershon and Schlossman, *Foxholes and Color Lines,* 82; McMillen, "Fighting for What We Didn't Have," 102; White, *A Rising Wind,* 36; Applebome, "John Hope Franklin," 36.

105. Michael Cassity, "History and the Public Purpose," *Journal of American History* 81 (December 1994): 972–973.

106. Wynn, *The Afro-American and the Second World War*, 103–106, 133, 135
(Dixon); Sullivan, *Days of Hope*, 212 (Talmadge); Isaacs, *The New World of Negro Americans*, 114; Polenberg, *War and Society*, 50; Patrick S. Washburn, *A Question of Sedition: The Federal Government's Investigation of the Black Press during World War II* (New York: Oxford University Press, 1986).

## 2. Jim Crow's Coming Out

1. Harold R. Isaacs, "The Political and Psychological Context of Point Four," *Annals of the American Academy of Political and Social Science* 270 (July 1950): 56.
2. Lauren, *Power and Prejudice*, 187.
3. Article 1 of the United Nations Charter, quoted in Fahy to Carr, 17 June 1947, PCCR, box 6, HSTL.
4. Wallace Stegner, *One Nation* (Boston: Houghton Mifflin, 1945).
5. Isaacs, "The Political and Psychological Context," 51.
6. Edmund Davison Soper, *Racism: A World Issue* (New York: Abingdon-Cokesbury, [1947]), 272. See also Lauren, *Power and Prejudice;* Plummer, *Rising Wind;* Von Eschen, *Race against Empire.*
7. Melvyn Leffler, *A Preponderance of Power: National Security, the Truman Administration, and the Cold War* (Stanford: Stanford University Press, 1992).
8. NSC 68, "United States Objectives and Programs for National Security," 14 April 1950, *FRUS, 1950*, 1:234–292.
9. For the U.S. government's awareness of the potential significance of more inclusive Soviet racial policies, see CIA, ORE 25–48, "The Break-Up of the Colonial Empires and Its Implications for U.S. Security," 3 September 1948, Harry S Truman Papers, President's Secretary's File, box 255, HSTL.
10. David McCullough, *Truman* (New York: Simon and Schuster, 1992), 53 (quotation), 83; Alonzo L. Hamby, *Man of the People: The Life of Harry Truman* (New York: Oxford University Press, 1995), 4–5; William E. Leuchtenburg, "The Conversion of Harry Truman," *American Heritage* 42 (November 1991): 56–57.
11. Hamby, *Man of the People*, 238–239, 272, 364–365, 631; McCullough, *Truman*, 234, 247, 971–972; Donald R. McCoy and Richard T. Ruetten, *Quest and Response: Minority Rights and the Truman Administration* (Lawrence: University Press of Kansas, 1973), 14–16; Leuchtenburg, "The Conversion of Harry Truman," 68; Robert H. Ferrell, *Harry S Truman: A Life* (Columbia: University of Missouri Press, 1994), 292–299. For a very critical view that still acknowledges personal growth, see Kenneth O'Reilly, *Nixon's Piano: Presidents and Racial Politics from Washington to Clinton* (New York: Free Press, 1995), 145–165.
12. Dalfiume, *Desegregation of the U.S. Armed Forces*, 140–141; McCullough, *Tru-*

*man,* 323; Hamby, *Man of the People,* 271–273; Barton J. Bernstein, "The Ambiguous Legacy: The Truman Administration and Civil Rights," in Bernstein, ed., *Politics and Policies of the Truman Administration* (Chicago: Quadrangle, 1970), 271–272.

13. See, for example, Clifford's "Memorandum for the President," 19 November 1947, Clark Clifford Papers, box 23, HSTL.

14. David A. Mayers, *George Kennan and the Dilemmas of U.S. Foreign Policy* (New York: Oxford University Press, 1988), 56.

15. Kennan diary, 1933–1938, "Fair Day, Adieu!" George F. Kennan Papers, box 25, Seeley G. Mudd Library, Princeton University, Princeton, New Jersey. See also Mayers, *George Kennan and Dilemmas of U.S. Policy,* 49–53; Walter Isaacson and Evan Thomas, *The Wise Men—Six Friends and the World They Made: Acheson, Bohlen, Harrison, Kennan, Lovett, McCloy* (New York: Simon and Schuster, 1986), 171–172.

16. George F. Kennan, *Memoirs: 1925–1950* (1967; New York: Pantheon, 1983), 181.

17. Kennan, *Memoirs: 1925–1950,* 182–185; Michael H. Hunt, *Ideology and U.S. Foreign Policy* (New Haven: Yale University Press, 1987), 162–163; Mayers, *George Kennan and Dilemmas of U.S. Policy,* 271–272; Anders Stephanson, *Kennan and the Art of Foreign Policy* (Cambridge, Mass.: Harvard University Press, 1989), 157–175.

18. Kennan, *Memoirs: 1925–1950,* 476–482; Kennan memo to Acheson, 29 March 1950, *FRUS, 1950,* 2:601–602; Roger R. Trask, "George F. Kennan's Report on Latin America (1950)," *Diplomatic History* 2 (Summer 1978): 307–311.

19. Kennan, "Tasks Ahead in U.S. Foreign Policy," lecture at the National War College, Washington, D.C., 18 December 1952, box 18, Kennan Papers, Mudd Library.

20. Kennan, *Memoirs: 1925–1950,* 74 (quoting from a paper he wrote in 1938).

21. Ibid., 551. Other Americans in Moscow shared Kennan's views: Leslie C. Stevens, the naval attaché in the U.S. embassy from 1947 to 1949, referred to Russians' "half-Asiatic minds." Stevens, *Russian Assignment* (Boston: Little, Brown, 1953), 187.

22. Kennan, lecture 2 at Bad Nauheim, 1942, box 16, Kennan Papers, Mudd Library, cited in n. 73 of David S. Foglesong, "Liberating Russia? American Thinking about the Russian Future and the Psychological Warfare of the Early Cold War, 1948–1953," unpublished manuscript, 1997 (in author's possession). For further discussion of these issues, see David S. Foglesong, "Roots of 'Liberation': American Images of the Future of Russia in the Early Cold War, 1948–1953," *International History Review* 21 (March 1999): 57–79.

23. See, for example, Kennan, *Memoirs: 1925–1950,* 483–484.

24. Dower, *War without Mercy,* 310.

25. John Egerton, *Speak Now against the Day: The Generation before the Civil Rights Movement in the South* (New York: Knopf, 1994), 576–577. Byrnes's career after he resigned from the State Department in 1947 reflected his primary commitment to racial segregation. The former Supreme Court justice, World War II administrator, and secretary of state went home to South Carolina, where he served as governor from 1950 to 1954 and energetically opposed all movement toward desegregation. As the national Democratic Party and the Supreme Court shifted away from supporting Jim Crow, Byrnes grew increasingly alienated from those institutions that had been so central to his life and career. His trajectory from the apex of national life to a besieged regional redoubt reflected the manner in which changing race relations altered American political life in the decades after World War II.

26. George Streator, "Negro Youth Told Future Is in South," *New York Times,* 21 October 1946, 31.

27. Carr to Marshall, 23 May 1947, and Carr to Rusk, 11 August 1947, both in PCCR, box 6, HSTL; Marshall to Diplomatic and Consular Offices, 20 July 1948, *FRUS, 1948,* 1:595; William T. Bowers, William M. Hammond, and George L. MacGarrigle, *Black Soldier, White Army: The 24th Infantry Regiment in Korea* (Washington: Center of Military History, United States Army, 1996), 23. Marshall's initial response to the 1941 Atlantic Charter (when he was army chief of staff) revealed something of his negative view of self-government among nonwhite peoples abroad. Was this declaration of American war aims, he asked privately, "an effort to keep the people entertained?" Kimball, "The Atlantic Charter: 'With All Deliberate Speed,'" in Brinkley and Facey-Crowther, *The Atlantic Charter,* 86.

28. Dudziak, "Desegregation as a Cold War Imperative," 101.

29. Hunt, *Ideology and U.S. Foreign Policy,* 180.

30. "Negroes Ask Jobs on Acheson Staff," *New York Times,* 14 April 1951, 19; Plummer, *Rising Wind,* 272–273; Douglas Brinkley, *Dean Acheson: The Cold War Years, 1953–71* (New Haven: Yale University Press, 1992), 305; Stephen J. Rabe, *Eisenhower and Latin America: The Foreign Policy of Anticommunism* (Chapel Hill: University of North Carolina Press, 1988), 20.

31. Gordon H. Chang, *Friends and Enemies: The United States, China, and the Soviet Union, 1948–1972* (Stanford: Stanford University Press, 1990), 15; Brinkley, *Dean Acheson,* 303–304.

32. Dean Acheson, *Present at the Creation: My Years in the State Department* (New York: Norton, 1969), 112; Godfrey Hodgson, "Enemies and Empires" (review of Douglas Brinkley, *Dean Acheson: The Cold War Years*), *New Republic,* 28 December 1992, 36–40.

33. Nicol C. Rae, *Southern Democrats* (New York: Oxford University Press, 1994), 36–40; Fite, *Richard B. Russell,* 225.

34. Dittmer, *Local People,* 2.

35. Fite, *Richard B. Russell,* 199, 221, 232–236, 244–245, 265–266, 280 (quotations at 264 and 274).

36. Quoted in Rae, *Southern Democrats,* 38.

37. Douglas Little, "Cold War and Colonialism in Africa: The United States, France, and the Madagascar Revolt of 1947," *Pacific Historical Review* 59 (November 1990): 527–552.

38. For American awareness of this reality, see U.S. Office of Strategic Services, R & A No. 2852, "Regulations and Practices Concerning Native Troops in British, French, Spanish, Belgian, Portuguese, and Ex-Italian Africa," 27 February 1945, *OSS/State Department Intelligence and Research Reports* (Washington: University Publications of America, 1980), part 13, *Africa, 1941–1961* (microfilm, 11 reels with printed guide), reel 3.

39. Dalfiume, *Desegregation of the U.S. Armed Forces,* 105–106, 132–133. See also Logan, *What the Negro Wants;* Egerton, *Speak Now against the Day;* Sullivan, *Days of Hope;* Richard M. Dalfiume, "The 'Forgotten Years' of the Negro Revolution," *Journal of American History* 55 (June 1968): 90–106; Doug McAdam, *Political Process and the Development of Black Insurgency, 1930–1970* (Chicago: University of Chicago Press, 1982); Aldon D. Morris, *The Origins of the Civil Rights Movement: Black Communities Organizing for Change* (New York: Free Press, 1984).

40. Dittmer, *Local People,* 20; Michael J. Hogan, *A Cross of Iron: Harry S. Truman and the Origins of the National Security State* (New York: Cambridge University Press, 1998), 431.

41. See, for example, Patricia Sullivan, "Southern Reformers, the New Deal, and the Movement's Foundation," in *New Directions in Civil Rights Studies,* ed. Armstead L. Robinson and Patricia Sullivan (Charlottesville: University Press of Virginia, 1991), 96.

42. Perhaps the most well-known contemporary exploration and condemnation of this phenomenon was William Faulkner's novel of northern Mississippi, *Intruder in the Dust* (New York: Random House, 1948).

43. "Killing of Negroes Is Protested Here," *New York Times,* 2 March 1946, clipping in Philleo Nash Files, box 6, HSTL; "NAACP Swings into High as Lynch Wave Hits South," *NAACP Bulletin* 5 (August–September 1946): 1, clipping in President's Secretary's Files, box 131, HSTL; Gail Williams O'Brien, *The Color of the Law: Race, Violence, and Justice in the Post–World War II South* (Chapel Hill: University of North Carolina Press, 1999); Dorothy Beeler, "Race Riot in

Columbia, Tennessee, February 25–27, 1946," *Tennessee Historical Quarterly* 39 (1980): 49–61; Burran, "Racial Violence in the South," 229–256; Mary L. Dudziak, "Civil Rights and the Cold War: The Impact of Foreign Relations on Civil Rights Reform in the Truman Administration," paper presented at the annual meeting of the Society for Historians of American Foreign Relations, June 1993, Charlottesville, Virginia.

44. Carr to members of President's Committee on Civil Rights, 16 April 1947, PCCR, box 16, HSTL; "Massacre," editorial, *Crisis* 53 (August 1947): 233; *To Secure These Rights: The Report of the President's Committee on Civil Rights* (Washington: U.S. Government Printing Office, 1947), 20–32; Shapiro, *White Violence and Black Response,* 365–370; Burran, "Racial Violence in the South," 226, 257–290; McCoy and Ruetten, *Quest and Response,* 44–45. Woodward had been discharged from the army just three hours before the assault, making this one of the swiftest demonstrations of white Southern resolve to intimidate returning black veterans.

45. Harold Preece, "Klan 'Murder, Inc.,' in Dixie," *Crisis* 53 (October 1946): 299–301; Shapiro, *White Violence and Black Response,* 353–357, 369–370.

46. "South Carolina," *Time,* 2 June 1947, 27.

47. Theron Lamar Caudle, "Civil Rights and Federal Law," address to North Carolina Bar Association, Winston-Salem, N.C., 30 August 1946, Nash Files, box 26, HSTL.

48. Fite, *Richard B. Russell,* 230.

49. Carl T. Rowan, *Go South to Sorrow* (New York: Random House, 1957), 187–191; Dittmer, *Local People,* 21; Shapiro, *White Violence and Black Response,* 395; Eric W. Rise, "Race, Rape, and Radicalism: The Case of the Martinsville Seven, 1949–1951," *Journal of Southern History* 58 (August 1992): 461–490, especially 465–466.

50. *To Secure These Rights,* 79–80.

51. "One Killed, Seven Injured in Melee at Leavenworth Disciplinary Barracks," *Kansas City Call,* 9 May 1947, clipping in Nash Papers, box 27, HSTL.

52. Shapiro, *White Violence and Black Response,* 419. The recent literature emphasizing the limits on Northern racial liberalism after World War II is well represented by Thomas J. Sugrue, *The Origins of the Urban Crisis: Race and Inequality in Postwar Detroit* (Princeton: Princeton University Press, 1996).

53. Elie Abel, "Cicero Riot Scored as Defeat for U.S.," *New York Times,* 14 November 1951, clipping in Nash Files, box 5, HSTL.

54. Leo J. Margolin, letter to the editor, *New York Times,* 17 July 1951, clipping in Nash Files, box 5, HSTL.

55. Thomas J. Sugrue, "Crabgrass-Roots Politics: Race, Rights, and the Reaction

against Liberalism in the Urban North, 1940–1964," *Journal of American History* 82 (September 1995): 551–578, especially 556.

56. *To Secure These Rights,* 29.

57. Ibid., 24, 124–125. On Hoover's racial inclinations, see O'Reilly, *"Racial Matters."*

58. Johnson and Weston to Truman, 27 July 1947, WHCF, Official File, box 588, HSTL.

59. "Tennessee Race Riot Ends, Ten Injured; Recall '33 Lynching," *New York Evening Post,* 26 February 1946, clipping in Nash Files, box 6, HSTL.

60. Rowan, *Go South to Sorrow,* 42–43.

61. Jules Tygiel, *Baseball's Great Experiment: Jackie Robinson and His Legacy* (New York: Oxford University Press, 1983). Less well known, but just as revealing of the spirit of the times, was the response of the first black baseball player whom Brooklyn Dodgers president Branch Rickey approached about playing in the major leagues. Rickey asked Cuban shortstop Silvio García how he would react if a racist white American were to slap him. García snarled: "I kill him." Rickey went with Robinson instead. Thomas G. Paterson, *Contesting Castro: The United States and the Triumph of the Cuban Revolution* (New York: Oxford University Press, 1994), 49.

62. Dudziak, "Civil Rights and the Cold War," 26; Dudziak, "Desegregation as a Cold War Imperative," 84. On the miscegenation case, see Peggy Pascoe, "Miscegenation Law, Court Cases, and Ideologies of 'Race' in Twentieth-Century America," *Journal of American History* 83 (June 1996): 44–69, especially 61–67.

63. Dudziak, "Desegregation as a Cold War Imperative," 61–65, 103, 111, 118; Dudziak, "Civil Rights and the Cold War," 16–20; William C. Berman, *The Politics of Civil Rights in the Truman Administration* (Columbus: Ohio State University Press, 1970), 232. See also Bert Lockwood, Jr., "The UN Charter and U.S. Civil Rights Litigation: 1946–1955," *Iowa Law Review* 5 (1984): 901–956.

64. John D. Hargreaves, "Toward the Transfer of Power in British West Africa," in *The Transfer of Power in Africa: Decolonization, 1940–1960,* ed. Prosser Gifford and William Roger Louis (New Haven: Yale University Press, 1982), 135–136; Pakenham, *The Scramble for Africa,* 674.

65. For further discussion of these issues, see Borstelmann, *Apartheid's Reluctant Uncle,* and Von Eschen, *Race against Empire.* On Randolph's campaign, see Berman, *The Politics of Civil Rights,* 97–100, and McCoy and Ruetten, *Quest and Response,* 106–108. On Truman's commitment to Democratic Party unity, see Bernstein, "The Ambiguous Legacy," 284, and Berman, *The Politics of Civil Rights,* 238–239.

66. *To Secure These Rights,* 146.

67. "Truman's Address" [text of 29 June 1947 speech], *Crisis,* July 1949, 200. See also Walter White address (introducing Truman), 29 June 1947, Clark Clifford Files, box 3, HSTL; McCoy and Ruetten, *Quest and Response,* 73–74. The precise mix of motives behind Truman's actions in support of civil rights has been the source of some scholarly contention over the past three decades. His biographers (Hamby, McCullough) and some other scholars (McCoy and Ruetten, Donovan) have tended to emphasize his moral convictions about human equality, while dissenting historians (O'Reilly, Berman, Bernstein) have noted his calculations of political advantage. Bernstein and Berman have also been careful to credit Truman's egalitarian inclinations and his commitment to preserving social order and individual rights, as Hamby has been meticulous in acknowledging his political motives. Hamby, *Man of the People;* McCullough, *Truman;* McCoy and Ruetten, *Quest and Response;* Robert J. Donovan, *Conflict and Crisis: The Presidency of Harry S Truman, 1945–1948* (New York: Norton, 1977), and *Tumultuous Years: The Presidency of Harry S Truman, 1949–1953* (New York: Norton, 1982); O'Reilly, *Nixon's Piano;* Berman, *The Politics of Civil Rights;* Bernstein, "The Ambiguous Legacy."

68. Clark Clifford, memorandum for the president, 19 November 1947, Clifford Papers, Political File, box 23, HSTL.

69. Leuchtenburg, "The Conversion of Harry Truman," 66. On political calculations, see Hamby, *Man of the People,* 445–452, and Bernstein, "The Ambiguous Legacy," 284.

70. Berman, *The Politics of Civil Rights,* 83–85 (quotation); McCoy and Ruetten, *Quest and Response,* 99–100.

71. Channing Tobias et al. to Truman, 19 September 1946, President's Secretary's Files, General File, box 131, HSTL.

72. On African American votes, see Philleo Nash, memorandum for the president, 6 November 1948, President's Secretary's Files, Political File, box 55, HSTL. Truman had hoped for only a mild plank on civil rights at the Democratic Convention in order to avoid further alienating the white South. He resented the success of liberal forces led by Hubert Humphrey in writing instead a plank that incorporated the recommendations of the president's own Committee on Civil Rights, although that stand contributed importantly to Truman's victory in November. McCullough, *Truman,* 638–640. On the Harlem speech (and Truman's disinclination to talk about civil rights during other campaign speeches), see Ferrell, *Harry S Truman,* 296. For examples of how Truman's election encouraged racial liberals abroad, see Raymond A. Valliere, "South African Political and Economic Developments," 16 November 1948, enclosed in Winship to secretary of state, 16 November 1948, 848A.00/11–1648,

*Confidential U.S. State Department Central Files, South Africa: Internal Affairs and Foreign Affairs, 1945–1949* (Frederick, Md.: University Publications of America, 1985 [microfilm, 14 reels with printed guide]), reel 4, and Frenise A. Logan, "Racism and Indian-U.S. Relations, 1947–1953: Views in the Indian Press," *Pacific Historical Review* 54 (February 1985): 77–78.

73. McCoy and Ruetten, *Quest and Response,* 171–204; Fite, *Richard B. Russell,* 245–246; Berman, *The Politics of Civil Rights,* 153–157; Hamby, *Man of the People,* 495.

74. Bernstein, "The Ambiguous Legacy," 292–296, 299; Hamby, *Man of the People,* 563; McCoy and Ruetten, *Quest and Response,* 283–288.

75. Barkan, *The Retreat of Scientific Racism.*

76. *To Secure These Rights,* 146–148; *Segregation in Washington: A Report of the National Committee on Segregation in the Nation's Capital* (Chicago: National Committee on Segregation in the Nation's Capital, 1948), 63–65; Harold R. Isaacs, *Two-Thirds of the World: Problems of a New Approach to the Peoples of Asia, Africa, and Latin America* (Washington: Public Affairs Institute, 1950), 43–44.

77. As noted in the Prologue, quotes around "race" are generally avoided throughout the text, but they are used here to remind the reader of the thoroughly socially constructed meaning of the term—a particularly important purpose of this paragraph.

78. Rowan, *Go South to Sorrow,* 150.

79. *Segregation in Washington,* 14; Logan, "Racism and Indian-U.S. Relations," 75–76.

80. *Segregation in Washington,* 6. For a similar incident in the restaurant of the House of Representatives, see Joseph D. Lohman and Edwin R. Embree, "The Nation's Capital," *Survey Graphic,* January 1947, 34.

81. Harris Wofford, *Of Kennedys and Kings: Making Sense of the Sixties* (New York: Farrar, Straus, Giroux, 1980), 110; Wofford, *Lohia and America Meet* (1951; Bombay: Sindhu, 1987), 43.

82. John Howard Griffin, *Black Like Me* (Boston: Houghton Mifflin, 1961).

83. Rowan, *Go South to Sorrow,* 52.

84. David M. Reimers, *Still the Golden Door: The Third World Comes to America,* 2nd ed. (New York: Columbia University Press, 1992), 61; DeConde, *Ethnicity, Race, and American Foreign Policy,* 141.

85. Memorandum of conversation of Acheson with Senator Benton, 21 June 1952, Dean Acheson Papers, Memoranda of Conversation, box 79, HSTL.

86. Takaki, *Strangers from a Different Shore,* 413.

87. Michelle Mart, "Tough Guys and American Cold War Policy: Images of Israel, 1948–1960," *Diplomatic History* 20 (Summer 1996): 357–380; Dinnerstein,

*Antisemitism in America,* 128–174; David S. Wyman, *The Abandonment of the Jews: America and the Holocaust, 1941–1945* (New York: Pantheon, 1984), 325; David A. Hollinger, "National Solidarity at the End of the Twentieth Century: Reflections on the United States and Liberal Nationalism," *Journal of American History* 84 (September 1997): 567.

88. John W. Dower, "Occupied Japan and the Cold War in Asia," in *The Truman Presidency,* ed. Michael J. Lacey (New York: Cambridge University Press, 1989), 368; Dower, *War without Mercy,* 301–311.

89. Max Hastings, *The Korean War* (New York: Simon and Schuster, 1987), 29.

90. Reimers, *Still the Golden Door,* 31. For an interpretation that emphasizes the unspoken threat of such an internment (through the McCarran Internal Security Act of 1950 and its provisions for incarcerating Communists in a national emergency), but on political rather than simply racial grounds, see Takaki, *Strangers from a Different Shore,* 415.

91. O'Reilly, *"Racial Matters,"* 28, 39; Mary L. Dudziak, "Josephine Baker, Racial Protest, and the Cold War," *Journal of American History* 81 (September 1994): 543–570.

92. Clark, "An Analysis of the Relationship between Anti-Communism and Segregationist Thought," esp. 14–15, 24–25.

93. Julian M. Pleasants and Augustus Burns III, *Frank Porter Graham and the 1950 Senate Race in North Carolina* (Chapel Hill: University of North Carolina Press, 1990); David R. Goldfield, *Black, White, and Southern: Race Relations and Southern Culture, 1940 to the Present* (Baton Rouge: Louisiana State University Press, 1990), 67–70.

94. Sullivan, *Days of Hope,* 180–181; McCoy and Ruetten, *Quest and Response,* 98–99.

95. Graham White and John Maze, *Henry A. Wallace: His Search for a New World Order* (Chapel Hill: University of North Carolina Press, 1995); Richard J. Walton, *Henry Wallace, Harry Truman, and the Cold War* (New York: Viking, 1976).

96. Sullivan, *Days of Hope,* 249–275; White and Maze, *Henry A. Wallace,* 276–282. Taylor was even arrested in Birmingham for breaking the city's segregation ordinance while trying to join a black youth group's meeting. The news that a U.S. senator could not speak freely with some Americans because of the color of their skin provoked comment around the world. "Taylor under Bail in Alabama in Racial Case, Will Make Test," *New York Times,* 3 May 1948, 1; Dudziak, "Desegregation as a Cold War Imperative," 83.

97. Sullivan, *Days of Hope,* 249.

98. In this regard, the president chose the advice of Clark Clifford and his political aides (to isolate Wallace by associating him solely with his Communist

Party supporters) over that of his Committee on Civil Rights, which warned that "public excitement about 'Communists' has gone far beyond the dictates of 'good judgment' and 'calmness' . . . A state of near-hysteria now threatens to inhibit the freedom of genuine democrats." Clifford, memorandum for the president, 19 November 1947, Clifford Papers, box 23, HSTL; *To Secure These Rights*, 49.

99. Clifford, memorandum for the president, 19 November 1947.

100. Von Eschen, *Race against Empire*, provides the best discussion to date of these issues. See also Charles I. Glickberg, "Negro Americans and the African Dream," *Phylon* 8 (1947): 323–330; Charles H. Wesley, "International Aspects of the Negro's Status in the United States," *Negro History Bulletin*, February 1948, 108, 113–118; Plummer, *Rising Wind;* Gerald Horne, *Black and Red: W. E. B. Du Bois and the Afro-American Response to the Cold War, 1944–1963* (Albany: State University of New York Press, 1986).

101. James L. Roark, "American Black Leaders: The Response to Colonialism and the Cold War, 1943–1953," *African Historical Studies* 4 (1971): 253–270; Mark Solomon, "Black Critics of Colonialism and the Cold War," in *Cold War Critics: Alternatives to American Foreign Policy in the Truman Years,* ed. Thomas G. Paterson (Chicago: Quadrangle, 1971), 205–239; Duberman, *Paul Robeson,* 388–390; Plummer, *Rising Wind,* 167–216; Von Eschen, *Race against Empire,* 107–144.

102. CIA, ORE 25–48, "The Break-Up of the Colonial Empires."

103. Lauren, *Power and Prejudice,* 201–202.

104. William Roger Louis, "American Anti-Colonialism and the Dissolution of the British Empire," *International Affairs* 61 (1985): 402–403, 411.

105. Plummer, *Rising Wind,* 127–128.

106. Robert J. McMahon, *Colonialism and Cold War: The United States and the Struggle for Indonesian Independence, 1945–1949* (Ithaca: Cornell University Press, 1981), 292–295.

107. Borstelmann, *Apartheid's Reluctant Uncle,* 111–114; J. K. Sweeney, "The Un-wanted Alliance: Portugal and the United States," in *The Romance of History: Essays in Honor of Lawrence S. Kaplan,* ed. Scott L. Bills and Timothy Smith (Kent, Ohio: Kent State University Press, 1997), 214–228; Alfred E. Eckes, Jr., *The United States and the Global Struggle for Minerals* (Austin: University of Texas Press, 1979), 157–161; Scott L. Bills, *Empire and Cold War: The Roots of U.S.-Third World Antagonism, 1945–1947* (New York: St. Martin's, 1990), 210–212.

108. George W. Malone, "Colonial Slavery," *Congressional Record,* 28 June 1950, 9339; Plummer, *Rising Wind,* 189.

109. Truman, address to joint session of Congress, 12 March 1947, reprinted in

*Major Problems in American Foreign Relations,* 4th ed., 2 vols., ed. Thomas G. Paterson and Dennis Merrill (Lexington, Mass.: D.C. Heath, 1995), 2:259–261; Logan, "Racism and Indian-U.S. Relations," 76.

110. Assistant Secretary of State George McGhee recognized this by privately acknowledging that a 1950 U.S. diplomatic conference held in Tangiers on the subject of colonialism would have been comparable to the French setting up a conference in Mobile, Alabama, to discuss the status of African Americans in the South. See Plummer, *Rising Wind,* 237–238.

111. White (Central Intelligence Group) to Stewart, 5 August 1947, enclosing "Foreign Radio Comment on American Civil Rights," PCCR, Correspondence, box 6, HSTL.

112. Isaacs, *Two-Thirds of the World,* 42–43; Richard L.-G. Deverall, "The Struggle for Asia," *Crisis,* January 1951, 28–29. See also William Stueck, *The Korean War: An International History* (Princeton: Princeton University Press, 1995), 81.

113. Dudziak, "Civil Rights and the Cold War," 11–12.

114. Henry B. Ryan, *The Vision of Anglo-America: The US-UK Alliance and Emerging Cold War, 1943–1946* (Cambridge: Cambridge University Press, 1987), 170–171; Plummer, *Rising Wind,* 169; Fite, *Richard B. Russell,* 217. Churchill himself, as the son of an English father and American mother, literally embodied such an alliance.

115. Acheson, speech to the Delta Council, 8 May 1947, reprinted in Joseph M. Jones, *The Fifteen Weeks (February 21–June 5, 1947)* (New York: Viking, 1955), 247–281, quotation at 276; Dittmer, *Local People,* 26–27. Less than a month earlier, Du Bois had asked in a speech to the Progressive Citizens of America if it was possible to "export democracy to Greece and not practice it in Mississippi." Jonathan Rosenberg, "'Struggling to Save America': World Affairs and the U.S. Civil Rights Movement, 1945–1960," paper presented at the annual conference of the Organization of American Historians, April 1999, Toronto, Canada, 22.

116. Memorandum for the file, "Under Secretary's Meeting of Friday, April 7, 1950," Records of the Office of the Executive Secretariat, box 1, Record Group 59, National Archives, Washington, D.C. (McGhee quotation); I thank Frank Costigliola for bringing this document to my attention; McGregor memorandum, 3 February 1954, *FRUS, 1952–54,* 11:416–417; editorial footnote, *FRUS, 1952–54,* 414; Robert W. Moore, "White Magic in the Belgian Congo," *National Geographic* 101 (March 1952): 321–362. For more extensive discussions of these issues, see Borstelmann, *Apartheid's Reluctant Uncle.*

117. See, for example, Gallman to State Department, 14 March 1952, *FRUS, 1952–54,* 11:5; Sims to Feld, 16 June 1952, ibid., 21–22; memorandum of conversa-

tion, 21 August 1952, ibid., 25; George McGhee, *Envoy to the Middle World: Adventures in Diplomacy* (New York: Harper and Row, 1983), 131. One partial exception to this was Liberia, whose settlement by African Americans in the nineteenth century had given it a unique relationship to the United States. On the growing American economic involvement in Liberia after 1945, see Earl P. Hanson, "The United States Invades Africa," *Harper's Magazine*, February 1947, 170–177.

118. William Attwood, *The Reds and the Blacks: A Personal Adventure* (New York: Harper and Row, 1967), 36. On the common tendency of European officials in Africa to mistrust American motives there, see memorandum of conversation, 20 February 1952, *FRUS, 1952–54*, 11:1.

119. Dudley to State Department, 3 June 1952, *FRUS, 1952–54*, 11:19–20.

120. Borstelmann, *Apartheid's Reluctant Uncle*, 8–12.

121. Sims to Bourgerie, 18 March 1952, *FRUS, 1952–54*, 11:11 (quotation); minutes of U.S.-U.K. colonial policy discussions, 25 September 1952, ibid., 311.

122. Prosser Gifford, "Misconceived Dominion: The Creation and Disintegration of Federation in British Central Africa," in *The Transfer of Power in Africa: Decolonization, 1940–1960*, ed. Prosser Gifford and Wm. Roger Louis (New Haven: Yale University Press, 1982), 387–416.

123. Dorsz to State Department, 10 October 1952, *FRUS, 1952–54*, 11:347–348. See also Minter, *King Solomon's Mines Revisited*, 118–123; Robert B. Edgerton, *Mau Mau: An African Crucible* (New York: Free Press, 1989).

124. The best sources on the U.S. perspective on South Africa at the dawn of apartheid include Thomas J. Noer, *Cold War and Black Liberation: The United States and White Rule in Africa, 1948–1968* (Columbia: University of Missouri Press, 1985); Minter, *King Solomon's Mines Revisited;* Borstelmann, *Apartheid's Reluctant Uncle.* For an example of white South Africans' concern with spreading their influence northward, see memorandum of conversation, 29 March 1949, Acheson Papers, box 73, HSTL.

125. Borstelmann, *Apartheid's Reluctant Uncle,* 197–199. On American appreciation of South Africa's role in Korea, see memorandum of conversation, 20 April 1951, Acheson Papers, box 77, HSTL.

126. Kilcoin to Brown, 17 April 1952, *FRUS, 1952–54*, 11:909; Perkins to secretary of state, 11 June 1952, ibid., 920; memorandum by Lee and Thoreson, 16 September 1952, ibid., 932.

127. Memorandum of conversation, 23 October 1952, ibid., 946.

128. Department of State, Office of Intelligence Research, "The South African Constitutional Crisis," 2 July 1952, *OSS/State Department Intelligence and Research Reports* (Washington: University Publications of America, 1980), part 13 *Africa, 1941–1961* (microfilm, 11 reels with printed guide), reel 10.

129. McGhee, *Envoy to the Middle World,* 146, 131.

130. This difference had the capacity to shock the occasional African American visitor to South Africa, such as actor Sidney Poitier, who arrived there in 1952 to film *Cry the Beloved Country.* See Poitier, *This Life* (New York: Knopf, 1980), 147–150.

131. George M. Frederickson, *Black Liberation: A Comparative History of Black Ideologies in the United States and South Africa* (New York: Oxford University Press, 1995), chaps. 5–7.

132. Logan, "Racism and Indian-U.S. Relations," 76; Borstelmann, *Apartheid's Reluctant Uncle,* 102–103.

133. Memorandum of conversation, 14 October 1952, Acheson Papers, box 80, HSTL.

134. See, for example, Colon to Truman, 29 July 1946, WHCF, Official File, box 588, HSTL; "Greek Communists Use of Violations of Civil Rights in the U.S." [November 1946], PCCR, box 6, HSTL; Danciger to Wilson, 23 December 1946, PCCR, box 2, HSTL; Logan, "Racism and Indian-U.S. Relations," 73–74.

135. *To Secure These Rights,* 100–101.

136. White (Central Intelligence Group) to Krould, 18 June 1947, PCCR, box 6, HSTL.

137. Stueck, *The Korean War,* 80.

138. "Voice of America Listener Hits Lynching," 27 May 1947, PCCR, box 6, HSTL.

139. Bowles to Carr, 19 March 1947, PCCR, box 8, HSTL; Dudziak, "Desegregation as a Cold War Imperative," 89.

140. James W. Ivy, "American Negro Problem in the European Press," *Crisis,* July 1950, 413–418, 468–472; Dudziak, "Desegregation as a Cold War Imperative," 81–83.

141. Isaacs, "The Political and Psychological Context of Point Four," 56.

142. *To Secure These Rights,* 147.

143. Ibid., 146–147.

144. Lauren, *Power and Prejudice,* 194.

145. Minutes of meeting of U.S. delegation to UN, 10 November 1950, *FRUS, 1950,* 2:564–569; "United States Policy toward Dependent Territories," *FRUS, 1952–54,* 3:1097.

146. Dudziak, "Desegregation as a Cold War Imperative," 85. The staff of the President's Committee on Civil Rights was dismayed to learn the limits of Marshall's interest in domestic racial reform as a way of dealing with this problem. Committee staffers requested a letter from the secretary of state to bolster

their report's emphasis on the need for reducing racial discrimination, but Marshall instead argued that reports of racial problems in the United States were largely the work of Communist Party exaggerations. The committee decided Marshall's letter would actually hurt rather than help their cause, and instead used Acheson's older letter to the Fair Employment Practices Commission on the negative effects of discrimination on U.S. diplomacy. Carr to Marshall, 23 May 1947, and Carr to Rusk, 11 August 1947, both in PCCR, box 6, HSTL.

147. Dudziak, "Civil Rights and the Cold War," 12.

148. Dudziak, "Desegregation as a Cold War Imperative," 95.

149. *A Petition to the United Nations on Behalf of 13 Million Oppressed Negro Citizens of the United States of America* (New York: National Negro Congress, 1946); *An Appeal to the World: A Statement on the Denial of Human Rights to Minorities in the Case of Citizens of Negro Descent in the United States and an Appeal to the United Nations for Redress* (New York: National Association for the Advancement of Colored People, 1947); *We Charge Genocide: The Historical Petition to the United Nations for Relief from a Crime of the United States Government against the Negro People* (New York: Civil Rights Congress, 1951). See also Harris, "Racial Equality and the United Nations Charter."

150. Berman, *The Politics of Civil Rights,* 66.

151. *An Appeal to the World,* 20.

152. See Ellen Schrecker, *Many Crimes: McCarthyism in America* (New York: Little, Brown, 1998). Further insightful discussion of this repressive campaign can be found in Von Eschen, *Race against Empire;* Plummer, *Rising Wind;* Horne, *W. E. B. Du Bois;* and Duberman, *Paul Robeson.*

153. Shapiro, *White Violence and Black Response,* 517, n. 65.

154. J. D. Ratcliff, "Edith Sampson—Thorn in Russia's Side," *Reader's Digest,* April 1951, 107–109; Dudziak, "Desegregation as a Cold War Imperative," 99.

155. Michael L. Krenn, "'Outstanding Negroes' and 'Appropriate Countries': Some Facts, Figures, and Thoughts on Black U.S. Ambassadors, 1949–1988," *Diplomatic History* 14 (Winter 1990): 131–141. A handful of African Americans had previously served as heads of mission in places like Haiti and Liberia at a rank below ambassador.

156. Dudziak, "Desegregation as a Cold War Imperative," 109.

157. *To Secure These Rights,* 87–95; *Segregation in Washington,* 21–53. Residents of the District of Columbia did not have a voting representative in Congress.

158. *Segregation in Washington,* 88.

159. Carr to President's Committee on Civil Rights, 24 April 1947, PCCR, box 1 (copy also in box 15), HSTL.

160. Ibid.; "Meeting of Negro Leaders with Secretary Acheson on April 13, 1951," and Randolph et al., statement to Acheson, 13 April 1951, both in Acheson Papers, box 77, HSTL.

161. *Segregation in Washington*, 9–10.

162. Lauren, *Power and Prejudice*, 180, 192.

163. DeConde, *Ethnicity, Race, and American Foreign Policy*, 128–129; Shapiro, *White Violence and Black Response*, 421; Lauren, *Power and Prejudice*, 225; Natalie Hevener Kaufman, *Human Rights Treaties and the Senate: A History of Opposition* (Chapel Hill: University of North Carolina Press, 1990).

164. White, *A Rising Wind*.

165. Plummer, *Rising Wind*, 207.

166. "Swedish Press Scores American 'Racists,'" 6 June 1947, PCCR, box 6, HSTL.

167. Truman to Acheson, 11 August 1952, enclosing "Report on the Foreign Service Personnel of the American Legation in Luxembourg," Acheson Papers, box 80, HSTL.

168. *To Secure These Rights*, 80; Truman address to Congress, 2 February 1948, Nash Files, box 24, HSTL; George W. Westerman, "Canal Zone Discrimination," *Crisis*, April 1951, 235–237.

169. Davis to Secretary of State, *FRUS, 1949*, 2:706–707.

170. Collier statement, "Civil Rights Problems in Dependent Areas," PCCR, box 15, HSTL.

171. War Department, "The Utilization of Negro Infantry Platoons in White Companies," June 1945, PCCR, box 6, HSTL; War Department, "Army Talk," 12 April 1947, Alvan C. Gillem, Jr., Papers, box 1, DDEL; Mershon and Schlossman, *Foxholes and Color Lines*, 145–152. On African American organizing to pressure Truman to desegregate the military, see Dalfiume, *Desegregation of the U.S. Armed Forces*, 155–169.

172. Dalfiume, *Desegregation of the U.S. Armed Forces*, 201; Mershon and Schlossman, *Foxholes and Color Lines*, 158–217.

173. Nalty, *Strength for the Fight*, 256–262; Mershon and Schlossman, *Foxholes and Color Lines*, 74–81, 218–251.

174. Chang, *Friends and Enemies*, 80; Hunt, *Ideology and U.S. Foreign Policy*, 162.

175. Stueck, *The Korean War*, 127; Andrew J. Rotter, "In Retrospect: Harold R. Isaacs's *Scratches on Our Minds*," *Reviews in American History* 24 (March 1996): 187.

176. Hastings, *The Korean War*, 69–70.

177. Ibid., 306–313.

178. "Smearing Negro GIs in Korea," editorial, *Crisis*, December 1950, 715; Clay Blair, *The Forgotten War: America in Korea, 1950–1953* (New York: Times Books, 1987), 683–684; Bowers, Hammond, and MacGarrigle, *Black Soldier*,

*White Army,* 186–188. For a summary of the controversy over the performance of African American soldiers in segregated units early in the war, see Mershon and Schlossman, *Foxholes and Color Lines,* 220–224.

179. Plummer, *Rising Wind,* 205.

180. Englehardt, *The End of Victory Culture,* 65; Plummer, *Rising Wind,* 209. Fears of Americans' having their minds removed and replaced by alien forces, whether from East Asia or outer space, were a common theme in science fiction literature and films of the period. See Peter Biskind, *Seeing Is Believing: How Hollywood Convinced Us to Stop Worrying and Love the Fifties* (New York: Pantheon, 1983).

181. Plummer, *Rising Wind,* 208–209.

182. On the war's effects on social reform efforts at home, see Alonzo Hamby, *Beyond the New Deal: Harry S. Truman and American Liberalism* (New York: Columbia University Press, 1973), 441–446.

183. South Africa's extensive supply of uranium ore makes the image of an expanding core—as in a nuclear reactor gone haywire—especially appropriate, in light of what might be seen as apartheid's cultural radioactivity.

### *3. The Last Hurrah of the Old Color Line*

1. Louis Jefferson, *The John Foster Dulles Book of Humor* (New York: St. Martin's, 1986), 166–167 (emphasis in original).

2. Chester Bowles, "While the World Watches," *New York Times,* 17 January 1960, sec. 10, p. 6, clipping in Staff Files, Administrative Officer for Special Projects (Morrow), box 9, folder "Civil Rights Clippings and Data (2)," DDEL.

3. Robert F. Burk, *The Eisenhower Administration and Black Civil Rights* (Knoxville: University of Tennessee Press, 1984), 261–263; Stephen E. Ambrose, *Eisenhower,* vol. 2, *The President* (New York: Simon and Schuster, 1984), 18–19, 620.

4. Stephen E. Ambrose, *Eisenhower,* vol. 1, *Soldier, General of the Army, President-Elect, 1890–1952* (New York: Simon and Schuster, 1983), 47; Ambrose, *Eisenhower,* 2:125; Burk, *Eisenhower Administration,* 27; Herbert S. Parmet, *Eisenhower and the American Crusades* (New York: Macmillan, 1972), 438; *Universal Military Training: Hearings before the Committee on Armed Services, U.S. Senate,* 80th Cong., 2d sess., March and April 1948 (Washington: Government Printing Office, 1948), 995–997. For examples of Eisenhower's occasional stands against blatant discrimination, see Burk, *Eisenhower Administration,* 27; Dwight D. Eisenhower, *The White House Years: Waging Peace, 1956–1961* (Garden City, N.Y.: Doubleday, 1965), 148; Ambrose, *Eisenhower,* 1:34–35, 113–114, 370.

5. Chester J. Pach, Jr., and Elmo Richardson, *The Presidency of Dwight D. Eisenhower*, rev. ed. (Lawrence: University Press of Kansas, 1991), 34; Arthur Larson, *Eisenhower: The President Nobody Knew* (New York: Scribner's, 1968), 127; Burk, *Eisenhower Administration*, 192; Ambrose, *Eisenhower*, 1:437–438, 469, 2:75, 142, 385–387, 497–498 (quotation).

6. Ambrose, *Eisenhower*, 1:102, 274, 2:387; Roy Wilkins, *Standing Fast: The Autobiography of Roy Wilkins* (New York: Viking, 1982), 256.

7. Mark Stern, "Presidential Strategies and Civil Rights: Eisenhower, The Early Years, 1952–54," *Presidential Studies Quarterly* 19 (Fall 1989): 780; David Halberstam, *The Fifties* (New York: Ballantine, 1993), 685; O'Reilly, *Nixon's Piano*, 165–187.

8. Branch, *Parting the Waters*, 181; Stern, "Presidential Strategies," 781–782; Burk, *Eisenhower Administration*, 190–191, 255–257; Peter Grose, *Gentleman Spy: The Life of Allen Dulles* (Boston: Houghton Mifflin, 1994), 7; Lauren, *Power and Prejudice*, 226; O'Reilly, *"Racial Matters,"* 39–40.

9. E. Frederic Morrow, *Black Man in the White House: A Diary of the Eisenhower Years by the Administrative Officer for Special Projects, the White House, 1955–1961* (New York: Coward-McCann, 1963), 47–48 (Rabb), 276–277 (Persons); Branch, *Parting the Waters*, 234; Ambrose, *Eisenhower*, 2:305.

10. Morrow, *Black Man*, 17–18, 40, 82–84, 88, 118–119, 136–137, 164, 179, 209–211, 258–259; Burk, *Eisenhower Administration*, 77–85; Halberstam, *Fifties*, 424–427.

11. FBI, "The Nation of Islam," October 1960, WHO, OSANSA, FBI Series, box 7, DDEL; Ambrose, *Eisenhower*, 1:439; Burk, *Eisenhower Administration*, 90, 108, 121–127.

12. Shapiro, *White Violence and Black Response*, 410–411 (quotation); Dittmer, *Local People*, 83–84; Southeastern Office, American Friends Service Committee, Department of Racial and Cultural Relations, National Council of Churches in Christ in the United States of America, and Southern Regional Council, *Intimidation, Reprisal, and Violence in the South's Racial Crisis* (Atlanta, 1959); Arnold R. Hirsch, "Massive Resistance in the Urban North: Trumbull Park, Chicago, 1953–1966," *Journal of American History* 82 (September 1995): 522–550; John E. Fleming, "African-American Museums, History, and the American Ideal," *Journal of American History* 81 (1994): 1025.

13. Wilkins, *Standing Fast*, 222; Stern, "Presidential Strategies," 778; Pach and Richardson, *Presidency*, 148–149; Burk, *Eisenhower Administration*, 23, 162–165, 263.

14. *A Testament of Hope: The Essential Writings of Martin Luther King, Jr.*, ed. James M. Washington (San Francisco: Harper and Row, 1986), 85–86; Ambrose, *Eisenhower*, 2:309, 498; Stern, "Presidential Strategies," 774–777, 788–789; Pach and Richardson, *Presidency*, 62–63, 156–157; Gary W. Reichard, "Democrats,

Civil Rights, and Electoral Strategies in the 1950s," *Congress and the Presidency* 13 (Spring 1986): 59–60; Jeff Broadwater, *Adlai Stevenson and American Politics: The Odyssey of a Cold War Liberal* (New York: Twayne, 1994), 47, 116, 140; Burk, *Eisenhower Administration,* 15–20.

15. Steven F. Lawson, *Running for Freedom: Civil Rights and Black Politics in America since 1941* (Philadelphia: Temple University Press, 1991), 55–56; Burk, *Eisenhower Administration,* 16, 89, 109, 152–153, 204–207.

16. "Discrimination on the Run," editorial, *Washington Post,* 22 April 1955, clipping enclosed in Rabb to Eisenhower, 29 April 1955, AWF, Ann Whitman Diary, box 5, DDEL; Rowan, *Go South to Sorrow,* 224–228; Dwight D. Eisenhower, *The White House Years: Mandate for Change, 1953–1956* (Garden City, N.Y.: Doubleday, 1963), 236; Burk, *Eisenhower Administration,* 45–67; Stern, "Presidential Strategies," 783; Lawson, *Running for Freedom,* 51–52.

17. Burk, *Eisenhower Administration,* 49, 60–67, 70–77.

18. Nalty, *Strength for the Fight,* 267–72; Burk, *Eisenhower Administration,* 24–44.

19. *The Eisenhower Diaries,* ed. Robert H. Ferrell (New York: Norton, 1981), 246–247 (Byrnes); Eisenhower to McGill, 26 February 1959, AWF, Name Series, box 23, DDEL; Burk, *Eisenhower Administration,* 238 (publishers); Morrow, *Black Man,* 218–219.

20. Ambrose, *Eisenhower,* 2:337 (quotation); Halberstam, *Fifties,* 686; Morrow, *Black Man,* 299–300.

21. Eisenhower to McGill, 26 February 1959, AWF, Name Series, box 23, DDEL ("center line"); Ambrose, *Eisenhower,* 2:327 (Jones).

22. Burk, *Eisenhower Administration,* 150, 201; Pach and Richardson, *Presidency,* 143. The Court's announcement on 17 May 1954 was a great surprise. Most press reporters in Washington had spent that morning speculating about the consequences of another event freighted with racial implications: the Vietnamese defeat of the French at Dien Bien Phu just ten days before. Sitkoff, *The Struggle for Black Equality,* 21.

23. Dudziak, "Desegregation as a Cold War Imperative," passim, but esp. 61 (quotation), 113, n. 299.

24. "'Voice' Speaks in Thirty-four Languages to Flash Court Ruling to World," *New York Times,* 18 May 1954, 1; "Editorial Excerpts from the Nation's Press on Segregation Ruling," ibid., 19; Isaacs, *The New World of Negro Americans,* 332 (Frazier); Harold Cruse, *The Crisis of the Negro Intellectual* (New York: William Morrow, 1967), 240; Dudziak, "Desegregation as a Cold War Imperative," 113.

25. Russell Baker, "Eisenhower Hints Desire for 'Slower' Integration," *New York Times,* 28 August 1958, 1; Earl Warren, *The Memoirs of Earl Warren* (Garden City, N.Y.: Doubleday, 1977), 291; Branch, *Parting the Waters,* 113; Larson, *Eisenhower,* 124; Burk, *Eisenhower Administration,* 134, 144, 152; Lawson, *Running*

*for Freedom,* 51; Sitkoff, *Struggle for Black Equality,* 24; Wilkins, *Standing Fast,* 222. Eisenhower's retrospective claim in his memoirs that he agreed with the *Brown* decision in 1954 does not accord with either his behavior at the time or the accounts of others close to him, especially Larson. See Eisenhower, *Waging Peace,* 150.

26. Richard Wright, *The Color Curtain: A Report on the Bandung Conference* (Cleveland: World, 1956), 133–136 (quotation); Carlos P. Romulo, *The Meaning of Bandung* (Chapel Hill: University of North Carolina Press, 1956), 35, 97–99; Tinker, *Race, Conflict, and the International Order,* 103.

27. Romulo, *Meaning of Bandung,* 48, 69 (quotation); Lauren, *Power and Prejudice,* 211; *Bandung: Texts of Selected Speeches and Final Communique of the Asian-African Conference, Bandung, Indonesia, April 18–24, 1955* (New York: Far Eastern Reporter, 1955), 14–15 (Sukarno).

28. "National Security Implications of Future Developments Regarding Africa," enclosed in Boggs to NSC, 10 August 1960, WHO, OSANSA, NSC Series, Policy Papers Subseries, box 28, folder "NSC 6001," DDEL; Lauren, *Power and Prejudice,* 213–214; *Bandung: Texts,* 24–31; Wright, *Color Curtain,* 157; Segal, *The Race War,* 340–342; Chang, *Friends and Enemies,* 137; George McTurnan Kahin, *The Asian-African Conference: Bandung, Indonesia, April 1955* (Ithaca: Cornell University Press, 1956).

29. Editorial footnote, *FRUS, 1955–57,* 18:1–2; Chang, *Friends and Enemies,* 132; Gerig to Wilcox, 9 May 1957, *FRUS, 1955–1957,* 18:66–68 (quotation).

30. Rabb memo of Eisenhower meeting with Powell, 11 May 1955, AWF, Ann Whitman Diary, box 5, DDEL; Charles V. Hamilton, *Adam Clayton Powell, Jr.: The Political Biography of an American Dilemma* (New York: Atheneum, 1991), 237–248; Dulles to Aldrich, 9 January 1956, John Foster Dulles Papers, Subject Series, box 6, folder "Policy of Independence for Colonial Peoples," DDEL.

31. Von Eschen, *Race against Empire,* 168–173 (black American press); Frederickson, *Black Liberation,* 267 (King); Plummer, *Rising Wind,* 247–256; Isaacs, *The New World of Negro Americans,* 51; Branch, *Parting the Waters,* 140.

32. Brown to Eisenhower, 2 March 1956, and Trade Arts Theater to Eisenhower, 27 February 1956, Records of White House Telegraph Office—Incoming, box 132, DDEL; Lawson, *Running for Freedom,* 51; O'Reilly, *Nixon's Piano,* 171 (Eisenhower); Branch, *Parting the Waters,* 203; Wofford, *Of Kennedys and Kings,* 121 ("white Christmas").

33. Stephen J. Whitfield, *A Death in the Delta: The Story of Emmett Till* (New York: Free Press, 1988), passim; Dittmer, *Local People,* 53–54.

34. Whitfield, *Death in the Delta,* 34 ("that river"), 46–47, 67–68 (Faulkner), 78–79, 85 (Tobias); Burk, *Eisenhower Administration,* 207 ("jungle fury"); Rowan, *Go South to Sorrow,* 41, 50–51. The French socialist *Le Populaire* credited colo-

nialism and its underlying motivation, racism, with responsibility for the situation in the American South. While Western Europeans had overseas colonies, "the essential difference is that the U.S. has its colony in the very interior of the country, while a third kind of empire, the U.S.S.R., has it on the borders." Rowan, *Go South to Sorrow,* 52.

35. Harry McPherson, *A Political Education* (Boston: Little, Brown, 1972), 138; Lawson, *Running for Freedom,* 66–67; Wilkins, *Standing Fast,* 265; Shapiro, *White Violence and Black Response,* 458–459 (Williams); Timothy B. Tyson, *Radio Free Dixie: Robert Williams and the Roots of Black Power* (Chapel Hill: University of North Carolina Press, 1999); Englehardt, *The End of Victory Culture,* 110–111; O'Reilly, *"Racial Matters,"* 42; Rowan, *Go South to Sorrow,* 17.

36. Feaster to Byrnes, 20 August 1953, AWF, Administrative Series, box 28, folder "Nixon, Richard M. (5)," DDEL (newspaperwoman); Rowan, *Go South to Sorrow,* 25, 28, 84–85; Michael J. Klarman, "How *Brown* Changed Race Relations: The Backlash Thesis," *Journal of American History* 81 (June 1994): 81–82; Fite, *Richard Russell,* 332, 369–371; Egerton, *Speak Now against the Day,* 574 (Talmadge).

37. Fite, *Richard Russell,* 333–334; David R. Goldfield, *Black, White, and Southern: Race Relations and Southern Culture, 1940 to the Present* (Baton Rouge: Louisiana State University Press, 1990), 84–85; Ambrose, *Eisenhower,* 2:305–306; Rowan, *Pitiful and Proud,* 19; Rowan, *Go South to Sorrow,* 173–174.

38. Ambrose, *Eisenhower,* 2:306–307 (quotation); Burk, *Eisenhower Administration,* 161, 208–209, 218–220, 240, 249–250; Pach and Richardson, *Presidency,* 147; Jordan to Eisenhower, 22 January 1957, Staff Files, Administrative Officer for Special Projects (Morrow), box 11, DDEL. For examples of contemporary appeals for Eisenhower to assert more leadership on this issue, see Rowan, *Go South to Sorrow,* 244, and G. Mennen Williams, "A Plea to the President," *Reporter,* 18 February 1960, clipping in Staff Files, Administrative Officer for Special Projects (Morrow), box 9, folder "Civil Rights Clippings and Data (2)," DDEL.

39. Val Washington speech, 18 October 1955, Staff Files, Bryce N. Harlow, box 8, folder "Civil Rights," DDEL; Ambrose, *Eisenhower,* 2:327–328; Broadwater, *Adlai Stevenson,* 152–168; Burk, *Eisenhower Administration,* 165–169; Lawson, *Running for Freedom,* 49–55; Wilkins, *Standing Fast,* 231–242. At the Democratic convention in Chicago in August, Governor George Wallace of Alabama enjoyed pointing out the white violence against black families in the Trumbull Park public housing project in the South Deering neighborhood—"within shouting distance" of the convention—and advising liberal Northern Democrats to attend to their own problems rather than criticizing segregation in the South. Hirsch, "Massive Resistance," 543.

40. King to Nixon, 30 August 1957, William P. Rogers Papers, 1938–1962, box 50, DDEL; Robert Dallek, *Lone Star Rising: Lyndon Johnson and His Times, 1908–1960* (New York: Oxford University Press, 1991), 526; Ambrose, *Eisenhower,* 2:407, 412–413; Wilkins, *Standing Fast,* 251–252; Larson, *Eisenhower,* 129; Lawson, *Running for Freedom,* 56–65; Burk, *Eisenhower Administration,* 226–228; Pach and Richardson, *Presidency,* 146; O'Reilly, *Nixon's Piano,* 179–180; Fite, *Richard Russell,* 339–343.

41. "Suez," *Time,* 20 August 1956, 17; Ambrose, *Eisenhower,* 2:331 (quotation), 462–463.

42. Lodge to Eisenhower, 21 December 1956, Dulles Papers, General Correspondence and Memoranda Series, box 5, DDEL; "Suez," *Time,* 20 August 1956, 18 (Labour official); Ambrose, *Eisenhower,* 2:361, 371 (Eisenhower); Wm. Roger Louis, "Dulles, Suez, and the British," in *John Foster Dulles and the Diplomacy of the Cold War,* ed. Richard H. Immerman (Princeton: Princeton University Press, 1990), 150–153.

43. Benjamine Fine, "Troops on Guard at School," *New York Times,* 25 September 1957, 1; Sitkoff, *Struggle for Black Equality,* 31; Anthony Lewis, *Portrait of a Decade: The Second American Revolution* (New York: Random House, 1964), 51; Pach and Richardson, *Presidency,* 152–153; Wilkins, *Standing Fast,* 253–254.

44. Text of Eisenhower address, 24 September 1957, AWF, Administrative Series, box 23, DDEL; Halberstam, *Fifties,* 687; Ambrose, *Eisenhower,* 2:414; O'Reilly, *Nixon's Piano,* 183–184.

45. Nelson Mandela, "A New Menace in Africa," March 1958, in *Mandela, Tambo, and the African National Congress—The Struggle against Apartheid, 1948–1990: A Documentary Survey,* ed. Sheridan Johns and R. Hunt Davis (New York: Oxford University Press, 1991), 56–59; Foreign Broadcast Information Service, "World Radio and Press Reaction to Events in Little Rock, Arkansas," 27 September 1957, Harlow Files, box 11, folder "Integration," DDEL (French commentators); U.S. Information Agency, "Public Reactions to Little Rock in Major World Capitals," 29 October 1957, enclosed in Loomis to Dearborn, 22 November 1957, Staff Files, Administrative Officer for Special Projects (Morrow), box 11, DDEL; Caputa to Rogers, 9 October 1957, Rogers Papers, box 2, DDEL; *Little Rock, U.S.A.: Materials for Analysis,* ed. Wilson Record and Jane Cassels Record (San Francisco: Chandler, 1960), 175 (white captain); Mary L. Dudziak, "The Little Rock Crisis and Foreign Affairs: Race, Resistance, and the Image of American Democracy," *Southern California Law Review* 70 (September 1997): 1641–1716; Isaacs, *The New World of Negro Americans,* 10–12; Harold R. Isaacs, "World Affairs and U.S. Race Relations: A Note on Little Rock," *Public Opinion Quarterly* 22 (Fall 1958): 366; Branch, *Parting the Waters,* 223; Halberstam, *Fifties,* 678–679; McKay, *Africa,* 403–404.

46. Text of Eisenhower address, 24 September 1957, AWF, Administrative Series, box 23, DDEL; Foreign Broadcast Information Service, "World Radio and Press Reaction," 27 September 1957, Harlow Files, box 11, DDEL; Isaacs, "World Reaction," 366.

47. Memo of NSC meeting, 8 May 1958, AWF, NSC Series, box 10, DDEL; Morrow, *Black Man,* 212–213, 289; Noer, *Cold War and Black Liberation,* 34–35; Dulles to Lodge, 3 April 1956, with enclosures, Dulles Papers, General Correspondence and Memorabilia Series, box 4, DDEL; Sears to Dulles, 15 February 1956, *FRUS, 1955–57,* 18:37–38 (U.S. delegation to UN); Attwood, *The Reds and the Blacks,* 16 (chief of protocol); Rowan, *Pitiful and Proud,* 152 (Ramsey); Lauren, *Power and Prejudice,* 217.

48. Isaacs, *Scratches on Our Minds,* 63–64, 232–233 ("lunacy"), 236–237; Rotter, "In Retrospect: Harold R. Isaacs's *Scratches on Our Minds,*" 187 ("jets"); Chang, *Friends and Enemies,* 170–174 (other quotations). American fears of the doubly subversive threat of nonwhite Communists were widespread; *Newsweek,* for example, spread a fictitious rumor in early 1953 that the tiny Guatemalan Communist Party had "hordes of armed Indians" invading plantations throughout that country. Piero Gleijeses, *Shattered Hope: The Guatemalan Revolution and the United States,* (Princeton: Princeton University Press, 1991), 232.

49. Chang, *Friends and Enemies,* 138, 173 (Eisenhower and Dulles); "The Kremlin," *Time,* 12 November 1956, 30–31.

50. DeConde, *Ethnicity, Race, and American Foreign Policy,* 142–143; "Liberating 'Enslaved Peoples,'" *Crisis,* April 1953, 228–229; Cole to Eisenhower, 22 February 1956, Records of White House Telegraph Office, Incoming, box 132, folder "Incoming Telegrams 'Alabama' Feb. 1956," DDEL; Nalty, *Strength for the Fight,* 274; Morrow, *Black Man,* 109–110, 116–117; Shapiro, *White Violence and Black Response,* 451 (King); McGregor memo, 28 December 1955, *FRUS, 1955–57,* 18:26; Rowan, *Pitiful and Proud,* 153–159; Harold R. Isaacs, "World Affairs and U.S. Race Relations: A Note on Little Rock," *Public Opinion Quarterly* 22 (Fall 1958): 364–365; Bowles, *Africa's Challenge,* 103–104; Ambrose, *Eisenhower,* 2:498; transcript of telephone conversation, Dulles and Lodge, 7 October 1953, Dulles Papers, Telephone Call Series, box 1, DDEL.

51. Shapiro, *White Violence and Black Response,* 416–417 (quotations), 458; Morrow, *Black Man,* 274; James Forman, *The Making of Black Revolutionaries* (1972; Washington: Open Hand, 1985), 173; Tyson, *Radio Free Dixie,* chaps. 4–5.

52. Randolph to Eisenhower, 17 June 1953, *FRUS, 1952–54,* 11:43–46; Burk, *Eisenhower Administration,* 159–160 (Powell); Man to Eisenhower, 24 February 1956, and Trade Arts Theater to Eisenhower, 27 February 1956 (other critics), Records of White House Telegraph Office, Incoming, box 132, DDEL; Rowan,

*Pitiful and Proud,* 142–164; McGregor memo, 28 December 1955, *FRUS, 1955–57,* 18:26–27.

53. Herman E. Talmadge, *You and Segregation* (Birmingham, Ala.: Vulcan Press, 1955), cited in Dudziak, "Desegregation as a Cold War Imperative," 117; Fite, *Richard Russell,* 345; Chapple to Eisenhower, 22 February 1956, Records of White House Telegraph Office—Incoming, box 132, DDEL; Richard M. Fried, *Nightmare in Red: The McCarthy Era in Perspective* (New York: Oxford University Press, 1990), 174–178.

54. Transcript of telephone conversation, Dulles with Hall, 6 May 1953, Dulles Papers, Telephone Call Series, box 1, DDEL; Burk, *Eisenhower Administration,* 112, 160, 166–167; Morrow, *Black Man,* 52.

55. Nixon, "Report to the President," 5 April 1957, AWF, Administrative Series, box 28, DDEL; O'Reilly, *Nixon's Piano,* 184; Isaacs, *The New World of Negro Americans,* 5–7 (quotation), 13; Isaacs, "World Affairs," 365; McKay, *Africa,* 402–403; Burk, *Eisenhower Administration,* 50–52, 69–70; Phaon Goldman, "The Significance of African Freedom for the Negro American," *Negro History Bulletin* 34 (October 1960): 6.

56. Paul Good, "Odyssey of a Man—and a Movement," in *Black Protest in the Sixties,* ed. August Meier, John H. Bracey, and Elliott M. Rudwick (New York: Markus Wiener, 1991), 265; Martin Staniland, *American Intellectuals and African Nationalists, 1955–1970* (New Haven: Yale University Press, 1991), 179–180 (Wilkins); *The Speeches of Malcolm X at Harvard,* ed. Archie Epps (New York: Morrow, 1968), 168–169; Isaacs, *The New World of Negro Americans,* 285–293; James Forman, "A Year of Resistance," in *Towards Revolution,* ed. John Gerassi, vol. 2, *The Americas* (London: Weidenfeld and Nicolson, 1971), 690; George M. Houser, "Freedom's Struggle Crosses Oceans and Mountains: Martin Luther King, Jr., and the Liberation Struggles in Africa and America," in *We Shall Overcome: Martin Luther King, Jr., and the Black Freedom Struggle,* ed. Peter J. Albert and Ronald Hoffman (New York: Pantheon, 1990), 170–171, 176–177, 184–185. For further discussion of this issue, see Plummer, *Rising Wind,* esp. 257–297; Von Eschen, *Race against Empire;* Adelaide Cromwell Hill and Martin Kilson, eds., *Apropos of Africa: Sentiments of Negro American Leaders on Africa from the 1800s to the 1950s* (London: Frank Cass, 1969).

57. Isaacs, *The New World of Negro Americans,* 152–154, 294, 298–299, 303–309 (quotation at 306), 314, 320–321; Attwood, *Reds and Blacks,* 46–47.

58. C. J. Bartlett, *"The Special Relationship": A Political History of Anglo-American Relations since 1945* (London: Longman, 1992), 84; Ambrose, *Eisenhower,* 2:333, 377–378, 587–588; Pach and Richardson, *Presidency,* 58, 180; Harry McPherson, *A Political Education* (Boston: Little, Brown, 1972), 136; Fite, *Richard B. Russell,*

346; Matthew Connelly, "Taking Off the Cold War Lens: Visions of North-South Conflict during the Algerian War for Independence," *American Historical Review* 105 (June 2000): 762–763.

59. Ambrose, *Eisenhower*, 1:496 (Eisenhower), 509; Thomas G. Paterson, *Contesting Castro: The United States and the Triumph of the Cuban Revolution* (New York: Oxford University Press, 1994), 235; Isaacs, *Scratches on Our Minds*, 39 ("all the world"); Richard H. Immerman, ed., *John Foster Dulles and the Diplomacy of the Cold War* (Princeton: Princeton University Press, 1990), 18–19, 280; Bartlett, *"Special Relationship,"* 82.

60. Hunt, *Ideology and U.S. Foreign Policy*, 164 (Jackson); Memo of NSC meeting, 14 April 1960, *FRUS, 1958–60*, 14:127 (Nixon); Paterson, *Contesting Castro*, 10 (Dulles), 257 (Herter and Eisenhower).

61. Marvin R. Zahniser and W. Michael Weis, "A Diplomatic Pearl Harbor? Richard Nixon's Goodwill Mission to Latin America in 1958," *Diplomatic History* 13 (Spring 1989): 163–190; Stephen G. Rabe, *Eisenhower and Latin America: The Foreign Policy of Anticommunism* (Chapel Hill: University of North Carolina Press, 1988), chap. 6; Pach and Richardson, *Presidency*, 188, 221; Ambrose, *Eisenhower*, 2:558 (quotation).

62. Chester Bowles, *Africa's Challenge to America* (Berkeley: University of California Press, 1956), vi–vii, 56–59; Sherman Adams, *Firsthand Report: The Story of the Eisenhower Administration* (New York: Harper and Brothers, 1961), 293; Chang, *Friends and Enemies*, 167; Ambrose, *Eisenhower*, 2:261–262; Robert J. McMahon, "Eisenhower and Third World Nationalism: A Critique of the Revisionists," *Political Science Quarterly* 101 (Fall 1986): passim.

63. Operations Coordinating Board, "Report on Africa South of the Sahara," 21 March 1958, WHO, OSANSA, NSC Series, Policy Papers Subseries, box 21, folder "NSC 5719/1," DDEL; USIA, "The Image of America," enclosed in Bundy to Coffey, 27 October 1958, WHO, OSANSA, OCB Series, Subject Subseries, box 3, folder "Image of America," DDEL.

64. John Foster Dulles, "The Cost of Peace," *Department of State Bulletin*, 18 June 1956, 999–1000; Murphy to Rockefeller, 19 August 1955, enclosing "Neutralism in the NEA Area," WHO, OSANSA, NSC Staff Papers, 1948–1961, box 2, folder "#9 Bandung (1)," DDEL (State Department); NSC 5719/1, "U.S. Policy toward Africa South of the Sahara," 23 August 1957, WHO, OSANSA, NSC Series, Policy Papers Subseries, box 21, DDEL.

65. John Gunther, *Inside Africa* (New York: Harper and Brothers, 1955), 4 (quotation), 587; National Intelligence Estimates 83, "Conditions and Trends in Tropical Africa," 22 December 1953, *FRUS, 1952–54*, 11:71–89; CIA, "Major U.S. Interests in Africa," 22 March 1954, *FRUS, 1952–54*, 11:107; Allen to Dulles, 12

August 1955, *FRUS, 1955–57*, 18:16; NSC 5719/1, 23 August 1957; Elsie May Bell Grosvenor, "Safari through Changing Africa," *National Geographic* 104 (August 1953): 145–198.

66. Dean to Dulles, 16 February 1953, *FRUS, 1952–54*, 2:1098; Office of Special Assistant to the Joint Chiefs of Staff for NSC Affairs, "Africa," 19 March 1954, ibid., 103; Harr to McCone, 14 October 1960, enclosing Johnson memo, WHO, OSANSA, OCB Series, Subject Subseries, box 1, folder "Africa," DDEL; Jonathan E. Helmreich, "U.S. Foreign Policy and the Belgian Congo in the 1950s," *Historian* 58 (Winter 1996): 316; Gunther, *Inside Africa*, 669–678.

67. Hadsel to Byroade, 3 August 1956, enclosing "U.S. Policy toward South Africa," *FRUS, 1955–57*, 18:788–790 (quotation); Wailes to State Department, 6 August 1956, ibid., 791; editorial footnote, ibid., 791; minutes of U.S. delegation to UN meeting, 25 October 1955, ibid., 778.

68. Sears to Dulles, 15 February 1956, *FRUS, 1955–57*, 18:31 ("police state"); Operations Coordinating Board, "Report on Africa South of the Sahara," 30 September 1959, WHO, OSANSA, NSC Series, Policy Papers Subseries, box 25, folder NSC 5818 ("retrogressive"); Crowe to State Department, 27 April 1959, *FRUS, 1958–60*, 14:732–733; Gallman to State Department, 2 March 1953, *FRUS, 1952–54*, 11:989–994.

69. Dulles to Gallman, 21 April 1953, *FRUS, 1952–54*, 11:995–996; Gallman to State Department, 2 March 1953, ibid., 989–992; Frederickson, *Black Liberation*, 266–267 (quotation). The USSR had officially outlawed racial discrimination soon after the Bolshevik Revolution.

70. Gunther, *Inside Africa*, 521.

71. David N. Gibbs, "Political Parties and International Relations: The United States and the Decolonization of Sub-Saharan Africa," *International History Review* 17 (May 1995): 314–315; Minter, *King Solomon's Mines Revisited*, 134–135 (quotation; emphasis added); Harold R. Isaacs, "Western Man and the African Crisis," *Saturday Review*, 2 May 1953, 10.

72. NSC 5719/1, 23 August 1957; Henry A. Byroade, "The World's Colonies and Ex-Colonies," *Department of State Bulletin*, 16 November 1953, 657–659; Crawford Young, "United States Policy Toward Africa: Silver Anniversary Reflections," *African Studies Review* 27 (September 1984): 2–4; Steven Metz, "American Attitudes toward Decolonization in Africa," *Political Science Quarterly* 99 (Fall 1984): 520–528; Staniland, *American Intellectuals*, 25; Helmreich, "U.S. Foreign Policy," 316–325.

73. Byroade address, 31 October 1953, *FRUS, 1952–54*, 11:54–65 (also printed as Byroade, "World's Colonies"); George V. Allen, "United States Foreign Policy in Africa," *Department of State Bulletin*, 30 April 1956, 716–718; Metz, "American Attitudes," 519–521; Waldemar A. Nielsen, *The Great Powers and Africa*

(New York: Praeger, 1969), 259–263; Vernon McKay, *Africa in World Politics* (New York: Harper and Row, 1963), 320–323.

74. Nixon, "Report to the President on Trip to Africa," 5 April 1957, AWF, Administrative Series, box 28, DDEL; Colin Legum, *Must We Lose Africa?* (London: W. H. Allen, 1954); Bowles, *Africa's Challenge*, 1–2; Gunther, *Inside Africa*, 3.

75. Bowles, *Africa's Challenge*, 49; Allen to Dulles, 12 August 1955, *FRUS, 1955–57*, 18:20; Byroade, "World's Colonies," 660; Gunther, *Inside Africa*, 14–15; Helmreich, "U.S. Foreign Policy," 315; Noer, *Cold War and Black Liberation*, 48; Nielsen, *Great Powers*, 274–277; Metz, "American Attitudes," 520–525; Cary Fraser, *Ambivalent Anti-Colonialism: The United States and the Genesis of West Indian Independence, 1940–1964* (Westport, Conn.: Greenwood, 1994), 28–29.

76. Feld memo, 17 August 1953, *FRUS, 1952–54*, 11:48; Anthony Low, "The End of the British Empire in Africa," in *Decolonization and African Independence: The Transfers of Power, 1960–1980*, ed. Prosser Gifford and Wm. Roger Louis (New Haven: Yale University Press, 1988), 43, 54–55; Gunther, *Inside Africa*, 358, 373; Staniland, *American Intellectuals*, 187–188; Stephen E. Ambrose, *Nixon: The Education of a Politician, 1913–1962* (New York: Simon and Schuster, 1987), 433.

77. Sears to Dulles, 15 February 1956, *FRUS, 1955–57*, 18:35–36 (quotations); Mallon to State Department, 19 January 1953, *FRUS, 1952–54* 11:30–31; Isaacs, "Western Man," 56; Bowles, *Africa's Challenge*, 47–48, 73, 81.

78. Operations Coordinating Board, "Report on Africa South of the Sahara (NSC 5719/1)," 21 March 1958, WHO, OSANSA, NSC Series, Policy Papers Subseries, box 21, DDEL; Jernegan to Lourie, 19 June 1953, *FRUS, 1952–54*, 11:325; Tibbetts to State Department, 30 July 1953, *FRUS, 1952–54*, 11:329; Byroade, "World's Colonies," 658; Steere to Utter, 22 October 1954, *FRUS, 1952–54*, 11:344–345; Prosser Gifford, "Misconceived Dominion: The Creation and Disintegration of Federation in British Central Africa," in *The Transfer of Power in Africa: Decolonization, 1940–1960*, ed. Gifford and Wm. Roger Louis (New Haven: Yale University Press, 1982), 396–400; Robert I. Rotberg, *The Rise of Nationalism in Central Africa: The Making of Malawi and Zambia, 1873–1964* (Cambridge, Mass.: Harvard University Press, 1965), 255–258, 292–310; Robert C. Good, *U.D.I.: The International Politics of the Rhodesian Rebellion* (Princeton: Princeton University Press, 1973), 30–32; Gunther, *Inside Africa*, 632–636 ("this country").

79. Ndabaningi Sithole, *African Nationalism* (Cape Town: Oxford University Press, 1959), 28, 36, 38 (quotation), 49; National Intelligence Estimates 76–59, "The Outlook in East, Central, and South Africa," 20 October 1959, *FRUS, 1958–60*, 14:63 (CIA); National Intelligence Estimates 72–56, "Conditions and Trends in Tropical Africa," 14 August 1956, *FRUS, 1955–57*, 18:45–46; Holmes to Dulles, 6 February 1958, *FRUS, 1958–60*, 14:8.

80. Memo of Nkrumah conversation with Nixon, 4 March 1957, *FRUS, 1955–57*, 18:376; Rotberg, *Rise of Nationalism*, 283; Branch, *Parting the Waters*, 214; Morrow, *Black Man*, 133.

81. Kwame Nkrumah, *The Autobiography of Kwame Nkrumah* (Edinburgh: Thomas Nelson, 1957), 24–34, 42–43 (quotation); Robin McKown, *Nkrumah: A Biography* (Garden City, N.Y.: Doubleday, 1973), 32–33; Adu Boahen, "Ghana since Independence," in *Decolonization and African Independence: The Transfers of Power, 1960–1980*, ed. Prosser Gifford and Wm. Roger Louis (New Haven: Yale University Press, 1988), 203–224. The other independent states on the continent in 1957 were South Africa (white-ruled), Ethiopia (not successfully colonized), Liberia (widely viewed as a pseudocolony of the United States), and Egypt, Morocco, Tunisia, Libya, and the Sudan (all predominantly Arab rather than black African).

82. Low, "End of British Empire," 55 (Macmillan), 57, 71; Rupert Emerson, *From Empire to Nation: The Rise to Self-Assertion of Asian and African Peoples* (Cambridge, Mass.: Harvard University Press, 1960), 5; McKay, *Africa*, 1, 11–12, 339.

83. Felix Belair, Jr., "United States Has Secret Sonic Weapon—Jazz," *New York Times*, 6 November 1955, 1; "Jazz Program on 'Voice' to Get World Booking," ibid., 2 April 1956, 17; "Jazz, Surgery Aid U.S. in Pakistan," ibid., 8 April 1956, 31; Bowles, *Africa's Challenge*, 127; McKay, *Africa*, 383; Penny M. Von Eschen, "'Satchmo Blows Up the World': Jazz, Race, and Empire during the Cold War," unpublished manuscript in author's possession; Dizzy Gillespie, *Dizzy: To Be or Not to Bop: The Autobiography of Dizzy Gillespie* (London: Quartet, 1982), 413–421 (quotations at 413, 421). I am grateful to Matt Abramovitz for bringing these newspaper citations to my attention. For examples of black speakers abroad, see Asa T. Spaulding statement, "Discrimination and the Negro in the United States," New Delhi, India, 26 November 1956, Staff Files, Administrative Officer for Special Projects (Morrow), box 11, folder "Inter-Racial Affairs," DDEL, and Rowan, *Pitiful and Proud*, passim.

84. Gary Giddins, *Satchmo* (New York: Doubleday, 1988), 159–163; Gillespie, *Dizzy*, 437–438; Lodge to Eisenhower, 28 March 1956, AWF, Dulles-Herter Series, box 6, folder "Dulles, John Foster-March 1956," DDEL. Lodge cited the case of his recent trip to Khartoum with his wife as an example: after a long state dinner ending at 1:00 A.M., they resisted weariness and agreed to the Sudanese foreign minister's suggestion to visit a nightclub. "It was an effort, but the Foreign Minister (who was coal black) danced with my wife and I heard later from our U.S. representative that the word went all over town that the Americans were not stuffy." The reaction of white American diplomats and officials who were not so "temperamentally inclined"—especially those from the South—can readily be imagined.

85. Memo of NSC meeting, 8 August 1958, AWF, NSC Series, box 10, DDEL (quotations); Nixon, "Report to the President," 5 April 1957, AWF, Administrative Series, box 28, DDEL; U.S. Congress, House of Representatives, Committee on Foreign Affairs, *Report of the Special Study Mission to Africa, South and East of the Sahara by Honorable Frances P. Bolton* (Washington: Government Printing Office, 1956), especially 12, 147; McKay, *Africa,* 342–346; Nielsen, *Great Powers,* 266–270. Some of Nixon's colleagues in the administration considered him the "father" of the new, friendlier American policy that was developing in response to African independence. See, for example, memo of NSC meeting, 23 August 1957, AWF, NSC Series, box 9, DDEL.

86. NSC 5818, "Statement of U.S. Policy toward Africa," 26 August 1958, *FRUS, 1958–60,* 14:25; CIA, Annex B to NSC 5818, 29 December 1958, enclosed in Smith to Lay, 20 January 1959, WHO, OSANSA, NSC Series, Policy Papers Subseries, box 25, DDEL; Hoover to Consulate General in Accra, 20 February 1956, *FRUS, 1955–57,* 18:362–364; John D. Hargreaves, *Decolonization in Africa* (London: Longman, 1988), 209–210; Young, "United States Policy," 1; McKay, *Africa,* 342. In a 1960 NSC meeting CIA chief Allen Dulles expressed his concern that the lower living standards of Chinese and even Eastern European technicians gave them an advantage in Africa over Americans accustomed to much greater material comforts. Dulles worried that the Eastern bloc workers' spirits might be higher in the poverty-stricken conditions of most of the continent, and that Africans would be impressed by this difference. See editorial note, *FRUS, 1958–60,* 14:708.

87. Lodge to State Department, 20 November 1957, *FRUS, 1955–57,* 18:834; Byroade to State Department, 7 November 1958, *FRUS, 1958–60,* 14:730–731; editorial footnotes and note, *FRUS, 1958–60,* 14:731, 739. For an example of the administration's awareness of the brutalities of apartheid for the majority of South Africans, see Walmsley to Herter, 9 July 1958, *FRUS, 1958–60,* 14:727–729.

88. Memo of NSC meeting, 9 May 1958, AWF, NSC Series, box 10, DDEL ("Spirit of 1776"); Jackson to Dulles, 9 February 1959, Dulles Papers, General Correspondence and Memoranda Series, box 2 ("juvenile delinquencies"); "National Security Implications of Future Developments Regarding Africa," enclosed in Boggs to NSC, 10 August 1960, WHO, OSANSA, NSC Series, Policy Paper Subseries, box 28, DDEL ("contagion"); Gibbs, "Political Parties," 314 ("serious and unnecessary"); memo of NSC meeting, 31 March 1960, AWF, NSC Series, box 12, DDEL (Nixon and Stans).

89. McGregor memo, 28 December 1955, *FRUS, 1955–57,* 18:26–27; memo of NSC meeting, 9 May 1958, AWF, NSC Series, box 10, DDEL; "The Kingdom of Silence: The Truth about Africa's Most Oppressed Colony," *Harper's,* May 1961,

31–32 ("have worked together"); Benjamin Welles, "Eisenhower Hails Portugal's Gains," *New York Times,* 21 May 1960, 3.

90. Ann Whitman diary, 10 October 1957, AWF, Ann Whitman Diary Series, box 9, DDEL; Eisenhower to Gallin-Douathe, 14 November 1960, AWF, International Series, box 6, folder "Central African Republic," DDEL; Dulles to U.S. Embassy in Ghana, 9 October 1957, *FRUS, 1955–57,* 18:378–379; John H. Morrow, *First American Ambassador to Guinea* (New Brunswick: Rutgers University Press, 1968), 101–102; Isaacs, *The New World of Negro Americans,* 16; Morrow, *Black Man,* 175; Rowan, *Pitiful and Proud,* 157; McKay, *Africa,* 402–403.

91. Goldman, "Significance of African Freedom," 6; Morris et al. to Eisenhower, 19 January 1960, WHCF, General File, box 44, folder "Civil Rights—Civil Liberties (14)," DDEL.

92. Crowe to State Department, 30 March 1960, *FRUS, 1958–60,* 14:747–748; memo of NSC meeting, 2 April 1960, AWF, NSC Series, box 12, DDEL; James Barber and John Barratt, *South Africa's Foreign Policy: The Search for Status and Security, 1945–1988* (Cambridge: Cambridge University Press, 1990), 70.

93. Editorial note, *FRUS, 1958–60,* 14:741 (State Department, Eisenhower, Herter); memo of conversation, 28 March 1960, ibid., 746 (Eisenhower to Macmillan); Crowe to State Department, 25 March 1960, ibid., 743–745.

94. Memo of NSC meeting, 24 March 1960, AWF, NSC Series, box 12, DDEL; NSC 6001, "Statement of U.S. Policy toward South, Central, and East Africa," 19 January 1960, *FRUS, 1958–60,* 14:86; National Intelligence Estimates 73–60, "The Outlook for the Union of South Africa," 19 July 1960, *FRUS, 1958–60,* 14:754–755; Hare to Williams, 19 August 1960, *FRUS, 1958–60,* 14:755–756; George M. Houser, *No One Can Stop the Rain: Glimpses of Africa's Liberation Struggle* (New York: Pilgrim Press, 1989), 88 (Mboya).

95. Burden to State Department, 10 July 1960, *FRUS, 1958–60,* 14:287; Minter, *King Solomon's Mines Revisited,* 147.

96. McIlvaine to State Department, 26 July 1960, *FRUS, 1958–60,* 14:356–357 ("an opportunist"); Tomlinson to State Department, 14 June 1960, ibid., 276 ("no better alternative"); Cumming to Herter, 25 July 1960, ibid., 356; memo of NSC meeting, 21 July 1960, ibid., 338–339 ("a Castro"); Timberlake to State Department, 16 September 1960, ibid., 491; Timberlake to State Department, 26 September 1960, ibid., 504; Richard D. Mahoney, *JFK: Ordeal in Africa* (New York: Oxford University Press, 1983), 40–50. A 26 August 1960 cable from Allen Dulles instructed the CIA station chief in Leopoldville that Lumumba's "removal must be an urgent and prime objective and . . . should be a high priority of our covert actions." Dulles cited "high quarters here" as the source of this "clearcut conclusion"—and the CIA director's only superior is the president. Editorial note, *FRUS, 1958–60,* 14:443. In a 19 September 1960

conversation with the British foreign secretary Lord Home that touched on the Congo, Eisenhower (according to notes of the meeting made by his son John) "expressed his wish that Lumumba would fall into a river of crocodiles; Lord Home said regretfully that we have lost many of the techniques of old-fashioned diplomacy." Despite his differences with the British over Suez, Eisenhower was perhaps more "old-fashioned" in this regard than his allies realized. Editorial note, *FRUS, 1958–60*, 14:495. For the best study to date of the U.S. role in the Congo, see David N. Gibbs, *The Political Economy of Third World Intervention: Mines, Money, and U.S. Policy in the Congo Crisis* (Chicago: University of Chicago Press, 1991).

97. Mahoney, *JFK*, 39 (Lumumba); *Time*, 16 May 1955, quoted in Staniland, *American Intellectuals*, 218; Crawford Young, "The Colonial State and Post-Colonial Africa," in *Decolonization and African Independence: The Transfers of Power, 1960–1980*, ed. Prosser Gifford and Wm. Roger Louis (New Haven: Yale University Press, 1988), 20–22.

98. Editorial footnotes, *FRUS, 1958–60*, 14:359 (Lodge), 366; Mahoney, *JFK*, 43.

99. Editorial footnote and notes, *FRUS, 1958–60*, 14:367 (Dillon), 528 (Hammarskjold), 354 (Bunche), 490 (Allen Dulles); memo of conversation, 11 October 1960, ibid., 522 (Wigny); Burden to State Department, 10 July 1960, ibid., 289.

100. Lewis, *Portrait of a Decade*, 162 (Perez); Mahoney, *JFK*, 38–39 (State Department).

101. Memo of NSC meeting, 18 August 1960, *FRUS, 1958–60*, 14:422–424 (Stans); Board of National Estimates to Allen Dulles, 22 August 1960, ibid., 439; Mahoney, *JFK*, 39.

102. Ilunga Kabongo, "The Catastrophe of Belgian Decolonization," in *Decolonization and African Independence: The Transfers of Power, 1960–1980*, ed. Prosser Gifford and Wm. Roger Louis (New Haven: Yale University Press, 1988), 388–389 (blackboard); Timberlake to State Department, 17 July 1960, *FRUS, 1958–60*, 14:318–319; Herter to Consul General in Leopoldville, 23 June 1960, ibid., 277–278; transcript of telephone conversations, Herter and Hammarskjold, and Eisenhower and Herter, ibid., 296–297; McIlvaine to State Department, 26 July 1960, ibid., 356–357; memo of conversation, 5 August 1960, ibid., 387. Allen Dulles also worried about the white South African response to the disorder in the Congo, especially the possibility of an alliance with Southern Rhodesia and the Portuguese colonies to create "a *cordon sanitaire*" across southern Africa for the containment of African self-rule. Memo of NSC meeting, 1 August 1960, *FRUS, 1958–60*, 14:376.

103. Paterson, *Confronting Castro*, 241 (Dulles); Hunt, *Ideology and U.S. Foreign Policy*, 166–167; Carlos Moore, *Castro, the Blacks, and Africa* (Los Angeles:

Center for Afro-American Studies, University of California, 1988), 59–63; Plummer, *Rising Wind*, 288–289.

104. Max Frankel, "Castro Stays in Hotel to Work Privately as Aides Take Up Fight before U.N.," *New York Times*, 22 September 1960, 14; Moore, *Castro*, 71–91; Plummer, *Rising Wind*, 289–297; Isaacs, *The New World of Negro Americans*, 337; Mary-Alice Waters, "Appendix: Fidel Castro's Arrival in Harlem," in Fidel Castro and Ernesto Che Guevara, *To Speak the Truth: Why Washington's 'Cold War' against Cuba Doesn't End* (New York: Pathfinder, 1992), 201–205; Van Gosse, "The African-American Press Greets the Cuban Revolution," in *Between Race and Empire: African-Americans and Cubans before the Cuban Revolution*, ed. Lisa Brock and Digna Castañeda Fuertes (Philadelphia: Temple University Press, 1998), 266–280.

105. In 1963 John Kennedy invited Eisenhower to endorse his legislative proposals for civil rights. The retired president declined, claiming that a "whole bunch of laws" were not the solution to the problem. Mark Stern, *Calculating Visions: Kennedy, Johnson, and Civil Rights* (New Brunswick: Rutgers University Press, 1992), 87. In 1966 Eisenhower passed along propaganda in support of apartheid to Clifford Roberts, the chairman of the Augusta National Golf Club, to which he attached a note: "Dear Clif, We hear so much misinformation about South Africa, I thought you might like to read this letter from the Ambassador of that nation." O'Reilly, *Nixon's Piano*, 187.

### 4. Revolutions in the American South and Southern Africa

1. Rusk to U.S. Embassy in South Africa, *FRUS, 1961–63*, 21:611.
2. ANC flyer, "Announcement of the Formation of Umkhonto we Sizwe," 16 December 1961, in *Mandela, Tambo, and the African National Congress—The Struggle against Apartheid, 1948–1990: A Documentary Survey*, ed. Sheridan Johns and R. Hunt Davis (New York: Oxford University Press, 1991), 138–139; CIA, "The Addis Ababa Conference and Its Aftermath," 11 July 1963, NSF, box 3, JFKL. Like the other Cold War, this one could also turn hot—as it did in Angola. On the support from the rest of Africa for southern African struggles against white rule, see Korry to Rusk, 25 May 1963, NSF, box 3, JFKL.
3. State Department paper, "Problems of Southern Africa," 25 March 1963, *FRUS, 1961–63*, 21:495; memorandum of conversation, 17 July 1963, ibid., 639.
4. Schlesinger to Robert Kennedy, 1 July 1963, ibid., 497; notes 1, 2, ibid., 612; Gerald E. Thomas, "The Black Revolt: The United States and Africa in the 1960s," in *The Diplomacy of the Crucial Decade: American Foreign Relations during the 1960s*, ed. Diane B. Kunz (New York: Columbia University Press, 1994), 324–325; Thomas J. Noer, "New Frontiers and Old Priorities in Africa," in *Kennedy's Quest for Victory: American Foreign Policy, 1961–1963*, ed. Thomas

G. Paterson (New York: Oxford University Press, 1989), 253–283; Lawson, *Running for Freedom*, 80.

5. James N. Giglio, *The Presidency of John F. Kennedy* (Lawrence: University of Kansas Press, 1991), 159–160; Gerald S. Strober and Deborah H. Strober, *"Let Us Begin Anew": An Oral History of the Kennedy Presidency* (New York: HarperCollins, 1993), 274; Richard Reeves, *President Kennedy: Profile of Power* (New York: Simon and Schuster, 1993), 62, 313–314.

6. J. Richard Snyder, "Introduction," in *John F. Kennedy: Person, Policy, Presidency*, ed. Snyder (Wilmington, Del.: Scholarly Resources, 1988), x; Branch, *Parting the Waters*, 687. Truman's significant support for civil rights as president and political ties to African American leaders did not preclude the private use of racial epithets indicative of more traditional white attitudes. Kennedy told White House aide Daniel Patrick Moynihan at one point, for example, "I can't get used to Harry Truman talking all the time about 'the niggers.'" Reeves, *President Kennedy*, 61–62.

7. Thomas C. Reeves, *A Question Of Character: A Life of John F. Kennedy* (New York: Free Press, 1991), 335–338; Herbert S. Parmet, *Jack: The Struggles of John F. Kennedy* (New York: Dial, 1980), 408–416; Giglio, *The Presidency of John F. Kennedy*, 160.

8. Brubeck to Bundy, 29 October 1963, NSF, boxes 158–161, folder "South Africa, General, 9/30/63–10/29/63," JFKL; Komer to Kennedy, 13 October 1962, *FRUS, 1961–63*, 21:102; Ronald J. Nurse, "Critic of Colonialism: JFK and Algerian Independence," *The Historian* 39 (February 1977): 307–326; Parmet, *Jack*, 399–416; Giglio, *The Presidency of John F. Kennedy*, 14, 221–223. After his much heralded 1957 Senate speech criticizing French colonialism in Algeria, for example, Kennedy subsequently muted his public comments on the subject, telling aides that he was "wary of being known as the Senator from Algeria." Parmet, *Jack*, 407.

9. Wofford, *Of Kennedys and Kings*, 133; Branch, *Parting the Waters*, 398, 808–809; Reeves, *President Kennedy*, 61–62.

10. Gary W. Reichard, "Democrats, Civil Rights, and Electoral Strategies in the 1950s," *Congress and the Presidency* 13 (Spring 1986): 59–81; Stern, *Calculating Visions*, 31–38; Burk, *Eisenhower Administration*, 258–260; Wofford, *Of Kennedys and Kings*, 25, 51–52, 61–63; Richard N. Goodwin, *Remembering America: A Voice from the Sixties* (Boston: Little, Brown, 1988), 136; Morrow, *Black Man*, 280–282.

11. Mahoney, *JFK*, 26–33, 52; Clifford M. Kuhn, "'There's a Footnote to History!': Martin Luther King's October 1960 Arrest and Its Aftermath," *Journal of American History* 84 (September 1997): 583–595; Lawson, *Running for Freedom*, 75–79; Wofford, *Of Kennedys and Kings*, 40–41; Parmet, *Jack*, 249–250.

12. Douglas Dales, "Candidates Urge End to Bias in U.S.," *New York Times,* 13 October 1960, 26; Wofford, *Of Kennedys and Kings,* 21.

13. Wofford, *Of Kennedys and Kings,* 67; Andrew Young, OHT, p. 23, LBJL; O'Reilly, *"Racial Matters,"* 102–103, 114, 126–131, 137, 150–151; Branch, *Parting the Waters,* 646, 692, 836, 902–906.

14. Reeves, *President Kennedy,* 270–271, 325, 466–468, 579; Victor S. Navasky, *Kennedy Justice* (New York: Atheneum, 1971), 244–248; Parmet, *JFK,* 251; Dittmer, *Local People,* 194–195; Giglio, *The Presidency of John F. Kennedy,* 37.

15. Randall Bennett Woods, *Fulbright: A Biography* (New York: Cambridge University Press, 1995), 252–260; J. William Fulbright, *The Price of Empire* (New York: Pantheon, 1989), 69; Richard N. Goodwin, *Remembering America: A Voice from the Sixties* (Boston: Little, Brown, 1988), 136; Wofford, *Of Kennedys and Kings,* 81–82; Steel, *Walter Lippman,* 523; Merle Miller, *Lyndon: An Oral Biography* (New York: G. P. Putnam's, 1980), 274–275.

16. Thomas J. Schoenbaum, *Waging Peace and War: Dean Rusk in the Truman, Kennedy, and Johnson Years* (New York: Simon and Schuster, 1988), 25, 242, 382–383 (quotations).

17. Isaacs, *The New World of Negro Americans,* 19 (quotation), 316.

18. Belk to Bundy, 17 July 1962, NSF, box 2, folder "Africa, General (6/62–7/62)," JFKL; Mahoney, *JFK,* 27.

19. Wofford to Kennedy, 17 July 1961, and Bowles to Kennedy, 21 August 1961, in President's Office Files, box 28, JFKL.

20. Noer, "New Frontiers and Old Priorities," 265 (Ball); Komer to Kennedy, 14 October 1963, *FRUS, 1961–63,* 21:11; Bundy to McNamara, 1 December 1962, *FRUS, 1961–63,* 21:153. It is not hard to imagine royal advisers in London in the 1790s referring to newly independent Americans as oversensitive. There is about the term, in this usage, a note of disdain for the dignity of the less powerful.

21. Bowles to Kennedy, 1 December 1962, President's Office Files, box 28, JFKL.

22. Belk to Bundy, 19 May 1961, NSF, box 2, JFKL.

23. Quoted in Branch, *Parting the Waters,* 477.

24. Elizabeth A. Cobbs, "Decolonization, the Cold War, and the Foreign Policy of the Peace Corps," *Diplomatic History* 20 (Winter 1996): 105. See also Elizabeth Cobbs Hoffman, *All You Need Is Love: The Peace Corps and the Spirit of the 1960s* (Cambridge, Mass.: Harvard University Press, 1998).

25. Wofford, *Of Kennedys and Kings,* 44–45.

26. Dean Rusk, "Building the Frontiers of Freedom," *Department of State Bulletin,* 17 June 1961, 948; Komer to Bundy, 14 October 1963, *FRUS, 1961–63,* 21:128; Gary R. Hess, "Commitment in the Age of Counterinsurgency: Kennedy's Vietnam Options and Decisions, 1961–1963," in *Shadow on the White House:*

*Presidents and the Vietnam War, 1945–1975,* ed. David L. Anderson (Lawrence: University of Kansas Press, 1993), 63; Mahoney, *JFK*, 188.

27. Wofford, *Of Kennedys and Kings,* 256.

28. "The White Redoubt," 28 June 1962, enclosed in Owen to McGhee et al., 6 July 1962, NSF, box 2, JFKL.

29. Chang, *Friends and Enemies,* 236; Marilyn B. Young, *The Vietnam Wars, 1945–1990* (New York: HarperCollins, 1991), 76.

30. Robert Buzzanco, *Masters of War: Military Dissent and Politics in the Vietnam Era* (New York: Cambridge University Press, 1996), 107.

31. Moore, *Castro, the Blacks, and Africa,* 93–94, 108–111. See also Thomas G. Paterson, *Confronting Castro,* and Paterson, "Fixation with Cuba: The Bay of Pigs, Missile Crisis, and Covert War against Castro," in *Kennedy's Quest for Victory: American Foreign Policy, 1961–1963,* ed. Paterson, (New York: Oxford University Press, 1989), 123–155.

32. Moore, *Castro, the Blacks, and Africa,* 129–135, 332; Mahoney, *JFK*, 31.

33. Komer to Kennedy, 15 July 1963, *FRUS, 1961–63,* 21:123; Komer to Bundy, 1 November 1963, ibid., 33.

34. Moore, *Castro, the Blacks, and Africa,* 112–114; Attwood, *The Reds and the Blacks,* 27.

35. Tyson, "Radio Free Dixie," 290–291; Moore, *Castro, the Blacks, and Africa,* 113, 121–122.

36. Plummer, *Rising Wind,* 305; Moore, *Castro, the Blacks, and Africa,* 112.

37. Moore, *Castro, the Blacks, and Africa,* 114.

38. Paterson, "Fixation with Cuba."

39. For recent summaries of this perspective, see Noer, "New Frontiers and Old Priorities," and David A. Dickson, "U.S. Foreign Policy toward Southern and Central Africa: The Kennedy and Johnson Years," *Presidential Studies Quarterly* 23 (Spring 1993): 301–315.

40. Rusk to Kennedy, 9 September 1961, enclosing report of Williams trip to Africa, NSF, box 2, JFKL; "Summary of Governor Williams' Trip to Africa," 25 September 1961," *FRUS, 1961–63,* 21:302–303; memorandum of conversation, 19 July 1963, *FRUS, 1961–63,* 21:420–423; Bowles to Kaysen, 13 November 1962, NSF, box 3, JFKL; Elizabeth Cobbs Hoffman, "Diplomatic History and the Meaning of Life: Toward a Global American History," *Diplomatic History* 21 (Fall 1997): 517; Mahoney, *JFK*, 20–33, 248; Henry F. Jackson, *From the Congo to Soweto: U.S. Foreign Policy toward Africa since 1960* (New York: William Morrow, 1982), 38–39; Roger Hilsman, *To Move a Nation: The Politics of Foreign Policy in the Administration of John F. Kennedy* (Garden City, N.Y.: Doubleday, 1967), 246.

41. Rusk to Williams, 25 February 1961, and Williams to Rusk, 26 February 1961,

in NSF, box 2, JFKL; note 5, *FRUS, 1961–63*, 21:347; Robert Kinloch Massie, *Loosing the Bonds: The United States and South Africa in the Apartheid Years* (New York: Doubleday, 1997), 115 (quotation); Cobbs, "Decolonization," 105; Richard J. Walton, *Cold War and Counterrevolution: The Foreign Policy of John F. Kennedy* (Baltimore: Viking, 1972), 206.

42. "The Strategic Importance of Africa," undated [c. May 1963], *FRUS, 1961–63*, 21:331; Dickson, "U.S. Foreign Policy," 304–305; Wofford, *Of Kennedys and Kings*, 380–381. Trade with Africa in 1960 constituted only 3–4 percent of total U.S. exports and imports, a point Europeanists liked to emphasize. Brinkley, *Dean Acheson*, 305. Richard Reeves's careful study of the daily course of Kennedy's presidency reveals how little attention the president and his most senior advisers usually paid to African issues. Reeves, *President Kennedy*, passim.

43. State Department, "Africa: Guidelines for Policy and Operations," March 1962, NSF, box 2, JFKL.

44. Williams to Rusk, 12 June 1963, NSF, box 3, JFKL; Rusk to certain African posts, 28 May 1963, *FRUS, 1961–63*, 21:332–334; Lauren, *Power and Prejudice*, 218–219.

45. Satterthwaite et al. to Williams, undated [September 1961], NSF, box 2, JFKL.

46. National Intelligence Estimates 60/70–2–61, "The Probable Interrelationships of the Independent African States," 31 August 1961, *FRUS, 1961–63*, 21:299–300.

47. Plummer, *Rising Wind*, 308.

48. Brubeck to Bundy, 29 October 1963, *FRUS, 1961–63*, 21:505–507.

49. Attwood, *The Reds and the Blacks*, 47; Wofford, *Of Kennedys and Kings*, 371.

50. Murrow to Bundy, 5 December 1962, *FRUS, 1961–63*, 21:325.

51. Freund to Rusk, 3 December 1962, and Rusk, Circular 1032, 4 December 1962, in NSF, box 3, folder "Africa, General (11/62–12/62)," JFKL; *Department of State Bulletin*, 24 December 1962, 961.

52. Geren to Rusk, 5 December 1962, NSF, box 155A, JFKL. Ellender repeated his attacks on the capacity of Africans for self-government in televised remarks on 16 June 1963, eliciting an angry response from several African ambassadors. Little to Bundy, 25 June 1963, NSF, box 3, JFKL.

53. "Problems of Southern Africa," 4 October 1962, enclosed in Rostow to members of Tuesday Planning Group, 18 October 1962, NSF, box 2, JFKL.

54. "The White Redoubt," 28 June 1962, enclosed in Owen to McGhee et al., 6 July 1962, NSF, box 2, JFKL. Roy Welensky was the prime minister of the Central African Federation, consisting until 1963 of Southern Rhodesia, Northern Rhodesia (Zambia), and Nyasaland (Malawi); Hendrik Verwoerd was the prime minister of South Africa; and Antonio Salazar was the president of Portugal.

55. Mandela, "Address to Conference of the Pan-African Freedom Movement of East and Central Africa," January 1962, Addis Ababa, in *Mandela, Tambo, and the African National Congress—The Struggle against Apartheid, 1948–1990: A Documentary Survey,* ed. Sheridan Johns and R. Hunt Davis (New York: Oxford University Press, 1991), 106–111.

56. Rusk to U.S. Consulate General in Salisbury, 30 November 1962, *FRUS, 1961–63,* 21:523; Ball to U.S. Embassy in United Kingdom, 7 January 1963, ibid., 524.

57. Williams to Rusk, 25 February 1963, ibid., 329.

58. "The White Redoubt," NSF, box 2, JFKL.

59. Stevenson to Rusk, 21 August 1963, NSF, boxes 158–161, JFKL.

60. "Problems of Southern Africa," NSF, box 2, JFKL.

61. "The White Redoubt," NSF, box 2, JFKL.

62. McNamara to Rusk, 11 July 1963, reprinted in *South Africa and the United States: The Declassified History,* ed. Kenneth Mokoena (New York: New Press, 1993), 62–63; State Department, "Guidelines for Policy and Operations: Republic of South Africa," May 1962, NSF, box 2, JFKL; memorandum of conversation, 21 August 1963, *FRUS, 1961–63,* 21:492–493; Williams to Rusk, 23 November 1963, *FRUS, 1961–63,* 21:339.

63. For examples, see memorandum of conversation, 7 November 1963, *FRUS, 1961–63,* 21:582–583; Rusk to Department of State, 6 October 1962, ibid., 621–622.

64. Brubeck to Bundy, 29 October 1963, NSF, boxes 158–161, JFKL.

65. A novel of unusual insights into this situation is Barbara Kingsolver, *The Poisonwood Bible* (New York: HarperFlamingo, 1998).

66. Noer, "New Frontiers and Old Priorities," 260–269.

67. Elbrick to Rusk, 11 December 1962, NSF, box 5, JFKL.

68. "Problems of Southern Africa," NSF, box 2, JFKL.

69. *New York Times,* 16 February 1961, 11; C. Eric Lincoln, "The Race Problem and International Relations," *New South* 21 (Fall 1966): 11; F. Chidozie Ogene, *Interest Groups and the Shaping of Foreign Policy: Four Case Studies of United States African Policy* (Lagos: Macmillan Nigeria, 1983), 32–33.

70. Gibbs, *Political Economy of Third World Intervention,* 122; Staniland, *American Intellectuals,* 236–243; Ogene, *Interest Groups and the Shaping of Foreign Policy,* 22–31; Noer, "New Frontiers and Old Priorities," 261–264. Katanga's American supporters sometimes slid over into explicit statements of racial prejudice about Congolese who did not agree with Tshombe. See, for example, Mahoney, *JFK,* 118.

71. Noer, "New Frontiers and Old Priorities," 266.

72. "Status Report of African Reactions to Civil Rights in the United States," 12

July 1963, NSF, box 295, JFKL; Minter, *King Solomon's Mines Revisited,* 146–150.

73. Williams to Rusk, 25 February 1963, *FRUS, 1961–63,* 21:328–329.

74. Mahoney, *JFK,* 136.

75. John Marcum, *The Angolan Revolution,* 2 vols. (Cambridge, Mass.: MIT Press, 1969–1978).

76. Stevenson to Kennedy, 26 April 1962, and Bowles to Kennedy, 4 June 1962, in NSF, boxes 154A–155, JFKL; Massie, *Loosing the Bonds,* 119; Noer, "New Frontiers and Old Priorities," 269–274; Mahoney, *JFK,* 188–189.

77. Bundy to Johnson, 28 July 1961, and Satterthwaite et al. to Williams, undated [September 1961], both in NSF, box 2, JFKL.

78. Hilsman to Bundy, 23 May 1961, *FRUS, 1961–63,* 21:543; Rusk to U.S. Embassy in Lisbon, 31 July 1961, NSF, box 5, JFKL; Rusk to U.S. Embassy in Congo, 5 October 1961, *FRUS, 1961–63,* 21:551–552; Mahoney, *JFK,* 190–204; Minter, *King Solomon's Mines Revisited,* 162; Noer, "New Frontiers and Old Priorities," 271.

79. Rusk to U.S. Embassy in Portugal, 23 April 1961, *FRUS, 1961–63,* 21:543 (quotation); Rusk to U.S. Embassy in Portugal, 11 August 1961, and Bundy to Kennedy, 31 August 1961, in NSF, box 5, JFKL; "The Kingdom of Silence"; Mahoney, *JFK,* 195.

80. Note 1, *FRUS, 1961–63,* 21:548.

81. Belk to Kennedy, 14 September 1961, ibid., 550.

82. Taft (for Williams) to Rusk, 16 August 1961, NSF, box 5, folder "Angola, General, 8/61–12/61," JFKL; report of Presidential Task Force on Portuguese Territories in Africa, 12 July 1961, NSF, box 5, JFKL; "The Kingdom of Silence," 30–31. One dissenting Portuguese colonial official had concluded that in Angola "only the dead are exempt from forced labor." Massie, *Loosing the Bonds,* 117.

83. Report of the Chairman of the Task Force on Portuguese Territories in Africa [Williams], 4 July 1961, enclosed in Belk to Bundy, 4 July 1961, NSF, box 5, JFKL. Ambassador William Attwood concisely explained the same point in a November 1961 speech to the Princeton Club of Washington: "The crisis in Berlin seems as remote to them [Africans] as Waterloo seemed remote to us 150 years ago." Attwood, *The Reds and the Blacks,* 60.

84. See, for example, Rusk to Johnson, 18 June 1961, *FRUS, 1961–63,* 21:544; Devine to Rusk, 19 February 1963, NSF, boxes 154A–155, JFKL.

85. Williams to Rusk, 23 October 1962, *FRUS, 1961–63,* 21:561.

86. Eldrick to Rusk, 11 July 1961, NSF, box 5, JFKL.

87. Rusk to U.S. Embassy in Lisbon, 23 August 1961, NSF, box 5, JFKL; CIA telegram, 31 January 1962, NSF, boxes 154A–155, JFKL; memorandum of conversa-

tion, 24 October 1962, *FRUS, 1961–63*, 21:562–563; Noer, *Cold War and Black Liberation*, 73; Brinkley, *Dean Acheson*, 307.

88. Quoted in Schoenbaum, *Waging Peace and War*, 376.

89. Belk to Dungan, 9 January 1962, NSF, box 2, JFKL; CIA, "Prospects for Nationalism and Revolt in Mozambique," 30 April 1963, NSF, box 3, JFKL. Tanganyika became Tanzania after merging with Zanzibar in 1964.

90. Hughes to Rusk, 5 November 1963, NSF, box 5, JFKL.

91. Stevenson to Kennedy, 26 April 1962, NSF, boxes 154A–155, JFKL; Noer, *Cold War and Black Liberation*, 75; Mahoney, *JFK*, 75.

92. Geren to Department of State, 25 October 1963, NSF, box 155A, JFKL.

93. Brinkley, *Dean Acheson*, 306–312, 389, n. 50 (quotation).

94. Bundy to Kennedy, 2 May 1962, NSF, boxes 154A–155, JFKL; note 1, *FRUS, 1961–63*, 21:562; Mahoney, *JFK*, 218–220. For samples of Kennedy's position, see Brubeck memorandum for the record, 15 July 1963, NSF, box 3, JFKL, and memorandums for the record, 18 July 1963 and 9 September 1963, *FRUS, 1961–63*, 21:573, 579.

95. Sorensen to Kennedy, 4 June 1962, NSF, boxes 154A–155, JFKL.

96. T. R. H. Davenport, *South Africa: A Modern History*, 3d ed. (Toronto: University of Toronto Press, 1987), 403–404; Joseph Lelyveld, *Move Your Shadow* (New York: Times Books, 1985), 327.

97. "The White Redoubt," NSF, box 2, JFKL.

98. Belk to Bundy, 11 July 1963, NSF, box 3, JFKL. On uranium in the earlier Cold War years, see Borstelmann, *Apartheid's Reluctant Uncle*.

99. Bundy to Gilpatric, 7 June 1961, *FRUS, 1961–63*, 21:595–597; Rusk to Kennedy, 16 March 1963, NSF, box 3, JFKL.

100. Belk to Bundy, 11 July 1963, NSF, box 3, JFKL; Hughes to Rusk, 12 August 1963, *FRUS, 1961–63*, 646–647. For further discussion of these issues, see Minter, *King Solomon's Mines Revisited*.

101. Bowles to Bundy, 21 September 1961, *FRUS, 1961–63*, 21:603–605; Stevenson to Rusk, 2 June 1961, ibid., 594. On the military importance of the tracking station, see Gilpatric to Bowles, 16 March 1961, ibid., 588–589; Brown to Deputy Assistant Secretary of Defense, 8 July 1963, NSF, box 3, JFKL.

102. See, for example, Rusk to U.S. Embassy in South Africa, 25 August 1961, *FRUS, 1961–63*, 21:598–600; Bowles to U.S. Embassy in South Africa, 28 September 1961, ibid., 605–606.

103. Memorandum of conversation, 20 November 1961, ibid., 615. See also Rusk to State Department, ibid., 620–622.

104. "Problems of Southern Africa," NSF, box 2, JFKL.

105. Allard Lowenstein, *Brutal Mandate: A Journey to South West Africa* (New York: Macmillan, 1962); William H. Chafe, *Never Stop Running: Allard Lowenstein*

*and the Struggle to Save American Liberalism* (New York: Basic Books, 1993), chap. 6, "The South Africa Years."

106. CIA, "The South-West Africa Issue in the United Nations," 19 April 1963, NSF, box 3, JFKL.

107. Satterthwaite to Rusk, 16 May 1963, NSF, box 3, JFKL.

108. Noer, "New Frontiers and Old Priorities," 277; Mahoney, *JFK*, 241–242; Christopher Coker, *The United States and South Africa, 1968–1985: Constructive Engagement and Its Critics* (Durham: Duke University Press, 1986), 27.

109. McKay, *Africa in World Politics*, 352; Noer, "New Frontiers and Old Priorities," 275.

110. Bundy to Kennedy, 13 July 1963, NSF, box 3, JFKL; Rusk to Harriman, 15 July 1963, *FRUS, 1961–63*, 21:635.

111. Rusk to U.S. Embassy in South Africa, 25 October 1961, *FRUS, 1961–63*, 21:611.

112. *Mandela, Tambo, and the African National Congress—The Struggle against Apartheid: A Documentary Survey*, ed. Sheridan Johns and R. Hunt Davis (New York: Oxford University Press, 1991), 89–90.

113. Satterthwaite to Rusk, 6 May 1963, enclosed in C. K. (Carl Kaysen) to Kennedy, 16 May 1963, NSF, box 3, JFKL.

114. Satterthwaite to Rusk, 18 December 1962, enclosing "Country Internal Defense Plan," NSF, box 3, JFKL.

115. Mandela, excerpt from courtroom statement, Rivonia trial, 20 April 1964, in Johns and Davis, *Mandela, Tambo, and the African National Congress*, 115–133. See also "The Communist Party in South Africa" [from *Africa Report*, March 1961], NSF, box 2, JFKL.

116. Massie, *Loosing the Bonds*, 129–132.

117. CIA, "Subversive Movements in South Africa," 10 May 1963, NSF, box 3, JFKL; Peter J. Schraeder, *United States Foreign Policy toward Africa: Incrementalism, Crisis, and Change* (New York: Cambridge University Press, 1994), 206; Minter, *King Solomon's Mines Revisited*, 192; Noer, *Cold War and Black Liberation*, 138–139. The supposedly coincidental timing of a visit to Durban by a U.S. naval task force on 31 May 1961, the day South Africa officially became an independent republic, was doubted by African observers. They tended instead to see U.S. marines demonstrating flame throwers and machine guns and U.S. helicopters flying over African neighborhoods as evidence of American support for the Pretoria government. Minter, *King Solomon's Mines Revisited*, 192.

118. Satterthwaite to State Department, 17 March 1962, *FRUS, 1961–63*, 618–619, esp. n. 4; Minter, *King Solomon's Mines Revisited*, 188.

119. CIA, "Subversive Movements in South Africa," NSF, box 3, JFKL. This docu-

ment has also been reprinted in Mokoena, *South Africa and the United States,* 188–194.

120. Joseph Albright and Marcia Kunstel, "CIA Tip Led to '62 Arrest of Mandela: Ex-Official Tells of US 'Coup' to Aid S. Africa," *Atlanta Journal and Constitution,* 10 June 1990, 1, 14.

121. Albright and Kunstel, "CIA Tip." Two days before the president's death, Robert Kennedy told Bundy that regarding black liberation fighters in South Africa, Southern Rhodesia, Angola, and Mozambique, "I gather that we really don't have much of a policy or we are just beginning to develop one." Such ignorance of the CIA's possible involvement in an area deemed peripheral seems perfectly plausible, despite Robert Kennedy's central role in administration policy on civil rights and on many international issues. Robert Kennedy to Bundy, 20 November 1963, NSF, Confidential File, box 76, LBJL.

122. Reeves, *President Kennedy,* 59–60.

123. Branch, *Parting the Waters,* 414 (quotation), 606; Chafe, "Kennedy and the Civil Rights Movement"; Strober, *"Let Us Begin Anew,"* 282; Reeves, *President Kennedy,* 60; Giglio, *The Presidency of John F. Kennedy,* 161; O'Reilly, *Nixon's Piano,* 201.

124. Stern, *Calculating Visions,* 52–53; Goodwin, *Remembering America,* 4–5; Giglio, *The Presidency of John F. Kennedy,* 162–164; Wilkins, *Standing Fast,* 281; Wofford, *Of Kennedys and Kings,* 141. Senior figures in the administration shared this attention to racial symbolism and its impact abroad, from Robert Kennedy initially recommending William Hastie for the first opening on the highest court ("It would mean so much overseas that we had a Negro on the Supreme Court") to Lyndon Johnson's reaction while watching the lift-off of the first American astronaut to orbit the Earth ("If John Glenn were only a Negro!"). Giglio, *The Presidency of John F. Kennedy,* 41; Miller, *Lyndon,* 278.

125. Sitkoff, *The Struggle for Black Equality,* 90–91, 95–105, 113–117, 128–131, 144–147; Chafe, "Kennedy and the Civil Rights Movement"; O'Reilly, *Nixon's Piano,* 236–237.

126. King to "My dear Fellow Clergymen," ("Letter from a Birmingham Jail"), 16 April 1963, copy in Burke Marshall Papers, box 8, JFKL (also reprinted in William H. Chafe and Harvard Sitkoff, eds., *A History of Our Time,* 3d ed. [New York: Oxford University Press, 1991]).

127. Wofford to Kennedy, 29 May 1961, Howard K. Smith, CBS weekly news analysis, 21 May 1961, and Wofford to Kennedy, 23 January 1962, in President's Office Files, box 67, JFKL.

128. Dittmer, *Local People,* 169; Stern, *Calculating Visions,* 44; O'Reilly, *"Racial Matters,"* 122.

129. "Negro Leaders Seek Halt in Freedom Ride Testing; Murrow Cites Reaction,"

*New York Times*, 25 June 1961, 1; O'Reilly, *Nixon's Piano*, 211–212 (quotation); Reeves, *President Kennedy*, 145; Wofford, *Of Kennedys and Kings*, 125, 155–156; Wilkins, *Standing Fast*, 280–283; Stern, *Calculating Visions*, 56–68; Branch, *Parting the Waters*, 472–479; Dittmer, *Local People*, 92–94.

130. Both antiracist organizers and some journalists were well aware of this ironic analogy of the South to the Soviet Union; see, for example, Dittmer, *Local People*, 90–91, and Dan T. Carter, *The Politics of Rage: George Wallace, the Origins of the New Conservatism, and the Transformation of American Politics* (New York: Simon and Schuster, 1995), 114–115.

131. Carter, *Politics of Rage*, 110–111; Reeves, *President Kennedy*, 356, 364.

132. Andrew Young, OHT, p. 5, LBJL; Dittmer, *Local People*, 138–142.

133. Branch, *Parting the Waters*, 665 (whites, president); Reeves, *President Kennedy*, 380 (attorney general). From the perspective of local civil rights workers, as John Dittmer has shown, the whole crisis at Oxford was a "sideshow"—created by a solo operator, Meredith—to the real agenda of the slow, steady organizing of black communities across the Magnolia State. See Dittmer, *Local People*, 138. The Kennedys, similarly, saw Meredith as a grandstander who was partly responsible for the crisis and the harm it caused to American interests abroad.

134. Chafe, "Kennedy and the Civil Rights Movement," 71; Sitkoff, *The Struggle for Black Equality*, 133–135; Glenn T. Askew, *But for Birmingham: The Local and National Movements in the Civil Rights Struggle* (Chapel Hill: University of North Carolina Press, 1997).

135. Korry to Rusk, 23 May 1963, and "Status Report of African Reactions to Civil Rights in the United States," 6 July 1963, enclosed in Read to Bundy, 8 July 1963, both in NSF, box 3, JFKL; "Reaction to Racial Tension in Birmingham, Alabama," 14 May 1963, and Wilson to Kennedy, 17 May 1963, both in President's Office Files, box 96, JFKL; Branch, *Parting the Waters*, 783–786.

136. Branch, *Parting the Waters*, 791.

137. Ibid., photograph no. 60, following p. 688.

138. O'Reilly, *Nixon's Piano*, 226; Stern, *Calculating Visions*, 86–87.

139. Memorandum of Kennedy-Wallace conversation, 18 May 1963, President's Office Files, box 96, JFKL.

140. Tom Wicker, "Kennedy Sees 'Moral Crisis' in U.S.," *New York Times*, 12 June 1963, 1, 20; Stern, *Calculating Visions*, 91–93 (Robert Kennedy); Reeves, *A Question of Character*, 354–356.

141. Tad Szulc, "Kennedy Asks Break in Cold War," *New York Times*, 11 June 1963, 1; Giglio, *The Presidency of John F. Kennedy*, 217.

142. Rusk to all American diplomatic and consular posts, 19 June 1963, and Ken-

nedy to all American diplomatic and consular posts, 19 June 1963, in NSF, box 3, JFKL.

143. "Status Report of African Reactions to Civil Rights in the United States," 6 July 1963, enclosed in Read to Bundy, 7 July 1963, NSF, box 3, JFKL; "Status Report of African Reactions to Civil Rights in the United States," 12 July 1963, and "Recent Worldwide Comment on the U.S. Racial Problem," 19 July 1963, in NSF, box 295, JFKL.

144. "Status Report of African Reactions to Civil Rights in the United States," 12 July 1963, and "Recent Worldwide Comment on the U.S. Racial Problem," 19 July 1963, in NSF, box 295, JFKL.

145. Stern, *Calculating Visions,* 89; Branch, *Parting the Waters,* 825. Ross Barnett's appearance at the subsequent trial of Evers's accused killer, Byron De La Beckwith, was no more encouraging. Medgar's wife, Myrlie, recalls Barnett walking into the courtroom, slapping Beckwith warmly on the shoulder, and sitting down next to him. Jurors had no trouble discerning the message from their governor that this man should be acquitted, and he was. Beckwith was re-tried and convicted thirty years later, when new evidence of official tampering with the trial came to light. Claudia Dreifus, "The Widow Gets Her Verdict," *New York Times Magazine,* 27 November 1994.

146. James Farmer, "The March on Washington: The Zenith of the Southern Movement," in *New Directions in Civil Rights Studies,* ed. Armstead L. Robinson and Patricia Sullivan (Charlottesville: University Press of Virginia, 1991), 31–32; Reeves, *President Kennedy,* 580; Giglio, *The Presidency of John F. Kennedy,* 185.

147. O'Reilly, *"Racial Matters,"* 120 (quotation); Dittmer, *Local People,* 128; Lawson, *Running for Freedom,* 83–86.

148. Giglio, *The Presidency of John F. Kennedy,* 169–170.

149. Reeves, *President Kennedy,* 431; Giglio, *The Presidency of John F. Kennedy,* 187.

150. Thomas J. Friedman, "Cold War without End," *New York Times Magazine,* 22 August 1993, 45 ("Why can"); O'Reilly, *Nixon's Piano,* 222 ("to persecute"); Carter, *Politics of Rage,* 161 ("the same people").

151. Lewis, *Portrait of a Decade,* 146.

152. Sitkoff, *The Struggle for Black Equality,* 139.

153. Carter, *Politics of Rage,* 120.

154. Dittmer, *Local People,* 255.

155. USIA, "Recent Worldwide Comment on the U.S. Racial Problem," 19 July 1963, NSF, box 295, JFKL; "Reaction to Racial Tension in Birmingham, Alabama," 14 May 1963, President's Office Files, box 96, JFKL; Harold R. Isaacs, "American Race Relations and the United States Image in World Affairs," *Journal of Human Relations* 10 (Winter–Spring 1962): 266–280.

156. Forman, *Making of Black Revolutionaries,* 177–178 (quotation); Wofford, *Of Kennedys and Kings,* 305.

157. Wallner to Rusk, 31 January 1961, NSF, box 2, JFKL; Romano, "No Diplomatic Immunity."

158. Wofford to Kennedy, 23 January 1962, President's Office Files, box 67, JFKL; Wofford, *Of Kennedys and Kings,* 149; Cabell Phillips, "U.S. Is Worried by Capital's Bias," *New York Times,* 26 May 1961, 26; "The Color Line in Diplomacy," *U.S. News and World Report,* 27 March 1961, 78–79; "When African Diplomats Come to Washington," *U.S. News and World Report,* 12 June 1961, 86–88.

159. Sanjuan to Chief of Protocol, 21 September 1961, enclosed in Battle to Dutton, 29 September 1961, NSF, box 2, JFKL.

160. Mahoney, *JFK,* 23. For Rusk's steep learning curve on this issue, see Schoenbaum, *Waging Peace and War,* 381–382.

161. Isaacs, *The New World of Negro Americans,* 17–18.

162. "Big Step Ahead on a High Road," *Life,* 8 December 1961, 32–39; "Department Urges Maryland to Pass Public Accommodations Bill," *Department of State Bulletin,* 2 October 1961, 551–552; "Troubled Route," *Time,* 13 October 1961; Timothy P. Maga, "Battling the 'Ugly American' at Home: The Special Protocol Service and the New Frontier, 1961–63," *Diplomacy and Statecraft* 3, 1 (1992): 126–142; Massie, *Loosing the Bonds,* 120–123; McKay, *Africa in World Politics,* 405–407; Wofford, *Of Kennedys and Kings,* 126–127.

163. Williams to Rusk, 23 November 1963, *FRUS, 1961–63,* 21:338.

164. Memorandum of conversation, 23 November 1962, ibid., 622–624.

165. Jon Nordheimer, "A Creek, Negro Run, Is the Source of Debate," *New York Times,* 3 November 1994, B6.

166. King, "'The Time For Freedom Has Come,'" *New York Times Magazine,* 10 September 1961, 25, 118–119.

167. King to "My dear Fellow Clergymen," 16 April 1963, in Chafe and Sitkoff, *A History of Our Time,* 187.

168. Horace Mann Bond, "Howe and Isaacs in the Bush: The Ram in the Thicket" [1961], reprinted in Hill and Kilson, *Apropos of Africa,* 278–288; Ferguson to State Department, 18 December 1953, *FRUS, 1952–54,* 11:70; McKay, *Africa,* 392–393.

169. James Reston, "'Copper Sun, Scarlet Sea, What Is Africa to Me?'" *New York Times,* 17 February 1961, 26; "Riot in Gallery Halts U.N. Debate," *New York Times,* 16 February 1961, 1, 10.

170. Wofford address to the National Civil Liberties Clearing House, 23 March 1961, President's Office Files, box 97, JFKL.

171. See Von Eschen, *Race against Empire;* Plummer, *Rising Wind;* Duberman, *Robeson;* Horne, *Black and Red.*

172. Massie, *Loosing the Bonds,* 129–132.

173. Houser, *No One Can Stop the Rain,* 266; Houser, "Freedom's Struggle Crosses Oceans and Mountains," 186–187.

174. Jonathan Zimmerman, "Beyond Double Consciousness: Black Peace Corps Volunteers in Africa, 1961–1971," *Journal of American History* 82 (December 1995): 1015–1018.

175. O'Reilly, *Nixon's Piano,* 225.

176. Branch, *Parting the Waters,* 705.

177. State Department, "Guidelines for Policy and Operations: Republic of South Africa," May 1962, NSF, box 2, JFKL.

178. Williams to Rusk, 12 June 1963, NSF, box 3, JFKL.

179. Rusk to Kennedy, 21 June 1963, NSF, boxes 158–161, JFKL (quotation); Massie, *Loosing the Bonds,* 144–146.

180. Isaacs, *The New World of Negro Americans,* 16.

181. See, for example, Dittmer, *Local People,* 211, and Peter G. Bourne, *Jimmy Carter: A Comprehensive Biography from Plains to Postpresidency* (New York: Simon and Schuster, 1997), 140.

### 5. *The Perilous Path to Equality*

1. Steven F. Lawson, "Mixing Moderation with Militancy," in *The Johnson Years,* vol. 3, *LBJ at Home and Abroad,* ed. Robert A. Divine (Lawrence: University Press of Kansas, 1993), 105; Bruce Miroff, "Presidential Leverage over Social Movements: The Johnson White House and Civil Rights," *Journal of Politics* 43, 1 (February 1981): 21–22. Julius Lester suggested black radicals' awareness of Johnson's desire to co-opt them when he referred to the president's extraordinary civil rights speech of 15 March 1965 with its declaration, "We shall overcome": "One began having nightmares of Lyndon Johnson standing before a joint session of Congress and closing an address with the words 'Black Power!'" Julius Lester, *Look Out, Whitey! Black Power's Gon' Get Your Mama!* (New York: Dial, 1968), 112–114.

2. Eric F. Goldman, *The Tragedy of Lyndon Johnson* (New York: Knopf, 1969), 352; Joseph A. Califano, Jr., *The Triumph and Tragedy of Lyndon Johnson: The White House Years* (New York: Simon and Schuster, 1991), 24, 196–203.

3. Clifford Alexander, OHT, 13–15, LBJL; Doris Kearns, *Lyndon Johnson and the American Dream* (New York: Harper and Row, 1976), x; Lawson, "Mixing Moderation with Militancy," 100.

4. Kearns, *Lyndon Johnson and the American Dream,* 340.

5. Ibid., 10–11.

6. Miller, *Lyndon,* 280–282 (quotation); Waldo Heinrichs, "Lyndon B. Johnson: Change and Continuity," in *Lyndon Johnson Confronts the World: American Foreign Policy, 1963–1968,* ed. Warren I. Cohen and Nancy Bernkopf Tucker (New York: Cambridge University Press, 1994), 25–26; Kearns, *Lyndon Johnson and the American Dream,* 194.

7. Philip Geyelin, *Lyndon B. Johnson and the World* (New York: Praeger, 1966), 15.

8. Miller, *Lyndon,* 455–456.

9. Ibid., 294; Heinrichs, "Lyndon B. Johnson," 25.

10. Lloyd C. Gardner, *Pay Any Price: Lyndon Johnson and the Wars for Vietnam* (Chicago: Ivan Dee, 1995).

11. Miller, *Lyndon,* 466.

12. Sandra C. Taylor, "Lyndon Johnson and the Vietnamese," in *Shadow on the White House: Presidents and the Vietnam War, 1945–1975,* ed. David L. Anderson (Lawrence: University of Kansas Press, 1993), 123. Johnson was not exaggerating: the speech Ky had just given in Honolulu had been prepared by the U.S. embassy in Saigon. Woods, *Fulbright,* 403–404.

13. Ronnie Dugger, *The Politician—The Life and Times of Lyndon Johnson: The Drive for Power, from the Frontier to Master of the Senate* (New York: Norton, 1982), 32.

14. Miller, *Lyndon,* 489–490; Bruce J. Schulman, *Lyndon B. Johnson and American Liberalism: A Brief Biography with Documents* (New York: St. Martin's, 1994), 142.

15. Wilkins, *Standing Fast,* 298; Roy Wilkins, OHT, 6, LBJL.

16. David M. Barrett, *Uncertain Warriors: Lyndon Johnson and His Vietnam Advisers* (Lawrence: University Press of Kansas, 1993), 31–32 (quotation); Geyelin, *Lyndon B. Johnson and the World,* 134; Terence Lyons, "Keeping Africa off the Agenda," in *Lyndon Johnson Confronts the World: American Foreign Policy, 1963–1968,* ed. Warren I. Cohen and Nancy Bernkopf Tucker (New York: Cambridge University Press, 1994), 245–248; Gerald E. Thomas, "The Black Revolt: The United States and Africa in the 1960s," in *The Diplomacy of the Crucial Decade: American Foreign Relations during the 1960s,* ed. Diane B. Kunz (New York: Columbia University Press, 1994), 326–327.

17. Roger Wilkins, *A Man's Life: An Autobiography* (New York: Simon and Schuster, 1982), 132; Louis Martin, OHT, 15, LBJL; Andrew Young, OHT, 19, LBJL; Ramsey Clark, OHT (III), 19–20, LBJL.

18. "Lyndon Johnson and the Civil Rights Revolution: A Panel Discussion," in *Lyndon Baines Johnson and the Uses of Power,* ed. Bernard J. Firestone and Robert C. Vogt (Westport, Conn.: Greenwood, 1988), 181 (quotation); Robert Dallek, *Lone Star Rising: Lyndon Johnson and His Times, 1908–1960* (New York:

Oxford University Press, 1991), 519–520; Robert Dallek, *Flawed Giant: Lyndon Johnson and His Times, 1961–1973* (New York: Oxford University Press, 1998), 111–121. Johnson liked to explain his conservative voting record as a congressman and senator from Texas as a matter of simple survival: "There's nothing in the world more useless than a dead liberal." Miller, *Lyndon,* 69.

19. Califano, *Triumph and Tragedy of Lyndon Johnson,* 56; Miller, *Lyndon,* 177.

20. Dallek, *Lone Star Rising,* 583–584.

21. Califano, *Triumph and Tragedy of Lyndon Johnson,* 177–178.

22. Ibid., 337 (quotation); Miller, *Lyndon,* 187–188.

23. Goodwin, *Remembering America,* 413.

24. O'Reilly, *"Racial Matters,"* 289.

25. Lawson, "Mixing Moderation with Militancy," 83–86, 96–99, 104–105.

26. Miller, *Lyndon,* 454–455.

27. Markman to Johnson, 1 February 1967, WHCF, Welfare, box 28, LBJL.

28. Robert Sherrill, *The Accidental President* (New York: Grossman, 1967), 191.

29. James Farmer, OHT (II), 27–28, LBJL; Lawson, "Mixing Moderation with Militancy," 97–100; Miller, *Lyndon,* 435; Wilkins, *A Man's Life,* 242.

30. Johnson, "The American Promise," remarks to a joint session of Congress, 15 March 1965, NSF, CF, box 77, LBJL; H. W. Brands, *The Wages of Globalism: Lyndon Johnson and the Limits of American Power* (New York: Oxford University Press, 1995), 4, 27–28.

31. Goodwin, *Remembering America,* 257–258 ("sneakers"); "Edison Dictaphone Recording: LBJ-Sorensen," 3 June 1963, George Reedy Office Files, box 1, LBJL.

32. Goldman, *Tragedy of Lyndon Johnson,* 245–248.

33. James Farmer, OHT (II), 19–20, 25, LBJL; Sitkoff, *The Struggle for Black Equality,* 172–73; Schulman, *Lyndon B. Johnson and American Liberalism,* 76.

34. Wilkins, *Standing Fast,* 243, 296, 300–301; Barrett, *Uncertain Warriors,* 45; Fite, *Richard B. Russell,* 404–405; Goodwin, *Remembering America,* 313–314.

35. Undated, unsigned memo, Marvin Watson Office Files, box 18, LBJL.

36. Geyelin, *Lyndon B. Johnson and the World,* 147 (quotation); Carl Rowan to Johnson, 21 July 1964, NSF, CF, box 76, LBJL; David J. Garrow, *Protest at Selma: Martin Luther King, Jr., and the Voting Rights Act of 1965* (New Haven: Yale University Press, 1978), 169; Piero Gleijeses, "'Flee! The White Giants Are Coming!': The United States, the Mercenaries, and the Congo, 1964–65," *Diplomatic History* 18, 2 (Spring 1994): 222, n. 81; C. Eric Lincoln, "The Race Problem and International Relations," *New South* 21, 4 (Fall 1966): 2–3.

37. Harold R. Isaacs, "Color in World Affairs," *Foreign Affairs* 47 (January 1969): 247–250; Lawson, "Mixing Moderation with Militancy," 104–106.

38. Lester, *Look Out, Whitey!* 22–23.

39. Carter, *Politics of Rage,* 222.

40. Thomas R. West and James W. Mooney, eds., *To Redeem a Nation: A History and Anthology of the Civil Rights Movement* (St. James, N.Y.: Brandywine, 1993), 219.

41. Haynes to Komer, 2 November 1965, NSF, CF, box 97, LBJL; transcript of telephone conversation, Ball and Greenfield, 10 November 1965, George Ball Papers, box 1, LBJL; Komer to Johnson, 16 June 1965, NSF, CF, box 76, LBJL; Anthony Lake, *The "Tar Baby" Option: American Policy toward Southern Rhodesia* (New York: Columbia University Press, 1976), 67–70; Lyons, "Keeping Africa off the Agenda," 246–251; Henry F. Graff, *The Tuesday Cabinet: Deliberation and Decision on Peace and War under Lyndon B. Johnson* (Englewood Cliffs, N.J.: Prentice-Hall, 1970), 75–76.

42. Staniland, *American Intellectuals and African Nationalists,* 99–139.

43. Ibid., 229–231.

44. Carl Rowan to Johnson, 21 July 1964, NSF, CF, box 76, LBJL; Rowan to Bundy, 29 September 1964, NSF, International Meetings and Travel File, boxes 33, 34, LBJL; Lincoln, "The Race Problem and International Relations," 12; Gleijeses, "'Flee! The White Giants Are Coming!'" 237.

45. "Angola Genocide Laid to Portugal," *New York Times,* 24 May 1964, clipping in NSF, CF, boxes 79, 80, LBJL; Attwood to Rusk, 1 June 1964, NSF, CF, box 76, LBJL.

46. Komer to Johnson, 16 June 1965, NSF, CF, box 76, LBJL; Noer, *Cold War and Black Liberation,* 117; Gleijeses, "'Flee! The White Giants Are Coming!'" 207–208, n. 5; Lauren, *Power and Prejudice,* 230–232.

47. Crawford Young, "Rebellion and the Congo," in *Protest and Power in Black Africa,* ed. Robert I. Rothberg and Ali A. Mazrui (New York: Oxford University Press, 1970), 969–1011, esp. 969–74, 1000–1007; Lyons, "Keeping Africa off the Agenda," 257.

48. CIA, "Short-Term Prospects for the Tshombe Government in the Congo," 5 August 1964, NSF, National Intelligence Estimates, boxes 8, 9, LBJL. From the agency's perspective, Tshombe evidently did not qualify as an "extremist."

49. Geyelin, *Lyndon B. Johnson and the World,* 38–39, 118–119; Gleijeses, "'Flee! The White Giants Are Coming!'" 208–209; Lyons, "Keeping Africa off the Agenda," 256; Mahoney, *JFK,* 289.

50. "How C.I.A. Put 'Instant Air Force' into Congo," *New York Times,* 26 April 1966, 1, 30; Mahoney, *JFK,* 230.

51. Transcript of telephone conversation, Lippmann and Ball, 25 August 1964, Ball Papers, box 2, LBJL.

52. Gleijeses, "'Flee! The White Giants Are Coming!'" 207–208, 216–217.

53. Mahoney, *JFK,* 230. Burke Marshall of the Justice Department remembered

the all-white Mississippi Highway Patrol in 1964 as "better than a lot of sheriffs" in the state but still "full of very, very low-grade types of police officers, to
put it mildly." Marshall, OHT, 31, LBJL.

54. "Opinion: Englehard in Zambia" [editorial], *Africa Today* 11, 8 (October 1964):
3.

55. *Memos of the Special Assistant for National Security Affairs: McGeorge Bundy to
President Johnson, 1963–1966* (Frederick, Md.: University Publications of America, 1985; microfilm, 4 reels), contains many of Bundy's key memos to Johnson
and other administration officials. See Bundy to Johnson, 16 November 1964,
reel 2, frame 47; Young, "Rebellion and the Congo," 974–975; Lake, *The "Tar
Baby" Option,* 75–76.

56. Gleijeses, "'Flee! The White Giants Are Coming!'" 218, 231.

57. Segal, *The Race War,* 108–110 (quotation); Lyons, "Keeping Africa off the
Agenda," 258–259.

58. Malcolm X, *The Speeches of Malcolm X at Harvard,* ed. Archie Epps (New York:
Morrow, 1968), 165–168 (quotation); "Dr. King Advocates Congo Withdrawal,"
*New York Times,* 14 December 1964, 3; Houser, "Freedom's Struggle Crosses
Oceans and Mountains," 184; Moore, *Castro, the Blacks, and Africa,* 188–192;
Gleijeses, "'Flee! The White Giants Are Coming!'" 233, 236.

59. "The Congo Massacre," *Time,* 4 December 1964, 28–32; Lyons, "Keeping Africa off the Agenda," 260; Minter, *King Solomon's Mines Revisited,* 152–153;
Gleijeses, "'Flee! The White Giants Are Coming!'" 230–233.

60. Bundy to Johnson, 19 January 1965, in Bundy, *Memos of the Special Assistant,*
reel 2, frame 314.

61. Taylor Branch, *Pillar of Fire: America in the King Years, 1963–65* (New York: Simon and Schuster, 1998), 341–509.

62. The precise level of violence against blacks in the South in the 1960s eludes
measurement, but tantalizing bits of evidence suggest that the visible part may
have been merely the tip of a hidden iceberg. The FBI investigation of the
murders of civil rights workers James Chaney, Michael Schwerner, and Andrew
Goodman in Neshoba County, Mississippi, in the summer of 1964, for example, included the dredging of swamps, which recovered several black corpses
and parts of many more. South American–style "disappearances" seem to have
been more than a remote possibility. Other forms of violence abounded as well,
of course, such as coerced sexual relations between white law officers and African American women. On both of these matters, see O'Reilly, *"Racial Matters,"*
173. On the analogy to war, see David Halberstam, *The Children* (New York:
Random House, 1998), 7–8.

63. Richard H. King, *Civil Rights and the Idea of Freedom* (New York: Oxford University, 1992), 167–168, 174–175; Clayborne Carson, *In Struggle: SNCC and the*

*Black Awakening of the 1960s* (Cambridge, Mass.: Harvard University Press, 1981), 175.

64. Epps, *The Speeches of Malcolm X at Harvard,* 172; Herbert H. Haines, *Black Radicals and the Civil Rights Mainstream, 1954–1970* (Knoxville: University of Tennessee Press, 1988), 57.

65. James Farmer, OHT (II), 2–6, LBJL.

66. Sherrill, *The Accidental President,* 19 (quotation); Sitkoff, *The Struggle for Black Equality,* 168.

67. Wilkins, *Standing Fast,* 305; O'Reilly, *"Racial Matters,"* 185–190; David J. Garrow, *The FBI and Martin Luther King, Jr.: From "Solo" to Memphis* (New York: Norton, 1981), 118–119.

68. The increasingly different perspectives of the White House and the civil rights movement could also be seen in Johnson's use of prominent Republican and former CIA chief Allen Dulles as an emissary to Mississippi in the summer of 1964 to investigate Klan violence. The president and his advisers were clearly pleased to use Dulles's mission as an effective form of public pressure on the recalcitrant head of the FBI, J. Edgar Hoover, embarrassing the bureau into taking a more active role in heading off further Klan violence. Civil rights activists Aaron Henry, Bob Moses, Dave Dennis, and Lawrence Guyot, meeting briefly with Dulles in Jackson on 25 June, were less impressed with the prominent Republican. Pressed to explain his suggestion to them that "we want this mess cleaned up," Dulles continued: "Well, these civil rights demonstrations are causing this kind of friction, and we're just not gonna have it, even if we have to bring troops in here." Aghast, Henry muttered, "You talkin' to the wrong people." Burke Marshall, OHT, 30–31, LBJL; O'Reilly, *"Racial Matters,"* 167.

69. Memorandum of Conversation, 12 November 1964, NSF, CF, box 78, LBJL; Miller, *Lyndon,* 398.

70. Lawson, *Running for Freedom,* 112; O'Reilly, *"Racial Matters,"* 196. See also Garrow, *Protest at Selma.*

71. Wofford, *Of Kennedys and Kings,* 194.

72. Wilkins, *A Man's Life,* 150–153.

73. O'Reilly, *"Racial Matters,"* 197–198.

74. Wofford, *Of Kennedys and Kings,* 189, 193.

75. Carson, *In Struggle,* 159 (quotation); Wilkins, *Standing Fast,* 306.

76. Wofford, *Of Kennedys and Kings,* 178.

77. Bundy to Johnson, 8 March 1965, NSF, CF, box 76, LBJL.

78. "Selma Violence Likened to That in South Africa," *Washington Post,* 22 March 1965, clipping, NSF, CF, box 76, LBJL.

79. Johnson, "Outline of Informal Speech," undated [10 March 1965], NSF, CF, box 76, LBJL.

80. Carson, *In Struggle,* 160 (quotation); Lawson, *Running for Freedom,* 112–113.

81. Johnson, "The American Promise," 15 March 1965, NSF, CF, box 77, LBJL; Califano, *Triumph and Tragedy of Lyndon Johnson,* 56; Goodwin, *Remembering America,* 332. Even Johnson's most critical biographer has acknowledged the extraordinary power of this speech. Robert A. Caro, *The Years of Lyndon Johnson: Means of Ascent* (New York: Knopf, 1990), xix–xx.

82. Caro, *Means of Ascent,* xx–xxii; Wilkins, *Standing Fast,* 307, 311.

83. Bundy to Read, 10 May 1965, NSF, CF, box 77, LBJL.

84. Lyndon Baines Johnson, *The Vantage Point: Perspectives of the Presidency, 1963–1969* (New York: Holt, Rinehart, and Winston, 1971), 166; "An Interview with Ralph Ellison" [1967], Harry McPherson Office Files, box 55, LBJL.

85. Barrett, *Uncertain Warriors,* 38.

86. Larry Berman, "Coming to Grips with Lyndon Johnson's War," *Diplomatic History* 17 (Fall 1993): 523 (quotation), 525; Drinnon, *Facing West,* 447.

87. Califano, *Triumph and Tragedy of Lyndon Johnson,* 23.

88. Barrett, *Uncertain Warriors,* 32.

89. Bundy to Johnson, 12 August 1965, Bundy, *Memos of the Special Assistant,* reel 3, frame 442.

90. Young, *The Vietnam Wars,* 197–198 (emphasis in original).

91. David J. Garrow, *Bearing the Cross: Martin Luther King, Jr., and the Southern Christian Leadership Conference* (New York: Morrow, 1986), 429–430, 438, 453.

92. Carson, *In Struggle,* 183–184.

93. O'Reilly, *"Racial Matters,"* 191.

94. "Civil Rights: The Deacons," *Newsweek,* 2 August 1965, 28–29.

95. California Governor's Commission on the Los Angeles Riots, *Violence in the City—An End or a Beginning* (Los Angeles, 1965), 1–2.

96. Not simply an undirected "riot," the events in Watts constituted what CBS Radio called "an insurrection against all authority" that targeted almost exclusively white-owned properties. Gerald Horne, *Fire This Time: The Watts Uprising and the 1960s* (Charlottesville: University Press of Virginia, 1995), 36–39.

97. One of the most original comments came from former president Herbert Hoover, who implied, in what might be considered a vehicular theory of social control, that blacks had no reason to riot because "our 19 million Negroes probably own more automobiles than all the 220 million Russians and the 200 million African Negroes put together." O'Reilly, *"Racial Matters,"* 237.

98. Kearns, *Lyndon Johnson and the American Dream,* 304–305 (quotation); Wilkins, *Standing Fast,* 313.

99. Schulman, *Lyndon B. Johnson and American Liberalism,* 112.

100. Califano, *Triumph and Tragedy of Lyndon Johnson,* 59–63.

101. Ibid., 61–62; California Governor's Commission, *Violence in the City,* 22–23.

102. Takaki, *Strangers from a Different Shore*, 419–421; Reimers, *Still the Golden Door*, chap. 3.

103. Robert C. Good, *U.D.I.: The International Politics of the Rhodesian Rebellion* (Princeton: Princeton University Press, 1973), 16, 24, 39–45, 82. The Salisbury regime dropped "Southern" from the country's name, as there was no longer a Northern Rhodesia. Many of those opposed to the UDI continued to use "Southern Rhodesia" to emphasize the illegality of the declaration, but eventually the shorter "Rhodesia" became common usage, a practice followed here with no political intent.

104. Lake, *The "Tar Baby" Option*, 1, 42–44; Good, *U.D.I.*, 25–26, 53–65, 251–252; Minter, *King Solomon's Mines Revisited*, 201–208.

105. Good, *U.D.I.*, 20–23, 25, 73–75 (quotation); Young, "Rebellion and the Congo," 975; Lake, *The "Tar Baby" Option*, 53–56.

106. CIA, "African Response to the Rhodesian Rebellion," 3 January 1966, NSF, CF, box 97, LBJL.

107. Daisuke Kitagawa, "Race Tension Worldwide: Thoughts from Geneva," *Christian Century*, 5 October 1966, 1222.

108. Rusk to American Consul in Salisbury, 29 October 1965, NSF, CF, box 97, LBJL; Bundy to Secretary of Agriculture [undated], Bundy, *Memos of the Special Assistant*, reel 4, frame 127; Lake, *The "Tar Baby" Option*, 60–67, 80–103; Ogene, *Interest Groups and the Shaping of Foreign Policy*, 104–106; Minter, *King Solomon's Mines Revisited*, 209–213. Minter makes a strong case for the limited effectiveness of those sanctions when he points out the ready availability of both external capital and trading partners for the Rhodesian regime. The comparison he offers to the effectiveness of Western sanctions on Cuba is revealing.

109. Valenti to Bundy, 19 November 1965, NSF, CF, box 97, LBJL (emphasis in original); Lake, *The "Tar Baby" Option*, 3. Valenti did concede about white Rhodesians that "the best are admirable farmers and should be welcome in Australia or Nebraska or British Columbia," suggesting the enduring power of the idea of international white identity even among those Americans opposed to the Smith regime.

110. Brinkley, *Dean Acheson*, 318.

111. Bundy to Johnson, 6 October 1965, Bundy, *Memos of the Special Assistant*, reel 3, frame 845.

112. Notes of NSC meeting, 25 January 1967, NSF, NSC Meetings File, box 2, LBJL.

113. Garrow, *Bearing the Cross*, 453; Lake, *The "Tar Baby" Option*, 70–73.

114. Transcript of telephone conversation, Ball and Young, 15 December 1965, Ball Papers, box 6, LBJL.

115. Ogene, *Interest Groups and the Shaping of Foreign Policy,* 122–124.

116. Raymond Arsenault, "White on Chrome: Southern Congressmen and Rhodesia, 1962–1971," *Issue: A Quarterly Journal of Africanist Opinion* 2, 4 (Winter 1972): 47–51 (quotation), 55; Lake, *The "Tar Baby" Option,* 103–120.

117. Vernon McKay, "The Domino Theory of the Rhodesia Lobby," *Africa Report* 12, 6 (June 1967): 56–57.

118. Ogene, *Interest Groups and the Shaping of Foreign Policy,* 117–122.

119. McKay, "Domino Theory," 55.

120. Haynes to Komer, 29 March 1966, NSF, CF, box 78, LBJL; Lelyveld, *Move Your Shadow,* 229; Chafe, *Never Stop Running,* 270; Peter J. Schraeder, *United States Foreign Policy toward Africa: Incrementalism, Crisis, and Change* (New York: Cambridge University Press, 1994), 205–206.

121. Houser, "Freedom's Struggle Crosses Oceans and Mountains," 191; Miller, *Lyndon,* 436.

122. "Status Report on NSAM No. 295 of April 24, 1964—South Africa," 30 July 1964; this document may be found in the helpful collection *South Africa and the United States: The Declassified History,* ed. Kenneth Mokoena (New York: New Press, 1993), 74. Minter, *King Solomon's Mines Revisited,* 213.

123. CIA, "Sanctions and the South African Economy," 3 September 1965, NSF, CF, box 78, LBJL.

124. "Briefing for NSC Standing Group," 10 March 1964, NSF, CF, box 76, LBJL.

125. "Briefing for NSC Standing Group," 10 March 1964, NSF, CF, box 76, LBJL.

126. CIA, "South Africa on the Eve of Elections," 25 March 1966, NSF, CF, box 78, LBJL; CIA, "South Africa's New Foreign Policy Offensive," 19 May 1967, NSF, CF, box 78, LBJL.

127. CIA, "South Africa Builds an Airfield on the Caprivi Strip in South West Africa," 14 June 1965, NSF, CF, box 78, LBJL.

128. Benjamin H. Read to Bundy, 20 May 1964, NSF, CF, box 78, LBJL (emphasis added). See also "David" to Bundy, 2 April 1964, NSF, CF, box 78, LBJL.

129. "Briefing for NSC Standing Group," 10 March 1964, NSF, CF, box 76, LBJL; Coker, *The United States and South Africa,* 9; Houser, "Freedom's Struggle Crosses Oceans and Mountains," 179–180. For more on this parallel, see Frederickson, *Black Liberation.*

130. Memorandum of conversation, 17 June 1964, NSF, CF, box 78, LBJL.

131. Brubeck to Bundy, 5 December 1963, NSF, CF, box 78, LBJL.

132. Haynes to Komer, 31 August 1965, NSF, Ric Haynes Office Files, box 1, LBJL.

133. Satterthwaite to Rusk, 12 June 1964, NSF, CF, box 76, LBJL; memorandum of conversation, 30 July 1964, NSF, CF, box 78, LBJL; Haynes to Bundy, 12 March 1965, NSF, CF, box 78, LBJL.

134. "Briefing for NSC Standing Group," 10 March 1964, NSF, CF, box 76, LBJL

(quotation); Department of State to all AF Diplomatic and Consular Posts, 1 April 1964, NSF, CF, box 76, LBJL; Satterthwaite to Rusk, 14 May 1965, NSF, CF, box 78, LBJL. This debate can be followed, for example, in Satterthwaite to Rusk, 16 March 1964, NSF, CF, box 78, LBJL; Satterthwaite to Rusk, 15 April 1964, NSF, CF, box 76, LBJL; Bundy to Johnson, 21 June 1965, Bundy, *Memos of the Special Assistant,* reel 3, frame 102.

135. Johnson, "Remarks of the President . . . ," 26 May 1966, NSF, CF, box 76, LBJL; Moyers to Johnson, 26 May 1966, NSF, CF, box 76, LBJL; Lyons, "Keeping Africa off the Agenda," 261–266.

136. Notes of NSC meeting, 14 July 1966, NSF, NSC Meetings File, box 2, LBJL.

137. Student Nonviolent Coordinating Committee, "Statement on Vietnam," in *Vietnam and Black America: An Anthology of Protest and Resistance,* ed. Clyde Taylor (Garden City, N.Y.: Anchor, 1973), 258–259; Carson, *In Struggle,* 175–190; Paul Good, "Odyssey of a Man—and a Movement" [June 1967], in *Black Protest in the Sixties,* ed. August Meier, John Bracey, Jr., and Elliott Rudwick (New York: Markus Wiener, 1991), 275; James Forman, *High Tide of Black Resistance* (Seattle: Open Hand, 1994), 102–103; Gerald Gill, "From Maternal Pacifism to Revolutionary Solidarity: African-American Women's Opposition to the Vietnam War," in *Sights on the Sixties,* ed. Barbara L. Tischler (New Brunswick: Rutgers University Press, 1992), 182–183. SNCC was following in the footsteps of Malcolm X, one of the earliest critics of the American war in Vietnam, who had argued, "If it is right for America to draft us, and teach us how to be violent in defense of her, then it is right for you and me to do whatever is necessary to defend our own people right here in this country." Peter B. Levy, "Blacks and the Vietnam War," in *The Legacy: The Vietnam War in the American Imagination,* ed. D. Michael Shafer (Boston: Beacon, 1990), 217.

138. Carson, *In Struggle,* 180–182.

139. Good, "Odyssey of a Man," 272 (emphasis in original).

140. Segal, *The Race War,* 298; Garrow, *Bearing the Cross,* 458–459; Carson, *In Struggle,* 188–189.

141. O'Reilly, *"Racial Matters,"* 243 (quotation); Levy, "Blacks and the Vietnam War," 216; Adam Fairclough, "Martin Luther King, Jr., and the War in Vietnam," *Phylon* 45, 1 (March 1984): 21–26; James H. Cone, "Martin Luther King, Jr., and the Third World," *Journal of American History* 74 (September 1987): 463–464; Garrow, *Bearing the Cross,* 394, 444–445, 455, 469–470; Robert S. Browne, "The Civil Rights Movement and Vietnam," in West and Mooney, *To Redeem A Nation,* 153; Louis Martin, OHT, p. 31, LBJL; Lawson, "Mixing Moderation with Militancy," 88–89. Johnson deeply appreciated the continuing refusal of Whitney Young and Roy Wilkins to criticize his Viet-

nam policies. Young even traveled to South Vietnam twice in support of Johnson's efforts there. Nancy J. Weiss, *Whitney M. Young, Jr., and the Struggle for Civil Rights* (Princeton: Princeton University Press, 1989), 160–164; Steven F. Lawson, "Civil Rights," in *Exploring the Johnson Years,* ed. Robert A. Divine (Austin: University of Texas Press, 1981), 108.

142. Lester, *Look Out, Whitey!* xi; Epps, *The Speeches of Malcolm X,* 164.

143. Garrow, *Bearing the Cross,* 497.

144. King et al. to Carmichael, 3 August 1966, Watson Office Files, box 18, LBJL; SNCC Central Committee to Wilkins, 4 August 1966, Watson Office Files, box 18, LBJL; Lawson, "Mixing Moderation with Militancy," 91–92.

145. Lester, *Look Out, Whitey!* 117 (emphasis in original).

146. Stokely Carmichael, "Black Power and the Third World," in *Towards Revolution,* ed. John Gerassi, vol. 2, *The Americas* (London: Weidenfeld and Nicolson, 1971), 704–705.

147. O'Reilly, *"Racial Matters,"* 240–241; Carmichael, "Black Power and the Third World," 706; Eldridge Cleaver, *Soul on Ice* (New York: McGraw-Hill, 1968), 125; Lawrence Neal, "Black Power in the International Context," in *The Black Power Revolt: A Collection of Essays,* ed. Floyd B. Barbour (Boston: Porter Sargent, 1968), 136–142.

148. Carson, *In Struggle,* 201, 272, 276–278; King, *Civil Rights and the Idea of Freedom,* 183–184.

149. Malcolm X, *The Autobiography of Malcolm X* (New York: Grove, 1965), chapts. 17–19; Harold Cruse, *The Crisis of the Negro Intellectual* (New York: Morrow, 1967), 408–409; Houser, "Freedom's Struggle Crosses Oceans and Mountains," 180–182.

150. Carson, *In Struggle,* 265–286; Stokely Carmichael and Charles V. Hamilton, *Black Power: The Politics of Liberation in America* (New York: Random House, 1967), xi; Lester, *Look Out, Whitey!* 138; James Forman, "A Year of Resistance," in *Towards Revolution,* ed. John Gerassi, vol. 2, *The Americas* (London: Weidenfeld and Nicolson, 1971), 700–703.

151. Carmichael and Hamilton, *Black Power,* 6.

152. Carson, *In Struggle,* 198.

153. Forman, "A Year of Resistance," 699–700.

154. King, *Civil Rights and the Idea of Freedom,* 153–156, 172–200 (quotation at 182).

155. Cone, "Martin Luther King, Jr., and the Third World," 462.

156. Levy, "Blacks and the Vietnam War," 217.

157. Lawson, *Running for Freedom,* 129.

158. Goldman, *Tragedy of Lyndon B. Johnson,* 173–174, 315 (quotation). On Wallace, see Carter, *Politics of Rage.*

159. Garrow, *Bearing the Cross*, 532.

160. Fite, *Richard B. Russell*, 409; Engelhardt, *The End of Victory Culture*, 151. Southern senators also opposed Johnson's initial selection of Abe Fortas to re-place Earl Warren, as Fortas was the first Jew nominated for chief justice of the Supreme Court. Miller, *Lyndon*, 483–485.

161. O'Reilly, *"Racial Matters,"* 240–241; Lawson, *Running for Freedom*, 129. White anger at black restiveness also showed up in the contrasting celebration of the hard-working, law-abiding "model minority" of Asian Americans, such as re-ported in the 26 December 1966 issue of *U.S. News and World Report*. See Gary Y. Okihiro, *Margins and Mainstreams: Asians in American History and Culture* (Seattle: University of Washington Press, 1994), 140.

162. Thomas E. Cronin to Johnson, 31 May 1967, WHCF, Welfare, box 29, LBJL.

163. Lawson, *Running for Freedom*, 133.

164. Miller, *Lyndon*, 467.

165. Garrow, *The FBI and Martin Luther King*, 106 (quotation), 151–166; O'Reilly, *"Racial Matters,"* 230.

166. Garrow, *The FBI and Martin Luther King*, 119–120 (quotation); O'Reilly, *"Ra-cial Matters,"* 154–155, 179, 229, 235.

167. O'Reilly, *"Racial Matters,"* 261, 285; Levy, "Blacks and the Vietnam War," 224–225; Lawson, "Mixing Moderation with Militancy," 92–93.

168. Garrow, *The FBI and Martin Luther King*, 167–169; Califano, *Triumph and Tragedy of Lyndon Johnson*, 277; O'Reilly, *"Racial Matters,"* 229–230.

169. Levy, "Blacks and the Vietnam War," 217–218 (quotation); Thomas R. Peake, *Keeping the Dream Alive: A History of the Southern Christian Leadership Con-ference from King to the Nineteen-Eighties* (New York: Peter Lang, 1987), 212–217; Fairclough, "Martin Luther King, Jr., and the War in Vietnam," 26–29; Garrow, *Bearing the Cross*, 542–550.

170. Garrow, *Bearing the Cross*, 551–552.

171. Martin Luther King, Jr., "Beyond Vietnam," in *Vietnam and Black America: An Anthology of Protest and Resistance*, ed. Clyde Taylor (Garden City, N.Y.: Anchor, 1973), 81–84, 94; Garrow, *Bearing the Cross*, 553.

172. Roche to Johnson, 5 April 1967, WHCF, CF, Name File, box 147, LBJL; Califano, *Triumph and Tragedy of Lyndon Johnson*, 277; Lawson, "Mixing Moderation with Militancy," 90.

173. Cone, "Martin Luther King, Jr., and the Third World," 464 (quotation); O'Reilly, *"Racial Matters,"* 244–245.

174. Garrow, *Bearing the Cross*, 555. See also O'Reilly, *"Racial Matters,"* 243.

175. Garrow, *The FBI and Martin Luther King*, 180–181.

176. Garrow, *Bearing the Cross*, 555.

177. Levy, "Blacks and the Vietnam War," 217–219.

178. Allen J. Matusow, *The Unraveling of America: A History of Liberalism in the 1960s* (New York: Harper and Row, 1984), 363.

179. Wilkins, *A Man's Life*, 197.

180. Califano, *Triumph and Tragedy of Lyndon Johnson*, 217 (quotation); Cyrus Vance, "Final Report concerning the Detroit Riots," 23 July–2 August 1967, WHCF, CF, Oversize Attachments, box 183, LBJL.

181. J. Walter Yeagley to Clark, 4 August 1967, Ramsey Clark Papers, box 75, LBJL.

182. Carson, *In Struggle*, 256 (Brown); Fred Vinson to Clark, 7 August 1967, Clark Papers, box 75, LBJL (Carmichael).

183. Terry H. Anderson, *The Movement and The Sixties: Protest in America from Greensboro to Wounded Knee* (New York: Oxford University Press, 1995), 176–177. The Black Panthers were protesting a proposed law to ban loaded weapons within city limits.

184. "Carmichael Asks Revolution in U.S.," *New York Times,* 18 August 1967, 17. Johnson and his staff shared Goldwater's frustration and desire to lock Carmichael up (though not to kill him), but were reluctantly convinced by Clark that the administration lacked sufficient evidence to convict him of violating the Logan Act and its restrictions on contacts with a foreign government. Larry Temple to Johnson, 19 January 1968, WHCF, CF, Name File, box 144, LBJL; Califano, *Triumph and Tragedy of Lyndon Johnson*, 221–222.

185. Kearns, *Lyndon Johnson and the American Dream*, 308.

186. Walter LaFeber, "Johnson, Vietnam, and Tocqueville," in *Lyndon Johnson Confronts the World: American Foreign Policy, 1963–1968,* ed. Warren I. Cohen and Nancy Bernkopf Tucker (New York: Cambridge University Press, 1994), 32–33; Califano, *Triumph and Tragedy of Lyndon Johnson*, 212–216.

187. J. W. Fulbright, "The Great Society Is a Sick Society," *New York Times Magazine,* 20 August 1967, 30; Garrow, *Bearing the Cross*, 575. The NAACP and the National Urban League stuck by the president, despite comments like that of one black Detroit resident during the riot, who urged African Americans to stop being "house niggers and slaves like Whitney Young and Roy Wilkins—and to stand up and fight like Stokely Carmichael and Cassius Clay." Lawson, "Mixing Moderation with Militancy," 97. See also Roy Wilkins, "LBJ and the Negro," *New York Post,* 2 December 1967, clipping in Watson Office Files, box 18, LBJL.

188. Califano, *Triumph and Tragedy of Lyndon Johnson*, 199; Lawson, "Mixing Moderation with Militancy," 100; O'Reilly, *"Racial Matters,"* 245.

189. Good, *U.D.I.*, 233–239.

190. CIA, "Some Aspects of Subversion in Africa," 19 October 1967, NSF, CF, box 78, LBJL.

191. "Armed Forces," *Time*, 26 May 1967, 15–16; Levy, "Blacks and the Vietnam War," 214.

192. Wallace Terry, *Bloods: An Oral History of the Vietnam War by Black Veterans* (New York: Ballantine, 1984), 23, 239.

193. Charley Trujillo, *Soldados: Chicanos in Viet Nam* (San Jose, Calif.: Chusma House, 1990), 13.

194. Lea Ybarra, "Perceptions of Race and Class among Chicano Vietnam Veterans," *Vietnam Generation* 1, 2 (Spring 1989): 77; Stanley Goff, *Brothers: Black Soldiers in the Nam* (Novato, Calif.: Presidio Press, 1982), 160.

195. Thomas A. Johnson, "The U.S. Negro in Vietnam," *New York Times*, 29 April 1968, 1, 16.

196. "Fact Sheet: Negro Participation in the Armed Forces and in Vietnam," 18 January 1967, NSF, CF, box 191, LBJL; Harry McPherson to Nathaniel Patrick, 8 July 1966, McPherson Office Files, box 28, LBJL; D. Michael Shafer, "The Vietnam-Era Draft: Who Went, Who Didn't, and Why It Matters," in *The Legacy: The Vietnam War in the American Imagination*, ed. D. Michael Shafer (Boston: Beacon, 1990), 69–73; Levy, "Blacks and the Vietnam War," 211–214.

197. Terry, *Bloods*, 259–260.

198. James E. Westheider, *Fighting on Two Fronts: African Americans and the Vietnam War* (New York: New York University Press, 1997), 68–70; final report of the President's Committee on Equal Opportunity in the Armed Forces, November 1964, Lee C. White Office Files, box 3, LBJL.

199. Nalty, *Strength for the Fight*, 300–302, 305; Ronald H. Spector, *After Tet: The Bloodiest Year in Vietnam* (New York: Free Press, 1993), 246–247; Terry Whitmore, *Memphis Nam Sweden: The Autobiography of a Black American Exile* (Garden City, N.Y.: Doubleday, 1971), 101–103.

200. Spector, *After Tet*, 242–259 (quotation at 244–245); Westheider, *Fighting on Two Fronts*, 5, 66–93; Levy, "Blacks and the Vietnam War," 312; Nalty, *Strength for the Fight*, 308–309; Terry, *Bloods*, xiv, 12; Engelhardt, *The End of Victory Culture*, 248–249.

201. David Halberstam, *The Best and the Brightest* (1972; New York: Penguin, 1983), 560.

202. Taylor, "Lyndon Johnson and the Vietnamese," 120 (first quotation); Miller, *Lyndon*, 416 (second quotation).

203. Robert Jay Lifton, *Home from the War: Learning from Vietnam Veterans* (1973; Boston: Beacon, 1992), 41.

204. Neil Sheehan, *A Bright Shining Lie: John Paul Vann and America in Vietnam* (New York: Random House, 1988), 685.

205. Drinnon, *Facing West,* 457 (Kruch); Philip Caputo, *A Rumor of War* (New York: Ballantine, 1977), xix; Lifton, *Home from the War,* 59–65.

206. Terry, *Bloods,* 5, 90; Lifton, *Home from the War,* 42–45.

207. DeConde, *Ethnicity, Race, and American Foreign Policy,* 151 (quotation); Michael Bilton and Kevin Sim, *Four Hours in My Lai* (New York: Penguin, 1992), 21; Lifton, *Home from the War,* 45, 194–201; George C. Herring, "'Peoples Quite Apart': Americans, South Vietnamese, and the War in Vietnam," *Diplomatic History* 14 (Winter 1990): 11–13, 18. The National Liberation Front strategy of digging tunnel systems as a response to American bombing, bulldozers, and defoliants offered a particularly striking example of how Americans could associate their enemies with animals, literally burrowing into the ground. See Tom Mangold and John Penycate, *The Tunnels of Cu Chi* (New York: Random House, 1985).

208. Memorandum of meeting with the president, 17 February 1965, Meeting Notes File, box 1, LBJL.

209. Steel, *Walter Lippmann and the American Century,* 570.

210. Transcript of telephone conversation, Lippmann and Ball, 25 August 1964, Ball Papers, box 2, LBJL; Engelhardt, *The End of Victory Culture,* 199–200, 238–239.

211. Thomas A. Johnson, "Negro Expatriates Finding Wide Opportunity in Asia," *New York Times,* 30 April 1968, 18; Trujillo, *Soldados,* passim, esp. 24; Lifton, *Home from the War,* 204–205. For more on Latino soldiers, see *Aztlán and Viet Nam: Chicano and Chicana Experiences of the War,* ed. George Mariscal (Berkeley: University of California Press, 1999).

212. Goff, *Brothers,* 131–133. See also Young, *Vietnam Wars,* illustration following 242; Terry, *Bloods,* 137.

213. Tom Holm, *Strong Hearts, Wounded Souls: Native American Veterans of the Vietnam War* (Austin: University of Texas Press, 1996).

214. Levy, "Blacks and the Vietnam War," 214, 225–226; Lincoln, "The Race Problem and International Relations," 13.

215. Ellen Frey-Wouters and Robert S. Laufer, *Legacy of a War: The American Soldier in Vietnam* (Armonk, N.Y.: M. E. Sharpe, 1986), 135–136, 333–340.

216. Thomas A. Johnson, "Negro Veteran Is Confused and Bitter," *New York Times,* 29 July 1968, 14.

217. Holm, *Strong Hearts, Wounded Souls,* 148–149.

218. Levy, "Blacks and the Vietnam War," 220–224.

219. Neal, "Black Power in the International Context," 144; Gill, "From Maternal Pacifism to Revolutionary Solidarity," 191.

220. Lifton, *Home from the War,* 47 (quotation); Drinnon, *Facing West,* 368. John Wayne's 1968 film *The Green Berets* made explicit use of Indian war imagery. In some ways the movie was a reprise of his 1949 film *The Sands of Iwo Jima,* with Vietnamese enemies replacing Japanese ones but with the Special Forces outpost still called Dodge City, Americans still as the cowboys, and Vietnamese dividing up into good (South Vietnamese) and bad (National Liberation Front and North Vietnamese) Indians. Sounding much like Tonto, the South Vietnamese got to say things like "We kill all stinking Cong," while Wayne, as the Lone Ranger, responded, "Affirmative. I like the way you talk." Bruce Taylor, "The Vietnam War Movie," in *The Legacy: The Vietnam War in the American Imagination,* ed. D. Michael Shafer (Boston: Beacon, 1990), 188.

221. Bilton and Sim, *Four Hours,* 51–52.

222. *Report of the National Advisory Commission on Civil Disorders* (New York: Bantam, 1968), 1, 10; McPherson to Califano, 1 March 1968, McPherson Office Files, box 32, LBJL; Roy Wilkins, OHT, 20, LBJL; Wilkins, *Standing Fast,* 327–329; Goodwin, *Remembering America,* 514; Lawson, "Mixing Moderation with Militancy," 100–101.

223. Califano, *Triumph and Tragedy of Lyndon Johnson,* 287; Lawson, "Mixing Moderation with Militancy," 102–104.

224. "Race Riot at Long Binh," *Newsweek,* 30 September 1968, 35; Spector, *After Tet,* 242–243, 251–252, 254–256; Nalty, *Strength for the Fight,* 305–306.

225. Carl T. Rowan, *Dream Makers, Dream Breakers: The World of Justice Thurgood Marshall* (Boston: Little, Brown, 1993), 355.

226. Burke Marshall, OHT, 33–34, LBJL.

227. Rowan, *Dream Makers, Dream Breakers,* 356.

228. Wilkins, *A Man's Life,* 156; Lawson, "Mixing Moderation with Militancy," 106.

229. Donald Spivey, "Black Consciousness and Olympic Protest Movement, 1964–1980," in *Sport in America: New Historical Perspectives,* ed. Spivey (Westport, Conn.: Greenwood, 1985), 239–262.

### 6. The End of the Cold War and White Supremacy

1. The evidentiary trail grows fainter after 1968 as well, as many materials for more recent decades, especially on national security issues, remain classified.

2. O'Reilly, *Nixon's Piano,* 5–6, 329; Bruce H. Kalk, "Wormley's Hotel Revisited: Richard Nixon's Southern Strategy and the End of the Second Reconstruction," *North Carolina Historical Review* 71 (January 1994): 89.

3. Herbert S. Parmet, *Richard Nixon and His America* (Boston: Little, Brown, 1990), 60, 267–269; Joan Hoff, *Nixon Reconsidered* (New York: Basic, 1994),

77; Tom Wicker, *One of Us: Richard Nixon and the American Dream* (New York: Random House, 1991), 184, 238, 240.

4. Carter, *Politics of Rage,* 375.

5. William H. Chafe, *Civilities and Civil Rights: Greensboro, North Carolina, and the Black Struggle for Freedom* (New York: Oxford University Press, 1980), 192.

6. Ambrose, *Nixon,* 2:244.

7. O'Reilly, *Nixon's Piano,* 277–329, esp. 279; Goodwin, *Remembering America,* 106.

8. Thomas Byrne Edsall and Mary D. Edsall, *Chain Reaction: The Impact of Race, Rights, and Taxes on American Politics* (New York: Norton, 1992), 85.

9. Carter, *From George Wallace to Newt Gingrich,* 28–29 (quotation); Wicker, *One of Us,* 325–327.

10. Joseph A. Aistrup, *The Southern Strategy Revisited: Republican Top-Down Advancement in the South* (Lexington: University of Kentucky Press, 1996), 29 (quotation); Kalk, "Wormley's Hotel Revisited," 85–105; Mary C. Brennan, *Turning Right in the Sixties: The Conservative Capture of the GOP* (Chapel Hill: University of North Carolina Press, 1995), 125–126; Reg Murphy and Hal Gulliver, *The Southern Strategy* (New York: Charles Scribner's Sons, 1971). The perspective of those implementing the Southern strategy can be found in Harry S. Dent, *The Prodigal South Returns to Power* (New York: John Wiley, 1978).

11. Carter, *Politics of Rage,* 334–335, 358–360 (quotation), 369; Brennan, *Turning Right in the Sixties,* 132.

12. Sitkoff, *The Struggle for Black Equality,* 212; Carter, *Politics of Rage,* 368.

13. Jonathan Schell, *The Time of Illusion* (New York: Vintage, 1975), 58 (quotation); Carter, *Politics of Rage,* 328–331; Ambrose, *Nixon,* 2:163.

14. Edsall and Edsall, *Chain Reaction,* 10, 20.

15. Kalk, "Wormley's Hotel Revisited," 105.

16. Seymour Hersh, *The Price of Power: Kissinger in the Nixon White House* (New York: Summit, 1983), 110–111.

17. Seymour M. Hersh, "Nixon's Last Cover-Up: The Tapes He Wants the Archives to Suppress," *New Yorker,* 14 December 1992, 94.

18. Hugh Davis Graham, "Richard Nixon and Civil Rights: Explaining an Enigma," *Presidential Studies Quarterly* 26 (Winter 1996): 98.

19. O'Reilly, *Nixon's Piano,* 327.

20. Daniel P. Moynihan, "Report to the President," 19 March 1969, box 1, EX Human Rights 2, Equality, White House Central Files, NPM, NA II. Moynihan noted his own dissent from Jensen's views, even as he reported them: "I personally do not believe this is so, but the truth is that it is an open question."

21. Clifford Alexander, OHT, 1 November 1971, p. 34, LBJL.

22. Walter Isaacson, *Kissinger: A Biography* (New York: Simon and Schuster, 1992),

560–561. Nixon apparently enjoyed baiting Kissinger with diatribes against blacks and Jews, which Kissinger refused to respond to. When his aide Winston Lord asked him why he did not say something, Kissinger replied, "I have enough trouble fighting with him on the things that really matter [foreign relations]; his attitudes towards Jews and blacks are not my worry." Ibid., 148.

23. Ambrose, *Nixon,* 2:172.

24. Ibid., 124.

25. Graham, "Richard Nixon and Civil Rights," 98.

26. Hersh, *The Price of Power,* 110–111.

27. O'Reilly, *"Racial Matters,"* 294–297 (quotations), 326–327, 334.

28. Tinker, *Race, Conflict, and the International Order,* 122–123 (quotation); Lawson, *Running for Freedom,* 142; O'Reilly, *"Racial Matters,"* 295.

29. Moynihan, "Report to the President," 23.

30. Flora Lewis, "The Rumble at Camp Lejeune," *Atlantic Monthly,* January 1970, 35–41; Westheider, *Fighting on Two Fronts,* 94–130; Nalty, *Strength for the Fight,* 309–313.

31. Richard Hammer, *The Court-Martial of Lt. Calley* (New York: Coward, McCann, and Geoghegan, 1971), 46–47, 349.

32. Drinnon, *Facing West,* 452, 457 (quotation).

33. Bilton and Sim, *Four Hours,* 14.

34. Ibid., 20.

35. Ibid., 340.

36. Ibid., 315–316.

37. Ibid., 455.

38. Drinnon, *Facing West,* 444–445.

39. Hugh Davis Graham, *The Civil Rights Era: Origins and Development of National Policy, 1960–1972* (New York: Oxford University Press, 1990), 303.

40. Moynihan, "Report to the President," 1.

41. Robinson to Nixon, 22 January 1969, WHCF, Human Rights, box 1, NPM, NA II.

42. Wicker, *One of Us,* 502.

43. Ibid., 488 (quotation; emphasis in original); Sitkoff, *The Struggle for Black Equality,* 212–213; Edsall and Edsall, *Chain Reaction,* 83–84; Leon E. Panetta and Peter Gall, *Bring Us Together: The Nixon Team and the Civil Rights Retreat* (Philadelphia: Lippincott, 1971).

44. Ambrose, *Nixon,* 2:247–248 (quotation; emphasis in original), 363.

45. Roy Reed, "G.O.P., Aided by Agnew, Surges in the South," *New York Times,* 7 December 1969, clipping in Staff Member Office Files, Harry Dent, box 8, NPM, NA II.

46. Wicker, *One of Us,* 488–489 (quotation; emphasis in original); Edsall and

Edsall, *Chain Reaction,* 81; Schell, *The Time of Illusion,* 42; Ambrose, *Nixon,* 2:406–407.

47. Graham, "Richard Nixon and Civil Rights," 99.

48. Kalk, "Wormley's Hotel Revisited," 102.

49. Schell, *The Time of Illusion,* 81–82. Nixon's chief lobbyist on Capitol Hill, for example, admitted that many senators "think Carswell's a boob, a dummy. And what counter is there to that? He is." The president himself wrote "*My god!*" on a news summary of some of Carswell's segregationist activities. Kalk, "Wormley's Hotel Revisited," 103–104.

50. Wicker, *One of Us,* 492–493; Ambrose, *Nixon,* 2:187, 520–523; Edsall and Edsall, *Chain Reaction,* 76, 87ff.

51. Melvin Small, *The Presidency of Richard Nixon* (Lawrence: University Press of Kansas, 1999), 163.

52. Schell, *The Time of Illusion,* 219.

53. Anderson, *The Movement and the Sixties,* 397.

54. Seymour M. Hersh, "The Price of Power: Kissinger, Nixon, and Chile," *Atlantic Monthly,* December 1982, 35.

55. O'Reilly, *Nixon's Piano,* 479.

56. Kissinger to Haldeman, 6 June 1969, WHCF, CO, box 22, NPM, NA II. See also Butterfield to Nixon, 20 July 1971, WHCF, Country Files, Subject Categories, box 4, NPM, NA II.

57. John Marcum, "Southern Africa and United States Policy: A Consideration of Alternatives," in *Racial Influences on American Foreign Policy,* ed. George W. Shepherd, Jr. (New York: Basic Books, 1970), 202; Minter, *King Solomon's Mines Revisited,* 254 (quotation).

58. Minter, *King Solomon's Mines Revisited,* 276–277; Jackson, *From the Congo to Soweto,* 69–70.

59. Hersh, *The Price of Power,* 111.

60. DeConde, *Ethnicity, Race, and American Foreign Policy,* 178–179; Houser, "Freedom's Struggle Crosses Oceans and Mountains," 193.

61. Morris, *Uncertain Greatness,* 117 (quotations); Minter, *King Solomon's Mines Revisited,* 220–221.

62. *The Kissinger Study of Southern Africa: National Security Study Memorandum 39,* ed. Mohamed El-Khawas and Barry Cohen (Westport, Conn.: Lawrence Hill, 1976), 105.

63. Morris, *Uncertain Greatness,* 112.

64. Acheson to Kissinger, 30 April 1969, WHCF, CO, box 65, NPM, NA II ("the most stable"); Brinkley, *Dean Acheson,* 321 ("subjugation"); "Introduction," in *Kissinger Study of Southern Africa,* 31; Morris, *Uncertain Greatness,* 114–116.

65. The *Kissinger Study of Southern Africa,* 87. On this issue, see also Richard W.

Hull, *American Enterprise in South Africa: Historical Dimensions of Engagement and Disengagement* (New York: New York University Press, 1990), and Minter, *King Solomon's Mines Revisited.*

66. Jacobs to Nixon, 16 March 1970, WHCF, CO, box 63, NPM, NA II. See also Lake, *The "Tar Baby" Option,* chaps. 4–5; Raymond Arsenault, "White on Chrome: Southern Congressmen and Rhodesia, 1962–1971," *Issue: A Quarterly Journal of Africanist Opinion* 2 (Winter 1972): 51; Ogene, *Interest Groups and the Shaping of Foreign Policy;* Sensing to Dent, 24 October 1969, Tower to Nixon, 12 January 1970, and Wolfenberger to Nixon, 14 March 1970, all in WHCF, CO, box 63, NPM, NA II.

67. Abshire to Morgan, 4 June 1971, WHCF, CO, box 62, NPM, NA II.

68. Stokes et al. to Nixon, 13 December 1972, WHCF, CO, box 62, NPM, NA II.

69. McDonald et al. to Nixon, 24 July 1969, WHCF, CO, box 63, NPM, NA II.

70. Lake, *The "Tar Baby" Option,* chap. 6; Ogene, *Interest Groups and the Shaping of Foreign Policy,* 104–106; Good, *U.D.I.,* 324.

71. Schraeder, *United States Foreign Policy toward Africa,* 41; Lake, *The "Tar Baby" Option,* 216–226; Arsenault, "White on Chrome," 46–55.

72. Schaufele to Kissinger, 1 April 1976, document 39 in Mokoena, *South Africa and the United States,* 228–235; Larry Bowman, "US Policy towards Rhodesia," in *American Policy in Southern Africa: The Stakes and the Stance,* ed. René Lemarchand (Washington: University Press of America, 1978), 184–189; Thomas J. Noer, "International Credibility and Political Survival: The Ford Administration's Intervention in Angola," *Presidential Studies Quarterly* 23 (Fall 1993): 780–783.

73. Isaacson, *Kissinger,* 687.

74. Ibid., 688, 989–992.

75. Good, *U.D.I.,* 236–237.

76. Lauren, *Power and Prejudice,* 245–246.

77. Mahoney, *JFK,* 237–238 (quotation), 243; Horan to Roosevelt, 5 September 1973, WHCF, CO, box 4, NPM, NA II.

78. State Department, "U.S. Policy toward Angola," 16 December 1975, document 37 in Mokoena, *South Africa and the United States,* 219–225.

79. Noer, "International Credibility and Political Survival," 780 (quotation); *The Kissinger Transcripts: The Top-Secret Talks with Beijing and Moscow,* ed. William Burr (New York: New Press, 1999), xvii.

80. House Select Committee on Intelligence, selection from the Pike Report Relating to Angola, February 1976, document 38 in Mokoena, *South Africa and the United States,* 226–227; Noer, "International Credibility and Political Survival," 777–778; John Robert Greene, *The Presidency of Gerald R. Ford* (Lawrence: University Press of Kansas, 1995), 115.

81. Peter W. Rodman, *More Precious Than Peace: The Cold War and the Struggle for the Third World* (New York: Scribner's, 1994), 163–182. For a more critical view of U.S. involvement, see John Stockwell, *In Search of Enemies: A CIA Story* (New York: Norton, 1978).

82. State Department, "U.S. Policy toward Angola," 224 (quotation); William A. DePalo, Jr., "Cuban Internationalism: The Angola Experience, 1975–1988," *Parameters: US Army War College Quarterly* 23 (Autumn 1993): 61–74; Moore, *Castro, the Blacks, and Africa*, 328–329; Jackson, *From the Congo to Soweto*, 70; "Introduction," in Mokoena, *South Africa and the United States*, xxiii; Noer, "International Credibility and Political Survival," 776.

83. Rodman, *More Precious Than Peace*, 360 (quotation); James Barber and John Barratt, *South Africa's Foreign Policy: The Search for Status and Security, 1945–1988* (Cambridge: Cambridge University Press, 1990), 154.

84. Coker, *The United States and South Africa*, 14; Steven Metz, "Congress, the Antiapartheid Movement, and Nixon," *Diplomatic History* 12 (Spring 1988): 167; O'Reilly, *"Racial Matters,"* 337–338.

85. Lauren, *Power and Prejudice*, 238–259 (quotation at 238).

86. Barber and Barratt, *South Africa's Foreign Policy*, 204–205.

87. *The Kissinger Study of Southern Africa*, 87.

88. Morris, *Uncertain Greatness*, 131–132.

89. Wilkins, *A Man's Life*, 279–282; O'Reilly, *Nixon's Piano*, 7.

90. Morris, *Uncertain Greatness*, 119–120. Joan Hoff makes a similar point; see Hoff, *Nixon Reconsidered*, 247.

91. Carter, *From George Wallace to Newt Gingrich*, 35. Kissinger, a former Harvard political science professor, once wrote on a cable from the U.S. ambassador in Chile reporting on atrocities, "Cut out the political science lectures." "Kissinger and Pinochet," *Nation*, 29 March 1999, 5.

92. Chang, *Friends and Enemies*, 285 (quotations); C. L. Sulzberger, *The World and Richard Nixon* (New York: Prentice Hall, 1987), 199.

93. Krogh to Hoover, 27 June 1969, and Krogh to Nixon, 27 June 1969, WHSF, Staff Member Office Files, John Ehrlichman, box 15, NPM, NA II.

94. *The Kissinger Study of Southern Africa*, 134 (quotation); DeConde, *Ethnicity, Race, and American Foreign Policy*, 177–178.

95. Nixon to Nyerere, 4 May 1970, WHCF, CO, box 62, NPM, NA II.

96. Peter G. Bourne, *Jimmy Carter: A Comprehensive Biography from Plains to Postpresidency* (New York: Simon and Schuster, 1997), 385.

97. John Dumbrell, *The Carter Presidency: A Re-evaluation* (Manchester: Manchester University Press, 1993), 199; Gaddis Smith, *Morality, Reason, and Power: American Diplomacy in the Carter Years* (New York: Hill and Wang, 1986), 118–119; Michael McClintock, *Instruments of Statecraft: U.S. Guerrilla Warfare*,

*Counterinsurgency, and Counterterrorism, 1940–1990* (New York: Pantheon, 1992), 313–314.

98. Bourne, *Jimmy Carter,* 23–29, 55.

99. Lawson, *Running for Freedom,* 190–191; Bourne, *Jimmy Carter,* 30, 98–99, 115 (quotation), 173.

100. Kenneth E. Morris, *Jimmy Carter: American Moralist* (Athens: University of Georgia Press, 1996), 151–154; Robert Scheer, *Thinking Tuna Fish, Talking Death: Essays on the Pornography of Power* (New York: Farrar, Straus, and Giroux, 1988), 233–239; Dumbrell, *The Carter Presidency,* 86–87; Bourne, *Jimmy Carter,* 71, 94–97, 377–378.

101. Murphy and Gulliver, *The Southern Strategy,* 186–187; Burton I. Kaufman, *The Presidency of James Earl Carter, Jr.* (Lawrence: University Press of Kansas, 1993), 8–9; Bourne, *Jimmy Carter,* 182, 190–197.

102. Lawson, *Running for Freedom,* 191; Dumbrell, *The Carter Presidency,* 87 (quotation); Bourne, *Jimmy Carter,* 212–213.

103. Carter graduation address to Cheyney State College, Cheyney, Pennsylvania, 20 May 1979, Louis Martin Files, box 19, JECL; Lawson, *Running for Freedom,* 192–193.

104. Dumbrell, *The Carter Presidency,* 89.

105. Kaufman, *The Presidency of James Earl Carter, Jr.,* 13–14.

106. Bourne, *Jimmy Carter,* 88, 302, 344.

107. Ibid., 342.

108. Ibid., 340.

109. Ibid., 328, 354.

110. Brzezinski to Costanza et al., 10 May 1978, DPS-Eizenstat, box 208, JECL; Kaufman, *The Presidency of James Earl Carter, Jr.,* 38.

111. McClintock, *Instruments of Statecraft,* 312.

112. Bourne, *Jimmy Carter,* 384.

113. Carter, "U.S. Interest and Ideals," address to the World Affairs Council, Philadelphia, 9 May 1980, Louis Martin Files, box 3, JECL.

114. Dumbrell, *The Carter Presidency,* 194.

115. Carter speech to Congressional Black Caucus legislative dinner, Washington, 30 September 1978, DPS—Civil Rights and Justice—Malson, box 2, JECL.

116. Fallows to Carter, 8 July 1977, Staff Offices—Speechwriter—Subject File, box 27, JECL.

117. Carter address at Cheyney State College.

118. Remarks of the president with Coretta King and Dr. Jonas E. Salk, 11 July 1977, DPS—Civil Rights and Justice—Malson, box 2, JECL; M. Glenn Abernathy, "The Carter Administration and Domestic Civil Rights," in *The Carter*

*Years: The President and Policy Making,* ed. Abernathy, Dilys M. Hill, and Phil Williams (New York: St. Martin's, 1984), 106–122; Kaufman, *The Presidency of James Earl Carter, Jr.,* 26–31; Dumbrell, *The Carter Presidency,* 94–98.

119. Joseph A. Califano, Jr., *Governing America: An Insider's Report from the White House and the Cabinet* (New York: Simon and Schuster, 1981), 231–243; Kaufman, *The Presidency of James Earl Carter, Jr.,* 68–70; Dumbrell, *The Carter Presidency,* 92–94.

120. Dees to Carter, 12 July 1977, DPS-Eizenstat, box 164, JECL; Walter LaFeber, *The American Age: United States Foreign Policy at Home and Abroad since 1750* (New York: Norton, 1989), 648–649.

121. Gutierrez to Eizenstat, 11 May 1978, and Aragon memo to Jordan et al., 25 May 1978, DPS-Eizenstat, box 165, JECL.

122. Eleanor Randolph, "Blacks Wary—Is Carter Their Man?" *Chicago Tribune,* 28 February 1977, clipping in DPS—Civil Rights and Justice—Malson, box 2, JECL.

123. Bruce Shapiro, "A House Divided: Racism at the State Department," *Nation,* 12 February 1996, 11–16.

124. Adamson to Powell and Eizenstat, 12 July 1978, DPS-Eizenstat, box 165, JECL; "NAACP Leaders Say Carter Is Sympathetic to Cause," *Washington Star,* 12 December 1978, clipping in Louis Martin Files, box 68, JECL; Martin to Carter, 4 September 1979, Martin Files, box 57; Kaufman, *The Presidency of James Earl Carter, Jr.,* 109–111, 136.

125. Califano, *Governing America,* 230–231; Sitkoff, *The Struggle for Black Equality,* 214–215.

126. Lawson, *Running for Freedom,* 201–202.

127. Jacqueline Trescott, "The Survival of Andy Young," *Washington Post,* 8 August 1979, E1 (quotation); Cyrus Vance, "U.S. Relations with Africa," address to the U.S. Jaycees, Atlantic City, N.J., 20 June 1978, *State Department Bulletin,* August 1978, 10–14; Jackson, *From the Congo to Soweto,* 157; Shapiro, "A House Divided," 12–13; Dumbrell, *The Carter Presidency,* 103–104; Carl Gardner, *Andrew Young: A Biography* (New York: Drake Publishers, 1978).

128. Trescott, "The Survival of Andy Young"; Pranay B. Gupte, "Young Bids Africa Build U.S. Ties," *New York Times,* 7 September 1979; Leon Dash, "African Respect for Young Aids Trade Mission," *Washington Post,* 11 September 1979; "Andrew Young's Coup for Pullman-Kellogg," *Business Week,* 1 October 1979.

129. "Young's Statements—and Reactions to Them," *Washington Post,* 16 August 1979, A7.

130. Califano, *Governing America,* 431; Dumbrell, *The Carter Presidency,* 102–104.

131. Wayne King, "North Carolina's Leaders Worried by Blemishes on the State's

Image," *New York Times,* 22 February 1978, 1; Lauren, *Power and Prejudice,* 247; Kaufman, *The Presidency of James Earl Carter, Jr.,* 105.

132. Bernard Gwertzman, "Young Resigns Post at U.N. in Furor over P.L.O. Talks," *New York Times,* 16 August 1979, 1; Joseph Kraft, "Andrew Young's Transgression," *Washington Post,* 16 August 1979.

133. George W. Ball and Douglas B. Ball, *The Passionate Attachment: America's Involvement with Israel, 1947 to the Present* (New York: Norton, 1992), 96.

134. Smith, *Morality, Reason, and Power,* 10.

135. Peake, *Keeping the Dream Alive,* 369–373; DeConde, *Ethnicity, Race, and American Foreign Policy,* 180.

136. Douglas Brinkley, *The Unfinished Presidency: Jimmy Carter's Journey beyond the White House* (New York: Penguin, 1998); Bourne, *Jimmy Carter,* 491.

137. Smith, *Morality, Reason, and Power,* 135.

138. Ibid., 134, 144 (quotation), 147.

139. Gardner, *Andrew Young,* 211.

140. Congressional Black Caucus to Carter, 31 May 1978, "Congressional Black Caucus Denounces Cold War in Africa," 6 June 1978, and Congressional Black Caucus to Carter, 28 June 1978," DPS—Civil Rights and Justice—Malson, box 2, JECL; Houser, "Freedom's Struggle Crosses Oceans and Mountains," 196; Minter, *King Solomon's Mines Revisited,* 280.

141. Hooks to Carter, 21 September 1978, Martin Files, box 68, JECL; Brzezinski to Carter, 2 August 1979, WHCF—Subject File, box CO-54, JECL.

142. "Rhetoric and Reality," editorial, *New York Times,* 20 March 1977; Kaufman, *The Presidency of James Earl Carter, Jr.,* 91–92.

143. Moore, *Castro, the Blacks, and Africa,* xiv–xv, 330–331, 372–373.

144. Zbigniew Brzezinski, ed., *Africa and the Communist World* (Stanford: Hoover Institution Publications, Stanford University, 1963).

145. Minter, *King Solomon's Mines Revisited,* 282.

146. Coker, *The United States and South Africa,* 148–149.

147. "An Overview of US Policy toward Africa," December 1977, DPS-Eizenstat, box 208, JECL; Lauren, *Power and Prejudice,* 261.

148. Peter Osnos and Caryle Murphy, "Vorster Derides Carter for 'Selective Morality' in Africa," *Washington Post,* 21 April 1978, A23. Andrew J. DeRoche makes this argument forcefully in his "Standing Firm for Principles: Jimmy Carter and Zimbabwe," *Diplomatic History* 23 (Fall 1999): 657–685.

149. Tarnoff to Brzezinski, 3 June 1978, WHCF—Subject File, box CO-54, JECL; Patricia Derian, "Human Rights in South Africa," 13 May 1980, Martin Files, box 3, JECL.

150. Barber and Barratt, *South Africa's Foreign Policy,* 275; Gardner, *Andrew Young,* 128–132.

151. Greeley to Carter, 19 July 1977, WHCF—Subject File, box CO-54, JECL.

152. Califano, *Governing America,* 228.

153. Macfarlane to Cary, 20 December 1977, WHCF—Subject File, box CO-54, JECL.

154. Vance to all African diplomatic posts, 1 November 1977, in Mokoena, *South Africa and the United States,* 129–133; Coker, *The United States and South Africa,* 148–149.

155. Van Buuren to Carter, 12 February 1980, WHCF—Subject File, box CO-51, JECL; Hoppenstein address, "Southern Africa—What Course the Future?" 25 March 1977, DPS-Eizenstat, box 208, JECL.

156. Barber and Barratt, *South Africa's Foreign Policy,* 275.

157. Carter, remarks upon signing Rhodesian chrome legislation, 18 March 1977, Speechwriters—Chronological File, box 3, JECL; Smith, *Morality, Reason, and Power,* 140.

158. DeRoche, "Standing Firm for Principles," 667.

159. Stephen Low, "The Zimbabwe Settlement, 1976–1979," in *International Mediation in Theory and Practice,* ed. Saadia Touval and I. William Zartman (Boulder, Colo.: Westview, 1985), 91–109.

160. Baker et al. to Sithole, 14 September 1978, Hodding Carter to Moose, 13 October 1978, and Hodding Carter to Vance, 27 October 1978, WHCF—Subject File, box CO-51, JECL; Watson to Jackson, 23 October 1978, WHCF—Subject File, box CO-54, JECL; Smith, *Morality, Reason, and Power,* 141; Kaufman, *The Presidency of James Earl Carter, Jr.,* 91.

161. Dole to Carter, 27 December 1977, Derwinski et al. to Carter, 19 January 1978, and Hatch et al. to Carter, 22 February 1978, WHCF—Subject File, box CO-50, JECL.

162. DeRoche, "Standing Firm for Principles," 677; Barber and Barratt, *South Africa's Foreign Policy,* 267; Kaufman, *The Presidency of James Earl Carter, Jr.,* 157. For earlier discussions of these points, see Mondale to Hatfield [April 1978], WHCF—Subject File, box CO-50, JECL; Martin to Carter, 29 May 1979, Staff Offices Counsel—Lipshutz, box 44, JECL.

163. Harriman to Brzezinski, 22 April 1980, WHCF—Subject File, box CO-51, JECL.

164. "An Overview of US Policy toward Africa," memorandum for president's meeting with black leaders' forum, 14 December 1977, DPS-Eizenstat, box 208, JECL; McClintock, *Instruments of Statecraft,* 314–315; Smith, *Morality, Reason, and Power,* chap. 9.

165. Dumbrell, *The Carter Presidency,* 193.

166. Bourne, *Jimmy Carter,* 369; Dumbrell, *The Carter Presidency,* 91.

167. Bourne, *Jimmy Carter,* 454.

168. Carter, "U.S. Interests and Ideals," address to the World Affairs Council, Philadelphia, 9 May 1980, Martin Files, box 3, JECL.

169. William E. Pemberton, *Exit with Honor: The Life and Presidency of Ronald Reagan* (Armonk: M. E. Sharpe, 1998), 138–139.

170. Bourne, *Jimmy Carter,* 463.

171. Edsall and Edsall, *Chain Reaction,* 10.

172. Sean Wilentz, "Color-Blinded," *New Yorker,* 2 October 1995, 91; Omi and Winant, *Racial Formation in the United States,* 132–134.

173. "Major Klan Group Gives Reagan Its Endorsement," *New York Times,* 1 August 1980, clipping in Martin Files, box 3, JECL. When Carter launched his own reelection campaign on 1 September in Tuscumbia, Alabama, with a speech appealing for racial harmony, hooded Klan members in the crowd held up "Reagan for President" signs. Bourne, *Jimmy Carter,* 463.

174. Adam Fairclough, "Martin Luther King, Jr., and the War in Vietnam," *Phylon* 45 (March 1984): 39.

175. Pemberton, *Exit with Honor,* 138.

176. Shapiro, "A House Divided," 13–14.

177. Lawson, *Running for Freedom,* 204–212; O'Reilly, *Nixon's Piano,* 355–378.

178. Schraeder, *United States Foreign Policy toward Africa,* 273, n. 73. One powerful ally of the administration's "far right hand" was Senator Jesse Helms, who on occasion found the White House too tough on racists. For nine months he blocked Chester Crocker's nomination as assistant secretary of state for African affairs because of Crocker's frank personal condemnation of apartheid, despite Crocker's design of the "constructive engagement" policy for drawing closer to the Pretoria regime. Coker, *The United States and South Africa,* 160.

179. Massie, *Loosing the Bonds,* 485.

180. Houser, "Freedom's Struggle Crosses Oceans and Mountains," 271, n. 44; Minter, *King Solomon's Mines Revisited,* 305–341.

181. Schraeder, *United States Foreign Policy toward Africa,* 34.

182. Massie, *Loosing the Bonds,* 616.

183. Moose statement to subcommittee on Africa of House Foreign Affairs Committee, 30 April 1980, Martin Files, box 3, JECL.

184. Lauren, *Power and Prejudice,* 262.

185. Ibid., 274.

186. Coker, *The United States and South Africa,* 227.

187. Massie, *Loosing the Bonds,* 506.

188. Rodman, *More Precious than Peace,* 364–365; Barber and Barratt, *South Africa's Foreign Policy,* 313–314.

189. Michael G. Schatzberg, *Mobutu or Chaos? The United States and Zaire, 1960–1990* (Lanham, Md.: University Press of America, 1991), 87.

190. Moore, *Castro, the Blacks, and Africa,* 348.

191. *New York Times* reporter Joseph Lelyveld won the Pulitzer Prize for his 1985 book *Move Your Shadow;* Hollywood's *Cry, Freedom* (1987) and *A World Apart* (1988) were widely viewed; and singer Paul Simon's album *Graceland* (1986), a collaboration with Ladysmith Black Mombazo, introduced millions of Americans to elements of black South African music.

192. Barber and Barratt, *South Africa's Foreign Policy,* 303–307; Coker, *The United States and South Africa,* 174–175; Lauren, *Power and Prejudice,* 282; Massie, *Loosing the Bonds,* 523–671; Donald R. Culverson, *Contesting Apartheid: U.S. Activism, 1960–87* (Boulder, Colo.: Westview, 1999).

193. Massie, *Loosing the Bonds,* 560–561.

194. Coker, *The United States and South Africa,* 199–200.

195. Massie, *Loosing the Bonds,* 587.

196. Ibid., 613.

197. O'Reilly, *Nixon's Piano,* 376.

198. Carter, *From George Wallace to Newt Gingrich,* xi–xiii.

199. O'Reilly, *Nixon's Piano,* 378–391.

200. Omi and Winant, *Racial Formation in the United States,* 146.

201. O'Reilly, *Nixon's Piano,* 391–399.

202. Henry Louis Gates, Jr., "Powell and the Political Elite," *New Yorker,* 25 September 1995, 68 (quotation); Richard L. Berke, "President Powell? Not Just If, But Why?" *New York Times,* 30 July 1995, sec. 4, p. 1; DeConde, *Ethnicity, Race, and American Foreign Policy,* 181.

203. Allister Sparks, *Tomorrow Is Another Country: The Inside Story of South Africa's Road to Change* (New York: Hill and Wang, 1995), 10.

204. LaFeber, *The American Age,* 752–760.

## Epilogue

1. Kevin Sack, "In Little Rock, Clinton Warns of Racial Split," *New York Times,* 26 September 1997, 20; Katharine Q. Seelye, "Blacks Stand by the President in His Time of Need," ibid., 16 February 1998, 11 (Lewis); Steven A. Holmes, "On Civil Rights, Clinton Steers Bumpy Course between Right and Left," ibid., 20 October 1996, 16.

2. Elizabeth Olson, "U.N. Report Criticizes U.S. for 'Racist' Use of Death Penalty," ibid., 7 April 1998, 17.

3. William J. Broad, "Spies vs. Sweat: The Debate over China's Nuclear Arsenal," ibid., 7 September 1999, 1.

4. James Dao, "At Missouri Base, Clinton Hails Power of Weaponry and Diversity," ibid., 12 June 1999, 7.

5. Lauren, *Power and Prejudice,* 275.

6. "Rising Tide of Color" (editorial), *Crisis,* May 1960, 306–307.
7. Quoted in Sherry, *In the Shadow of War,* 208.
8. *New York Times,* 24 September 1998, A20.
9. Missouri qualifies most accurately as a border state, but its slaveholding traditions were strong, especially in Truman's own family of origin.

# ARCHIVES AND MANUSCRIPT COLLECTIONS

James E. Carter, Jr., Library, Atlanta, Georgia
  Jimmy Carter Presidential Papers
  White House Central Files
  Staff Office Files
  Domestic Policy Staff
  White House Office of Counsel to the President
  Office of the Chief of Staff
  Presidential Speechwriters
  Special Assistant for Black Affairs (Louis Martin)
  Special Assistant for Hispanic Affairs (Esteban Torres)
  Assistant for Communications (Gerald Rafshoon)
  Records of the Cuban-Haitian Task Force

Dwight D. Eisenhower Library, Abilene, Kansas
  Dwight D. Eisenhower Presidential Papers
  Ann Whitman File
  Administration Series
  ACW Diary Series
  Cabinet Series
  Name Series
  Dulles-Herter Series
  NSC Series
  White House Central Files
  Confidential File
  Official File
  General File
  Alphabetical File

President's Personal File
White House Office, Telegraph Office Records
White House Office, Office of the Special Assistant for National Security Affairs
  Records
John Foster Dulles Papers
General Correspondence and Memoranda Series
Special Assistants Chronological Series
Telephone Conversation Series
White House Memoranda Series
Christian A. Herter Papers
Bryce Harlow Records
D. Jackson Papers
Frederic Morrow Records
Wilton E. Persons Records
William P. Rogers Papers
Alven C. Gillem, Jr., Papers

Lyndon B. Johnson Library, Austin, Texas
  Lyndon B. Johnson Presidential Papers
  National Security Files
  Office Files of the White House Aides
  Special Files
  White House Central Files
  George Ball Papers
  Warren Christopher Papers
  Ramsey Clark Papers
  John Roche Papers
  Oral Histories
  Ramsey Clark
  Clifford and Virginia Durr
  James O. Eastland
  Allen J. Ellender
  Charles Evers
  James Farmer
  John A. Hannah
  Aaron E. Henry
  Burke Marshall
  Thurgood Marshall
  Louis Martin
  Joseph Palmer, II

Philip Randolph
John P. Roche
Terry Sanford
John E. Stennis
Strom Thurmond
Lee White
Roy Wilkins
Mennen Williams
Andrew J. Young, Jr.

John F. Kennedy Library, Boston, Massachusetts
John F. Kennedy Presidential Papers
President's Office Files
Subject Series
Country Series
National Security Files
White House Central Files
White House Staff Files
McGeorge Bundy Files
Harris Wofford Files
Lee White Files
Wayne Fredericks Papers
Nicholas deB. Katzenbach Papers
Burke Marshall Papers

Richard M. Nixon Presidential Materials, National Archives, College Park,
    Maryland
White House Special Files (from White House Central Files and Staff Member
    Office Files)
Charles W. Colson Files
John W. Dean Files
Harry Dent Files
John D. Ehrlichman Files
H. R. Haldeman Files
Egil M. Krogh Files
President's Office Files
President's Personal Files
White House Central Files—Subject Files
Country Files
Commission on Civil Rights Files

Foreign Affairs Files
Human Rights Files

Harry S. Truman Library, Independence, Missouri
Harry S. Truman Presidential Papers
President's Secretary's Files
Intelligence File
Political File
Subject File
White House Central Files
Confidential File
Official File
Dean Acheson Papers
Eleanor Bontecou Papers
Tom C. Clark Papers
Clark M. Clifford Files
Charles Fahy Papers
Philleo Nash Files
Philleo Nash Papers
Naval Aide to the President Office Files
David Niles Papers
U.S. President's Committee on Civil Rights Records
U.S. President's Committee on Equality of Treatment and Opportunity in the
    Armed Services Records
E. W. Kenworthy Oral History

# INDEX